AF180753

SOCIAL PROTECTION AND LABOR AT THE WORLD BANK, 2000–08

SOCIAL PROTECTION AND LABOR AT THE WORLD BANK, 2000–08

ROBERT HOLZMANN, EDITOR

THE WORLD BANK
Washington, D.C.

1818 H Street NW
Washington, DC 20433
Telephone: 202-473-1000
Internet: www.worldbank.org
E-mail: feedback@worldbank.org

1 2 3 4 12 11 10 09

ISBN: 978-0-8213-7648-5
eISBN: 978-0-8213-7654-6
DOI: 10.1596/978-0-8213-5

Library of Congress Cataloging-in-Publication Data
Social protection & labor at the World Bank, 2000-08 / Robert Holzmann, editor.
p. cm.
Includes bibliographical references and index.
ISBN 978-0-8213-7648-5 (alk. paper) — ISBN 978-0-8213-7654-6
1. Economic assistance—Social aspects—Developing countries. 2. Unemployment—Developing countries. 3. Poverty—Developing countries. 4. World Bank—Developing countries. I. Holzmann, Robert. II. World Bank. III. Title: Social protection and labor at the World Bank, 2000–08.
HC60.S619 2009
332.1'532091724—dc22

2008025023

CONTENTS

BOXES

FIGURES

TABLES

PREFACE

In autumn 2000, the World Bank's Board approved the first-ever strategy for the new Social Protection and Labor Sector, and in January 2001, the sector published the strategy. The subtitle, *From Safety Net to Springboard*, indicated the World Bank's move toward a broader understanding of poverty reduction and the relationship of risk to poverty. Because risks and access to appropriate risk management instruments matter for poverty reduction and development, the strategy proposed a new conceptual framework—Social Risk Management—that would review and reform existing interventions and propose new ones to better assist the vulnerable in addressing the many risks to which they are exposed.

After seven years of implementation, it was time to review the strategy and work of the areas of selected core competence: labor market, social insurance (in particular pensions), social safety nets, social funds, disability and development, and risk and vulnerability analysis. The strategic position, its development, and the results by the sector since the launch of its strategy were reviewed and presented to the World Bank's Committee on Development Effectiveness at the end of 2007. The review included a stocktaking of the analytical work and lending operations in each of the six core competence areas.

The result of this review and the six stocktaking papers are presented in this publication. They reveal the progress that the World Bank has made in understanding the importance of social risk management for poverty reduction and the critical contribution it makes to equitable and sustainable growth. The breadth of analytical work and lending operations across the areas of core competence that have been implemented in all regions is an indicator of the influence the strategy has had on poor and vulnerable people in the World Bank's partner countries.

The successful implementation of the strategy is also testimony to the operation of the network structure at the World Bank. The results would not have been possible without the productive and seamless interactions between managers and staff members in central units and regions during these years. The World Bank internal Quality Assurance Group recognized this accomplishment when it gave the sector the highest rating among all World Bank sectors. To achieve such a result required supportive network vice presidents, engaged social protection managers, and a highly dedicated staff.

Vice Presidents, Human Development Network

Joy Phumaphi
2007–present

Jean-Louis Sarbib
2003–06

Jo Ritzen
2001–02

Eduardo Doryan
1999–2001

David de Ferranti
1997–99

Social Protection Sector Board Members

Social Protection Anchor

Social Protection Board Chair and Sector Director for Social Protection and Labor
Robert Holzmann
1997–present

Sector Managers

Bassam Ramadan
2008–present

Sándor Sipos, Lynne Sherburne-Benz, and Steen Jørgensen
1997–2008

Social Protection Board Secretaries

Shams ur Rehman
2002–present

Mylene Domingo, Francine Pagsibigan, Katya Gutierrez, and Diana Macleod
1997–2002

Africa Region

Lynne Sherburne-Benz
2008–present

Harold Alderman
2006–present

Laura Frigenti, Arvil Van Adams, and Helena Ribe
1997–2005

East Asia and Pacific Region

Xiaoqing Yu
2008–present

Emmanuel Jimenez
2002–present

Ana Revenga, Tamar Manuelyan Atnic, Jill Armstrong, and Alan Ruby
1997–2008

Europe and Central Asia Region

Kathy Lindert
2008–present

Gordon Betcherman
2008–present

Hermann von Gersdorff, Arup Banerji, and Michal Rutkowski
1998–2008

Latin America and the Caribbean Region

Helena Ribe
2002–present

Andrew Mason
2006–present

Chris Chamberlin, Ariel Fiszbein, Ana-Maria Arriagada, and Charles Griffin
1999–2004

Middle East and North Africa Region

Roberta Gatti
2008–present

John Blomquist
2007–present

David Steel, Michal Rutkowski, Setareh Razmara, George Schieber, Zafiris Tzannatos, and Qaiser Khan
1997–2007

South Asia Region

Mansoora Rashid
2004–present

Qaiser Khan
2008–present

Michelle Riboud, Tara Vishwanath, and Roberto Zhaga
1999–2004

World Bank Institute

Bruno Laporte and Azedine Ouerghi
1999–present

Egbe Osifo and Michelle Riboud
2001–04

Development Economics Vice Presidency

Elizabeth King and Norbert Schady
2005–present

Ritva Reinikka, Dominique van de Walle, Martin Rama, and Emmanuel Jimenez
1997–2004

Poverty Reduction and Economic Management Network

Pierella Paci
2006–present

Jeni Klugman, Stefano Paternostro, and Aline Coudouel
2002–05

Social Protection Anchor Team Leaders

Labor

Milan Vodopivec
2007–present

Stefano Scarpetta, Gordon Betcherman, and Zafiris Tzannatos
1997–2006

Pensions

Richard Hinz
2007–present

Yvonne Sin and Anita Schwarz
1997–2007

Social Safety Nets

Margaret Grosh
1999–present

Social Risk Management/Social Funds

Laura Rawlings
2008–present

Valerie Kozel, Emil Tesliuc, Julie Van Domelen, David Warren, and Samantha de Silva
1998–2008

Disability and Development

Aleksandra Pošarac
2008–present

Jeanine Braithwaite and Judy Heumann
2002–08

ABBREVIATIONS

AAA	analytical and advisory activities
AFR	Africa (Region)
ASIF	Armenia Social Investment Fund
BFP	Bolsa Família Program
BNPP	Bank-Netherlands Partnership Program
BRASA	Brazil Social Assistance (program)
BW	Business Warehouse
CAS	Country Assistance Strategy
CBD	community-based development
CCT	conditional cash transfer
CDD	community-driven development
D&D	disability and development
DGF	development grant facility
DO	development objective
DPL	development policy lending
DPO	disabled persons' organization
EAP	East Asia and Pacific (Region)
ECA	Europe and Central Asia (Region)
EMIS	educational management information systems
ESSD	Environmentally and Socially Sustainable Development (Network)
ESW	economic and sector work
FIS	Fondo de Inversión Social (Social Investment Fund) (Bolivia)
FOSIS	Fondo de Solidaridad e Inversión Social (Fund for Solidarity and Social Investment) (Chile)
FY	fiscal year
GDP	gross domestic product
GPDD	Global Partnership for Disability and Development
HDN	Human Development Network
HDNSP	Human Development Network, Social Protection
HIPC	heavily indebted poor countries
HROST	Health Reform Options Simulation Toolkit
IBRD	International Bank for Reconstruction and Development
ICR	implementation completion report
IDA	International Development Association
IDB	Inter-American Development Bank
IEG	Independent Evaluation Group
IFPRI	International Food Policy Research Institute
ILO	International Labour Organization
IP	implementation progress
ISR	implementation status report
JFPR	Japan Fund for Poverty Reduction
LAC	Latin America and the Caribbean (Region)
MASAF	Malawi Social Action Fund
MDG	Millennium Development Goal
MEER	Marmara Earthquake Emergency Reconstruction (Project) (Turkey)
MENA	Middle East and North Africa (Region)
MILES	macroeconomic conditions, investment climate and infrastructure, labor market regulations and institutions, education and skill development, and social protection
NBFI	nonbank financial institution
NGO	nongovernmental organization
OECD	Organisation for Economic Co-operation and Development
OED	Operations Evaluation Department
PA	poverty assessment
PAD	project appraisal document
PATH	Programme of Advancement through Health and Education (Jamaica)
POVNET	Development Co-operation Directorate Network on Poverty Reduction
PREM	Poverty Reduction and Economic Management (Sector Board)
PROST	Pension Reform Options Simulation Toolkit
PRSP	Poverty Reduction Strategy Paper
PSNP	Productive Safety Nets Program
PSR	project status report
QAG	Quality Assurance Group
R&V	risk and vulnerability
RVA	risk and vulnerability assessment
SAR	South Asia Region
SP	social protection

SP&L	social protection and labor
SRM	Social Risk Management (framework)
SSN	social safety net
TA	technical assistance
UISIM	Unemployment Insurance Simulation Model
UN	United Nations
UN-HABITAT	United Nations Human Settlements Programme
UNDESA	United Nations Department of Economic and Social Affairs
WHO	World Health Organization
ZAMSIF	Zambia Social Investment Fund

CHAPTER 1 one

SOCIAL PROTECTION AND LABOR AT THE WORLD BANK: AN OVERVIEW

Robert Holzmann, Sándor Sipos, and the Social Protection Team

The World Bank has been engaged in social protection and labor (SP&L) activities for more than two decades, albeit with large differences across regions and over time. The first social funds were prepared in the late 1980s to help communities cope with short-term adverse impacts of structural reforms. These funds expanded rapidly to become a central part of the Bank's poverty reduction efforts in low-income countries.

Policy discussions on old-age security and pension reform took off in the early 1990s in response to impending demographic changes worldwide, transition economy issues in Eastern and Central Europe, and fiscal crises in Latin America. Policy debates and lending for social safety nets had antecedents in the late 1980s in some Latin American countries but fully took root in the 1990s—initially in the context of structural reforms and the Tequila and Asian financial crises and more recently in all regions to help households cope with shocks and natural and human-made disasters such as the current food and oil prices crisis. Well-functioning labor markets and job creation have long been topics of interest for development economists at the Bank, and work in this area included *World Development Report 1995: Workers in an Integrating World* (World Bank 1995). However, the World Bank's work in this area was often piecemeal and lacked a coherent framework. To rectify this problem and in recognition of the importance of the issues for development, the Bank brought together the various strands of social protection and labor work by creating the SP&L sector as a part of the Human Development Network in 1996. This institutional focus was conducive to rethinking the role of social protection in development and allowed the Bank to articulate a new conceptual framework and strategy.

The new framework is based on the conviction that risk and access to risk management instruments matter for development. The poorest in society are typically the most exposed to diverse forms of risk and have the least access to instruments for managing risks. *Social protection*—defined as public policies that assist individuals, households, and communities in better managing risks and that support the critically vulnerable—is crucial for sustainable and equitable economic growth. It contributes in fundamental ways to human development and is crucial for poverty reduction.

This concept is in essence the key message and position taken by the report *Social Protection Sector Strategy: From Safety Net to Springboard* (World Bank 2001a). It has remained the conceptual basis of the work program by the SP&L sector in its key areas of selected core competence:

Robert Holzmann is sector director of the Social Protection and Labor Department at the World Bank. Sándor Sipos was sector manager and Holzmann's deputy at the department. He is now special representative to the European Union, Brussels. An anchor team, under the leadership of Holzmann and Sipos, drafted the Sector Strategy Implementation Update on which this chapter is based. The Social Protection Team included many authors of the stocktaking papers mentioned in this chapter, in addition to Raiden Dillard and Surat Nsour. Richard Carroll, a consultant at the World Bank, helped update the data on lending.

labor market, social security (in particular pensions), social safety nets, social funds, disability and development, and risk and vulnerability analysis. The strategic position, its development, and the results by the sector since the launch of the strategy were reviewed and presented to the Bank's Board of Executive Directors at the end of 2007 (OPCDM 2007). The review included a stocktaking of the analytical work and lending operations in each of the six core competence areas. Six stocktaking papers that resulted have been revised and updated and are the content of chapters 2 through 7. The remainder of this chapter briefly presents the Bank's conceptual underpinnings of the new sector; sketches the progress and achievements in the fundamental development objectives (good jobs, greater security, and greater equity); and provides a very short overview of the key Bank instruments applied: analytical work and lending.

THE WORLD BANK'S CONCEPTUAL UNDERPINNINGS OF SOCIAL PROTECTION

The conceptual foundations of the SP&L sector strategy are set forth in *Social Protection Sector Strategy: From Safety Net to Springboard* (World Bank 2001a). These principles have been applied and deepened in publications both inside and outside the Bank. *World Development Report 2000/2001: Attacking Poverty* (World Bank 2001b) established security at an equal level to opportunities and empowerment to accelerate poverty reduction. *World Development Report 2004: Making Services Work for Poor People* (World Bank 2003) dealt with the crucial role of transfers and social services. *World Development Report 2005: A Better Investment Climate for Everyone* (World Bank 2004) highlighted the role of labor markets for investment climate. *World Development Report 2006: Equity and Development* (World Bank 2005) addressed the role of equity in development, including the contribution of transfer programs. Finally, *World Development Report 2007: Development and the Next Generation* (World Bank 2006) dealt with crucial aspects of youth employment. This increasing focus on SP&L was mirrored, among other ways, by the International Labour Organization (ILO) conference on Social Protection of 2003, the Organisation for Economic Co-operation and Development's Development Co-operation Directorate Network on Poverty Reduction (POVNET), and a report by the World Commission on the Social Dimension of Globalization (2004).

The strategy was innovative in placing particular emphasis on risk and risk management—the Social Risk Management (SRM) framework—as a complement to social protection's more traditional emphasis on equity and basic needs and in recognition of the demands and consequences of the rapidly changing global economy. The SRM framework is particularly relevant for low-income countries, where risk is often an important cause of poverty. Poor people are more vulnerable to systemic risks (such as drought) as well as idiosyncratic risks (such as illness), and they generally lack access to good instruments for effectively managing those risks. The SRM framework adds vulnerability as a forward-looking concept to the traditional poverty analysis and thus highlights the importance of having multiple strategies for dealing with risks (prevention, mitigation, and coping) as well as multiple arrangements—traditional and informal systems, market-based systems, and public sector policies and programs.

On the basis of this framework and in line with the World Bank's vision and mission of poverty reduction and inclusive and sustainable globalization, the Bank's SP&L strategy is driven by three broad policy objectives:

1. To improve earning opportunities and the quality of jobs
2. To improve security through better management of risks
3. To improve equity and reduce extreme poverty through better assistance programs for vulnerable groups.

PROGRESS AND ACHIEVEMENTS

The 2007 implementation update of the Bank's SP&L strategy provides details about progress in the pursuit of the fundamental development objectives: good jobs, greater security, and greater equity. Extracts from this update highlight the importance of a clear conceptual framework to guide policy work, the implementation of the strategy in country contexts, and the role of partnership with other international agencies in this area.

Creating More and Better Jobs

Efforts to improve earnings opportunities and the quality of jobs lie at the heart of the Bank's SP&L strategy. Although worldwide labor market policy has improved (all eight ILO core conventions have been ratified by 124 countries, and 163 have ratified the Convention on the Worst Forms of Child Labor), major challenges remain. Joblessness remains high and resilient, particularly among youth. Nearly half of the 2.85 billion people in the world have jobs that earn below the US$2 per day international poverty line. Although the number of children engaged in hazardous work has fallen, 218 million children are still working. Employment of people with disabilities remains problematic.

Between 2000 and 2007, more than 10 percent of World Bank projects (for a total of 206) involved labor markets, constituting a portfolio lending of US$4.35 billion. Out of a total of 164 labor-related investment projects since 2000, the most common were projects that seek to boost employment through development of microenterprises (26 percent) and improve labor market outcomes by training or retraining workers (20 percent). Substantial analytical work has laid the groundwork for policy action. Between 2005 and 2007, the Bank completed 93 analytical studies of labor markets, including main regional flagships and country studies in China, Ethiopia, India, and the Russian Federation.

Recent developments have seen a resurgence of recognition that employment is at the heart of development. This resurgence is closely linked to the fact that because labor is often the only asset of the poor, a growth process that is not associated with sustained job creation is likely to fail to help the poor to escape from poverty. The Bank's leadership in this drive to put employment at the heart of a development agenda is reflected in World Bank flagship publications, including four consecutive *World Development Reports* (2005, 2006, 2007, and 2008). Those reports discuss the labor market's role in enhancing the investment climate, reducing inequalities, protecting and deepening human capital investment in youth, and providing a path out of rural poverty.

The SP&L sector developed a multisectoral framework to guide the Bank's work and policy dialogue, represented by the acronym MILES.[1] This multisector analytical framework is a diagnostic tool that is meant to encompass all key aspects of the economic, political, and institutional context for job creation. The MILES framework is now progressively being implemented in country-specific cases using robust empirical methodologies. To exploit synergies, the Bank is involved in important partnerships with other international agencies that have also provided leadership in this area (such as ILO, the German Agency for Technical Cooperation, and the Institute for the Study of Labor). An example is the Bank's partnership with the Institute for the Study of Labor to mobilize the international research community to fill gaps in knowledge about labor markets in low- and middle-income countries, including the mobility of workers into and out of informality and the effects of globalization and restructuring on workers.

Child labor and youth employment are two areas in which to develop better data and analysis and, increasingly, policy advice and project experience. On child labor, the Understanding Children's Work project with ILO and the United Nations Children's Fund has developed innovative tools to measure, monitor, and analyze child labor. The project is now the preeminent source for data on child labor in the world (with, so far, direct work in Cambodia, El Salvador, Guatemala, Morocco, Nepal, and the Republic of Yemen). On youth unemployment, the SP&L sector increasingly conducts analytical work, works in cooperation with ILO and the United Nations on the Youth Employment Network, and supports operations that provide second-chance education and training opportunities as well as other support services for poor youth (for example, a global inventory of employment programs for youth was completed in 2007).

Creating More Security

The Bank promotes better risk management for households and communities by facilitating the development of equitable, affordable, and sustainable savings and income-support programs, countercyclical safety nets, and informal and market-based risk management programs. Risk and vulnerability assessments (RVAs) provide core diagnostics at the country level (box 1.1).

Ten percent of the world population now exceeds 60 years of age. By 2050, the ratio will double, and 80 percent of the elderly will live in the developing world. Since 1984, the Bank has been involved in pension reforms in more than 80 countries, with an initial focus on Eastern

BOX 1.1

CORE DIAGNOSTICS: RISK AND VULNERABILITY ASSESSMENTS

Directly following the launch of *Social Protection Sector Strategy* (World Bank 2001a), the SP&L sector engaged in an explicit strategy to conduct country risk and vulnerability assessments to aid in the diagnosis of appropriate social protection strategies for countries and of points of engagement for the Bank with countries. Forty RVAs were done across all regions in the years initially following the launch of the social protection strategy. These RVAs provided a basis for a richer dialogue with country stakeholders and identified important new areas of lending. They highlighted the importance of risk and the impact of exogenous shocks (for example, natural disasters such as drought, hurricanes, earthquakes, and mudslides; health shocks such as HIV/AIDS; and exogenous price shocks) on poverty levels, particularly for low-income countries. Risk and vulnerability analysis is now increasingly mainstreamed into poverty assessments.

Europe and Latin America. More recently, the focus has shifted to other Bank regions and to comprehensive system evaluations, reform of civil service pensions to enhance the overall equity of systems, and consideration of noncontributory social pensions and other systems to achieve coverage in the large informal employment and rural sectors.

The Bank has developed an overall pension policy framework, which is based on the principles of risk diversification through multipillar systems that use a combination of public and private institutions. This framework is articulated in the recent publication *Old-Age Income Support in the 21st Century: An International Perspective on Pension Systems and Reform* (Holzmann and Hinz, with others 2005) and is discussed by the World Bank's Board of Executive Directors (Holzmann, Hinz, and Dorfman 2008). Appropriately balanced multipillar pension systems are better able to deliver poverty reduction and consumption smoothing than are single pillar systems because they diversify risks, capitalize on the imperfectly correlated rates of return from the various schemes and pillars, and provide a risk floor.

To underpin the policy dialogue and support the framework for pensions and income support to the elderly, the Bank has developed and disseminated a computer model called PROST (Pension Reform Options Simulation Toolkit). PROST has now been used in more than 90 countries (including those in the European Union). It has the capability to project and compare the fiscal implications of a variety of pension system parameters and reform options. Building on PROST, the Bank released a new health-financing projection model (HROST, or Health Reform Options Simulation Toolkit) in November 2006 and tested it in 12 countries. A tool for evaluating unemployment benefit systems (UISIM, or Unemployment Insurance Simulation Model) has been developed and piloted in four countries: Bosnia and Herzegovina, China, Slovenia, and Turkey.

The SRM framework also acknowledges the importance of other tools for managing risks that are currently less commonly used in the social protection sector. Market-based strategies are being explored, for example, through an African regional study on weather-based insurance. This effort includes provision of insurance to small producers and input suppliers and ways to use weather data to provide countercyclical financing for safety nets. Ethiopia's Productive Safety Nets program incorporates such a mechanism to scale up safety nets in times of drought. Similar work is carried out in other sectors, such as herder insurance in Mongolia and weather-based crop insurance in India.

Informal and community-based social risk management mechanisms are also important, with risks pooled within extended families, ethnic groups, neighborhood groups, and professional networks. Some social funds are exploring how they can fortify these mechanisms. For example, the Tanzania Social Action Fund includes strengthening local institutions and promoting savings and income-generating activities at the community level in addition to its more standard activities to increase access to service and provide income through public works.

Enhancing Equity

The third priority of the SP&L strategy is to improve equity and reduce extreme levels of poverty and vulnerability. The proportion of the world's population living on less than US$1 per day has fallen from 28 percent in 1990 to 21 percent in 2002. This trend is consistent with nonmonetary indicators such as the percentage of stunted children or enrollment rates in schools. Recent rigorous impact evaluations of social safety net programs (cash transfers and workfare) have demonstrated the contribution of SP&L interventions to reducing poverty and malnutrition and improving access to health and education services, and the prevalence of such programs is growing (Grosh and others 2008).

The understanding that safety nets are an important component of social policy everywhere has greatly increased in recent years, in part because the SRM framework demonstrates that safety nets can play a role in improving efficiency and growth, in addition to their more traditionally understood redistributive role. As a result of the wider acknowledgment of the need for safety nets, the range and sophistication of work has greatly increased. The World Bank has engaged with 116 countries on safety net issues since 2002.

The most dramatic change in safety nets in recent years is the advent of conditional cash transfer (CCT) programs. These programs transfer cash to poor families on the condition that the families ensure that the children regularly attend school, receive prescribed standards for preventive health care, and participate in nutrition programs. A decade ago, only three countries had CCT programs. Now 20 have full-blown programs or pilots, and many more are in the process of considering them. The early programs have had gold-standard experimental design evaluations, showing very good targeting, effects on poverty and inequality that are commensurate with the (varied) transfer size, a largely positive influence on school enrollment and use of health services, and more muted but often positive effects on educational and health status (World Bank 2008).

Another area of substantially increased focus and scale of efforts is safety nets for low-income countries, especially in Sub-Saharan Africa. More than a dozen African countries are either piloting or considering cash transfer programs, with the majority of these programs being conditional. Social funds have recently been experimenting with innovative community-based approaches in delivering safety net services in low-income countries. For example, the use of community institutions for implementing cash transfers is being piloted in Nigeria, Sierra Leone, Tanzania, and Uganda, and the use of community targeting and participatory methods in public works programs is being piloted in Malawi, Tanzania, and Uganda. Most safety nets in low-income countries are largely externally financed, so donor harmonization is a key issue. Collaboration with partners has been extensive, especially with the U.K. Department for International Development, the German Agency for Technical Cooperation, and the World Food Programme.

A final area of significant advance in the past decade is the know-how for, and implementation of, better targeting and administrative systems. Almost all safety net projects supported by the Bank contain elements to strengthen these systems. The best targeting systems in the Bank's client countries that worked with the Bank on safety nets (for example, Brazil and Romania) have achieved targeting efficiency similar to that in the United Kingdom and the United States. This achievement demonstrates the potential for improvement in other client countries, where one-fifth of programs with targeting instruments that could yield good results were still producing regressive outcomes as recently as 2004.

KEY BANK INSTRUMENTS: KNOWLEDGE AND LENDING

Like other Bank sectors, the SP&L sector used key Bank instruments to implement the strategy in pursuit of the three development objectives just sketched. The key instruments are (a) the Country Assistance Strategy (CAS), (b) analytical and advisory activities (AAA) and training, and (c) lending operations. The use of the latter two instruments is detailed in subsequent chapters. This section provides an aggregate overview.

Country Assistance Strategy

The Country Assistance Strategy is the key document that states the development priorities of the country and the committed support by the Bank for their achievement. In International Development Association (IDA) countries, the CAS is directly derived from the country's Poverty Reduction Strategy Paper (PRSP). The PRSP is the result of a country-driven process and includes input from national stakeholders and international donors. Since the launch of the sector strategy in early 2001, significant progress has been made in incorporating social protection into CASs. A review of CASs for 18 priority countries shows that social protection coverage has nearly doubled and is now included in 92 percent of the most recent CASs (table 1.1). Moreover,

Table 1.1: Coverage of Social Protection in Country Assistance Strategies for 18 Priority Countries

	Diagnostic (%)		Lending (%)		Nonlending (%)		Average (%)	
	FY 2000–03	FY 2005–06	FY 2000–03	FY 2005–06	FY 2000–03	FY 2005–06	FY 2000–03	FY 2005–06
All priority countries	56	100	61	83	39	94	52	92
IBRD	63	100	88	75	63	100	71	92
IDA	50	100	40	90	20	90	37	93

Source: Authors, based on the World Bank's Business Warehouse and documents.
Note: FY = fiscal year, IBRD = International Bank of Reconstruction. The sample of 18 countries was selected on the basis of (a) the importance of the country's risk management issues from a global perspective, (b) the comparative advantage of the World Bank relative to other development partners in the country, and (c) the opportunity for World Bank involvement. The review assessed the extent to which CAS documents cover social protection core competencies in terms of three indicators: (a) diagnostic review, (b) planned lending, and (c) nonlending programs. Social protection core competencies include disability, labor market, pensions, safety nets, social funds, and SRM. Seventy-three percent of the documents reviewed were full CASs, 12 percent were Interim Strategy Note–type reports, and 16 percent were CAS progress reports.

coverage for IDA client countries is now equal to that for International Bank of Reconstruction and Development (IBRD) countries, whereas in the earlier CASs it was about half that level.

Analytical and Advisory Activities

The instrument of AAA and training works through a number of formal outputs, such as economic and sector work (ESW) and technical assistance (TA). Both ESW and TA are based on numerous studies, papers, books, and other publications such as the Social Protection Discussion Papers, the Primer Papers in the key practice areas, and conference proceedings. During the review period of the strategy update (fiscal years 2000–07), the Bank completed 161 SP&L ESW and TA products. The overall number of formal and informal knowledge products by the Bank in the area, however, is much larger but also more difficult to ascertain. For this reason, a time-consuming and painstaking stocktaking exercise was undertaken. These stocktaking reports provide a wealth of information about the World Bank's knowledge and lending activities in six areas of core competence: labor markets, pensions, social safety nets, social funds, disability and development, and risk and vulnerability analysis. The reports also include analysis by region, type of intervention involved, sector, and financing instrument.

A new knowledge product that is motivated by the SRM framework is the risk and vulnerability assessment. RVAs move the focus of analysis from a backward-looking poverty measurement to a forward-looking vulnerability assessment. During fiscal years 2000 to 2007, 132 RVAs were completed, covering all six regions of the Bank (table 1.2). An additional 23 background papers were prepared, primarily under the auspices of the Social Protection Team. These papers focus on analytical methods and approaches, good practice guidelines, and discussion of cross-regional and cross-country experiences.

Lending

Besides knowledge management through AAA and training, another key instrument used by the Bank is lending. The stocktaking exercise estimates that US$9.7 billion of Bank lending was committed to SP&L during fiscal years 2002 to 2007. The distribution across regions and practice areas is uneven, reflecting both differences in need and also that take-up of SP&L as a topic in development is changing over time and regions (table 1.3).

Table 1.4 shows that close to two-thirds of SP&L lending is under IBRD terms, and IBRD-to-IDA shares of SP&L lending are similar to overall proportions in the Bank. Hence, this distribution does not reflect that lower-income countries (IDA recipients) are less able or willing to afford social protection than middle-income countries (IBRD recipients). However, it may reflect that for the years reviewed those countries preferred to use their IDA allocation for more tangible outcomes from infrastructure,

Table.1.2: Risk and Vulnerability Assessments by World Bank Region, Fiscal Years 2000–07

	Number of RVAs						
Year	East Asia and the Pacific	Eastern Europe and Central Asia	Latin America and the Caribbean	Middle East and North Africa	South Asia	Sub-Saharan Africa	Total
2000	5	2	1	0	1	2	11
2001	5	4	5	2	0	1	17
2002	2	4	4	2	6	1	19
2003	3	9	7	1	1	6	27
2004	0	4	7	0	0	3	14
2005	0	5	3	0	4	6	18
2006	6	0	1	0	1	3	11
2007	0	4	0	0	3	3	10
Total	21	32	28	5	16	25	127

Source: Authors, based on the World Bank's Business Warehouse and documents.

Table 1.3: **Total Social Protection and Labor Lending by Region and SP&L Practice Area, Fiscal Years 2002–07**

	Amount (US$ millions)				
Region	**Social funds**	**Safety nets**	**Pensions**	**Labor markets**	**Total**
East Asia and the Pacific	19	189	0	38	246
Eastern Europe and Central Asia	386	454	691	778	2,309
Latin America and the Caribbean	36	1,737	993	1,452	4,218
Middle East and North Africa	80	71	65	103	319
South Asia	0	517	232	317	1,066
Sub-Saharan Africa	621	433	56	440	1,550
Total	1,142	3,401	2,037	3,128	9,708

Source: Authors, based on the World Bank's Business Warehouse and documents.

Table 1.4: **Total Social Protection and Labor Lending by SP&L Practice Area and Type of Lending, Fiscal Years 2002–07**

	Amount (US$ millions)				
Type of lending	**Social funds**	**Safety nets**	**Pensions**	**Labor markets**	**Total**
IBRD	329	2,167	1,710	2,171	6,377
IDA	813	667	204	948	2,632
Blended and other	0	567	123	10	700
Total	1,142	3,401	2,037	3,128	9,708

Source: Authors, based on the World Bank's Business Warehouse and documents.
Note: Because of rounding, totals may deviate slightly from the sum of the parts.

education, and health. In turn, pension lending that goes to 84 percent if IBRD countries reflects their priorities and the concerns of middle-income countries.

Most SP&L lending falls under investment (61 percent), in contrast to development policy lending (DPL), which is typically associated with reform programs. All social fund lending is considered investment lending. Pension lending is mainly DPL because most of it supports pension reform and broader economic reform programs (table 1.5).

There is no discernible time trend in social protection lending (table 1.6), and the fluctuations are determined by IDA cycles, lumpiness of lending, and economic cycles. SP&L lending is typically countercyclical and is slated to increase in response to rapidly increasing food and oil prices in 2008.

Table 1.7 shows that while, as expected, the SP&L Sector Board accounts for the majority of SP&L lending (55 percent), many other Bank sectors also cover SP&L lending thematic objectives. There is a diverse group of 10 other sector boards, all but one accounting for at least US$100 million of SP&L lending.

CONCLUDING REMARKS

As a result of the implementation of the 2001 SP&L sector strategy, social protection has been mainstreamed

Table 1.5: **Total Social Protection and Labor Lending by SP&L Practice Area and Type of Instrument, Fiscal Years 2002–07**

	Amount (US$ million)				
Type of instrument	**Social funds**	**Safety nets**	**Pensions**	**Labor markets**	**Total**
Investment	1,142	2,109	469	2,207	5,927
Development policy	0	1,292	1,568	922	3,782
Total	1,142	3,401	2,037	3,128	9,708

Source: Authors, based on the World Bank's Business Warehouse and documents.
Note: Because of rounding, totals may deviate slightly from the sum of the parts.

Table 1.6: **Social Protection and Labor Lending by SP&L Practice Area by Fiscal Year**

	Amount (US$ million)						
SP&L practice area	**FY 2002**	**FY 2003**	**FY 2004**	**FY 2005**	**FY 2006**	**FY 2007**	**Total**
Social funds	318	153	174	331	59	107	1,142
Safety nets	293	1,174	393	560	538	444	3,401
Pensions	214	158	540	691	342	91	2,037
Labor markets	422	999	344	512	428	424	3,128
Total	1,247	2,484	1,451	2,094	1,367	1,066	9,708

Source: Authors, based on the World Bank's Business Warehouse and documents.
Note: FY = fiscal year. Because of rounding, totals may deviate slightly from the sum of the parts.

at the Bank, and social risk management has provided an important and forward-looking concept to advance new thinking around social protection activities. This concept has helped the Bank to move from a traditional, instrument-based definition of social protection and labor to an objective-based definition that relies for its achievements on a diverse set of informal, market-based, and public arrangements. It has helped to expand the objectives as well as the focus of Bank-supported programs, which have moved from addressing mainly equity concerns and redistribution to carrying out new work on improved efficiency and economic growth.

The social risk management approach is broadly consistent with human rights–based approaches and social policy calls for minimum provisions. Whether social risk management should happen through universal access and means-tested provisions or, more selectively, through conditionality is open for discussion, and policy choices should be evidence based. Encouragingly, the SRM framework is being used increasingly outside the Bank, and its application has made more than a few flowers bloom (Devereux and Sabates-Wheeler 2007). It has proven useful for the review and redesign of traditional programs and has inspired the development of new programs. Although its refinement and application is still a work in progress, the SRM framework is widely used to improve social risk management for all and to render social protection relevant for the poorest.

To strengthen the effectiveness of social protection interventions and in full support of evidence-based policy, SP&L is moving toward a results-oriented framework that will be strengthened over the next years. Initiatives in this area include the identification and collection of better data about the sector's input, output, and outcome; further development on a results framework for the sector; a revised and

Table 1.7: **Total Social Protection and Labor Lending by SP&L Practice Area and Sector Board, Fiscal Years 2002–07**

	Amount (US$ million)				
Sector board	Social funds	Safety nets	Pensions	Labor markets	Total
Social Protection and Labor	1,142	1,837	794	1,579	5,352
Urban Development	0	374	0	21	395
Economic Policy	0	272	509	121	902
Public Sector Governance	0	170	183	54	407
Education	0	136	0	625	761
Social Development	0	136	0	48	184
Poverty Reduction	0	136	0	52	188
Financial Services and Programs	0	0	224	188	412
Private Sector Development	0	0	204	0	204
Rural Development	0	0	0	135	135
Transport	0	0	0	95	95
Other	0	340	123	208	671
Total	1,142	3,401	2,037	3,128	9,708

Source: Authors, based on the World Bank's Business Warehouse and documents.
Note: Because of rounding, totals may deviate slightly from the sum of the parts.

enhanced framework for knowledge and learning products; and comprehensive monitoring and impact evaluation of all Bank interventions in the sector. The stocktaking of knowledge and lending activities in the six practice areas is an important initial contribution to this end.

NOTE

[1] The MILES framework proposes five key sectors to be investigated for binding constraints in job creation: M as in macroeconomic conditions, I as in investment climate and infrastructure, L as in labor market regulations and institutions, E as in education and skill development, and S as in social protection.

REFERENCES

Devereux, Stephen, and Rachel Sabates-Wheeler, eds. 2007. "Debating Social Protection." IDS Bulletin 38 (3), Institute of Development Studies, University of Sussex, Brighton, U.K.

Grosh, Margaret, Carlo del Ninno, Emil Tesliuc, and Azedine Ouerghi, with Annamaria Milazzo and Christine Weigand. 2008. *For Protection and Promotion: The Design and Implementation of Effective Safety Nets.* Washington, DC: World Bank.

Holzmann, Robert, and Richard Hinz, with Hermann von Gersdorff, Indermit Gill, Gregorio Impavida, Alberto R. Musalem, Robert Palacios, David Robolino, Michal Rutkowski, Anita Schwartz, Yvonne Sine, and Kalanidhi Subbarao. 2005. *Old-Age Income Support in the 21st Century: An International Perspective on Pension Systems and Reform.* Washington, DC: World Bank.

Holzmann, Robert, Richard Hinz, and Mark Dorfman. 2008. "Pension Systems and Reform Conceptual Framework." Pension Reform Primer Paper, World Bank, Washington, DC.

OPCDM (Operations Policy and Country Services Delivery Management Unit). 2007. *Sector Strategy Implementation Update: Third Review.* Washington, DC: World Bank.

World Bank. 1995. *World Development Report 1995: Workers in an Integrating World.* Washington, DC: World Bank.

———. 2001a. *Social Protection Sector Strategy: From Safety Net to Springboard.* Washington, DC: World Bank. http://go.worldbank.org/97LBYDY3U0.

———. 2001b. *World Development Report 2000/2001: Attacking Poverty.* Washington, DC: World Bank.

———. 2003. *World Development Report 2004: Making Services Work for Poor People.* Washington, DC: World Bank.

———. 2004. *World Development Report 2005: A Better Investment Climate for Everyone.* Washington, DC: World Bank.

———. 2005. *World Development Report 2006: Equity and Development.* Washington, DC: World Bank.

———. 2006. *World Development Report 2007: Development and the Next Generation.* Washington, DC: World Bank.

———. 2007. *Agriculture for Development.* Washington, DC: World Bank.

———. 2008. *Conditional Cash Transfers for Attacking Present and Future Poverty.* Washington, DC: World Bank.

World Commission on the Social Dimension of Globalization. 2004. *A Fair Globalization: Creating Opportunities for All.* Geneva: International Labour Office.

CHAPTER 2 two

RISK AND VULNERABILITY ANALYSIS IN WORLD BANK ANALYTICAL WORK, 2000–07

Valerie Kozel, Pierre Fallavier, and Reena Badani

INTRODUCTION

Objectives

The World Bank recently completed a review of progress in implementing its social protection and labor (SP&L) strategy.[1] As part of this review, a series of thematic papers were prepared to assess the breadth and coverage of lending and analytical work in key areas of SP&L focus: labor markets, pensions, social safety nets, and social funds. The Social Risk Management (SRM) framework underpins the SP&L strategy (Holzmann and Jørgensen 2000), and analytical work on risk and vulnerability (R&V) has made important contributions to the implementation of the strategy. This review of the Bank's analytical work on R&V has been prepared as a complement to the thematic papers. Its objective is to take stock of the substantial body of R&V analysis undertaken since the advent of the SP&L strategy in 2000.[2]

The chapter first identifies the defining features of R&V analysis and the types of questions typically addressed. The methodology used to compile this inventory of relevant Bank work is then presented. The chapter then assesses the breadth of the R&V analysis portfolio, in aggregate and by region; summarizes key components and examples of good practices; highlights some broad lessons that have been learned; and discusses specific examples of how R&V analysis has helped shape the Bank's country assistance programs and led to better country strategies and policies. Future challenges and implications of the review's major findings are discussed briefly in the final section of the chapter.

Definition of Key Terms

The Bank has produced a substantial amount of work on individual and household-level risk and vulnerability, in particular since the advent of the SRM framework in 2000. In some cases, this work has taken the form of freestanding reports, often referred to as risk and vulnerability assessments (RVAs). In other cases, R&V analysis has been included in poverty assessments (PAs),3 in safety net assessments, and in broader reports on social protection (SP) policies and programs. Formal economic and sector work (ESW) has been complemented by informal background papers, including research papers and operational policy notes. For purposes of this chapter, the term R&V analysis refers to this broad body of work.

R&V analysis has several defining features:

- It focuses explicitly on poor and other vulnerable groups, who are generally seen to be more exposed to uninsured

Valerie Kozel was senior economist and head of the Strategy, Implementation, and Results Unit of the World Bank's Social Protection and Labor Department. She is now senior poverty economist at the country office in Hanoi, Vietnam. Pierre Fallavier was a World Bank consultant; he is currently an urban planning adviser with the United Nations Human Settlements Programme (UN-HABITAT) in Afghanistan. Reena Badani was also a World Bank consultant; she is completing her PhD in economics at Yale University.

risk, more likely to suffer shocks, and less able to manage these shocks effectively.

- The poor consist of those who are always poor (at any point in time) and those who move in and out of poverty. Accordingly, a static estimate of poverty (measured at a specific point in time) is likely to underestimate those who are at risk of falling into poverty (at some other point in time). R&V analysis looks at poverty explicitly as a dynamic process. It focuses on vulnerability as a forward-looking concept, capturing the possibility that an individual will have a level of welfare (for example, consumption) below some benchmark (for example, the poverty line) at a given time in the future.
- R&V analysis examines the links between risk and shocks, on the one hand, and welfare and poverty, on the other. It identifies the most important downside risks and shocks in a particular setting:
  - *Risk* refers to potential fluctuations in the circumstances of a household that affect its income, its welfare, or both. In particular, risk refers to *states of the world* that an individual or household faces, coupled with the likelihood that each of these states will occur.
  - *Shocks* refer to the realization of different states of the world. Examples of shocks include the occurrence of an earthquake, substantial movement in terms of trade, or the death of a household member.
- Given risk profiles, R&V analysis identifies ex ante and ex post risk management strategies that individuals, households, and communities can use to protect welfare, and it identifies policy measures to promote effective management of risk.

Links between Social Risk Management and R&V Analysis

In recent decades, profound economic, social, and political changes have taken place in the developing world. These changes include market and political liberalization, economic and social restructuring, vast technological changes, and growing market integration and globalization (Heitzmann, Canagarajah, and Siegel 2002). In parallel with these changes—and in some cases directly linked to change processes—low- and middle-income countries have been struggling to cope with a range of shocks such as natural disasters, economic fluctuations, political and social crises, and global health threats. Uninsured risk and shocks adversely affect development, both globally and at the national level. For example, the oil crises in 1973, 1979, and 1990 had far-reaching effects on the global economy; they hit some developing countries particularly hard.

The 1990s brought risk sharply into focus in the international policy arena. Countries in Latin America suffered a series of economic shocks and financial crises in the 1990s, as did East Asian countries beginning in 1997. In both cases, contagion effects were widespread. Evidence suggests that the frequency and severity of climate shocks increased in Sub-Saharan Africa in the 1990s, and many countries on the subcontinent are struggling to cope with HIV/AIDS, malaria, and other widespread infectious diseases. Countries in East Asia were particularly prone to climate shocks over the past decade, and armed conflict is pervasive in parts of Africa and the Middle East.

SRM Framework

Against this backdrop, the SP&L sector launched its Social Risk Management framework in 2000 to 2001 as an analytical and prescriptive model. The premise behind the SRM framework is that individuals, households, and communities are vulnerable to multiple risks from different sources that may affect welfare levels. Unpredictable or unpreventable shocks coupled with an inability to adequately cushion these shocks may both cause and deepen poverty. Because the poor typically have higher levels of exposure to risk than the nonpoor, are more averse to risk, and have fewer means for managing risks, they are among the most vulnerable in society and would benefit from greater access to ex post and ex ante risk management instruments. By focusing on (a) assisting individuals, households, and communities to better manage risk and (b) providing support for the critically poor, the SRM approach recognizes the importance of risk management instruments for protecting the poor from shocks and allowing them to engage in higher return, higher risk activities.

The importance of security and the role of risk and shocks as fundamental determinants of poverty were highlighted in the *World Development Report 2000/2001: Attacking Poverty* (World Bank 2001n), which laid out a three-pronged strategy for poverty reduction, focusing on opportunities, empowerment, and security (see box 2.1).

Risk management strategies are important before and after shocks occur. Measures taken before a shock are intended to reduce the likelihood that the shock will occur. If a shock cannot be prevented (for example, bad weather), then the aim is to mitigate its effects. These measures are classified in the SRM framework as risk reduction or risk mitigation strategies. Measures taken after the shock has

BOX 2.1

OPPORTUNITIES, EMPOWERMENT, AND SECURITY: A NEW STRATEGY FOR POVERTY REDUCTION

According to *World Development Report 2000/2001: Attacking Poverty* (World Bank 2001n: 6):

> The approach to reducing poverty has evolved over the past 50 years in response to a deepened understanding of the complexity of development.... In the 1990s governance and institutions moved toward center stage, as did issues of vulnerability at local and national levels. This report ... proposes a strategy for attacking poverty in three ways: promoting opportunity, facilitating empowerment, and enhancing security.

The security pillar highlights the importance of addressing risk and shocks in the context of poverty reduction:

> Enhancing security. Reducing vulnerability—to economic shocks, natural disasters, ill health, disability, and personal violence—is an intrinsic part of enhancing well-being and encourages investment in human capital and in higher-risk, higher-return activities. This requires effective national action to manage the risk of economywide shocks and effective mechanisms to reduce the risk faced by poor people, including health- and weather-related risks. It also requires building the assets of poor people, diversifying household activities, and providing a range of insurance mechanisms to cope with adverse shocks. (World Bank 2001n: 7)

occurred aim to help households cope with the impacts of the shock. The schematic in figure 2.1 depicts the sequencing of risk management strategies and shocks for a household in a given risk environment.

Prevention strategies address the underlying sources of risk by trying to decrease the probability that adverse states of the world will occur. Reducing the probability of an adverse risk typically increases expected incomes and reduces income variability. Some important preventive strategies fall outside SP&L, such as sound macropolicies, or well-functioning public policies for health, education, and training. Other strategies are central to the SP&L strategy; they include policies that, for example, reduce risks in the labor market, such as the risk of unemployment or underemployment, or malfunctioning in the labor market.

Mitigation strategies aim to alter the outcome experienced by a household in a given state of the world. They are also implemented before a shock occurs. Households have various strategies available to them to reduce the potential impact of given shocks. For example, when faced with uncertainty about the weather, a household may cultivate crops that are less sensitive to weather variability, thereby altering yields and reducing income variability when bad weather occurs. Alternatively, a household may choose to join a savings group or rely on informal, community-based insurance to ensure access to resources if a shock hits the household.

Coping strategies are used to relieve the impact of the shock after it has occurred. Among the most common coping strategies are reducing consumption, selling assets, seeking help from friends and family, borrowing, working longer hours, and relying on support from government programs. Clearly, not every strategy is available to all households, and some strategies have graver consequences for long-term outcomes than others do. A household that sells critical productive assets, such as farm equipment, livestock, or land, to meet short-run needs may have a difficult time recovering from a shock in the longer run. Because damaging coping strategies may make a household more susceptible to future adverse shocks or incidents of poverty (by decreasing the stock of future coping strategies to which it has access), interventions that decrease a household's reliance on damaging coping strategies are particularly important.

Prevention, mitigation, and coping strategies can be organized into various arrangements:

- *Informal arrangements* include help from family or friends, community organizations, and self-insurance for informal borrowing and lending, crop diversification, transfers, and gifts in times of need.
- *Market-based arrangements* include market-based institutions, such as currency, banks, and insurance systems. The institutional requirements for formal financial institutions to be effective are substantial because well-functioning financial markets as well as a financially literate population are required. Because collateral requirements and asymmetric information are likely to be high in the general banking sector, microfinance institutions are likely to play an important role in providing access to credit, savings, and adapted microinsurance services.
- *Public arrangements* include social insurance for risks such as old age, death, or illness of family members; injuries; and disabilities. Because these forms of social insurance

FIGURE 2.1: SEQUENCING OF SHOCKS AND RISK MANAGEMENT STRATEGIES

risk reduction strategies → uninsured risk (sources of risk) → risk mitigation decisions → implications for outcomes (levels, growth, short run, long run) → Shock (realization of the state of the world) → risk coping decisions → implications for outcomes (levels, growth, short run, long run)

Source: Dercon 2007.

are often linked to formal sector employment, they are unlikely to cover the most poor and vulnerable portions of the population. Additionally, government programs may better target the poor and vulnerable groups by helping households cope with the aftermath of a shock through social assistance, subsidies on basic goods and services, and public works programs.

Although each arrangement has its merits, each has a different role, and no arrangement is likely to be preferred in all circumstances. In a given country, the most effective means of implementing social risk management interventions will depend on the policy environment and strengths of existing institutions. Public interventions should complement informal and market-based arrangements and are particularly important in circumstances where these other arrangements are inadequate or lead to adverse outcomes for certain segments of the population.

How to Make SRM Diagnostics Operational through R&V Analysis

R&V analysis has played an important diagnostic and policy role in making the SRM framework operational. The definitive papers that framed future R&V analysis were Holzmann (2001) and Holzmann and Jørgensen (1999). Specific guidelines were prepared for undertaking RVAs (Heitzmann, Canagarajah, and Siegel 2002), as well as good practice papers on data and methods for measuring vulnerability (Hoddinott and Quisumbing 2003a, 2003b).

R&V analysis may take different forms, depending on country conditions. At the heart of all R&V analysis, however, is a set of core questions:

- Do households or individuals in the country or region face major risks? What are these risks, and how frequent and widespread are they? Are certain groups (for example, the poor, widows, or young children) more exposed to risk than others? Which risks have the greatest impact on welfare?
- Which populations are at risk of falling into (deeper) poverty? What is the profile of these populations, and how does their profile compare with that of the poor as conventionally defined (based on static poverty indicators)? For households at risk of poverty, how important are structural factors as compared to volatility in consumption and other measures of well-being?
- How does risk affect welfare? What types of ex ante risk management strategies are used by households, at what cost, and to what effect? What types of ex post risk-coping mechanisms are used, what is their cost, and how effective are they? What are the welfare implications of existing strategies? What role is played by informal institutions? Markets? Public policy and government programs?
- In the event of inadequate coping strategies, what are the short-run and longer-run implications for well-being? Do households trade off short-run gains at the cost of persistent and longer-run adverse impacts? How persistent are adverse welfare impacts, and how are they evidenced?
- How is risk incorporated into policy directions? Do existing public policies and programs adequately deal with the impact of risk? How can they be improved—with respect to which groups and which specific categories of risk? What are the requirements for programs to provide an adequate cushion against shocks? What is the role for SP&L?

METHODOLOGY FOR COMPILING THE INVENTORY OF R&V ANALYSES

How the Bank Accounts for R&V Analysis

Since December 2001, task team leaders have assigned thematic codes to activities; these codes are used for internal reporting and assessment. In the case of analytical and advisory activities and ESW, report types are also coded.

Two types of codes are directly relevant for identifying R&V analyses: report type *Risk and Vulnerability Assessment (SOP)* and thematic code *Vulnerability Assessment and Monitoring (55)*. Unfortunately, neither code does a good job of capturing the extent and breadth of R&V analysis in the Bank; first, because the report type definition is not consistent with the defining features and questions addressed by R&V analysis and, second, because task team leaders have used the relevant thematic code 55 very broadly for many different types of SP and non-SP related work.

Risk and Vulnerability Assessment (SOP) refers to a report that analyzes how the social sector affects living standards and productivity, income generation, social development, and mobility. Such a report also defines broad principles for guiding public expenditures that ensure the access of poor people to basic social services and increase project effects on health, nutrition, population, and education indicators. This definition has little bearing on the defining characteristics of R&V analysis described previously in the section "Definition of Key Terms" and, in any case, is far too general to define a concrete product line. Since 2001, only 19 reports were coded as SOP in the Bank's system, and only about half of them conform to the definition of R&V analysis used in this chapter.

In contrast, the definition of the thematic code *Vulnerability Assessment and Monitoring (55)*[4] is more consistent with the intent of R&V analysis: programs that help identify and monitor the vulnerable and that build capacity to reduce vulnerability, including (a) identification of vulnerable groups through both quantitative and qualitative means, (b) capacity building to address vulnerability, (c) institutional reforms to better address vulnerability concerns, and (d) monitoring conditions of the vulnerable. Unfortunately, the thematic code also applies to a substantial amount of the Bank's work on safety nets, labor markets, and SP strategy notes and has been used extensively both by SP and non-SP task team leaders across the Bank. More than 200 products were identified in Business Warehouse[5] that had a primary or secondary thematic code of 55, but only a subset of those are consistent with this chapter's definition of R&V analysis.

More recently, R&V analysis has been codified into practice in PAs through the Bank's Guidance Note on Poverty Assessments (July 2004), which accompanies OP 1.0 Operational Policy on Poverty Assessments. Paragraph 11 of the Guidance Note identifies the need to assess the main sources of vulnerability at the individual, household, community, and national levels; to assess food security, health risks, conflict, and environmental risks; and to assess the risk of loss of income caused by poor harvests, terms of trade shocks, unemployment, or declines in real wages. With these additions to the Bank's good practice guidance for poverty assessment, R&V analysis has been mainstreamed into practice in the World Bank. The review undertaken for this chapter shows that most PAs completed after 2004 include some discussion of vulnerability and risk.

This chapter aims to capture the full scope of the World Bank's R&V analysis, as defined by the list of identifying features. Such work includes both formal and informal ESW. Formal diagnostic reports typically include RVAs, risk-focused PAs, a growing body of work on safety nets that uses vulnerability diagnostics,[6] and SP strategy papers. A large body of research that focuses on different aspects of risk, vulnerability, and poverty reduction has also been included here from the SP discussion paper series, regional series, and various journals and research publications. Although other aid agencies and research institutes are beginning to use R&V analytical approaches, only work financed or led by the World Bank is included.

Data Sources

This chapter used several strategies to identify the universe of R&V analysis work:

- Business Warehouse provided a list of all Bank-supported ESW with thematic code 55 and report type SOP. All work that fit the criteria described for R&V analysis was included.
- An early R&V analysis list that was compiled by the Social Risk Management Team in the network anchor was used, as well as papers presented in various workshops on risk and poverty[7] and those found through key-word searches in Business Warehouse and the Bank's intranet.
- In addition, a review was carried out to identify all PAs that include substantial analysis of risk and vulnerability (for example, a section or chapter that examines the links between risk and poverty or calculation of vulnerability-to-poverty indicators).

The resulting inventory includes 155 documents:[8] 132 have a specific country focus, whereas 23 have a broader focus (for example, on R&V methodologies and approaches). These documents are listed in annex 2.A. Taken in total, the Bank's R&V analysis portfolio comprises a substantial body of global knowledge about the links between risk and poverty and about the nature of vulnerability as a forward-looking concept. The various studies highlight the importance of security and of SP policies in a range of settings, such as poor countries suffering from droughts and other natural disasters, fragile states beset with conflict, rapidly changing transition economies, or middle-income countries struggling with economic shocks and potential financial crises.

OVERVIEW OF THE R&V ANALYSIS PORTFOLIO

Description of the Bank-Wide Portfolio

As noted, 132 country-specific R&V analyses were completed between fiscal years 2000 and 2007, spread across all six regions. (Table 2.1 describes the stock of R&V analyses by year and region.) An additional 23 background papers were prepared, primarily under the auspices of the Social Protection Anchor. These papers focus on analytical methods and approaches, good practice guidelines, and discussion of cross-regional and cross-country experiences.

R&V analysis has been applied throughout the developing world. Analysis of risk, shocks, and poverty began early in the East Asia and Pacific (EAP) Region, primarily in response to the 1997 financial crisis. A substantial body of early work was undertaken in the Latin America and Caribbean (LAC) and the Europe and Central Asia (ECA) Regions, initially driven by concerns about macrovolatility but over time focusing more on vulnerability of the poor and related microconcerns. In contrast, R&V analysis came on line more slowly in the Africa (AFR) Region and the South Asia Region (SAR), and much of this later work has had a strong focus on human development and SP policies. The focus and coverage of R&V analysis has varied substantially by region and is still evolving. The following section provides an overview of regional approaches and findings.

One-third of the fiscal year 2000 to 2007 portfolio covers freestanding RVA reports and papers, and the remaining two-thirds comprises risk-focused PAs and poverty policy notes. The AFR Region accounts for the majority of freestanding RVAs, followed closely by the LAC Region. In contrast, a significant majority of the ECA Region portfolio (31 of 34 products) and of the Middle East and North Africa (MENA) Region portfolio (6 of 7 products) consists of PAs that integrate analysis of vulnerability and the effect of risk and shocks with more conventional poverty analyses (see figure 2.2).

R&V analysis had a particularly high profile in the early years of 2000, in response to economic shocks and financial crises in a number of countries. Natural disasters of global proportion, such as Hurricane Mitch in 1998, the 2004 tsunami, Hurricane Katrina in 2005, and repeated droughts in southern Africa, gave new impetus to work on risk and risk coping in the middle of the decade. The distribution of R&V analysis over time mimics the frequency and types of shocks experienced (see figure 2.3).

Table 2.1: **R&V Analysis by Region, Fiscal Years 2000–07**

Year	Africa	East Asia and Pacific	Europe and Central Asia	Latin America and the Caribbean	Middle East and North Africa	South Asia Region	Total
2000	2	5	3	1	0	1	12
2001	1	5	4	5	2	0	17
2002	1	3	5	4	3	6	22
2003	7	3	8	7	1	1	27
2004	2	0	4	6	1	0	13
2005	6	0	6	4	0	3	19
2006	3	6	0	1	0	1	11
2007	4	0	4	0	0	3	11
Total	26	22	34	28	7	15	132

Source: Authors' calculations based on the RVA inventory.

FIGURE 2.2: **RVAS COMPARED WITH PAs, FISCAL YEARS 2000–07**

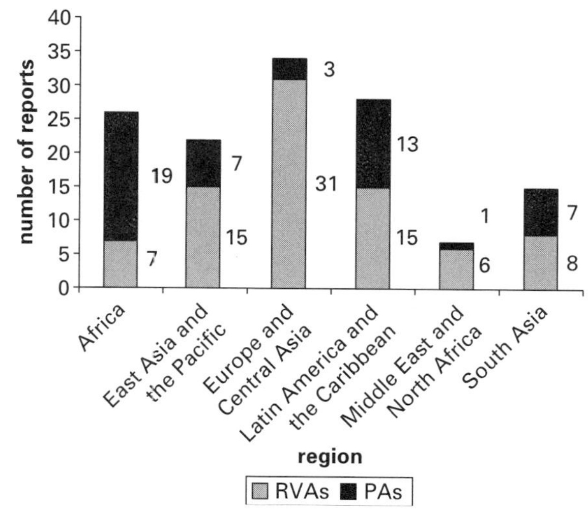

Source: Authors' calculations based on the RVA inventory.

FIGURE 2.3: **COMBINED R&V ANALYSIS PRODUCTS BY YEAR**

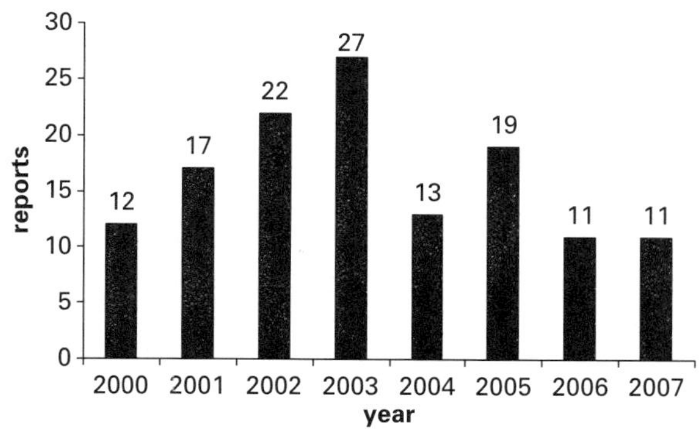

Source: Authors' calculations based on the RVA inventory.

In addition to the many reports, working papers, and research studies, R&V analysis has been the subject of several major conferences and a number of workshops in recent years, beginning with the Stiglitz Summer Workshop in 1999, which was carried out in preparation for *World Development Report 2000/2001: Attacking Poverty* (World Bank 2001n) (box 2.2).

Recent years have witnessed a reduction in freestanding work on R&V at the Bank, accompanied by a slight increase in risk-focused PAs. On the basis of these numbers, one is tempted to say that the Bank's interest in R&V concerns has been decreasing. However, R&V analysis portfolio numbers capture only part of the Bank's rich body of work on risk, shocks, and natural disasters. The SRM framework has influenced the work of other sectors in the Bank. For example, the Infrastructure Network has developed risk assessment tools for hazard risk management, and a substantial number of hazard risk management assessments have recently been finalized or are in preparation. Many new Bank operations are designed in response

BOX 2.2

KEY WORKSHOPS ON RISK, VULNERABILITY, AND POVERTY, FISCAL YEARS 2000–07

In 1999, World Bank Chief Economist Joseph Stiglitz began a summer research series to discuss leading issues in development economics. The first workshop was devoted to poverty, inequality, and development, the topic of *World Development Report 2000/2001.* Two full sessions were devoted to issues of risk and poverty: Session 5: Risk and Vulnerability and Safety Nets, and Session 6: Coping with National Shocks. In addition, the various links between security and poverty were discussed in a number of other sessions (security is one of the three pillars of the *World Development Report* poverty reduction strategy).

In September 2002, the International Food Policy Research Institute (IFPRI) and the World Bank jointly hosted a major conference, "Risk and Vulnerability: Estimation and Policy Implications." The objectives of the two-day conference were (a) to review the current approaches used in estimating vulnerability and their value added in terms of policy recommendations, compared to the traditional approach to understanding poverty, and (b) to brainstorm on the information needed for microeconometric risk and vulnerability assessment. Fifteen research papers were presented and discussed at the conference.

The IFPRI–World Bank conference was followed by several internal events at the World Bank, including a research workshop titled "Poverty, Risk, and Vulnerability in Sub-Saharan Africa" (November 2003) and a training workshop titled "Measuring, Understanding, and Alleviating Household Vulnerability: Data Needs and Policy Implications" (February 2004). Workshop papers on Africa were published in the *Journal of African Economics* (vol. 14, no. 4, 2005).

The Bank's Poverty Reduction Anchor hosted a workshop titled "Frontiers in Practice: Reducing Poverty Through Better Diagnostics" in March 2006. The workshop had four sessions, including a session on data and methodological advances in risk and poverty.

to natural and human-made disasters. The Social Development Department has developed conflict assessment tools, and these have been applied in many countries over the years, including in the preparation of freestanding conflict assessments as well as social assessments (see Conflict Prevention and Reconstruction Unit n.d.). Note that a number of R&V reports included in the stocktaking—particularly for Africa—include work on climate shocks and related natural disasters (for example, World Bank 2005e, on Ethiopia) and on conflict risks (for example, World Bank 2006b on Guinea-Bissau and World Bank 2007e on Guinea).

Overview of Regional Approaches

The Bank's overall SP strategy, *Social Protection Sector Strategy: From Safety Net to Springboard* (World Bank 2001k) was developed and further refined on the basis of a series of regional SP strategy papers, beginning with East Asia in 1999 and ending with the LAC strategy paper in 2003:

- "Towards an East Asia Social Protection Strategy" (World Bank 1999a)
- *Balancing Protection and Opportunity: A Strategy for Social Protection in Transition Economies* (World Bank 2000a)
- *Dynamic Risk Management and the Poor: Developing a Social Protection Strategy for Africa* (World Bank 2001c)
- *Poverty and Vulnerability in South Asia* (World Bank 2002m)
- *Reducing Vulnerability and Increasing Opportunity: Social Protection in the Middle East and North Africa* (World Bank 2002n)
- *Volatility, Risk, and Innovation: Social Protection in Latin America and the Caribbean* (World Bank 2003q)

Each region has taken a different approach, in large part determined by differences in country settings, such as the level of development, current SP systems, the nature of the risks faced by poor households, the country policy environment, and capacity for institutional response.

The organization of the Bank's regional teams also has had some bearing on SP analytical and diagnostic work: for example, until 2003, SAR had no dedicated SP staff, and little R&V analysis was done outside the context of PAs. Much of the extensive R&V analysis for the ECA Region was also done in the context of PAs, many led by a well-staffed ECA-SP team. Similarly, the AFR Region developed a very rich body of work on poverty in the 1990s, led jointly by SP and Poverty Reduction and Economic Management staff. By the late 1990s, however, the impetus for poverty work in the AFR Region had slowed, and few new PAs were being carried out. In lieu of PAs, SP launched a number of freestanding RVA reports for African countries. More recently, a new series of risk-focused PAs has been initiated for Africa.

The remainder of the section briefly discusses the primary issues and the type and coverage of R&V analysis undertaken in each region.

R&V Analysis in Latin America and the Caribbean

Issues Addressed. Countries in Latin America face a common set of challenges that shape future priorities for social protection. Shocks caused by economic volatility widely affect incomes, frequent natural disasters afflict large populations, and political volatility prevents public policies from being sustained in the long run. Inequalities in redistributing the benefits of growth continue to widen, and existing SP systems mostly cover workers in the formal sector and better-off households.

The SP regional strategy paper identified three key challenges for social protection in the region: (a) reducing the vulnerability of low-income households and ensuring that they can meet basic consumption needs, (b) helping households effectively manage income over their full life cycle, and (c) improving equity—particularly in response to the effects of shocks.

R&V Analysis Coverage. Risk and vulnerability are an important part of the poverty debate in Latin America. Most of the region's R&V Analysis poverty assessment work also addresses vulnerability issues, looking not only at the number of poor people and the evolution of poverty but also at the impacts of shocks and at responses to them. Diagnostic work in vulnerability, poverty, and risk is often complemented by specific assessments, for example, of social security programs.

The region also experimented with different methods to measure vulnerability—for example, life-cycle approaches or vulnerability-to-poverty indicators—as well as qualitative approaches. The 2003 Guatemala PA hence included a very detailed treatment of vulnerability, which was based on innovative qualitative methods and estimation of vulnerability-to-poverty indicators (see World Bank 2003j). It provided a strong basis for informed discussions in Guatemala on poverty and SP policies, and it brought concerns about risk and shocks to the forefront of policy discussions.

Much of the region's R&V analysis has focused on a specific shock or crisis. Argentina's 2003 PA (World Bank

2003b) looked at the impact of the 2002 economic crisis and at local policy responses. It highlighted the limitations of formal SP mechanisms in reaching the poorest and discussed the need to develop long-term poverty alleviation strategies to reduce the number of vulnerable persons. Similar analyses and conclusions are shared in poverty diagnoses for Bolivia (World Bank 2002d, 2005c) and Uruguay (World Bank 2003n). Analyses of the effect of the "coffee crisis" in 1999 to 2000 on poverty in Central America's economies further point to the effects and limitations of formal and informal SP mechanisms that were intended to assist poor people who face economic shocks. The studies note the positive effects of conditional cash transfer programs in Nicaragua and of informal strategies of income diversification by poor households before the crisis (Maluccio 2005; Vakis, Kruger, and Mason 2004; World Bank 2001g).

Other R&V analysis highlights the growing needs of poor populations not reached by formal SP programs, such as the youth and the unemployed in Uruguay (World Bank 2001m). In Ecuador and Peru, poverty is attributed to governments' mainly focusing on the extraction of natural resources and on agriculture rather than promoting the creation of better-paying jobs for poor people (World Bank 2004d, 2005j). More generic poverty assessments call for relatively similar public policies to reduce macroeconomic vulnerabilities, to reform formal protection mechanisms so that they better reach the poor, and to invest in youth by improving their access to education and health services. They include PAs for Brazil (World Bank 2003f); Colombia (World Bank 2002f, 2002g); Costa Rica (World Bank 2002h); Ecuador (World Bank 2000b, 2004d); and the República Bolivariana de Venezuela (World Bank 2001a).

R&V Analysis in Europe and Central Asia

Issues Addressed. The Bank's work on poverty and vulnerability divides Europe and Central Asia into three groups: (a) a "European" group of Southeastern European nations and of countries about to join or having recently joined the European Union; (b) a "Eurasian" group comprising members of the Commonwealth of Independent States; and (c) a group of nations emerging from conflict. Each group has reached different levels of development and of institutional capacity to analyze and respond to poverty and vulnerability. Most countries in the European group have formal systems of social protection; their key challenges relate to adapting these systems to the rules and constraints of a market economy. The Eurasian nations tend to have weaker government systems and to rely on informal structures of social protection. Their governments need help in analyzing risk and poverty and in finding ways to bridge gaps between formal and informal systems of protection. Postconflict countries have lost their capacities to generate wealth; conflicts have further destroyed their formal and informal systems of protection against risk and their governments' capacities to plan. Their needs start with basic assessments of poverty situations and with integrated national development plans.

R&V Analysis Coverage. The ECA Region has carried out two comprehensive regional studies of growth, poverty, and inequality (Alam 2005; Jones and Revenga 2000), and it is in the process of finalizing a third flagship study. All studies highlight the importance of social risk management and the need for fundamental improvements in SP policies. They assess trends in poverty and in vulnerability[9] and are complemented by 32 country-level R&V analyses. Broken down by country groups, they can be characterized as follows:

- In the European group, most work aims at developing governments' capacities to analyze the evolution of social indicators as a basis for policy making and to improve existing systems of social protection so that they adapt to a market economy and better reach vulnerable groups. Most then lay directions for Poverty Reduction Strategy Papers or National Poverty Reduction Strategies. Key examples of such work are the poverty assessments for Albania (de Soto and others 2002; World Bank 2003a), Belarus (World Bank 2004a), Poland (World Bank 2004g), and the Russian Federation (World Bank 2005l). The assessments for Bulgaria (World Bank 2002e), Hungary (World Bank 2001d), and Romania (World Bank 2003k) provide good examples of in-depth work on particularly vulnerable groups. The assessments for the Slovak Republic (World Bank 2001j, 2005m) highlight the continuing concerns about equity—concerns that must be addressed for a former centrally planned economy to fully integrate into the European Union. The PAs and RVAs for Armenia (World Bank 2002b, 2003c) highlight continuing levels of poverty and vulnerability linked to transition processes and discuss the key reforms needed for Armenia's SP system to become more effective and better targeted to the needs of the poorest and most vulnerable. More typical PAs and updates were conducted for Croatia (World Bank 2001b), Georgia (World Bank 2002i), and the former Yugoslav Republic of Macedonia (World Bank 2005g).
- In the Eurasian group, analytical work is more generic; it focuses on developing recommendations for policy makers because governments tend to have less capacity in analyzing

poverty trends, in developing national poverty reduction strategies, and in providing formal social protection to the poor. Nevertheless, strong traditional mechanisms of mutual help provide bases to develop SP programs. In this group, poverty analyses rely more on qualitative consultations than on statistical data alone, because the latter are often not readily available. Particularly interesting in providing a well-rounded understanding of poverty and vulnerability using qualitative methods to complement limited quantitative data are the PAs for Azerbaijan (World Bank 2003d), Kazakhstan (World Bank 2004e), and Uzbekistan (World Bank 2003o, 2007d). Similar assessments were conducted for the Kyrgyz Republic (World Bank 2003h, 2005i, 2007b); Latvia (World Bank 2007c); Moldova (World Bank 2004h); and Serbia and Montenegro (World Bank 2003l).

- Postconflict countries have suffered extensive destruction of their government systems and their social fabric. There, the Bank's poverty and vulnerability work has focused on determinants of growth and security and on the importance of providing basic services to the most vulnerable groups. These assessments—which provide directions to develop national poverty reduction strategies—cover Bosnia and Herzegovina; Kosovo (World Bank 2001f, 2005h, 2007a); and Tajikistan (World Bank 2000c). Other assessments look at recovery after crises, such as the earthquake that affected Turkey in 1999, which was followed by a financial crisis (World Bank 2000d, 2003m).

R&V Analysis in East Asia and the Pacific

Issues Addressed. The EAP Region prepared its SP strategy in 1999, on the heels of the 1997 financial crisis. Fueled by concerns about the crisis, the strategy highlighted the need to strengthen SP mechanisms with reference to labor markets and labor policies, pensions, and safety nets. Subsequent analyses focused on the effects of economic growth, on equity in the distribution of wealth, and on the coverage of public services. They underscored that a focus on risk was essential to understand the evolution of poverty over time and highlighted how risk especially affected some of the most vulnerable populations. As the financial crisis receded, natural disasters and global health threats (for example, the avian flu) have become an increasing focus in East Asia's R&V analysis.

R&V Analysis Coverage. To date, East Asia's R&V analysis has been integrated within country-led PAs or presented in published research papers and journal articles. In 2007, a regional vulnerability flagship study was launched that will build on the rich body of existing country-level R&V analysis and undertake new cross-country analyses. The aim of that study is to highlight the importance of risk and continuing widespread vulnerability in the region, despite substantial reductions in poverty, and to facilitate discussions across countries about the challenges and policy responses.

In the early part of the decade, EAP was home to research and innovations in R&V analysis methods, primarily focused on measuring the impacts of the financial crisis. Pritchett, Suryahadi, and Sumarto (2000) proposed models to quantify vulnerability to poverty in Indonesia, and Chaudhuri, Jalan, and Suryahadi (2002) used survey data to empirically demonstrate links between vulnerability and poverty in several countries, reinforcing findings from China (Jalan and Ravallion 2001). In the countries most affected by the 1997 crisis, Bourguignon and Goh (2002) found no apparent relation between vulnerability to poverty and openness to international trade, and in the Philippines, a research study demonstrated, in fact, that the financial crisis had affected poverty less extensively than a natural shock such as El Niño (Datt and Hoogeveen 2000). The new thinking and analytical work supported poverty assessment and country dialogue in a number of countries. In Thailand, the Bank has collaborated with the government and other donors to assess the evolution of poverty and the effects of social protection following the 1997 crisis; an SP strategy led to a Country Development Partnership mainly focused on developing mechanisms of social protection and social development (World Bank 2001l).

As the crisis receded, R&V analysis focused on a wider set of issues, such as natural disasters; climate shocks; idiosyncratic risks, for example, in the labor market; and health shocks. Thus, a people-centered poverty report prepared in 2002 for Indonesia looked at the determinants of poor peoples' livelihoods, including local livelihood risks, and gave directions on how to improve well-being and reduce poverty through empowerment, social protection, pro-poor growth, and safety nets (World Bank 2002l). Indonesia's most recent PA includes an extended analysis of the risks and vulnerabilities of the poor and of the various mechanisms that they use to manage shocks (World Bank 2006c). The *Vietnam Development Report 2000* (World Bank 1999b) showed that the poor were particularly vulnerable to health shocks and to fluctuations in farm revenue. It proposed a poverty reduction strategy focused on (a) increasing employment and productivity, (b) ensuring that all could equitably benefit from the results of growth, and (c) reducing the vulnerability of the poorest. The *Vietnam Development Report 2004* (World Bank 2003p) then showed that over 15 years the country had reduced poverty faster than many other countries starting at the same levels. The PA for the Philippines (World Bank 2001h) assessed the effect that the financial crisis and climate shocks had on poverty levels and trends and explored a range of policies aimed at reducing vulnerability in the country.

Vulnerability and the role of SP policies have been addressed in PAs for other countries in the region as well. For example, the 2006 Cambodia PA analyzed poverty from an integrated approach combining income poverty; measures of inequalities in accessing productive capital; and an analysis of relations between growth, institutions, and poverty (World Bank 2006a). The work was supported by a series of mixed-method studies on SP issues (such as Ridao-Cano 2006), on access to justice, and on the use of public funds to deliver health and education services. A new PA is just being finalized for China; it treats health shocks and SP responses extensively.

R&V Analysis in Africa

Issues Addressed. Countries in Sub-Saharan Africa are characterized by high levels of poverty, inequality, and broad exposure to a range of risks, including repeated drought and frequent food shortages; AIDS, malaria, and other health threats and epidemics; macroeconomic shocks; and conflict, political instability, and corruption. Few countries have effective formal SP systems, and those systems that do exist (for example, pension systems) often serve the needs of the better-off rather than the poor. Poor households resort to a range of informal strategies to manage and cope with risk, many of which can have long-run adverse impacts (for example, reducing food consumption or pulling children out of school).

The Bank developed a rich body of work on poverty in Africa in the 1990s through formal PAs (38 completed between 1993 and 2000), poverty notes and updates, Country Economic Memorandums, and related development reports. Poverty reports for Africa were framed around the 1990 *World Development Report*'s approach to poverty reduction (World Bank 1990), and all these early PAs included a discussion of vulnerable groups and formal and informal safety nets.

R&V Analysis Coverage. The Africa SP strategy paper, completed in 2001, highlighted the importance of risk management for Africa's poor and other vulnerable groups. A number of country-level RVAs were launched following completion of the SP strategy paper, using RVA guidelines prepared by the Social Protection Anchor (Heitzmann, Canagarajah, and Siegel 2002; Hoddinott and Quisumbing 2003a, 2003b). These early RVAs had a strong diagnostic focus, with the aim of enumerating the risks faced by poor men, women, and children and of identifying formal and informal coping mechanisms. The reports looked at a range of risks in different settings: climate shocks and food security in Ethiopia (World Bank 2005e); health shocks, including malaria, in Kenya (Christiaensen and Subbarao 2005); and conflict and ethnic violence in the Democratic Republic of Congo (World Bank 2003g), Guinea (World Bank 2007e), Guinea-Bissau (World Bank 2006b), and Nigeria (World Bank 2003i). A number of these studies used new types of data (for example, shock modules) and innovative analytical methods (for example, estimation of vulnerability-to-poverty indicators) to look at poverty in a dynamic rather than a static context. For example, the Burkina Faso RVA (World Bank 2004b) experimented with new measurement methodologies to better identify the most vulnerable among the poor. The Ethiopia RVA (World Bank 2005e) is noteworthy in extending its analysis to include a discussion of risk management strategies, drawing on conceptual distinctions between risk coping and risk reduction or mitigation. The work uses data on existing safety net programs, including costs and coverage, as well as household responses to hypothetical questions in a household survey about potential sources of funds to meet unforeseen shocks.

Those early RVAs were followed by a series of risk-focused PAs for Benin (World Bank 2003e), Burkina Faso[10] (World Bank 2005d), Malawi (in preparation), Uganda (World Bank 2006e), and Zambia (World Bank 2007h). Many common issues were addressed. For example, PAs for Malawi, Uganda, and Zambia each highlighted the importance of drought and related climate shocks as well as households' limited access to safety nets and other formal risk management instruments. HIV/AIDS and other communicable diseases were identified as major sources of risk for poor people in Malawi and Zambia and were also linked to risks experienced by elderly persons.

R&V Analysis in the Middle East and North Africa

Issues Addressed. The Middle East and North Africa was a high-growth region until the mid 1980s, when oil prices began to fall. Many countries experienced negative economic growth rates, and economic and social conditions began to deteriorate. The situation was exacerbated by conflict: civil wars in Algeria, Lebanon, and the Republic of Yemen; the Iran-Iraq War, the first Gulf War, and the current war in Iraq. According to the Middle East and North Africa SP strategy paper, countries in the region now face economic and social risks that threaten investments in human capital and compromise the welfare of the population. Particularly vulnerable population groups include the poor; children and youth; small farmers, who remain exposed to unanticipated changes in weather and fluctuations in prices; first-time job seekers and low-skilled workers, who face the risk of unemployment; and the elderly, who may lack access to sustainable health insurance and pension systems.

R&V Analysis Coverage. A substantial body of analytical and policy work addresses conventional SP themes in the MENA Region (that is, labor markets, children and youth, safety nets, and formal and informal pensions), much of it focused on key sources of risk for vulnerable groups. This work has been augmented by several risk-focused PAs for the Arab Republic of Egypt (World Bank 2002a); Morocco (World Bank 2001e, 2004f); the Republic of Yemen (World Bank 2002o); and the West Bank and Gaza (World Bank 2001i, 2003r).

The impacts of growth reversals and deteriorating social conditions are discussed in the Egypt PA, which describes the changing picture of poverty and highlights growing concerns about regional disparities, lack of opportunities, and high exposure to risk among the poorest and most vulnerable. The report highlights the importance of better-targeted safety nets and subsidy programs for them. PAs for Morocco and the Republic of Yemen likewise highlight the importance of good social policies and more effective social spending. Morocco's growth slowdown in the 1990s was accompanied by sharp increases in unemployment and poverty and in the share of the population vulnerable to poverty. In contrast to Egypt and Morocco, the Republic of Yemen has high levels of poverty (42 percent of the population), and an additional 25 percent of the population is vulnerable to poverty. Vulnerability is primarily driven by idiosyncratic factors but is exacerbated by a series of covariate shocks, such as drought in 1990 and 1991, war in 1991, and civil war in 1994.

Risks associated with conflict are addressed in PAs for Algeria, Lebanon, and the West Bank and Gaza. Conflict plunges economies into crisis and causes dramatic declines in living conditions. The West Bank and Gaza provides a classic example: following three years of *intifada*, 16 percent of the population was living below the subsistence poverty line, and many of the poor and near poor had exhausted their savings and were vulnerable to malnutrition, ill health, and permanent poverty traps. RVAs in crisis settings highlight the importance of emergency assistance through public works and targeted cash transfers, as well as job training once the recovery period begins.

R&V Analysis in South Asia

Issues Addressed. South Asia's regional SP strategy identifies a wide range of covariate and idiosyncratic risks that increase vulnerability of the poor—climate shocks and natural disasters, labor market risks, health shocks—and framed a cross-sectoral strategy for achieving social protection objectives in the region. The strategy highlighted the strong links between poverty and risk; the importance of improving access to markets and market-based instruments, such as insurance and credit, for ensuring longer-run security and well-being; and the need for short-run interventions to support risk mitigation and coping. More recently, massive natural disasters such as the 2004 tsunami and Pakistan's 2005 earthquake have helped focus the attention of policy makers and of the international community on the links between the risk of natural disaster and poverty and on vulnerability more generally in the SAR.

Evolution of R&V Analysis. Initial R&V analysis was done in the context of PAs and poverty updates for Bangladesh (World Bank 2002c); Nepal (World Bank 2006d); Pakistan (World Bank 2002k); Sri Lanka (World Bank 2002p, 2005k); and Uttar Pradesh, India (World Bank 2002j). The Uttar Pradesh PA highlighted the importance of risk (particularly idiosyncratic risk) in determining levels and trends in poverty in one of India's poorest and largest states. Health shocks were found to be particularly problematic—and a major cause of extreme poverty—particularly for the elderly and female-headed households. Social identity (caste) also was a major risk factor. A recent social safety net assessment for Uttar Pradesh (Ajwad 2007) builds on the earlier poverty study and explores potential SP responses. An all-India safety net assessment is under way; it explores sources of risk, identifies key vulnerable groups, and analyzes the coverage and efficacy of safety net programs nationwide.

PAs for Bangladesh and Pakistan discuss the impacts of natural disasters and climate shocks. Bangladesh is flood prone, and food security is a continuing concern. R&V analysis for Bangladesh focuses on the need for better ex ante risk management as well as ex post risk coping, for example, through formal safety nets and emergency relief measures (del Ninno, Dorosh, and Smith 2003; World Bank 2005b). Poor households in Pakistan struggle to cope with adverse weather shocks and other agriculture shocks, and many of the near poor and nonpoor are at risk of poverty (Mansuri and Healy 2002; World Bank 2007g). The massive earthquake in 2005, together with droughts and flooding in earlier years, has focused the attention of Pakistani policy makers on the need for a systemic response to large covariate risks—that is, the importance of safety nets and community-based systems that can be scaled up in times of need.

A poverty and vulnerability assessment carried out for Afghanistan in 2005 (World Bank 2005a) likewise discussed the importance of natural disasters, drought, and sharp increases in food prices. It also highlighted vulnerability linked to conflict and the potential for an escalation of violence in parts of the country. As a result of this work, vulnerability has become an explicit area of focus in Afghanistan's poverty reduction strategy. Vulnerability linked to conflict also was an important concern in the Sri Lanka PA as well as in the 2006 poverty work for Nepal. Sri Lanka was particularly hard hit by the 2004 tsunami, and a number of studies have been launched to better understand the long-run effect of the tsunami on living conditions of the poor.

RESULTS: EFFECT ON COUNTRY STRATEGIES AND APPROACHES

The focus of R&V analysis thus far has been primarily on analytics and good diagnostics. Moving from diagnostics to better and more risk-sensitive policies remains a challenge. There is still debate within the Bank about whether the dynamic focus of R&V analysis leads to a different set of policies (or different policy sequencing) than does traditional poverty analysis. A strong consensus is emerging that analyzing poverty dynamics and assessing vulnerability can lead to different policy recommendations, depending on the country and institutional setting, but more work remains to be done to better understand these critical policy reforms and to promote lesson sharing across countries and regions.

In a number of countries, R&V analytical work underpinned important policy dialogue on SP&L concerns and helped the Bank do business in a different and more effective way. Examples of good practices from Ethiopia, Chile, and Turkey are discussed in the following sections.

Ethiopia: Country Experience and Results

A recent PA for Ethiopia (World Bank 2005f) estimated that 44 percent of the population lived below the national poverty line. Half of these people were chronically poor and lived below the food poverty line of 1,650 kilocalories per day. Using these same data, the Ethiopia RVA (World Bank 2005e) estimated vulnerability to poverty to be very high, with 70 percent of the population predicted to have more than a 50 percent chance of falling into poverty at some point in the future. This finding implies that nearly a quarter of nonpoor Ethiopians (based on static poverty measures) face a high probability of being poor at some future point.

The RVA highlighted considerable scope for improving the welfare of households through social risk management instruments. High levels of vulnerability in Ethiopia are due to a combination of a high-risk environment and inadequate coping mechanisms. The majority of rural households are affected by drought, which results in harvest failure, livestock losses, and food and water insecurity. Furthermore, households commonly face large movements in prices, particularly for grains, which constitute an important dietary source, and for coffee, the main export crop. Because rainfall and price risks are locally covariate, they tend to affect entire communities, thereby reducing the potential for risk sharing using localized mutual insurance. Idiosyncratic health shocks are so pervasive that they have begun to deteriorate into communitywide shocks. Exposure to malaria and HIV/AIDS in Ethiopia exacerbates the vulnerability of the poor. In 2000, 6.4 percent of the adult population overall and 15 percent of the urban adult population were diagnosed as HIV positive, and 40 percent of the population was estimated to be at risk of malaria.

Inadequate market mechanisms and public strategies for coping with these high risks have resulted in a large fraction of the population being subject to food insecurity. Household strategies to deal with risk do not provide adequate protection, particularly in the face of locally covariate risk.

The RVA identified gaps and difficulties with several public risk management programs (for example, supplemental irrigation, water harvesting, agroecological packages, and resettlements). The programs reached only a fraction of the poor and vulnerable and were, in many cases, poorly designed. Unpredictable policy changes were also highlighted as having contributed to the volatility of the environment.

The primary focus of Ethiopia's SP programs for coping with the aftereffects of a shock is on drought protection and food security, leaving households to cope on their own with other risks, such as HIV/AIDS or malaria. For two decades, the government has relied heavily on the international community to provide emergency assistance to meet the consumption needs of both the chronic and the transitory poor. Although these programs helped reduce poverty—at least temporarily—unpredictable and often delayed responses meant that they did little to prevent environmental degradation or to protect livelihoods or community or household assets. As such, the programs were designed to provide short-term relief rather than to support a broader framework for providing households with reliable risk management strategies. In addition, the national food security program had a narrow coverage, leaving a substantial proportion of the population at risk of food insecurity. Despite large food-aid flows, chronic food insecurity has continued to rise in the aftermath of repeated droughts as vulnerable households without adequate risk management mechanisms fall deeper into poverty.

In recognition of the substantial shortcomings of the emergency aid regime, the government launched in 2003 the Coalition for Food Security initiative, with the aim of developing a food security framework. Because of its extensive work on vulnerability and poverty and its ongoing discussions with government, the World Bank was asked to lead the design of the national safety net framework and to be one of the major financing partners.

In 2005, the Ethiopian government initiated the Productive Safety Nets Program (PSNP), which replaced the emergency humanitarian appeal system as the chief means of assisting chronically poor households. The objective of the PSNP is to reduce household vulnerability and increase resilience to shocks. These aims are to be achieved through reforming the humanitarian emergency system to create a development-oriented program.

The PSNP has three primary components:

- Providing safety net activities that support chronically poor households through labor-intensive public works and grants for those who cannot participate in public works projects (for example, orphans, pregnant women, and elderly or sick individuals)
- Providing timely resources for transient food-insecure households in response to shocks
- Strengthening program implementation through capacity building, improved monitoring, evaluation, transparency, and accountability.

Chile: Country Experience and Results

Chile experienced a period of growth between 1987 and 1998, demarcated by increasing average incomes and a substantial drop in poverty. An RVA conducted in 2004 suggests that, although poverty continued to fall between 1998 and 2000, the level of extreme poverty stagnated during this latter period (World Bank 2004c). Building on existing poverty analysis, the RVA examined household risk management and SP strategies to assess the efficiency and efficacy of instruments available to manage risk. It indicated that the poorest households had high exposure to a range of risks and were characterized by high levels of malnutrition, low levels of schooling, unemployment, ill health, and disability.

Despite the presence of a number of SP programs, substantial gaps in coverage were identified, particularly for the poorest households and in rural areas. The RVA identified a set of reforms to SP policies and institutions that would help close the gap in coverage between the formal and informal sectors. To improve outreach to Chile's poorest groups, the RVA suggested that less reliance be placed on contributory social insurance and greater weight be given to social assistance. Furthermore, it recommended that the social assistance programs be financed through value added taxes rather than payroll taxes, to ensure a more reliable source of contributory financing.

Responding to the interests of the Chilean government, the RVA ultimately provided a diagnostic and framework for Chile's Social Protection Sector Adjustment Loan. Chile's Fund for Solidarity and Social Investment (Fondo de Solidaridad e Inversión Social, or FOSIS) experimented with applying different SRM approaches to its investment decisions, prioritized according to risk indicators. The Puente program for indigent households was piloted in response. In addition, the government implemented broad legislative and institutional reform to reach the poorest of the poor. The Chile Solidario initiative, announced in May 2002, included a package of legislative reforms to Chile's poverty reduction and social protection policies.

Chile's Social Protection Sector Adjustment Loan supported government actions in five key areas:

- Reforming poverty reduction and SP policies targeted to the poorest households
- Integrating databases and service provision and improving key information systems, including the country's primary tool to target the poor
- Performing improved monitoring and evaluation of social programs and policies, including providing a greater role for civil society in conducting participatory evaluations
- Expanding the roles of the evaluation of social programs and policies, including providing a greater role for civil society in conducting participatory evaluations
- Expanding the roles of municipal authorities and civil society in implementing social policy.

The loan ultimately improved the access of the poorest households to Chile's SP system and increased the effectiveness of the system in reducing extreme poverty and protecting the living conditions of the poorest.

Turkey: Country Experience and Results

The first PA for Turkey (World Bank 2000d) documented substantial improvements in social indicators and moderate reductions in poverty during the 1990s, despite volatile growth in gross domestic product, weak employment, and rising inequality. A follow-on study of poverty and vulnerability (World Bank 2003m) found that natural disasters—earthquakes, in particular—were a key source of vulnerability. Earthquakes are frequent in Turkey, and a high proportion of the population lives in self-constructed masonry houses, leaving these people especially hard hit. The study found that the poor had higher levels of exposure and were ill equipped to cope when natural disasters actually occurred. Moreover, vulnerability (defined as the proportion of the population with income below twice the food poverty line) was on the rise in Turkey, increasing from 36 percent of the urban population in 1994 to 56 percent by 2001.

On August 17, 1999, a major earthquake hit the Marmara region of Turkey, leaving 17,000 dead and 200,000 homeless as well as seriously damaging Turkey's industrial heartland. The earthquake highlighted the need to upgrade the existing emergency response system, to ameliorate the lack of effective enforcement of Turkey's building sector, and to address the inadequate coverage of earthquake insurance in the housing market.

At the request of government, the World Bank prepared a two-stage program to help restore living conditions in the Marmara region. In the first stage, the Bank reallocated funds from ongoing Bank projects toward emergency relief and reconstruction. The second stage focused on reconstruction and risk mitigation: the Marmara Earthquake Emergency Reconstruction (MEER) Project.

The MEER Project aimed (a) to help restore living conditions in the earthquake-affected region, (b) to promote economic recovery and growth, and (c) to develop an institutional framework for disaster risk management and mitigation. It supported the government's emergency cash transfer program through immediate cash assistance to victims for accommodations, repairs, death and disability benefits, and survivor and disability pensions. Although the MEER Project was primarily targeted at the region and the population affected by the earthquake, its components for the design and implementation of a disaster management system and the establishment of disaster insurance target the whole country and aim at preventing and mitigating the potential impacts of a recurrent event.

Turkey's RVA supported the development of additional lending instruments to assist poor households manage economic shocks. The Social Risk Mitigation Project for Turkey was developed in 2001 and 2002 to reduce the effect of the 2001 economic crisis on the poorest households and to improve their capacity to cope with similar risks in the future. The investment component of the project included a conditional cash transfer (CCT) program, which implemented a social assistance program targeted to the poorest 6 percent of the population. Assistance was provided conditional on better use of basic health and education services. The CCT promoted positive behavioral changes in such areas as school attendance, childhood vaccinations, basic health care, and nutrition. A targeting system based on a scoring formula was used to select which households would be eligible for CCT social assistance programs.

LESSONS AND THE FORWARD AGENDA

Pulling It All Together: Good Practices in RVA

Building on *World Development Report 2000/2001: Attacking Poverty* (World Bank 2001n), the Bank has produced a rich body of work on risk and vulnerability since the launch of the Social Risk Management framework in 2000. R&V analysis has been mainstreamed into the Bank's work on poverty reduction; good poverty assessment is poverty and vulnerability assessment and thus includes a careful assessment of sources of household vulnerability and the role of public policy in helping households manage risk and increase security. R&V analysis has affected policy discussions and lending across a broad range of countries, ranging from low-income countries in Africa and South Asia to middle-income countries in Latin America and Eastern Europe, for example.

Although R&V analysis supports the Bank's work on SP policies and programs, it is also used by other sectors through whose policies many risks are most appropriately addressed. The SRM framework, however, creates a common platform for looking at risk, and R&V analysis provides a flexible set of methodological approaches.

Table 2.2 summarizes the key components of R&V approaches and highlights good practices. The table describes what has been learned in terms of information sources, analytical methods, and risks faced by poor and other vulnerable households in client countries. It highlights the richness and diversity of R&V practice at the World Bank.

Table 2.2: **Components of R&V Analysis and Examples of Good Practice**

R&V draws on various sources of information	
***Unit records from consumer expenditure surveys* have been widely used to measure vulnerability, to identify poor and vulnerable households, and to analyze the effects of risk.**	Cross-sections repeated over time can be amalgamated to form a pseudo-panel, as was done for Kenya and Morocco. In Morocco, poverty mapping was used to estimate poverty and vulnerability for small geographic areas using data from cross-sectional household surveys and the population census. The Kenya RVA examines the probability of falling below the poverty line in nonpastoral rural areas using pseudo-panel data derived from repeated cross-sections augmented with historical information on shocks.
***Specialized risk modules* have been added to these surveys in some cases. These modules are useful in measuring the incidence of shocks and in understanding key risk management strategies.**	Risk modules have been launched in a number of African countries—for example, in Zambia (Living Conditions Monitoring Surveys II and III)—as well as in Afghanistan and in Guatemala. In Guatemala, using precoded questions for 28 economic, natural, social and political, and life-cycle shocks, the surveys asked households to report whether they had experienced a shock during the previous 12 months. These shocks were classified ex ante into covariate and idiosyncratic shocks. In Afghanistan, the national RVA conducted in 2003 identified key risks faced by rural households, such as drought, farming shocks, and epidemics.
***Panel data*—repeated observations of individuals, households, and communities—are increasingly available and have substantially improved vulnerability measurement and analysis.**	Data that contain repeated observations of the same units provide a more complete view of the dynamics of poverty. Examples of studies that have used panel data include PAs and RVAs for Ethiopia, Nicaragua, and South Africa. The Ethiopia RVA used panel data from 15 rural villages to provide a detailed depiction of consumption movements; the panel was supplemented with a more nationally representative pseudo-panel of cohorts. The Nicaragua study explored the impact of coffee price shocks on rural households, using use panel data to explore household responses to terms of trade shocks.
***Qualitative surveys and related information* complement standard survey data and add depth and coverage of different dimensions of poverty and sources of vulnerability.**	Qualitative studies have been used in several PAs and RVAs (such as those for Burkina Faso, Guatemala, and Zambia) to derive a more rounded depiction of vulnerability. For example, qualitative and quantitative studies were combined in Zambia to identify key risks facing the population and its ability to cope with these risks. Alongside conducting a quantitative analysis of vulnerability, the Burkina Faso RVA used information from a qualitative analysis. Specially designed surveys were administered in four villages. Detailed information was collected on shocks faced by households, their effects on income or assets, and the period of recovery.
Different analytical methods measure vulnerability and identify households and individuals most at risk of falling into poverty.	
***Vulnerability-to-poverty indicators* are based on econometric estimates of the probability of becoming poor, sometimes based on expected utilities (cross-section or panel data).**	Vulnerability-to-poverty measures were initially calculated for Indonesia to assess the impacts of the 1997 financial crisis. Similar estimates were provided in the Philippines and Thailand. As methodologies improved, vulnerability indicators were used for PAs and RVAs. In Burkina Faso, for instance, household-level survey data were used to estimate a vulnerability-to-poverty indicator; those identified as being vulnerable to poverty were separated into the chronic poor (63 percent) and the transient poor (37 percent). Households identified as vulnerable were smaller households that had limited access to land and transportation. In Indonesia, two panel data sets were used to estimate the probability of being poor next period, given current consumption levels. They showed that if the poverty line was set so that the headcount poverty rate was 20 percent, an additional 10 to 30 percent of the population was at substantial risk of poverty.
***Proportions of the poverty* line can be used to identify individuals whose current consumption levels are close to the poverty line and who are thus at risk of falling into poverty (usually cross-section data).**	This indicator has been used to provide an estimate of individuals not classified as currently poor but whose incomes lie near the poverty line and therefore for whom the risk of falling into poverty is likely not to be negligible. PAs for Morocco and for Serbia and Montenegro have used this approach. In Serbia and Montenegro, the vulnerability line was set at 50 percent above the poverty line: 33 percent of the Serbian population and 37 percent of the Montenegrin population were found to be vulnerable to poverty or poor, compared to headcount rates of 10.6 percent and 9.4 percent, respectively.

(continued)

Table 2.2: **Components of R&V Analysis and Examples of Good Practice** (*continued*)

Different analytical methods measure vulnerability and identify households and individuals most at risk of falling into poverty.	
Life-cycle approaches **identify individuals at risk because of age, gender, and other personal or household characteristics (usually cross-section data).**	Life-cycle approaches are used to identify vulnerable groups at particular points in their life cycles or given particular characteristics. Examples of PAs and RVAs that use this approach include those for Argentina, Benin, Colombia, and Mexico. The RVA for Benin found that older people, having had time to accumulate agricultural land, fruit tree plantations, or other income-generating means, were often considered relatively prosperous. In contrast, younger people who had not yet accumulated wealth were more likely to be counted among the poor—especially young women, whose productivity is greatly reduced by childbearing and childrearing. In Colombia, individuals displaced by conflict were found extremely vulnerable to shocks.
Heuristic approaches **draw on empirical information about individuals and households that experienced shocks and those who are poor or badly off (cross-section augmented by risk modules and by administrative information).**	Multiple sources are commonly used to derive a more complete view of vulnerability, for example, in Afghanistan, Colombia, Ethiopia, or Guatemala. In Afghanistan, an R&V study among rural households identified the key risks they faced—notably, drought, farming shocks resulting in a loss of crops or animals, natural disasters, epidemics, and increases in food prices. For urban areas, various qualitative assessments identified risks, those more vulnerable to poverty, and coping strategies used. In Ethiopia, panel data on 15 villages were used alongside a more representative panel of household heads of the same age living in the same administrative zone.
Qualitative assessments **are subjective assessments of poverty and vulnerability (qualitative fieldwork, surveys).**	Qualitative methods (often combined with quantitative assessments) have been incorporated into several PAs and RVAs (for example, those for Burkina Faso and Zambia) to identify the set of pivotal factors that perpetuate or exacerbate poverty. The Zambia PVA used a combination of qualitative and quantitative methods to conduct an in-depth analysis of the incidence and impact of those shocks on poverty. It estimated that 20 percent of households were vulnerable, while almost 40 percent were chronically poor. Moreover, 10 percent were both vulnerable and chronically poor and were therefore at most risk.
Covariate and idiosyncratic risk impacts welfare levels and living conditions of poor households.	
Covariate	
Macroshocks **include terms-of-trade and financial crises.**	Macroeconomic factors, such as terms-of-trade shocks or financial crises, may affect large segments of the population. Examples of studies examining these covariate shocks include Vakis, Kruger, and Mason (2004) and Bourguignon and Goh (2002). The first one examined the impact of terms-of-trade-shocks on rural households showing the impacts of the 2000–02 "coffee crisis" on the coffee-growing regions of Latin America. The second addressed whether the volatility of workers' hours and incomes increased as a result of increasing trade liberalization and whether the same has had an effect on vulnerability to poverty.
Climate shocks **include droughts and flooding. Other agriculture production shocks also occur, such as cattle disease and insect infestations.**	Climatic variation is a common covariate shock that affects rural households throughout the world. For example, the Ethiopia RVA identifies drought as the main shock leading to food insecurity, with famine being a yearly occurrence. The effects of crop damage caused by pests, insects, or frosts on consumption were also found substantial. The Senegal RVA lists drought and flooding as the key shocks facing rural households. Drought cycles reduce agricultural production. In addition, insects and the diseases they carry affect plants and animals.
Natural disasters **include storms, earthquakes, and the like.**	Regions prone to natural disasters are likely to be particularly vulnerable to poverty. For example, Turkey experienced severe losses of life and infrastructure in 1999 because of an earthquake. The earthquake was followed by a period of economic and financial crisis, culminating in a major currency devaluation in February 2001. *Turkey: Poverty and Coping after Crises* (World Bank 2003m) examined the mechanisms households used to cope with the earthquake; the major effect of the subsequent crises has been an increase in poverty in urban areas.

(continued)

Table 2.2: **Components of R&V Analysis and Examples of Good Practice** (*continued*)

Covariate and idiosyncratic risk impacts welfare levels and living conditions of poor households.	
War, civil conflict, and violence **also are in this category.**	The impact of war and conflict on livelihoods and vulnerability is discussed in several studies, such as the PAs for Bosnia and Herzegovina, Kosovo, Guinea-Bissau, and the Republic ofYemen. In Guinea-Bissau, conflict and political instability have considerably weakened the country's productive tissue.This problem in itself increased the degree of vulnerability of the population—mainly in rural areas, where most economic activities take place—hence impeding economic growth.
Idiosyncratic	
Health shocks **include HIV/AIDS, chronic and acute illnesses, and deaths.**	Although health shocks are generally considered idiosyncratic, the widespread nature of HIV/AIDS and malaria in some parts of the world implies that these shocks can often be viewed as covariate shocks. In Zambia's PVA, formal and informal coping mechanisms for dealing with shocks have come under increasing stress because of high rates of HIV/AIDS and death. Health risks may also be due to environmental degradation and outmoded industrial practices. For example, the Kosovo PA found that exposure to health risks is widespread, largely resulting from environmental pollution.
Labor and demographic **shocks include job loss, unemployment, and death of a breadwinner.**	Unemployment and underemployment have been identified as major risks faced by households of a certain demographic in Argentina, Bolivia, Colombia, and Uruguay, for instance. *Colombia: Social Safety Net Assessment* (World Bank 2002g) notes that even though economic growth recovered modestly in 2000, poverty and unemployment remained high, and some human development indicators had declined. This result was partly due to Colombia not having an effective safety net in place that could address the social consequences of the crisis.
Other shocks **include corruption and violence, theft, fire, loss of property, and local and family disputes.**	Many studies noted the adverse impacts of corruption, crime, and violence. Problems are particularly acute in urban areas, as evidenced in analytical work in Latin American and Caribbean countries such as Guyana, Haiti, and Jamaica. Most R&V analysis has had a rural focus, particularly for low-income countries. Risks associated with crime, fire, and loss of property were noted in a number of reports for African countries, such as those for Kenya and Senegal, as well as conflict-affected countries.

Source: Authors' compilation based on the RVA inventory.

Key Lessons

The R&V documents reviewed in this chapter provide extensive evidence that risk matters for development: shocks are important causes of both transient and extreme poverty. Despite high levels of risk exposure, the poor in many countries have only limited access to formal and informal risk management instruments.

The situation differs substantially across countries and regions in terms of both the risks identified and the nature of formal and informal responses. Differences are particularly notable between low-income and middle-income countries. The risks identified in middle-income countries are more amenable to traditional SP instruments than those identified in low-income countries. SP systems in middle-income countries are more extensive and better financed. R&V analysis there has focused more on the need for systemic reforms to SP systems, with the aim of improving the design and targeting of programs and promoting incentives, cost-effectiveness, and fiscal sustainability.

In contrast, poor people in low-income countries are exposed to a wide range of covariate and idiosyncratic risks, and most have only limited access to formal risk management mechanisms. Informal mechanisms play an important role; however, informal family- and community-based systems have come under pressure and are breaking down in many low-income countries in Africa and South Asia. Vulnerability is increasing even as poverty levels are falling. Certain vulnerable groups are particularly at risk and particularly poorly served by existing policies and programs—for example, the elderly and chronically ill, deserted women and widows, people living with HIV/AIDS, orphans and other vulnerable children, families displaced by conflict or other crises, and smallholders struggling with repeated drought.

Taken in aggregate, recent R&V analysis draws attention to rising levels of vulnerability and highlights concerns for those whom development has left behind despite global and regional progress in reducing poverty. Risk contributes not only to transitory episodes of poverty. New analysis, buttressed by findings in a number of R&V studies, identifies strong links between chronic, extreme poverty and risk in low-income settings. Addressing risks, in particular for vulnerable groups, emerges as another key concern for inclusive and sustainable globalization.

The Priorities Going Forward

Important progress has been made in improving the quality, relevance, and application of R&V analysis. However, the Bank faces a number of challenges moving forward.

Although R&V analysis has been mainstreamed into poverty assessment, challenges remain in carrying out good R&V work, including issues of measurement, analytics, and—most important—development of effective policy responses. It is essential to continue to improve the quality and relevance of R&V work in the context of poverty assessments and poverty and vulnerability assessments.

In addition, such assessments should be complemented by freestanding analyses of specific risks to support specific sectoral responses and strategies. The existing body of R&V work highlights the importance of climate shocks and other natural disasters in Sub-Saharan Africa and some East Asian countries; HIV/AIDS in southern Africa; and health shocks, particularly in low-income countries. Human-made disasters include conflict and other forms of violence, financial crises, and rising food prices, which have recently led to violence and political upheaval. In this context, identifying the primary risks that affect specific countries and the relevant current and future policy responses at the sector level is important.

Fragile states and low-income countries in Africa are among the Bank's strategic priorities. As noted earlier, risks are widespread in low-income countries. More work needs to be done in the context of fragile states and low-income countries to identify highly vulnerable groups and to tailor sectoral strategies to address the risks faced by those groups and their sources of vulnerability.

In terms of improvements to R&V fundamentals, this chapter highlights the following:

- *Vulnerability indicators.* There is still debate regarding how to measure vulnerability and what are the best indicators. Measures of vulnerability to poverty are widely acknowledged as conceptually attractive albeit difficult to estimate in a robust and consistent way. Data problems further confound estimation. Do existing approaches represent the best that can be done, or is this area an important priority for future work?
- *Data.* Lack of good data continues to limit how well vulnerability is measured and monitored as well as the ensuing analyses. Good cross-section survey data are widely available; however, progress has been much slower in developing representative panel surveys, particularly among the poorest and most vulnerable countries. Good second-best data sources are being developed. For example, data from small (nonrepresentative) panels of households and communities are collected with greater frequency, and more use is made of qualitative methods and data. More extensive efforts are needed to improve the data on which R&V analysis is based.
- *Poverty dynamics and drivers of vulnerability.* Again, although important progress has been made, understanding of poverty dynamics and the primary causes of vulnerability remains at a general conceptual level. Data and measurement problems are important limiting factors. Better empirical work is clearly needed, with particular focus on high-risk countries and specific shocks.
- *Policy impacts.* Although the Bank has done extensive analytical work on vulnerability, this work has had only limited effect on country-level policy discussions for SP&L, with some notable exceptions, such as the work in Chile, Ethiopia, and Madagascar. A lot can still be learned about sectoral responses to risk and vulnerability and about how the Bank can provide more effective support through its country assistance programs. More progress can and should be made on the policy front and in developing concrete operational responses to R&V findings, notwithstanding imperfections in data and analytical methods.

ANNEX 2.A: COMPREHENSIVE LIST OF R&V ANALYSES BY REGION

Generic

Alderman, Harold, and Christina H. Paxson. 1992. "Do the Poor Insure? A Synthesis of the Literature on Risk and Consumption in Developing Countries." Policy Research Working Paper 1008, Agriculture and Rural Development Department, World Bank, Washington, DC.

Alwang, Jeffrey, Paul B. Siegel, and Steen Jørgensen. 2001. "Vulnerability: A View from Different Disciplines." Social Protection Discussion Paper 0115, Social Protection Unit, Human Development Network, World Bank, Washington, DC.

Attanasio, Orazio, and José-Víctor Ríos-Rull. 2000. "Consumption Smoothing in Island Economies: Can Public Insurance Reduce Welfare?" *European Economic Review* 44 (7): 1225–58.

Blomquist, John, Marijn Verhoeven, Juan Pablo Cordoba, César Bouillon, and Patricia Moser. 2001. "Social Safety Nets in Response to Crisis: Lessons and Guidelines from Asia and Latin America." Paper prepared in collaboration with Asia-Pacific Economic Cooperation (APEC) member countries and submitted to the APEC finance ministers, World Bank, Washington, DC.

Bourguignon, François, Chor-ching Goh, and Dae Il Kim. 2004. "Estimating Individual Vulnerability to Poverty with Pseudo-Panel Data." Policy Research Working Paper 3375, World Bank, Washington, DC.

de Janvry, Alain, Elisabeth Sadoulet, Pantelis Solomon, and Renos Vakis. 2006. "Uninsured Risk and Asset Protection: Can Conditional Cash Transfer Programs Serve as Safety Nets?" Social Protection Discussion Paper 0604, Social Protection Unit, Human Development Network, World Bank, Washington, DC.

de la Brière, Bénédicte, and Laura B. Rawlings. 2006. "Examining Conditional Cash Transfer Programs: A Role for Increased Social Inclusion?" Social Protection Discussion Paper 0603, Social Protection Unit, Human Development Network, World Bank, Washington, DC.

del Ninno, Carlo, Paul A. Dorosh, and Kalanidhi Subbarao. 2005. "Food Aid and Food Security in the Short and Long Run: Country Experience from Asia and Sub-Saharan Africa." Social Protection Discussion Paper 0538, Social Protection Unit, Human Development Network, World Bank, Washington, DC.

Heitzmann, Karin, R. Sudharshan Canagarajah, and Paul B. Siegel. 2002. "Guidelines for Assessing the Sources of Risk and Vulnerability." Social Protection Discussion Paper 0218, Social Protection Unit, Human Development Network, World Bank, Washington, DC.

Hoddinott, John, and Agnes Quisumbing. 2003. "Data Sources for Microeconometric Risk and Vulnerability Assessments." Social Protection Discussion Paper 0323, Social Protection Unit, Human Development Network, World Bank, Washington, DC.

———. 2003. "Methods for Microeconometric Risk and Vulnerability Assessments." Social Protection Discussion Paper 0324, Social Protection Unit, Human Development Network, World Bank, Washington, DC.

Holzmann, Robert. 2001. "Risk and Vulnerability: The Forward Looking Role of Social Protection in a Globalizing World." Social Protection Discussion Paper 0109, Social Protection Unit, Human Development Network, World Bank, Washington, DC.

Holzmann, Robert, and Steen Jørgensen. 1999. "Social Protection as Social Risk Management: Conceptual Underpinnings for the Social Protection Sector Strategy Paper." Social Protection Discussion Paper 9904, Social Protection Unit, Human Development Network, World Bank, Washington, DC.

———. 2000. "Social Risk Management: A New Conceptual Framework for Social Protection and Beyond." Social Protection Discussion Paper 0006, Social Protection Unit, Human Development Network, World Bank, Washington, DC.

Holzmann, Robert, and Valerie Kozel. 2007. "The Role of Social Risk Management in Development: A World Bank View." *IDS Bulletin* 38 (3): 8–13.

Holzmann, Robert, Lynne Sherburne-Benz, and Emil Tesliuc. 2003. *Social Risk Management: The World Bank's Approach to Social Protection in a Globalizing World.* Washington, DC: Social Protection Unit, Human Development Network, World Bank.

Hoogeveen, Johannes, Emil Tesliuc, and Renos Vakis, with Stefan Dercon. 2004. "A Guide to the Analysis of Risk, Vulnerability, and Vulnerable Groups." Social Protection Unit, Human Development Network, World Bank, Washington, DC.

Ligon, Ethan, and Laura Schechter. 2004. "Evaluating Different Approaches to Estimating Vulnerability." Social

Protection Discussion Paper 0410, Social Protection Unit, Human Development Network, World Bank, Washington, DC.

Peracchi, Franco, Valeria Perotti, and Stefano Scarpetta. 2007. "Informality and Social Protection: Preliminary Results from Pilot Surveys in Bulgaria and Colombia." Social Protection Discussion Paper 0717, Social Protection Unit, Human Development Network, World Bank, Washington, DC.

Ravallion, Martin. 2003. "Targeted Transfers in Poor Countries: Revisiting the Trade-Offs and Policy Options." CPRC Working Paper 26, Chronic Poverty Research Centre and World Bank, Washington, DC.

Sadoulet, Elisabeth, Federico Finan, Alain de Janvry, and Renos Vakis. 2004. "Can Conditional Cash Transfer Programs Improve Social Risk Management? Lessons for Education and Child Labor Outcomes." Social Protection Discussion Paper 0420, Social Protection Unit, Human Development Network, World Bank, Washington, DC.

Siegel, Paul B., and Jeffrey Alwang. 1999. "An Asset-Based Approach to Social Risk Management: A Conceptual Framework." Social Protection Discussion Paper 9926, Social Protection Unit, Human Development Network, World Bank, Washington, DC.

Skoufias, Emmanuel, and Agnes R. Quisumbing. 2004. "Consumption Insurance and Vulnerability to Poverty: A Synthesis of the Evidence from Bangladesh, Ethiopia, Mali, Mexico and Russia." Social Protection Discussion Paper 0401, Social Protection Unit, Human Development Network, World Bank, Washington, DC.

Steele, Diane. 2005. "Household Vulnerability and Children's Activities: Information Needed from Household Surveys to Measure Their Relationship." Social Protection Discussion Paper 0517, Social Protection Unit, Human Development Network, World Bank, Washington, DC.

World Bank. 2000. *Balancing Protection and Opportunity: A Strategy for Social Protection in Transition Economies.* Washington, DC: Social Protection Team, Human Development Sector Unit, Europe and Central Asia Region, World Bank.

———. 2001. *Social Protection Sector Strategy: From Safety Net to Springboard.* Washington, DC: World Bank. http://go.worldbank.org/97LBYDY3U0.

———. 2001. *World Development Report 2000/2001: Attacking Poverty.* Washington, DC: World Bank.

———. 2007. *Sector Strategy Implementation Update: Third Review.* Washington, DC: Operations Policy and Country Services Delivery Management Unit, World Bank.

Africa

Christiaensen, Luc J., Richard N. Boisvert, and John Hoddinott. 2000. "Validating Operational Food Insecurity Indicators against a Dynamic Benchmark: Evidence from Mali." Policy Research Working Paper 2471, Poverty Reduction and Social Development Unit, Africa Region, World Bank, Washington, DC.

Christiaensen, Luc J., and Kalanidhi Subbarao. 2005. "Towards an Understanding of Household Vulnerability in Rural Kenya." *Journal of African Economies* 14 (4): 520–58.

Dabalen, Andrew, Nadine Poupart, and Patrick Kline. 2002. "Vulnerability to Rainfall Shock in Ethiopia." World Bank and the University of Michigan, Washington, DC.

del Ninno, Carlo, and Alessandra Marini. 2005. "Household's Vulnerability to Shocks in Zambia." Social Protection Discussion Paper 0536, Social Protection Unit, Human Development Network, World Bank, Washington, DC.

Dercon, Stefan. 2007. "Fate and Fear: Risk and Its Consequences in Africa." GPRG Working Paper 074. Global Poverty Research Group, University of Oxford, Oxford, U.K.

Ersado, Lire, Harold Alderman, and Jeffrey Alwang. 2001. "Changes in Consumption and Savings Behavior before and after Economic Shocks: Evidence from Zimbabwe." Paper presented at the International Conference on Crises and Disasters: Measurement and Mitigation of Their Human Costs, organized by the International Food Policy Research Institute and the Inter-American Development Bank, Washington, DC, November 13–14.

Harrower, Sarah, and John Hoddinott. 2005. "Consumption Smoothing in the Zone Lacustre, Mali." *Journal of African Economies* 14 (4): 489–519.

Hoogeveen, Johannes G. 2004. "Measuring Welfare for Small but Vulnerable Groups: Poverty and Disability in Uganda." Social Protection Discussion Paper 0419, Social Protection Unit, Human Development Network, World Bank, Washington, DC.

Lerisse, Fred, Donald Mmari, and Mgeni Baruani. 2003. "Vulnerability and Social Protection Programmes in Tanzania." Paper prepared for the Research and Analysis Working Group of a Study on Social Protection Programmes on Vulnerability, Research on Poverty Alleviation, Dar es Salaam, Tanzania.

Siaens, Corinne, Kalanidhi Subbarao, and Quentin Wodon. 2003. *Are Orphans Especially Vulnerable? Evidence from Rwanda.* Washington, DC: World Bank.

Vedeld, Trond. 2007. *Malawi: Social Protection Status Report.* Report 40027-MW. Sustainable Development Network, Conflict and Social Development Unit, Country Department 2, Africa Region, World Bank, Washington, DC.

World Bank. 2000. *Swaziland: Reducing Poverty through Shared Growth.* Report 19658-SW. Washington, DC: Human Development Group, Eastern and Southern Africa, World Bank.

———. 2003. *Benin: Poverty Assessment.* Report 28447-BEN. Washington, DC: Human Development II, Country Department 13, Africa Region, World Bank.

———. 2003. *Benin: Poverty Reduction Strategy Paper and Joint Staff Assessment.* Report 25475-BEN. Washington, DC: World Bank.

———. 2003. *Étude Pilote de Risques et de la Vulnérabilité en République Démocratique du Congo.* Kinshasa: World Bank.

———. 2003. *Nigeria: Risk and Vulnerability Assessment.* Washington, DC: Africa Human Development Division 3, Africa Region, World Bank.

———. 2003. "Securing Consumption while Promoting Growth: The Role of a Productive Social Safety Net in Ethiopia." Issues note, World Bank, Washington, DC.

———. 2004. *Burkina Faso: Risk and Vulnerability Assessment.* Report 28144-BUR. Washington, DC: Africa Human Development Division 2, Africa Region, World Bank.

———. 2005. *Burkina Faso: Reducing Poverty through Sustained Equitable Growth—Poverty Assessment.* Report 29743-BUR. Washington, DC: Poverty Reduction and Economic Management Unit 4, Africa Region, World Bank.

———. 2005. *Ethiopia: Risk and Vulnerability Assessment.* Report 26275-ET. Washington, DC: Human Development Group 3, Africa Region, World Bank.

———. 2005. *Ethiopia: Well-Being and Poverty in Ethiopia: The Role of Agriculture and Agency.* Report 29468-ET. Washington, DC: Poverty Reduction and Economic Management Unit 2, Country Department for Ethiopia, Africa Region, World Bank.

———. 2006. *Guinea-Bissau: Integrated Poverty and Social Assessment (IPSA).* Report 34553-GW. Washington, DC: Poverty Reduction and Economic Management Unit 4, Africa Region, World Bank.

———. 2006. *Senegal: Managing Risks in Rural Senegal: A Multi-sectoral Review of Efforts to Reduce Vulnerability.* Report 33435-SN. Washington, DC: Human Development II, Africa Region, World Bank.

———. 2006. *Uganda: Poverty and Vulnerability Assessment.* Report 36996-UG. Washington, DC: Poverty Reduction and Economic Management, Southern Africa, Africa Region, World Bank.

———. 2007. *Risk and Vulnerability Assessment for Conflict Prevention in Guinea.* Washington, DC: Human Development Unit, Africa Human Development Division 2, Africa Region, World Bank.

———. 2007. *Zambia: Poverty and Vulnerability Assessment.* Report 32573-ZM. Washington, DC: Africa Human Development Division 1, Poverty Reduction and Economic Management Unit, Africa Region, World Bank.

East Asia and the Pacific

Attridge, Edmund, Stefan Nachuk, and Dao Viet Dung. 2003. "Localizing MDGs for Poverty Reduction in Vietnam: Ensuring Good Governance for Poverty Reduction." Poverty Task Force Strategies for Achieving the Vietnam Development Goals Working Paper 22996, World Bank, Washington, DC.

Bourguignon, François, and Chor-ching Goh. 2002. "Trade and Labor Market Vulnerability in Indonesia, Korea, and Thailand." *World Bank PovertyNet Newsletter* 48: 223–241.

Chaudhuri, Shubham, Jyotsna Jalan, and Asep Suryahadi. 2002. "Assessing Household Vulnerability to Poverty from Cross-Sectional Data: A Methodology and Estimates from Indonesia." Discussion Paper 0102-52, Department of Economics, Columbia University, New York.

Datt, Gaurav, and Hans Hoogeveen. 2000. "El Niño or El Peso? Crisis, Poverty, and Income Distribution in the Philippines." Policy Research Working Paper 2466, East Asia and Pacific Region, Poverty Reduction and Economic Management Sector Unit, World Bank, Washington, DC.

Jalan, Jyotsna, and Martin Ravallion. 1998. "Behavioral Responses to Risk in Rural China." Policy Research Working Paper 1978, Development Research Group, Poverty and Human Resources, World Bank, Washington, DC.

———. 2001. "Household Income Dynamics in Rural China." Policy Research Working Paper 2706, Development Research Group, World Bank, Washington, DC.

Pritchett, Lant, Asep Suryahadi, and Sudarno Sumarto. 2000. "Quantifying Vulnerability to Poverty: A Proposed Measure, Applied to Indonesia." Policy Research Working Paper 2437, East Asia and Pacific Region, Environment and Social Development Sector Unit, World Bank, Washington, DC.

Ridao-Cano, Cristóbal. 2006. *Children's Work in Cambodia: A Challenge for Growth and Poverty Reduction.* Rome: Understanding Children's Work Project, Faculty of Economics, University of Rome Tor Vergata.

World Bank. 1999. "Towards an East Asian Social Protection Strategy." Human Development Unit, East Asia and Pacific Region, World Bank, Washington, DC.

———. 1999. *Vietnam Development Report 2000: Attacking Poverty—Country Economic Memorandum.* Report 19914-VN. Washington, DC: Poverty Reduction and Economic Management Unit, East Asia and Pacific Region, World Bank.

———. 2000. *China: Overcoming Rural Poverty.* Report 21105-CHA. Washington, DC: Rural Development and Natural Resources Unit, East Asia and Pacific Region, World Bank.

———. 2000. *Papua New Guinea: Poverty and Access to Public Services.* Report 19584-PNG. Washington, DC: Poverty Reduction and Economic Management Unit, East Asia and Pacific Region, World Bank.

———. 2001. *Indonesia: Poverty Reduction in Indonesia: Constructing a New Strategy.* Report 23028-IND. Washington, DC: Environment and Social Development Sector Unit, East Asia and Pacific Region, World Bank.

———. 2001. "Mongolia: Participatory Living Standards Assessment 2000." National Statistical Office of Mongolia and World Bank, Ulaanbaatar.

———. 2001. *Philippines: Poverty Assessment.* Report 20498. Washington, DC: Poverty Reduction and Economic Management Unit, East Asia and Pacific Region, World Bank.

———. 2001. *Thailand: Social Monitor—Poverty and Public Policy.* Report 23147-TH. Washington, DC: Human Development Sector Unit, East Asia and Pacific Region, World Bank.

———. 2002. *People, Poverty, and Livelihoods: Links for Sustainable Poverty Reduction in Indonesia.* Report 25289. Jakarta: World Bank and U.K. Department for International Development.

———. 2003. *Timor-Leste Poverty Assessment: Poverty in a New Nation—Analysis for Action.* Report 25662-TP. Washington, DC: Poverty Reduction and Economic Management Sector Unit, East Asia and Pacific Region, World Bank.

———. 2003. *Vietnam Development Report 2004.* Report 27130-VN. Washington, DC: Poverty Reduction and Economic Management Unit, East Asia and Pacific Region, World Bank.

———. 2006. *Cambodia: Halving Poverty by 2015? Poverty Assessment 2006.* Report 35213-KH. Washington, DC: East Asia and Pacific Region, World Bank.

———. 2006. *Indonesia: Making the New Indonesia Work for the Poor.* Report 37349-ID. Washington, DC: Poverty Reduction and Economic Management Sector Unit, East Asia and Pacific Region, World Bank.

———. 2006. *Lao PDR: Poverty Assessment Report—From Valleys to Hilltops: 15 Years of Poverty Reduction.* Report 38083-LA. Washington, DC: Poverty Reduction and Economic Management Sector Unit, East Asia and Pacific Region, World Bank.

———. 2006. *Managing Risk and Vulnerability in Cambodia: An Assessment and Strategy for Social Protection.* Report 38209. Washington, DC: World Bank.

———. 2006. *Mongolia: Poverty Assessment.* Report 35660-MN. Washington, DC: Poverty Reduction and Economic Management, East Asia and Pacific Region, World Bank.

Europe and Central Asia

Alam, Asad. 2005. *Growth, Poverty, and Inequality: Eastern Europe and the Former Soviet Union.* Washington, DC: World Bank.

de Soto, Hermine, Peter Gordon, Ilir Gedeshi, and Zamira Sinoimeri. 2002. "Poverty in Albania: A Qualitative Assessment." World Bank Technical Paper 520, World Bank, Washington, DC.

Jones, Christine, and Ana Revenga. 2000. *Making Transition Work for Everyone: Poverty and Inequality in Europe and Central Asia.* Washington, DC: World Bank.

World Bank. 2000. *Republic of Tajikistan: Poverty Assessment.* Report 20285-TJ. Washington, DC: Human Development Sector Unit, Europe and Central Asia Region, World Bank.

———. 2000. *Turkey: Economic Reforms, Living Standards, and Social Welfare Study.* Report 20029-TU. Washington, DC: Poverty Reduction and Economic Management Unit, Europe and Central Asia Region, World Bank.

———. 2001. *Croatia: Economic Vulnerability and Welfare Study.* Report 22079-HR. Washington, DC: Poverty Reduction and Economic Management Unit, Europe and Central Asia Region, World Bank.

———. 2001. *Hungary: Long-Term Poverty, Social Protection, and the Labor Market.* Report 20645-HU. Washington, DC: Poverty Reduction and Economic Management Unit, Europe and Central Asia Region, World Bank.

———. 2001. *Kosovo: Poverty Assessment.* Report 23390-KOS. Washington, DC: Poverty Reduction and Economic Management Unit, Europe and Central Asia Region, World Bank.

———. 2001. *Slovak Republic: Living Standards, Employment, and Labor Market Study.* Report 22351-SK. Washington, DC: Poverty Reduction and Economic Management Unit, Europe and Central Asia Region, World Bank.

———. 2002. *Armenia: Poverty Update.* Report 24339-AM. Washington, DC: Human Development Sector Unit, Europe and Central Asia Region, World Bank.

———. 2002. *Bulgaria: Poverty Assessment.* Report 24516-BUL. Washington, DC: Human Development Sector Unit, Europe and Central Asia Region, World Bank.

———. 2002. *Georgia: Poverty Update.* Report 22350-GE. Washington, DC: Poverty Reduction and Economic Management Unit, Europe and Central Asia Region, World Bank.

———. 2003. *Albania: Poverty Assessment.* Report 26213-AL. Washington, DC: Human Development Sector Unit, Europe and Central Asia Region, World Bank.

———. 2003. *Armenia: Poverty Assessment.* Report 27192-AM. Washington, DC: Human Development Sector Unit, Europe and Central Asia Region, World Bank.

———. 2003. *Azerbaijan Republic: Poverty Assessment.* Report 24890-AZ. Washington, DC: Human Development Sector Unit, South Caucasus Country Unit, Europe and Central Asia Region, World Bank.

———. 2003. *Bosnia and Herzegovina:* Poverty Assessment. Report 25343-BIH. Washington, DC: Poverty Reduction and Economic Management Unit, Europe and Central Asia Region, World Bank.

———. 2003. *Kyrgyz Republic: Enhancing Pro-Poor Growth.* Report 24638-KG. Washington, DC: Poverty Reduction and Economic Management Unit, Europe and Central Asia Region, World Bank.

———. 2003. *Romania: Poverty Assessment.* Report 26169-RO. Washington, DC: Human Development Sector Unit and Environmentally and Socially Sustainable Development Unit, Europe and Central Asia Region, World Bank.

———. 2003. *Serbia and Montenegro: Poverty Assessment.* Report 26011-YU. Washington, DC: Poverty Reduction and Economic Management Unit, Europe and Central Asia Region, World Bank.

———. 2003. *Turkey: Poverty and Coping after Crises.* Report 24185-TR. Washington, DC: Human Development Unit, Europe and Central Asia Region, World Bank.

———. 2003. *Uzbekistan: Living Standards Assessment—Policies to Improve Living Standards.* Report 25923-UZ. Washington, DC: Human Development Sector Unit, Europe and Central Asia Region, World Bank.

———. 2004. *Belarus: Poverty Assessment—Can Poverty Reduction and Access to Services Be Sustained?* Report 27431-BY. Washington, DC: Human Development Sector Unit, Europe and Central Asia Region, World Bank.

———. 2004. *Kazakhstan: Dimensions of Poverty in Kazakhstan.* Report 30294-KZ. Washington, DC: Poverty Reduction and Economic Management Unit, Europe and Central Asia Region, World Bank.

———. 2004. *Poland: Growth, Employment and Living Standards in Pre-accession Poland.* Report 28233-POL. Washington, DC: Poverty Reduction and Economic Management Unit, Europe and Central Asia Region, World Bank.

———. 2004. *Recession, Recovery, and Poverty in Moldova.* Report 28024-MD. Washington, DC: Human Development Sector Unit, Europe and Central Asia Region, World Bank.

———. 2005. *FYR of Macedonia: Poverty Assessment for 2002–2003.* Report 34324-MK. Washington, DC: Poverty Reduction and Economic Management Unit, Europe and Central Asia Region, World Bank.

———. 2005. *Kosovo: Poverty Assessment—Promoting Opportunity, Security, and Participation for All.* Report 32378-XK. Washington, DC: Poverty Reduction and Economic Management Unit, Europe and Central Asia Region, World Bank.

———. 2005. *Kyrgyz Republic: Poverty Update—Profile of Living Standards in 2003.* Report 36602-KG. Washington, DC: Poverty Reduction and Economic Management Unit, Europe and Central Asia Region, World Bank.

———. 2005. *Russian Federation: Reducing Poverty through Growth and Social Policy Reform.* Report 28923-RU. Washington, DC: Poverty Reduction and Economic Management Unit, Europe and Central Asia Region, World Bank.

———. 2005. *Slovak Republic: The Quest for Equitable Growth in the Slovak Republic—A World Bank Living Standards Assessment.* Report 32433-SK. Washington, DC: Poverty Reduction and Economic Management Unit, Europe and Central Asia Region, World Bank.

———. 2007. *Kosovo: Poverty Assessment.* Report 39737-XK. Washington, DC: Poverty Reduction and Economic Management Unit, Europe and Central Asia Region, World Bank.

———. 2007. *Kyrgyz Republic: Poverty Assessment.* Report 40864-KG. Washington, DC: Poverty Reduction and Economic Management Unit, Europe and Central Asia Region, World Bank.

———. 2007. *Latvia: Sharing the High Growth Dividend—A Living Standards Assessment.* Report 38437-LV. Washington, DC: Poverty Reduction and Economic Management Unit, Europe and Central Asia Region, World Bank.

———. 2007. *Republic of Uzbekistan: Living Standards Assessment Update.* Report 40723-UZ. Washington, DC: Human Development Sector Unit, Central Asia Country Unit, Europe and Central Asia Region, World Bank.

Latin America and the Caribbean

Gertler, Paul G. 2004. "Do Conditional Cash Transfers Improve Child Health? Evidence from PROGRESA's Control Randomized Experiment." *American Economic Review* 94 (2): 336–41.

Maloney, William F., Wendy Cunningham, and Mariano Bosch. 2003. *Who Suffers Income Falls during Crises? An Application of Quantile Analysis to Mexico: 1992–95.* Washington, DC: World Bank.

Maluccio, John A. 2005. "Coping with the 'Coffee Crisis' in Central America: The Role of the Nicaraguan *Red de Protección Social.*" FCND Discussion Paper 188, Food Consumption and Nutrition Division, International Food Policy Research Institute, Washington, DC.

Silvério Marques, José. 2003. "Social Safety Net Assessments from Central America: Cross-Country Review of Principal Findings." Social Protection Discussion Paper 0316, Social Protection Unit, Human Development Network, World Bank, Washington, DC.

Tesliuc, Emil D., and Kathy J. Lindert. 2004. "Risk and Vulnerability in Guatemala: A Quantitative and Qualitative Assessment." Social Protection Discussion Paper 0404, Social Protection Unit, Human Development Network, World Bank, Washington, DC.

Vakis, Renos, Diana Kruger, and Andrew D. Mason. 2004. "Shocks and Coffee: Lessons from Nicaragua." Social Protection Discussion Paper 0415, Social Protection Unit, Human Development Network, World Bank, Washington, DC.

World Bank. 2000. *Ecuador: Crisis, Poverty, and Social Services.* Report 19920-EC. Washington, DC: Human Development Department, Latin America and Caribbean Region, World Bank.

———. 2001. *Bolivarian Republic of Venezuela: Investing Human Capital for Growth, Prosperity, and Poverty Reduction.* Report 21833-VE. Washington, DC: Colombia, Mexico, and Venezuela Country Management Unit, Poverty Reduction and Economic Management Unit, Latin America and Caribbean Region, World Bank.

———. 2001. *Dominican Republic: Poverty Assessment—Poverty in a High-Growth Economy (1986–2000).* Report 21306-DR. Washington, DC: Poverty Reduction and Economic Management Unit, Latin America and Caribbean Region, World Bank.

———. 2001. *Honduras: Poverty Diagnostic 2000.* Report 20531-HO. Washington, DC: Poverty Reduction and Economic Management Sector Unit, Latin America and Caribbean Region, World Bank, with contributions from International Food Policy Research Institute and Programa de Asignación Familiar.

———. 2001. *Nicaragua: Poverty Assessment: Challenges and Opportunities for Poverty Reduction.* Report 20488-NI. Washington, DC: Poverty Reduction and Economic Management Sector Unit, Latin America and Caribbean Region, World Bank.

———. 2001. *Uruguay: Maintaining Social Equity in a Changing Economy.* Report 21262. Washington, DC: Argentina, Chile, Paraguay, and Uruguay Country Management Unit, Poverty Reduction and Economic Management Sector Unit, Latin America and Caribbean Region, World Bank.

———. 2002. *Bolivia: Poverty Diagnostic 2000.* Report 20530-80. Washington, DC: Poverty Reduction and Economic Management Sector Unit, Latin America and Caribbean Region, World Bank, with contributions from Instituto Nacional de Estadística and Unidad de Análisis de Políticas Económicas.

———. 2002. *Colombia: Poverty Report.* Report 24524-CO. Washington, DC: Colombia Country Management Unit, Poverty Reduction and Economic Management Sector Unit, Latin America and Caribbean Region, World Bank.

———. 2002. *Colombia: Social Safety Net Assessment.* Report 22255-CO. Washington, DC: Latin America and the Caribbean Regional Office, World Bank.

———. 2002. *Costa Rica: Social Spending and the Poor.* Report 24300-CR. Washington, DC: Human Development Sector Management Unit, Central America Country Management Unit, Latin America and Caribbean Region, World Bank.

———. 2003. *Argentina: Crisis and Poverty 2003: Poverty Assessment.* Report 26127-AR. Washington, DC: Poverty Reduction and Economic Management Unit, Latin America and Caribbean Region, World Bank.

———. 2003. *Brazil: Strategies for Poverty Reduction in Ceara: The Challenge of Inclusive Modernization.* Report 24500-BR. Washington, DC: Brazil Country Management Unit, Latin America and Caribbean Region, World Bank.

———. 2003. *Nicaragua: Poverty Assessment: Raising Welfare and Reducing Vulnerability.* Report 26128-NI. Washington, DC: Central America Department, Latin America and Caribbean Region, World Bank.

———. 2003. *Poverty in Guatemala.* Report 27586. Washington, DC: World Bank.

———. 2003. *Uruguay: Poverty Update 2003.* Report 26223-UR. Washington, DC: Argentina, Chile, Paraguay, and Uruguay Country Management Unit, Poverty Reduction and Economic Management Unit, Latin America and Caribbean Region, World Bank.

———. 2003. *Volatility, Risk, and Innovation: Social Protection in Latin America and the Caribbean.* Social Protection Unit, World Bank, Washington, DC.

———. 2004. *Chile: Household Risk Management and Social Protection.* Report 25286-CH. Washington, DC: Country Management Unit for Argentina, Chile, Paraguay, and Uruguay, Human Development Department, World Bank.

———. 2004. *Ecuador: Poverty Assessment.* Report 27061-EC. Washington, DC: Poverty Reduction and Economic Management Sector Unit, Latin America and Caribbean Region, World Bank.

———. 2004. *Mexico: Poverty in Mexico—An Assessment of Conditions, Trends, and Government Strategy.* Report 28612-ME. Washington, DC: Colombia and Mexico Country Management Unit, Poverty Reduction and Economic Management Division, Latin America and Caribbean Region, World Bank.

———. 2005. *Bolivia: Poverty Assessment—Establishing the Basis for Pro-Poor Growth.* Report 28068-BO. Washington, DC: Poverty Reduction and Economic Management Sector Unit, Latin America and Caribbean Region, World Bank; with contributions from Unidad de Análisis de Políticas Sociales y Económicas and Instituto Nacional de Estadística.

———. 2005. *El Salvador: Poverty Assessment Strengthening Social Policy.* Report 29594-SV. Washington, DC: Poverty Reduction and Economic Management and Human Development Sector Management Units, Latin America and Caribbean Region, World Bank.

———. 2005. *Peru: Opportunities for All—Peru Poverty Assessment.* Report 29825-PE. Washington, DC: Poverty Reduction and Economic Management Sector Unit, Latin America and Caribbean Region, World Bank.

———. 2006. *Honduras: Poverty Assessment—Attaining Poverty Reduction.* Report 35622-HN. Washington, DC: Central America Department, Latin America and Caribbean Region, World Bank.

Middle East and North Africa

World Bank. 1999. *Democratic and Popular Republic of Algeria: Growth, Employment, and Poverty Reduction.* Report 18564-AL. Washington, DC: Human Development Group, Middle East and North Africa Region, World Bank.

———. 2001. *Kingdom of Morocco: Poverty Update.* Report 21506-MOR. Washington, DC: Human Development Sector, Middle East and North Africa Region, World Bank.

———. 2001. *Poverty in the West Bank and Gaza.* Report 22312-GZ. Washington, DC: Middle East and North Africa Region, World Bank.

———. 2002. *Arab Republic of Egypt: Poverty Reduction in Egypt—Diagnosis and Strategy.* Report 24234-EGT. Washington, DC: Social and Economic Development Group, Middle East and North Africa Region, World Bank, and Ministry of Planning, Government of the Arab Republic of Egypt.

———. 2002. *Reducing Vulnerability and Increasing Opportunity: Social Protection in the Middle East and North Africa.* Washington, DC: Middle East and North Africa Region, World Bank.

———. 2002. *Republic of Yemen: Poverty Update.* Report 24422-YEM. Washington, DC: Social and Economic Development Group, Middle East and North Africa Region, World Bank.

———. 2003. *West Bank and Gaza: Deep Palestinian Poverty in the Midst of Economic Crisis.* Report 30150-WBZ. Washington, DC: World Bank and Palestinian Central Bureau of Statistics.

———. 2004. *Morocco: Poverty Report—Strengthening Policy by Identifying the Geographic Dimension of Poverty.* Report 28223-MOR. Washington, DC: Middle East and North Africa Region, World Bank.

South Asia

Ajwad, Mohamed Ihsan. 2007. "Performance of Social Safety Net Programs in Uttar Pradesh." Social Protection Discussion Paper 0714, Social Protection Unit, Human Development Network, World Bank, Washington, DC.

del Ninno, Carlo, Paul A. Dorosh, and Lisa C. Smith. 2003. "Public Policy, Markets, and Household Coping Strategies in Bangladesh: Avoiding a Food Security Crisis Following the 1998 Floods." *World Development* 31 (7): 1221–38.

Mansuri, Ghazala, and Andrew Healy. 2002. "Vulnerability Prediction in Rural Pakistan." Paper prepared for the International Food Policy Research Institute–World Bank Conference on Risk and Vulnerability: Estimation and Policy Implications, Washington, DC, September 23–24.

World Bank. 2000. *India: Policies to Reduce Poverty and Accelerate Sustainable Development.* Report 19471-IN. Washington, DC: Poverty Reduction and Economic Management Unit, South Asia Region, World Bank.

———. 2002. *Bangladesh: Poverty in Bangladesh—Building on Progress.* Report 24299-BD. Washington, DC: Poverty Reduction and Economic Management Sector Unit, South Asia Region, World Bank.

———. 2002. *India: Poverty in India—The Challenge of Uttar Pradesh.* Report 22323-IN. Washington, DC: Poverty Reduction and Economic Management Sector Unit, South Asia Region, World Bank.

———. 2002. *Pakistan Poverty Assessment: Poverty in Pakistan—Vulnerabilities, Social Gaps, and Rural Dynamics.* Report 24296-PAK. Washington, DC: Poverty Reduction and Economic Management Sector Unit, South Asia Region, World Bank.

———. 2002. *Poverty and Vulnerability in South Asia.* Washington, DC: Human Development Sector, South Asia Region, World Bank.

———. 2002. *Sri Lanka: Poverty Assessment.* Report 22535-CE. Washington, DC: Poverty Reduction and Economic Management Sector Unit, South Asia Region, World Bank.

———. 2005. *Afghanistan: Poverty, Vulnerability, and Social Protection—An Initial Assessment.* Report 29694-AF. Washington, DC: Human Development Unit, South Asia Region, World Bank.

———. 2005. *Bangladesh: Social Safety Nets in Bangladesh—An Assessment.* Report 33411-BD. Washington, DC: Human Development Unit, South Asia Region, World Bank.

———. 2005. *A Poverty Map for Sri Lanka—Lessons and Findings.* Report 35605. Washington, DC: Poverty Reduction and Economic Management Unit, South Asia Region, World Bank.

———. 2006. *Nepal: Resilience amidst Conflict—An Assessment of Poverty in Nepal, 1995–96 and 2003–04.* Report 34834-NP. Washington, DC: Poverty Reduction and Economic Management Sector Unit, South Asia Region, World Bank.

———. 2007. *Social Protection in Pakistan: Managing Household Risks and Vulnerability.* Report 35472-PK. Washington, DC: Human Development Unit, South Asia Region, World Bank.

———. 2007. *Sri Lanka: Strengthening Social Protection.* Report 38107-LK. Washington, DC: Human Development Unit, South Asia Region, World Bank.

NOTES

[1] The Social Protection Sector Strategy Implementation Update was discussed at the meeting of the World Bank's Committee on Development Effectiveness on September 17, 2007 (World Bank 2007f).

[2] The World Bank board approved the Social Protection Sector Strategy in September 2000, and it was published in early 2001 (World Bank 2001k).

[3] Although poverty and vulnerability assessments have been conducted, they are mainly an informal subset of the official PAs. Thus, in this chapter they are classified under PAs.

[4] Thematic code 55 was created only in July 2001 and thus applies only to products created in fiscal years 2002 to 2007.

[5] Business Warehouse is an electronic storage facility for all documents produced by the Bank, organized thematically and by report type.

[6] This work primarily addresses countries in Latin America and South Asia.

[7] See for a list of these workshops, beginning with the 1999 Summer Stiglitz Workshop organized in preparation for *World Development Report 2000/2001: Attacking Poverty* (World Bank 2001n).

[8] The current R&V analysis inventory does not include Bank documents that are still being prepared or that have not been finalized and put in the public domain for two reasons: (a) draft documents can be difficult to locate, and (b) many have been explicitly distributed to only a limited audience. This exclusion has the largest effect on the Africa R&V analysis portfolio: a number of PAs for francophone countries have not been finalized for public distribution, nor has the Malawi poverty and vulnerability assessment, which includes a comprehensive treatment of risk and risk management instruments.

[9] Vulnerability is not measured using stochastic methods—that is, vulnerability to poverty—but is defined as having consumption levels that are close to the poverty line.

[10] The Burkina Faso PA drew on an RVA prepared in 2003 and 2004 (see World Bank 2004b).

REFERENCES

Ajwad, Mohamed Ihsan. 2007. "Performance of Social Safety Net Programs in Uttar Pradesh." Social Protection Discussion Paper 0714, Social Protection Unit, Human Development Network, World Bank, Washington, DC.

Alam, Asad. 2005. *Growth, Poverty, and Inequality: Eastern Europe and the Former Soviet Union.* Washington, DC: World Bank.

Bourguignon, François, and Chor-ching Goh. 2002. "Trade and Labor Market Vulnerability in Indonesia, Korea, and Thailand." *World Bank PovertyNet Newsletter* 48: 223–241.

Chaudhuri, Shubham, Jyotsna Jalan, and Asep Suryahadi. 2002. "Assessing Household Vulnerability to Poverty from Cross-Sectional Data: A Methodology and Estimates from Indonesia." Discussion Paper 0102-52, Department of Economics, Columbia University, New York.

Christiaensen, Luc J., and Kalanidhi Subbarao. 2005. Towards an Understanding of Household Vulnerability in Rural Kenya. *Journal of African Economies* 14 (4): 520–58.

Conflict Prevention and Reconstruction Unit. n.d. "CPR and Related Publications on Conflict and Development." World Bank, Washington, DC.

Datt, Gaurav, and Hans Hoogeveen. 2000. "El Niño or El Peso? Crisis, Poverty, and Income Distribution in the Philippines." Policy Research Working Paper 2466, East Asia and Pacific Region, Poverty Reduction and Economic Management Sector Unit, World Bank, Washington, DC.

del Ninno, Carlo, Paul A. Dorosh, and Lisa C. Smith. 2003. "Public Policy, Markets, and Household Coping Strategies in Bangladesh: Avoiding a Food Security Crisis Following the 1998 Floods." *World Development* 31 (7): 1221–38.

de Soto, Hermine, Peter Gordon, Ilir Gedeshi, and Zamira Sinoimeri. 2002. "Poverty in Albania: A Qualitative Assessment." World Bank Technical Paper 520, World Bank, Washington, DC.

Dercon, Stefan. 2007. "Fate and Fear: Risk and Its Consequences in Africa." GPRG Working Paper 074. Global Poverty Research Group, University of Oxford, Oxford, U.K.

Heitzmann, Karin, R. Sudharshan Canagarajah, and Paul B. Siegel. 2002. "Guidelines for Assessing the Sources of Risk and Vulnerability." Social Protection Discussion Paper 0218,

Social Protection Unit, Human Development Network, World Bank, Washington, DC.

Hoddinott, John, and Agnes R. Quisumbing. 2003a. "Data Sources for Microeconometric Risk and Vulnerability Assessments." Social Protection Discussion Paper 0323, Social Protection Unit, Human Development Network, World Bank, Washington, DC.

———. 2003b. "Methods for Microeconometric Risk and Vulnerability Assessments." Social Protection Discussion Paper 0324, Social Protection Unit, Human Development Network, World Bank, Washington, DC.

Holzmann, Robert. 2001. "Risk and Vulnerability: The Forward Looking Role of Social Protection in a Globalizing World." Social Protection Discussion Paper 0109, Social Protection Unit, Human Development Network, World Bank, Washington, DC.

Holzmann, Robert, and Steen Jørgensen. 1999. "Social Protection as Social Risk Management: Conceptual Underpinnings for the Social Protection Sector Strategy Paper." Social Protection Discussion Paper 9904, Social Protection Unit, Human Development Network, World Bank, Washington, DC.

———. 2000. "Social Risk Management: A New Conceptual Framework for Social Protection and Beyond." Social Protection Discussion Paper 0006, Social Protection Unit, Human Development Network, World Bank, Washington, DC.

Jalan, Jyotsna, and Martin Ravallion. 2001. "Household Income Dynamics in Rural China." Policy Research Working Paper 2706, Development Research Group, World Bank, Washington, DC.

Jones, Christine, and Ana Revenga. 2000. *Making Transition Work for Everyone: Poverty and Inequality in Europe and Central Asia.* Washington, DC: World Bank.

Maluccio, John A. 2005. "Coping with the 'Coffee Crisis' in Central America: The Role of the Nicaraguan *Red de Protección Social.*" FCND Discussion Paper 188, Food Consumption and Nutrition Division, International Food Policy Research Institute, Washington, DC.

Mansuri, Ghazala, and Andrew Healy. 2002. "Vulnerability Prediction in Rural Pakistan." Paper prepared for the International Food Policy Research Institute–World Bank Conference on Risk and Vulnerability: Estimation and Policy Implications, Washington, DC, September 23–24.

Pritchett, Lant, Asep Suryahadi, and Sudarno Sumarto. 2000. "Quantifying Vulnerability to Poverty: A Proposed Measure, Applied to Indonesia." Policy Research Working Paper 2437, East Asia and Pacific Region, Environment and Social Development Sector Unit, World Bank, Washington, DC.

Ridao-Cano, Cristóbal. 2006. *Children's Work in Cambodia: A Challenge for Growth and Poverty Reduction.* Rome: Understanding Children's Work Project, Faculty of Economics, University of Rome Tor Vergata.

Vakis, Renos, Diana Kruger, and Andrew D. Mason. 2004. "Shocks and Coffee: Lessons from Nicaragua." Social Protection Discussion Paper 0415, Social Protection Unit, Human Development Network, World Bank, Washington, DC.

World Bank. 1990. *World Development Report 1990: Poverty.* Washington, DC: World Bank.

———. 1999a. "Towards an East Asian Social Protection Strategy." Human Development Unit, East Asia and Pacific Region, World Bank, Washington, DC.

———. 1999b. *Vietnam Development Report 2000: Attacking Poverty—Country Economic Memorandum.* Report 19914-VN. Washington, DC: Poverty Reduction and Economic Management Unit, East Asia and Pacific Region, World Bank.

———. 2000a. *Balancing Protection and Opportunity: A Strategy for Social Protection in Transition Economies.* Washington, DC: Social Protection Team, Human Development Sector Unit, Europe and Central Asia Region, World Bank.

———. 2000b. *Ecuador: Crisis, Poverty, and Social Services.* Report 19920-EC. Washington, DC: Human Development Department, Latin America and the Caribbean Region, World Bank.

———. 2000c. *Republic of Tajikistan: Poverty Assessment.* Report 20285-TJ. Washington, DC: Human Development Sector Unit, Europe and Central Asia Region, World Bank.

———. 2000d. *Turkey: Economic Reforms, Living Standards, and Social Welfare Study.* Report 20029-TU. Washington, DC: Poverty Reduction and Economic Management Unit, Europe and Central Asia Region, World Bank.

———. 2001a. *Bolivarian Republic of Venezuela: Investing Human Capital for Growth, Prosperity, and Poverty Reduction.* Report 21833-VE. Washington, DC: Colombia, Mexico, and Venezuela Country Management Unit, Poverty Reduction and Economic Management Unit, Latin America and Caribbean Region, World Bank.

———. 2001b. *Croatia: Economic Vulnerability and Welfare Study*. Report 22079-HR. Washington, DC: Poverty Reduction and Economic Management Unit, Europe and Central Asia Region, World Bank.

———. 2001c. *Dynamic Risk Management and the Poor: Developing a Social Protection Strategy for Africa.* Washington, DC: Human Development Department, Africa Region, World Bank.

———. 2001d. *Hungary: Long-Term Poverty, Social Protection, and the Labor Market.* Report 20645-HU. Washington, DC: Poverty Reduction and Economic Management Unit, Europe and Central Asia Region, World Bank.

———. 2001e. *Kingdom of Morocco: Poverty Update.* Report 21506-MOR. Washington, DC: Human Development Sector, Middle East and North Africa Region, World Bank.

———. 2001f. *Kosovo: Poverty Assessment.* Report 23390-KOS. Washington, DC: Poverty Reduction and Economic Management Unit, Europe and Central Asia Region, World Bank.

———. 2001g. *Nicaragua: Poverty Assessment: Challenges and Opportunities for Poverty Reduction.* Report 20488-NI. Washington, DC: Poverty Reduction and Economic Management Sector Unit, Latin America and Caribbean Region, World Bank.

———. 2001h. *Philippines: Poverty Assessment.* Report 20498. Washington, DC: Poverty Reduction and Economic Management Unit, East Asia and Pacific Region, World Bank.

———. 2001i. *Poverty in the West Bank and Gaza.* Report 22312-GZ. Washington, DC: Middle East and North Africa Region, World Bank.

———. 2001j. *Slovak Republic: Living Standards Employment and Labor Market Study.* Report 22351-SK. Washington, DC: Poverty Reduction and Economic Management Unit, Europe and Central Asia Region, World Bank.

———. 2001k. *Social Protection Sector Strategy: From Safety Net to Springboard.* Washington, DC: World Bank. http://go.worldbank.org/97LBYDY3U0.

———. 2001l. *Thailand: Social Monitor—Poverty and Public Policy.* Report 23147-TH. Washington, DC: Human Development Sector Unit, East Asia and Pacific Region, World Bank.

———. 2001m. *Uruguay: Maintaining Social Equity in a Changing Economy.* Report 21262. Washington, DC: Argentina, Chile, Paraguay, and Uruguay Country Management Unit, Poverty Reduction and Economic Management Sector Unit, Latin America and Caribbean Region, World Bank.

———. 2001n. *World Development Report 2000/2001: Attacking Poverty.* Washington, DC: World Bank.

———. 2002a. *Arab Republic of Egypt: Poverty Reduction in Egypt—Diagnosis and Strategy.* Report 24234-EGT. Washington, DC: Social and Economic Development Group, Middle East and North Africa Region, World Bank, and Ministry of Planning, Government of the Arab Republic of Egypt.

———. 2002b. *Armenia: Poverty Update.* Report 24339-AM. Washington, DC: Human Development Sector Unit, Europe and Central Asia Region, World Bank.

———. 2002c. *Bangladesh: Poverty in Bangladesh—Building on Progress.* Report 24299-BD. Washington, DC: Poverty Reduction and Economic Management Sector Unit, South Asia Region, World Bank.

———. 2002d. *Bolivia: Poverty Diagnostic 2000.* Report 20530-80. Washington, DC: Poverty Reduction and Economic Management Sector Unit, Latin America and Caribbean Region, World Bank, with contributions from Instituto Nacional de Estadística and Unidad de Análisis de Políticas Económicas.

———. 2002e. *Bulgaria: Poverty Assessment.* Report 24516-BUL. Washington, DC: Human Development Sector Unit, Europe and Central Asia Region, World Bank.

———. 2002f. *Colombia: Poverty Report.* Report 24524-CO. Washington, DC: Colombia Country Management Unit, Poverty Reduction and Economic Management Sector Unit, Latin America and Caribbean Region, World Bank.

———. 2002g. *Colombia: Social Safety Net Assessment.* Report 22255-CO. Washington, DC: Latin America and the Caribbean Regional Office, World Bank.

———. 2002h. *Costa Rica: Social Spending and the Poor.* Report 24300-CR. Washington, DC: Human Development Sector Management Unit, Central America Country Management Unit, Latin America and Caribbean Region, World Bank.

———. 2002i. *Georgia: Poverty Update.* Report 22350-GE. Washington, DC: Poverty Reduction and Economic Management Unit, Europe and Central Asia Region, World Bank.

———. 2002j. *India: Poverty in India—The Challenge of Uttar Pradesh.* Report 22323-IN. Washington, DC: Poverty Reduction and Economic Management Sector Unit, South Asia Region, World Bank.

———. 2002k. *Pakistan Poverty Assessment: Poverty in Pakistan—Vulnerabilities, Social Gaps, and Rural Dynamics.* Report 24296-PAK. Washington, DC: Poverty Reduction and Economic Management Sector Unit, South Asia Region, World Bank.

———. 2002l. *People, Poverty, and Livelihoods: Links for Sustainable Poverty Reduction in Indonesia.* Report 25289. Jakarta: World Bank and U.K. Department for International Development.

———. 2002m. *Poverty and Vulnerability in South Asia.* Washington, DC: Human Development Sector, South Asia Region, World Bank.

———. 2002n. *Reducing Vulnerability and Increasing Opportunity: Social Protection in the Middle East and North Africa.* Washington, DC: Middle East and North Africa Region, World Bank.

———. 2002o. *Republic of Yemen: Poverty Update.* Report 24422-YEM. Washington, DC: Social and Economic Development Group, Middle East and North Africa Region, World Bank.

———. 2002p. *Sri Lanka: Poverty Assessment.* Report 22535-CE. Washington, DC: Poverty Reduction and Economic Management Sector Unit, South Asia Region, World Bank.

———. 2003a. *Albania: Poverty Assessment.* Report 26213-AL. Washington, DC: Human Development Sector Unit, Europe and Central Asia Region, World Bank.

———. 2003b. *Argentina: Crisis and Poverty 2003: Poverty Assessment.* Report 26127-AR. Washington, DC: Poverty Reduction and Economic Management Unit, Latin America and Caribbean Region, World Bank.

———. 2003c. *Armenia: Poverty Assessment.* Report 27192-AM. Washington, DC: Human Development Sector Unit, Europe and Central Asia Region, World Bank.

———. 2003d. *Azerbaijan Republic: Poverty Assessment.* Report 24890-AZ. Washington, DC: Human Development Sector Unit, South Caucasus Country Unit, Europe and Central Asia Region, World Bank.

———. 2003e. *Benin: Poverty Assessment.* Report 28447-BEN. Washington, DC: Human Development II, Country Department 13, Africa Region, World Bank.

———. 2003f. *Brazil: Strategies for Poverty Reduction in Ceara: The Challenge of Inclusive Modernization.* Report 24500-BR. Washington, DC: Brazil Country Management Unit, Latin America and Caribbean Region, World Bank.

———. 2003g. *Étude Pilote de Risques et de la Vulnérabilité en République Démocratique du Congo.* Kinshasa: World Bank.

———. 2003h. *Kyrgyz Republic: Enhancing Pro-Poor Growth.* Report 24638-KG. Washington, DC: Poverty Reduction and Economic Management Unit, Europe and Central Asia Region, World Bank.

———. 2003i. *Nigeria: Risk and Vulnerability Assessment.* Washington, DC: Africa Human Development Division 3, Africa Region, World Bank.

———. 2003j. *Poverty in Guatemala.* Report 27586. Washington, DC: World Bank.

———. 2003k. *Romania: Poverty Assessment.* Report 26169-RO. Washington, DC: Human Development Sector Unit and Environmentally and Socially Sustainable Development Unit, Europe and Central Asia Region, World Bank.

———. 2003l. *Serbia and Montenegro: Poverty Assessment.* Report 26011-YU. Washington, DC: Poverty Reduction and Economic Management Unit, Europe and Central Asia Region, World Bank.

———. 2003m. *Turkey: Poverty and Coping after Crises.* Report 24185-TR. Washington, DC: Human Development Unit, Europe and Central Asia Region, World Bank.

———. 2003n. *Uruguay: Poverty Update 2003.* Report 26223-UR. Washington, DC: Argentina, Chile, Paraguay, and Uruguay Country Management Unit, Poverty Reduction and Economic Management Unit, Latin America and Caribbean Region, World Bank.

———. 2003o. *Uzbekistan: Living Standards Assessment—Policies to Improve Living Standards.* Report 25923-UZ. Washington, DC: Human Development Sector Unit, Europe and Central Asia Region, World Bank.

———. 2003p. *Vietnam Development Report 2004.* Report 27130-VN. Washington, DC: Poverty Reduction and Economic Management Unit, East Asia and Pacific Region, World Bank.

———. 2003q. "Volatility, Risk, and Innovation: Social Protection in Latin America and the Caribbean." *Spectrum*, Social Protection Unit, World Bank, Washington, DC.

———. 2003r. *West Bank and Gaza: Deep Palestinian Poverty in the Midst of Economic Crisis.* Report 30150-WBZ. Washington, DC: World Bank and Palestinian Central Bureau of Statistics.

———. 2004a. *Belarus: Poverty Assessment—Can Poverty Reduction and Access to Services Be Sustained?* Report 27431-BY. Washington, DC: Human Development Sector Unit, Europe and Central Asia Region, World Bank.

———. 2004b. *Burkina Faso: Risk and Vulnerability Assessment.* Report 28144-BUR. Washington, DC: Africa Human Development Division 2, Africa Region, World Bank.

———. 2004c. *Chile: Household Risk Management and Social Protection.* Report 25286-CH. Washington, DC: Country Management Unit for Argentina, Chile, Paraguay, and Uruguay, Human Development Department, World Bank.

———. 2004d. *Ecuador: Poverty Assessment.* Report 27061-EC. Washington, DC: Poverty Reduction and Economic Management Sector Unit, Latin America and Caribbean Region, World Bank.

———. 2004e. *Kazakhstan: Dimensions of Poverty in Kazakhstan.* Report 30294-KZ. Washington, DC: Poverty Reduction and Economic Management Unit, Europe and Central Asia Region, World Bank.

———. 2004f. *Morocco: Poverty Report—Strengthening Policy by Identifying the Geographic Dimension of Poverty.* Report 28223-MOR. Washington, DC: Middle East and North Africa Region, World Bank.

———. 2004g. *Poland: Growth, Employment and Living Standards in Pre-accession Poland.* Report 28233-POL. Washington, DC: Poverty Reduction and Economic Management Unit, Europe and Central Asia Region, World Bank.

———. 2004h. *Recession, Recovery, and Poverty in Moldova.* Report 28024-MD. Washington, DC: Human Development Sector Unit, Europe and Central Asia Region, World Bank.

———. 2005a. *Afghanistan: Poverty, Vulnerability, and Social Protection—An Initial Assessment.* Report 29694-AF. Washington, DC: Human Development Unit, South Asia Region, World Bank.

———. 2005b. *Bangladesh: Social Safety Nets in Bangladesh—An Assessment.* Report 33411-BD. Washington, DC: Human Development Unit, South Asia Region, World Bank.

———. 2005c. *Bolivia: Poverty Assessment—Establishing the Basis for Pro-Poor Growth.* Report 28068-BO. Washington, DC: Poverty Reduction and Economic Management Sector Unit, Latin America and Caribbean Region, World Bank; with contributions from Unidad de Análisis de Políticas Sociales y Económicas and Instituto Nacional de Estadística.

———. 2005d. *Burkina Faso: Reducing Poverty through Sustained Equitable Growth—Poverty Assessment.* Report 29743-BUR. Washington, DC: Poverty Reduction and Economic Management Unit 4, Africa Region, World Bank.

———. 2005e. *Ethiopia: Risk and Vulnerability Assessment.* Report 26275-ET. Washington, DC: Human Development Group 3, Africa Region, World Bank.

———. 2005f. *Ethiopia: Well-Being and Poverty in Ethiopia: The Role of Agriculture and Agency.* Report 29468-ET. Washington, DC: Poverty Reduction and Economic Management Unit 2, Country Department for Ethiopia, Africa Region, World Bank.

———. 2005g. *FYR of Macedonia: Poverty Assessment for 2002–2003.* Report 34324-MK. Washington, DC: Poverty Reduction and Economic Management Unit, Europe and Central Asia Region, World Bank.

———. 2005h. *Kosovo: Poverty Assessment—Promoting Opportunity, Security, and Participation for All.* Report 32378-XK. Washington, DC: Poverty Reduction and Economic Management Unit, Europe and Central Asia Region, World Bank.

———. 2005i. *Kyrgyz Republic: Poverty Update—Profile of Living Standards in 2003.* Report 36602-KG. Washington, DC: Poverty Reduction and Economic Management Unit, Europe and Central Asia Region, World Bank.

———. 2005j. *Peru: Opportunities for All—Peru Poverty Assessment.* Report 29825-PE. Washington, DC: Poverty Reduction and Economic Management Sector Unit, Latin America and Caribbean Region, World Bank.

———. 2005k. *A Poverty Map for Sri Lanka's Findings and Lessons.* Report 35605. Washington, DC: Poverty Reduction and Economic Management Unit, South Asia Region, World Bank.

———. 2005l. *Russian Federation: Reducing Poverty through Growth and Social Policy Reform.* Report 28923-RU. Washington, DC: Poverty Reduction and Economic Management Unit, Europe and Central Asia Region, World Bank.

———. 2005m. *Slovak Republic: The Quest for Equitable Growth in the Slovak Republic—A World Bank Living Standards Assessment.* Report 32433-SK. Washington, DC: Poverty Reduction and Economic Management Unit, Europe and Central Asia Region, World Bank.

———. 2006a. *Cambodia: Halving Poverty by 2015? Poverty Assessment 2006.* Report 35213-KH. Washington, DC: East Asia and the Pacific Region, World Bank.

———. 2006b. *Guinea-Bissau: Integrated Poverty and Social Assessment (IPSA).* Report 34553-GW. Washington, DC: Poverty Reduction and Economic Management Unit 4, Africa Region, World Bank.

———. 2006c. *Indonesia: Making the New Indonesia Work for the Poor.* Report 37349-ID. Washington, DC: Poverty Reduction and Economic Management Sector Unit, East Asia and Pacific Region, World Bank.

———. 2006d. *Nepal: Resilience amidst Conflict—An Assessment of Poverty in Nepal, 1995–96 and 2003–04.* Report 34834-NP. Washington, DC: Poverty Reduction and Economic Management Sector Unit, South Asia Region, World Bank.

———. 2006e. *Uganda: Poverty and Vulnerability Assessment.* Report 36996-UG. Washington, DC: Poverty Reduction and Economic Management, Southern Africa, Africa Region, World Bank.

———. 2007a. *Kosovo: Poverty Assessment.* Report 39737-XK. Washington, DC: Poverty Reduction and Economic Management Unit, Europe and Central Asia Region, World Bank.

———. 2007b. *Kyrgyz Republic: Poverty Assessment.* Report 40864-KG. Washington, DC: Poverty Reduction and Economic Management Unit, Europe and Central Asia Region, World Bank.

———. 2007c. *Latvia: Sharing the High Growth Dividend—A Living Standards Assessment.* Report 38437-LV. Washington, DC: Poverty Reduction and Economic Management Unit, Europe and Central Asia Region, World Bank.

———. 2007d. *Republic of Uzbekistan: Living Standards Assessment Update.* Report 40723-UZ. Washington, DC: Human Development Sector Unit, Central Asia Country Unit, Europe and Central Asia Region, World Bank.

———. 2007e. *Risk and Vulnerability Assessment for Conflict Prevention in Guinea.* Washington, DC: Africa Human Development Division 2, Africa Region, World Bank.

———. 2007f. *Sector Strategy Implementation Update: Third Review.* Washington, DC: Operations Policy and Country Services Delivery Management Unit, World Bank.

———. 2007g. *Social Protection in Pakistan: Managing Household Risks and Vulnerability.* Report 35472-PK. Washington, DC: Human Development Unit, South Asia Region, World Bank.

———. 2007h. *Zambia: Poverty and Vulnerability Assessment.* Report 32573-ZM. Washington, DC: Africa Human Development Division 1, Poverty Reduction and Economic Management Unit, Africa Region, World Bank.

CHAPTER 3 three

LABOR MARKETS IN WORLD BANK LENDING AND ANALYTICAL WORK, 2000–07

Milan Vodopivec, Jean Fares, and Michael Justesen

INTRODUCTION

Objectives

Full and productive employment is now a target of the Millennium Development Goals (Target 1.b) and occupies a central place in the workings of development agencies. The World Bank directly supports low- and middle-income countries in promoting efficient labor markets and employment growth through analytical work, technical assistance, and lending operations, both in project and development policy loans. Labor market analysis is also increasingly featured in World Bank flagship publications and analytical products. The objectives of this chapter are threefold: (a) to document the Bank's involvement in improving labor markets from 2000 to 2007, (b) to present good practices that have emerged in promoting labor markets in a wide variety of contexts, and (c) to present activities and partnerships for the future.

The labor market is critical for a sustainable and inclusive development strategy. First, it is here that employment shocks related to (and often required by) structural reforms must be addressed. Second, labor is most often the only asset that poor people have, and a growth process that is not associated with sustained job creation may fail to reach them. Third, a labor market that facilitates job creation and increases productivity is a key ingredient in a business climate where new firms are created and private agents find the proper incentives to invest and innovate. A well-functioning labor market is needed to guarantee the success of structural reforms, to maintain social support for those reforms, and to ensure that their benefits are widely distributed. Moving toward a well-functioning labor market will likely be crucial to a more effective implementation of poverty reduction strategies and hence progress toward meeting the Millennium Development Goals.

How Bank Thinking Has Evolved and How Labor Markets Fit into the SRM Framework

During the past decades, the World Bank has improved its understanding about how labor markets are linked to economic growth and the reduction of poverty, and placing the labor market interventions in the broader framework of social risk management has been helpful for this endeavor.

Evolution of Bank Thinking on Labor Markets. The World Bank's understanding of the links between economic development and the labor market has evolved dramatically over the past three decades. In the 1980s, a widely shared view was that stabilizing the economy and getting relative

Milan Vodopivec is lead economist and head of the Labor Team of the World Bank's Social Protection and Labor Department. Jean Fares is senior economist on this team. Michael Justesen was a consultant at the World Bank; he is now a senior adviser in the Danish Ministry of Employment.

prices right would increase the demand for the abundant factor of production—that is, labor—and, thus, would help workers and reduce poverty. Adverse transitional effects were perceived to be short-lived and, at least in middle-income countries, social safety nets were considered sufficient to protect workers affected by structural changes. Toward the end of the 1980s, it became clear that macrostabilization and trade liberalization alone did not lead to improvements in labor market conditions, especially for the most vulnerable groups. Such policy prescriptions were often accompanied by tough fiscal austerity programs, which generally reduced expenditures for social safety nets. Thus, efforts to protect social expenditures and improve their effectiveness in order to mitigate adverse effects of structural adjustment became one of the main thrusts of the Bank's activities in the 1990s.

Low-income countries have also been subject to changes that have implications for human capital investment policies in those countries. The emergence of China and India as global players in the manufacturing and services sectors not only has affected developed countries but also has presented workers in developing countries with significant challenges. The limited labor productivity gains in countries of Sub-Saharan Africa and Latin America have also reduced the ability of workers in those regions to compete with China and India. At the same time, increased mobility within countries and regions, as well as international migration, now allows workers to find better employment matches in distant places. The continued trend of excess labor's moving out of agriculture and into rural nonfarm activities and the urban sector has added to those flows and has pressured urban and modern markets to absorb those large flows (World Bank 2007c).

Since the 1990s, the Bank's work in the labor market area has focused on the assessment of specific labor market policies and institutions to help the unemployed or those excluded from the formal labor market. A clear sense of how labor markets fit into a comprehensive development strategy was not yet part of this focus, as it is today. The Bank continues to work to improve the understanding of how specific labor market conditions in developing countries affect economic growth and the response of the economy to structural reforms, as well as to study the distribution of costs and benefits of such reforms among different social groups. The main challenge for the future is to discover how labor markets contribute to economic growth and empower poor people and to assess how efficient labor markets can contribute to the Millennium Development Goals, specifically poverty reduction.

How Labor Markets Fit into the Social Risk Management Framework. The concept of social risk management asserts that individuals, households, and communities are exposed to multiple risks from different sources, both natural (such as earthquakes, floods, and illness) and constructed (such as unemployment, environmental degradation, and war). Poor people are typically more exposed to risk and have less access to effective risk management instruments than do people with greater assets. This vulnerability renders individuals risk averse and unwilling or unable to engage in high-risk and high-return activities. Under those circumstances, poor people have developed elaborate mechanisms of self-protection, such as asset accumulation in good times, diversification of income sources, and creation of informal family and community risk-pooling arrangements. However, those arrangements are often relatively expensive and inefficient, and the coping strategies available once a shock occurs often reduce poor people's human capital (for example, cutting back on meals or taking children out of school to help generate income). Thus, public intervention is needed. The Social Risk Management (SRM) framework allows labor market risk management mechanisms—informal and formal, private and public—to be divided into three categories:

- Those that reduce the risk of unemployment (that is, reduce the probability of becoming unemployed or increase the probability of leaving unemployment if unemployed)
- Those that mitigate that risk (that is, reduce the impact of a future period of unemployment)
- Those applied in response to the undesirable event that has already occurred (coping mechanisms).

Within all three categories, informal and formal mechanisms are usually available. Formal mechanisms include both market-based and public mechanisms. Table 3.1 illustrates how labor market policies fit into the SRM framework. For example, to *mitigate* the risk of losing a job, formal instruments such as unemployment insurance could be used. Active labor market programs allow the unemployed to *cope* with the unemployment shock. Informal coping mechanisms for this shock could take the form of child labor when children are forced to leave school to generate income because of a parent's job loss.

The SRM framework enables one to position labor market policies and programs in the context of other mechanisms that may be used to manage social risks. Viewing the framework in its entirety is useful when evaluating the performance of public policies and programs or when selecting among them. Above all, the framework helps identify links and interactions among various components. For

Table 3.1: Labor Market Policies within the Social Risk Management Framework

Strategy	Informal mechanisms	Formal mechanisms: Market based	Formal mechanisms: Public
Risk reduction			
	■ Less risky production ■ Migration ■ Proper feeding and weaning practices ■ Maintenance of good health	■ Training ■ Financial market literacy ■ Company-based and market-driven labor standards	■ Sound macroeconomic policies ■ Public health policy ■ **Labor market policies (including employment protection policies, such as severance pay)**
Risk mitigation			
Portfolio diversification	■ Multiple jobs ■ Investment in human, physical, and real assets ■ Investment in social capital (rituals, reciprocal gift giving)	■ Investment in multiple financial assets ■ Microfinance programs	■ Multipillar pension systems ■ Asset transfers ■ Protection of property rights ■ Support for extending financial markets to the poor
Insurance	■ Savings (in form of financial or other assets) ■ Marriage and family ■ Community arrangements ■ Sharecrop tenancy	■ Old-age annuities ■ Disability, accident, and other personal insurance ■ Crop, fire, and other damage insurance	■ *Unemployment insurance* ■ *Unemployment assistance* ■ *Unemployment insurance savings accounts* ■ Pensions (including **early retirement**), disability, and sickness insurance
Risk coping			
	■ Selling of real assets ■ Borrowing from neighbors ■ Intracommunity transfers and charity ■ Child labor ■ Dissaving in human capital	■ Sale of financial assets ■ Commercial loans	■ Social assistance ■ General subsidies ■ **Active labor market programs (job search assistance, training, employment subsidies, and public works)** ■ Social funds

Source: Adapted from World Bank 2001.
Note: Major public mechanisms used to manage the labor market risks are shown in bold.

example, there are important links between risk reduction and risk mitigation instruments. An important case in point is the distribution of risk, which is linked to the maintenance of workplaces: relying on employers to bear excessive risk may hinder job creation, innovations, and technological progress, but shifting risk to workers calls for the establishment of appropriate mechanisms to protect workers. Similarly, participation in a public income-support program may increase investments in human capital (such as enabling better education of family members and improving health) and reduce the use of undesirable coping strategies (such as selling cattle essential for providing important nutrients). The SRM framework also points out general equilibrium and growth interactions. For example, the introduction of unemployment insurance may encourage the emergence or expansion of more risky jobs or industries, which could conceivably increase efficiency.

Current Labor Market Conditions

Over the past decade, the estimated number of unemployed worldwide rose from about 160 million in 1996 to around 190 million in 2007 (ILO 2008). The unemployment rate peaked at 6.5 percent in 2002 and has since slowly declined to less than 6 percent by 2007 (figure 3.1). Almost 3 billion people were estimated to be employed in 2007. Of those, 486.7 million workers still do not earn enough to lift themselves and their families above the US$1-a-day poverty line, and 1.3 billion workers do not earn enough to lift themselves and their families above the US$2-a-day line. In other words, despite working, more than 4 out of 10 workers are poor.

Although employment rates of developing countries are comparable to those of developed countries, the large proportion of working poor in the developing world is a better indicator of the unfavorable labor market conditions of developing countries (figure 3.2). The average employment

FIGURE 3.1: GLOBAL EMPLOYMENT AND UNEMPLOYMENT TRENDS, 1996–2007

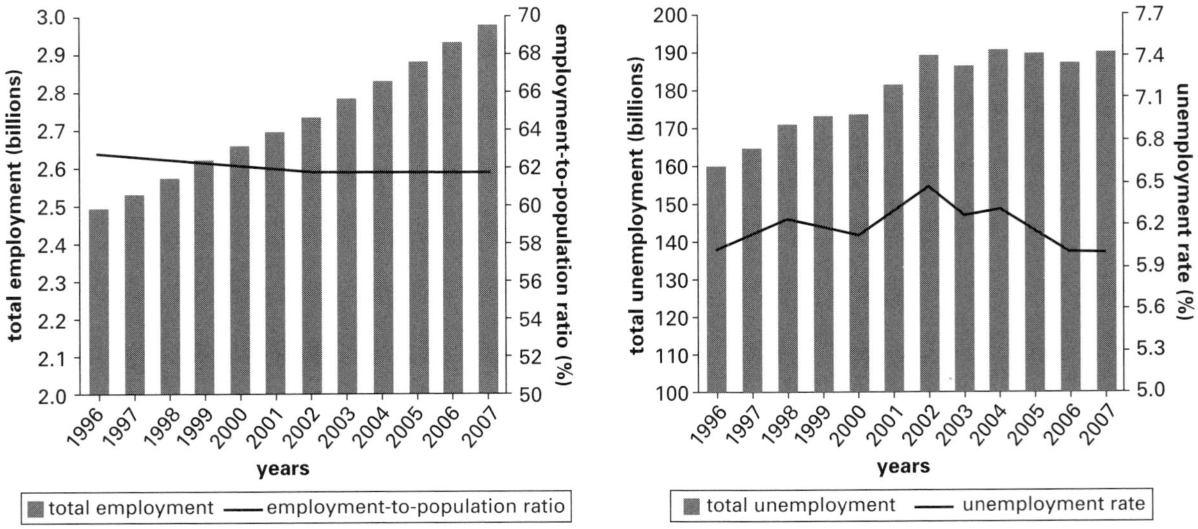

Source: ILO 2008.
Note: 2007 estimates are preliminary.

FIGURE 3.2: EMPLOYMENT RATE, UNEMPLOYMENT RATE, AND WORKING POOR LIVING BELOW US$1 PER DAY, 2006

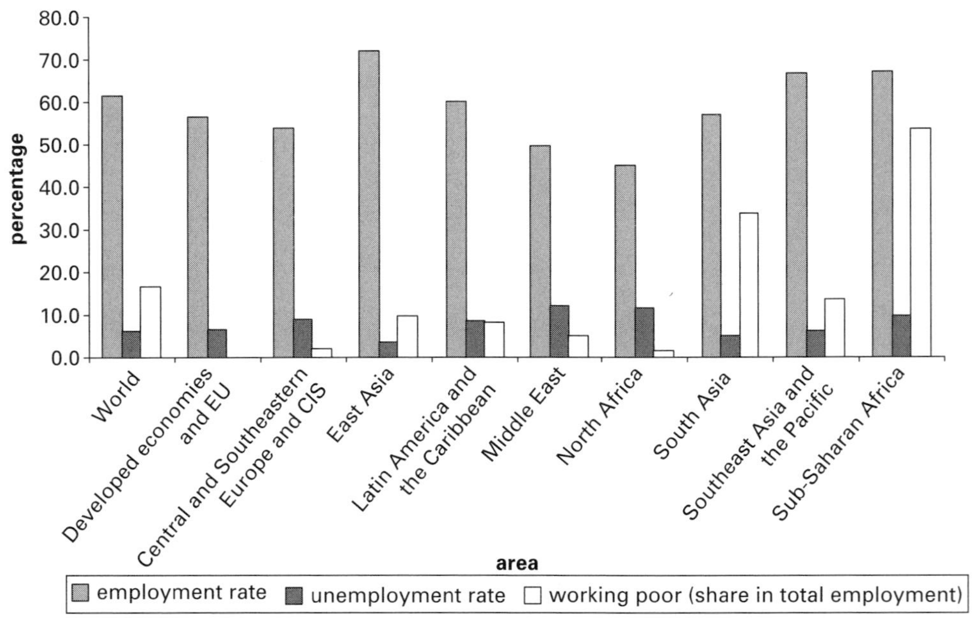

Source: ILO 2007b.
Note: CIS = Commonwealth of Independent States; EU = European Union. Data are preliminary. Data for Central and Southeastern Europe exclude EU countries.

rate of high-income countries is 56 percent, compared with employment rates of more than 65 percent in East Asia, Sub-Saharan Africa, and Southeast Asia and the Pacific and employment rates of around 50 percent in the Middle East and North Africa. Differences in employment rates are paralleled by differences in unemployment rates, with the latter being the largest in the Middle East and North Africa (12 percent each) and the lowest in East Asia (4 percent), South Asia (5 percent), and Southeast Asia and the Pacific (6 percent). However, 17 percent of the working population that resides outside developed countries lives in extreme poverty (on less than US$1 a day), with this share exceeding 50 percent in Sub-Saharan Africa and 30 percent in South Asia.

Major Issues for Labor Markets

Significant social, technological, and economic changes are affecting labor market performance and are responsible for some of the challenges outlined here. These changes are creating new opportunities, but they are also increasing risks and have potentially long-term implications for the development of countries and regions. Three main drivers of change are taking hold in labor markets worldwide:

1. *Demographic pressures.* In several low-income countries, demographic transition has resulted in a significant rise of the children and youth share of the population and a decrease in the dependency ratios (World Bank 2006b). As a result, a window of opportunity has opened in several low-income countries with the potential to reap a demographic dividend. In other countries—some middle-income and most high-income countries—the population is aging quickly, raising challenges on how to increase labor productivity to sustain this phenomenon.
2. *Technological change.* Changes in technology have accelerated rising returns to education and skills everywhere. The adjustment in the labor market and other sectors (including education) has been slow. As a result, important imbalances occur and a need for significant reform is rising.
3. *Globalization and migration.* Increased flows of goods, services, and capital have altered production and may have changed the development process in low-income countries. The implications on the labor market vary from opportunities in new and expanding export-oriented industries to the effect of foreign direct investment on working conditions in developing countries. At the same time, the flows of migrants internally and from South to North and the South-South flows along defined corridors have increased.

These drivers of change have led to the following concerns that the development community will need to address:

- *The persistent rates of incidence of child labor.* Research by the World Bank and others demonstrates the threat that child labor poses to the individual child as well as to the economic development of the country. The highest incidence of child labor is in Africa, where 29 percent of children work. Asia has the highest absolute number: 127 million, or 19 percent of children (International Labour Office 2006). Even these numbers likely underestimate the incidence of children working, because many types of child labor, such as domestic work, are not counted.
- *The high rate of youth joblessness.* Currently, 1.3 billion young people (ages 12–24) live in developing countries. They are the largest cohort ever to enter the labor force. They are more educated and healthier than previous generations were. Yet in many countries, young people face significant difficulties in their transition to work. Some begin working too early, others cannot enter the workforce, and still others get stuck in low-productivity work. Poverty can exacerbate outcomes such as school dropout rates and joblessness. Slow economic growth and rigid labor markets limit employment opportunities for young people. Lack of skills and experience often constrains youth from taking advantage of employment opportunities, while limited access to information and networks undermine their ability to create their own work and livelihoods. For many young women, the transition to work never takes place (World Bank 2006b).
- *The difficulties for women entering the labor market.* Women face many constraints at home and in the marketplace when they decide to seek paid employment. Numerous studies point to women's reproductive role as affecting female labor force participation, in general, and work for pay, in particular. Besides child care, women also face the time burden of domestic tasks—especially collecting water and firewood. In rural areas of Burkina Faso, Uganda, and Zambia, the potential time savings from locating a potable water source within 400 meters of all households range from 125 hours per household per year to 664 (Barwell 1996). However, wage gaps and discrimination against women in labor markets may also lower labor force participation, both contemporaneously and for future generations. The segregation of women into low-paying occupations may be another important driver of underinvestment in girls' education.
- *The high incidence of working poor.* Despite a decline in the percentage of working poor in global employment over the past 10 years, the International Labor Office estimates that the number of working people living on US$2 a day has continued to grow in absolute numbers, reaching 1.37 billion in 2006 (ILO 2008).
- *The expanding informality and the difficulties of many workers to access a minimum level of protection.* Some people pursue informal jobs so that they can combine work with other activities, whereas others do so because informal jobs are the only jobs available. Informal employment can work as a safety net for the poor, but it

may not be an effective safety net because of unclear long-term, aggregate consequences for productivity growth, human capital enhancement, and poverty. It is worrisome that in many developing and transition countries informal employment has been growing more rapidly than formal employment. Moreover, workers in sectors traditionally considered "formal" are increasingly employed in temporal, precarious jobs, blurring the line between formal and informal employment. See, for example, World Bank (2007a) for informality in the Latin America and the Caribbean Region.

METHODOLOGY

To what extent do the World Bank activities in the labor market area reflect the evolution of the thinking within the Bank and the global and country trends and challenges? Identifying the World Bank activities that are related to employment is not a straightforward exercise. Because employment is multisectoral by nature, several activities that lie beyond the labor market sometimes have important employment components. This section explains how World Bank lending for labor market activities was estimated.

Data Sources

Activities at the Bank are identified by their themes and sectors and by the sector board that is responsible for the activity. Thematic code 51 (*Improving the Labor Market*) is the only thematic code relevant to employment. Sectors that are related to employment are sector codes JB (*Other Social Services*), EV (*Vocational Training*), and BE (*Compulsory Pension and Unemployment Insurance*). The sector board that is mainly responsible for labor market work at the Bank is the Social Protection Sector Board. Finally, because activities could cut across sectors and themes, some activities have components that fall under different sector codes and sector boards.

The World Bank Business Warehouse (BW) was the main data source from which labor market activities were selected. Labor market activities were selected on the basis of either theme or sector identification. Relying entirely on the BW was in line with the purpose of the portal, kept the focus narrow, avoided the randomness in selection when the selection was based on a word search, and—above all—allowed the application of consistent and narrow search criteria. The focus was the period from 2000 to 2007 for identifying lending projects and the period from 2005 to 2007 for identifying analytical products.

Selection of Projects with Labor Market Components

The selection of labor projects from the BW consisted of two steps. First, the initial list of 714 projects (for 2000–07) was created and included all projects identified by either thematic code 51 (*Labor Markets*) or sector codes JB (*Other Social Services*), EV (*Vocational Training*), or BE (*Compulsory Pension and Unemployment Insurance*).[1] No grants were included. Among projects coded JB, only those under the Social Protection Sector Board were chosen, whereas all EV projects were chosen. Selection was further refined by identifying, for investment lending projects, intervention type, financing, and components. Similarly, for development policy lending projects, conditions, objectives, actions, and outcomes were identified. For all projects with thematic code 51, this identification required retrieving project documents from ImageBank, from IRIS, or directly from the task team leader (project appraisal documents were the preferred way of identification).[2]

Second, for projects identified in the first step, further selection criteria were applied to identify those with a significant labor component, resulting in a final count of 206 labor projects for 2000 to 2007 (149 projects with thematic code 51 and 57 projects with sector code JB or EV). The selection was based on information about the proportion of the lending amount assigned to labor markets in a specific project. This task was simple for projects with thematic code 51, where the full proportion of the loan was on labor markets. However, the sector code JB (*Other Social Services*) captured more than just labor market activities, and such projects had to be carefully examined.

For identification of analytical products, a similar procedure was applied, resulting in the final count of 93 analytical products for fiscal years 2005 to 2007. For this period, under the labor market thematic code (51), the initial selection identified 51 economic and sector work (ESW) and technical assistance (TA) products.[3] Sector codes JB (*Other Social Services*), EV (*Vocational Training*), and BE (*Compulsory Pension and Unemployment Insurance*) identified 405 additional products. As with projects, additional criteria were used to determine the final list of analytical products—that is, analytical products were included only if labor was ranked among the top three sector codes (dropped projects of substantial size were skimmed for labor market components, but none were found relevant). A large number of the initially identified products were found not to be relevant or were covered by other units and were therefore dropped, resulting in a total count of 93 analytical products (29, 33, and 31 for fiscal years 2005, 2006, and 2007, respectively). Note that rather than being as comprehensive as possible, the applied search criteria are strict and consistent, considering only BW products cataloged under narrow thematic and sector codes.[4]

REVIEW OF LABOR MARKETS PORTFOLIO FOR FISCAL YEARS 2000–07

This section first provides an overall picture of the Bank's labor markets portfolio and then describes the distribution of this portfolio by region, type of lending, lending instrument, and sector board. It also analyzes how the Bank's analytical and advisory activities were distributed by region and sector. It concludes with a discussion of results produced by the Bank's labor market activity during 2000 to 2007.

Overall Portfolio

In total, 206 investment and development policy lending projects, worth more than US$4 billion, targeted labor markets between 2000 and 2007, and 93 analytical pieces analyzed labor markets between 2005 and 2007. Investment lending was the main lending instrument for labor market activities. The main objectives of the lending were training and skills development and promotion of microenterprises and labor-intensive public works. More than two-thirds of the lending went to middle-income countries, and nearly half was managed by the Social Protection Sector Board. Of the 93 analytical pieces, ESW accounted for two-thirds of the work, and TA contributed the remainder. Analytical work was equally spread across regions, and 4 out of 10 pieces were produced outside the social protection sector. Millions of people and thousands of enterprises benefited directly from labor market lending, and indirect benefits consisted of strengthened institutions and an improved legal framework, as well as enhanced capacity, which included the construction of new training facilities. Moreover, analytical work produced useful baseline information and informed debates that have led to better policy decisions and development outcomes.

More than 10 percent of all World Bank projects involved labor markets during 2000 to 2007. The total Bank lending portfolio on labor market components in this period comprised an estimated US$4,353.6 million, spread over 206 projects (table 3.2). With regard to lending volume, nearly 3 percent of total Bank lending was directed toward labor markets.

Apart from a spike in 2003, labor market lending was fairly steady during fiscal years 2000 to 2007. Both the volume of lending and the number of projects concerned with labor market components were relatively stable, averaging US$544.2 million and 26 projects per year (table 3.2). The one spike in lending in 2003 is owed to the Jefes de Hogar project in Argentina, which alone accounted for US$582 million.

Table 3.2: Labor Market Lending by U.S. Dollar Amount and Number of Projects, 2000–07

	Lending (US$ millions)			Number of projects		
Year	Investment lending	Development policy lending	Total lending	Investment lending	Development policy lending	Total lending
2000	273.1	433.1	706.1	19	5	24
2001	492.4	26.9	519.3	27	3	30
2002	207.7	214.1	421.8	19	7	26
2003	764.2	234.5	998.7	20	6	26
2004	255.4	88.2	343.7	24	4	28
2005	285.9	225.9	511.8	13	4	17
2006	404.4	23.4	427.8	26	3	29
2007	289.1	135.4	424.4	20	6	26
Total	2,972.1	1,381.5	4,353.6	168	38	206

Source: Authors' calculations based on sources discussed in the text.
Note: Because of rounding, totals may deviate slightly from the sum of the parts.

Distribution of Labor Market Lending by Region

From 2000 to 2007, the Latin America and the Caribbean (LAC) and the Europe and Central Asia (ECA) Regions were the largest borrowers with regard to lending to labor markets, whereas the East Asia and the Pacific (EAP) and the Middle East and North Africa (MENA) Regions were the smallest. The LAC Region was by far the biggest borrower on labor markets, having received more than 42 percent and close to US$2 billion of the total labor market lending from the World Bank (table 3.3). This figure contrasts with the region's share in total lending of 23 percent; thus, the region's share in labor market lending is disproportionately high. The ECA Region was also a large recipient of labor market lending, receiving 28 percent (US$1.2 billion) of labor market lending compared with the 18 percent of total Bank lending the region received. There has been relatively little labor market lending to the Africa (AFR) Region. Its share in labor market lending was 14 percent (US$628.6 million). The EAP and MENA Regions were the two smallest recipients of labor market lending, with a combined share of 5.4 percent (US$232.4 million). The EAP Region and South Asia Region (SAR) accounted for 2.5 and 9.9 percent of labor market lending, respectively.

Distribution of Labor Markets Lending by Type of Lending: IDA and IBRD

Lending by the International Bank for Reconstruction and Development (IBRD) accounted for 68 percent of lending for labor markets (figure 3.3). This type of lending was mostly provided to middle-income countries. The International Development Association (IDA) accounts for the remaining 32 percent of total labor market lending.[5] This division means that middle-income countries received total lending on labor market components in the amount of US$2.9 billion, whereas low-income countries received US$1.4 billion in loans.

FIGURE 3.3: **IBRD AND IDA LABOR MARKET LENDING, 2000–07**

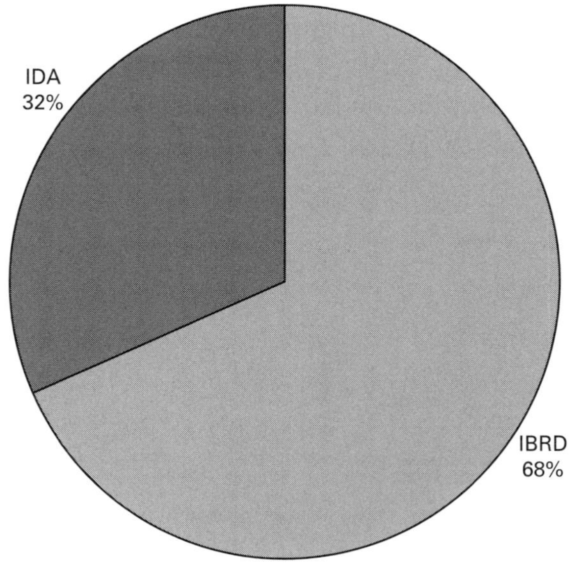

Source: Authors' calculations based on sources discussed in the text.
Note: IBRD = International Bank for Reconstruction and Development; IDA = International Development Association.

Table 3.3: **Total Labor Markets Lending by Region, 2000–07**

Region	Amount of lending (US$ millions)	Percentage of total
Africa	628.6	14.4
East Asia and the Pacific	106.8	2.5
Europe and Central Asia	1,216.0	27.9
Latin America and the Caribbean	1,847.6	42.4
Middle East and North Africa	125.6	2.9
South Asia	429.1	9.9
Total	4,353.6	100.0

Source: Authors' calculations based on sources discussed in the text.
Note: Because of rounding, totals may deviate slightly from the sum of the parts.

Distribution of Labor Markets Lending by Lending Instrument: Investment and Policy Lending

The first part of this section details investment lending and the specific labor market activities that it finances. The second part focuses on development policy lending and the specific labor market conditionalities that it supports. Both sections further divide the analysis by Bank region.

Investment lending is used more extensively for labor markets than is development policy lending, but development policy lending is substantial (figures 3.4 and 3.5). Total investment lending for fiscal years 2000 to 2007 was approximately US$3 billion compared with US$1.3 billion in development policy lending. Investment lending for labor markets was estimated at 2.8 percent of all Bank investment lending, compared with 2.6 percent of all Bank development policy lending. Almost all (93.1 percent) development policy lending for labor markets was in the ECA and LAC Regions. Less than US$100 million was lent for the other four regions. The MENA and EAP Regions did not have a single development policy loan with a labor market component during 2000 to 2007, relying instead on investment lending. There has been significant variation in lending during the period, but no clear trend. Annual investment lending has averaged US$372 million, and development policy lending has averaged US$173 million. For numbers of projects, a similar pattern is observed but with more small projects in Africa than in the other regions.

Investment Lending and Specific Activities Financed

A total of 168 investment lending projects contained a labor market component during fiscal years 2000 to 2007, and although the AFR Region had the most projects (62), the LAC Region received the most lending. The ECA and LAC Regions also had many projects (37 and 31, respectively). SAR (17), the MENA Region (13), and the EAP Region (8) had the fewest projects containing a labor market component. As for investment lending amounts, the distribution is slightly different: the LAC Region is the largest borrower (36.9 percent), followed by the ECA Region (22.9 percent), AFR Region (20.1 percent), South Asia Region (12.1 percent), MENA Region (4.2 percent), and EAP Region (3.6 percent).

For investment lending, the primary labor market objectives have been to support training, microenterprises, and public works: 6 of 10 labor market components in investment lending projects were on training, microenterprises, and labor-intensive public works over the period covered (table 3.4). Also, support to disadvantaged persons, labor administration, institutional capacity building, adjustment schemes for retrenched workers, employment services, and information and monitoring were common among labor market components, covering 97 percent of the labor market components. Only 3 percent of the components focused on employment subsidies, labor code revisions, and unemployment assistance.

Europe and Central Asia. Both in number of investment lending projects and in amounts of lending, Europe and Central Asia was the second-largest region. In total, the region received US$681 million of investment lending on labor market components during fiscal years 2000 to 2007, surpassed only by Latin America and the Caribbean (US$1,096 million). Lending varied significantly over the years: from a high of US$222.8 million in 2001 to a low of US$13.7 million in 2007. The average for the eight years was US$85.1 million.

The most frequently observed components in the ECA Region were on microenterprises, labor administration, and training, but the region also contributed significantly in most other areas. Labor market investment loans in Europe and Central Asia were aimed mainly at microenterprises (22 percent), labor administration (17 percent), and training (17 percent). However, the region also contributed significantly to most other types of labor market components apart from public works and disadvantaged groups, including employment services, labor administration, employment subsidies, labor code revisions, labor market information, and unemployment assistance.

Africa. The AFR Region had the most labor market projects and was the third-largest borrower in investment lending during fiscal years 2000 to 2007. Total investment lending on labor markets to the region was US$598.8 million, spread over 62 projects. Thus, the average project size going to labor markets was smaller than the two largest borrowers (the LAC and ECA Regions). Lending amounts were fairly consistent over the years, with a high in 2001 (US$130.7 million) and a low in 2000 (US$51.4 million). On average, the region obtained US$74.8 million in new loans per year.

Disadvantaged groups, adjustment schemes, and employment services received relatively more attention in the AFR Region than in other regions. Disadvantaged groups such as women, youth, and the rural poor were supported in 14 percent of the components in the region. Also, adjustment schemes for retrenched workers (8 percent) and employment services (7 percent) were better represented than in most regions.

FIGURE 3.4: LABOR MARKET LENDING INSTRUMENTS, BY REGION, 2000–07

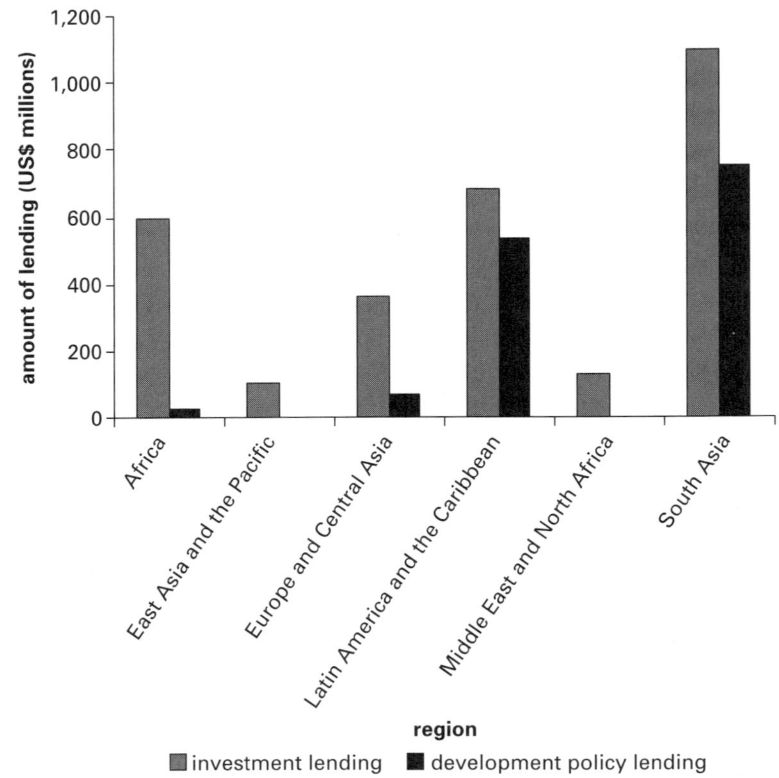

Source: *Authors' calculations based on sources discussed in the text.*

FIGURE 3.5: LABOR MARKET LENDING INSTRUMENTS, 2000–07

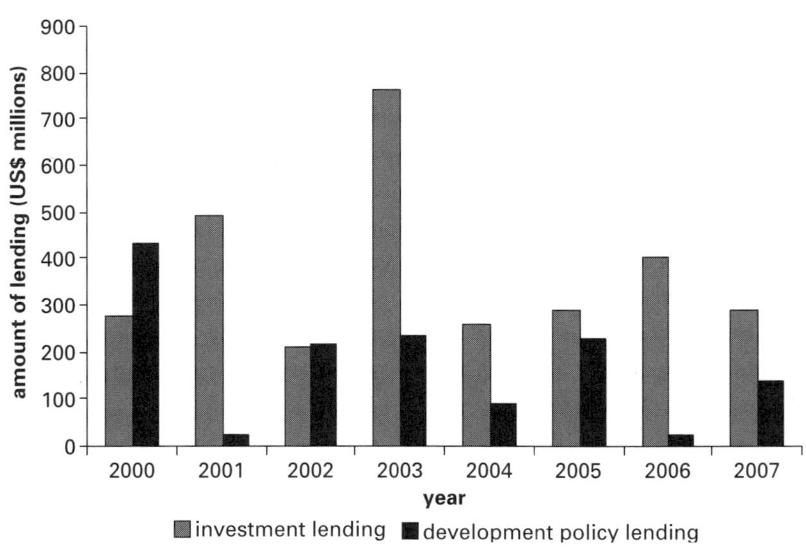

Source: *Authors' calculations based on sources discussed in the text.*

Table 3.4: Labor Market Components, Investment Lending, 2000–07

Component	Number of components	Percentage of total
Training or retraining for workers, unemployed persons, and labor market entrants	85	22.7
Microenterprises	82	21.9
Public works	56	14.9
Disadvantaged groups (women, youth, and poor)	42	11.2
Labor administration and institutional capacity building	34	9.1
Adjustment schemes for retrenched workers	23	6.1
Employment services	22	5.9
Labor market information and monitoring	19	5.1
Employment subsidies	6	1.6
Unemployment assistance and insurance scheme	4	1.1
Labor code revision	2	0.5
Total	375	100.0

Source: Authors' calculations based on sources discussed in the text.
Note: Because of rounding, totals may deviate slightly from the sum of the parts.

Similar to most regions, training (26 percent), microenterprises (26 percent), and public works (17 percent) were the most observed labor market components in the AFR Region.

The AFR Region contributed almost a third of the World Bank labor market components on each topic apart from labor administration and labor market information. Given the many—but smaller—labor market projects, a large number of labor market components were identified, giving the AFR Region more weight in the distribution of labor market components than the lending amount indicates. Therefore, with labor components spread across all areas, the AFR Region's labor market components made up almost a third of each topic's components apart from labor market administration and labor market information.

South Asia. South Asia accounted for US$363.4 million (12 percent) of World Bank investment lending on labor markets, spread over 17 projects, making it the fourth-largest region. Lending varied from US$2.7 million in 2005 to US$97.8 million in 2007 and averaged US$45.4 million. The number of projects per year varied between one and four.

The SAR targeted disadvantaged groups, training, and microenterprises. Although training (25.5 percent) and microenterprises (25.5 percent) are the most frequently observed labor market components in the region, disadvantaged groups (21.6 percent) are the component that has received the most attention compared with other regions. In fact, 26.2 percent of the disadvantaged group labor market component was in the SAR during fiscal years 2000 to 2007.

Latin America and the Caribbean. Latin America and the Caribbean received the most investment lending during fiscal years 2000 to 2007, with a total of US$1,096 million on labor markets for 31 projects. Thus, the labor market components were on average much larger than in other regions in lending amount. Variation in lending over time was enormous: lending in 2005 was only US$0.4 million, whereas it was US$586.2 million in 2003 when the Jefes de Hogar project was launched. Average investment lending for the eight years was US$137.1 million.

Training, microenterprises, and labor administration were the most frequent labor market components in the LAC Region. Training (30.4 percent) and microenterprises (20.3 percent) were the most often addressed areas in the region, but labor administration (14.5 percent) received more attention among the topics than in any other region apart from the ECA Region. Nearly one in three components on labor administration took place in the LAC Region.

Also, the proportion of all components across the region was relatively high on labor market information (26.3 percent), employment services (18.2 percent), and employment subsidies (16.7 percent).

Middle East and North Africa. The Middle East and North Africa received the second-least investment lending of the six regions. Total investment lending on labor market components in the MENA Region was US$125.6 million during fiscal years 2000 to 2007; only the EAP region was smaller (US$106.8 million). There was no investment lending on labor markets in the MENA Region in 2005; however, it was as high as US$68.1 million in 2006. On average, US$15.8 million in investment lending went to labor markets in the region annually.

Although public works and training received the most attention in the region, disadvantaged groups were also targeted to a large extent. With 37.5 percent of the labor market components being labor-intensive public works, the Middle East and North Africa was the region with strongest emphasis on job creation and income support through public works. Training made up 25.0 percent of the components, but disadvantaged groups also received significant attention, with 15.6 percent of the components in the region. The MENA Region contributed 21.4 percent of all the public works components and 11.9 percent of all components helping disadvantaged groups. Microenterprises were not a main target, accounting for just 9.4 percent of the components.

East Asia and the Pacific. East Asia and the Pacific was the smallest region with regard to investment lending on labor markets, with eight projects and US$106.8 million over the period covered. Average annual investment lending on labor markets was US$13.3 million, with the majority of lending occurring at the beginning of the period. In fact, 89 percent of lending took place during fiscal years 2000 to 2003, leaving just US$12 million in lending for the four most recent years.

Investment lending in the EAP Region was focused on microenterprises and public works. Nearly 39 percent of the labor market components addressed microenterprises and 22 percent focused on labor-intensive public works. Training was less of a focus than in all other regions, but 17 percent of the components still involved training. The remaining 22 percent of the labor market components dealt with disadvantaged groups (11.1 percent), labor market information (5.6 percent), and labor administration (5.6 percent).

Development Policy Lending with Labor Market Conditionalities

The World Bank approved 247 development policy loans during fiscal years 2000 to 2007, of which 38 (12 percent) included at least one labor market condition. The ECA and LAC Regions were the largest consumers of development policy loans. Development policy lending on labor markets was concentrated in two regions: the LAC Region (54 percent) and the ECA Region (39 percent). SAR and the EAP Region followed, with 5 percent and 2 percent, respectively. There were no development policy loans with labor market conditions in the EAP and MENA Regions. The LAC Region had the most total development policy lending (35 percent of total World Bank development policy loans). In the LAC Region, 6.4 percent of total development policy lending was allocated to labor markets (see figure 3.6). Only the ECA Region has a higher proportion of development policy loans for labor markets with 8.3 percent. Development policy lending on labor markets for the remaining two regions (Africa and South Asia) combined contributed less than 1.0 percent to the regions' total development policy loans.

With a high of US$433.1 million in development policy loans in 2000 and a low of US$23.4 million in 2006, variation was great. This large range is explained by a number of large projects, between US$50 million and US$150 million, concentrated in certain years, such as 2006, and by the variation in the size of labor market components. Across regions, lending has also varied significantly. All regions have experienced at least one year without any development policy loans with labor market conditions.

The most frequently supported labor market conditions were for labor market flexibility enhancement (27 percent), active labor market programs (27 percent), and wage determination mechanisms (20 percent). Table 3.5 also shows that the least financed conditions were working hours (9 percent) and unemployment insurance (16 percent).

Africa. Total development policy lending in Africa was US$29.8 million during fiscal years 2000 to 2007. Development policy loans to the region varied from no loans in 2003 and 2004 to US$9.3 million in loans in 2002. The region is the fourth-biggest borrower on labor market development policy lending, but it is clear that the portfolio has been small for all the years and there have been no projects of significant size on labor markets. Development policy lending on labor markets was US$3.7 million annually in the AFR Region, on average.

FIGURE 3.6: SHARE OF LABOR MARKET LENDING IN TOTAL DEVELOPMENT POLICY LENDING BY REGION, 2000–07

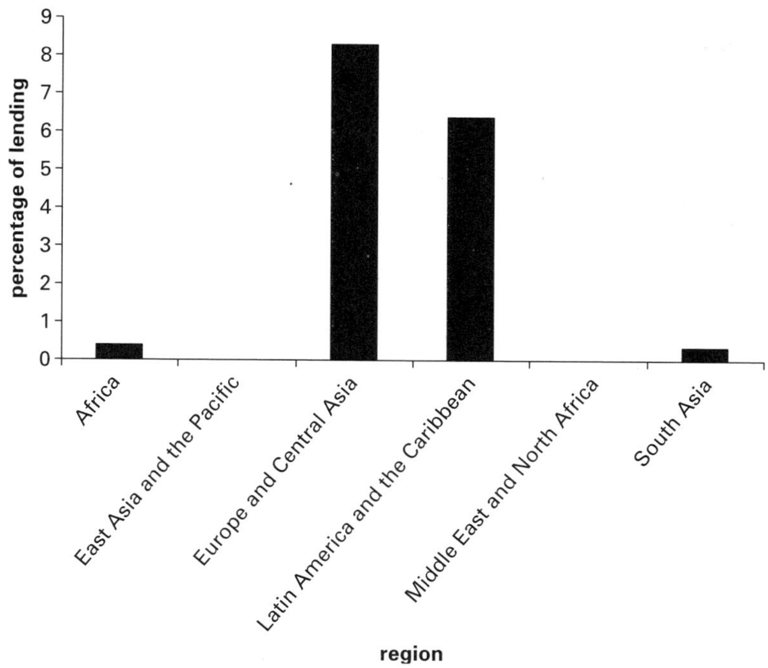

Source: Authors' calculations based on sources discussed in the text.

Table 3.5: Frequency of Labor Market Conditions, 2000–07

Region	Labor market flexibility enhancement	Wage determination mechanisms	Working hours	Unemployment insurance	Active labor market programs	All categories
Africa	3	1	2	2	5	13
South Asia	4	0	0	0	1	5
Europe and Central Asia	7	8	3	3	6	27
Latin America and the Caribbean	1	2	0	4	3	10
Total	15	11	5	9	15	55
Percentage of total	27.3	20.0	9.1	16.4	27.3	100.0

Source: Authors' calculations based on sources discussed in the text.
Note: Only thematic code 51 development policy loans for 2006 to 2007 are included. A development policy loan may have more than one condition, and the project may therefore be double-counted. Because of rounding, totals may deviate slightly from the sum of the parts.

The most frequently used conditions in the AFR Region were to promote active labor market programs and to enhance labor market flexibility. In 39 percent of the cases, labor market conditionality was on active labor market programs, and conditionality to enhance labor market flexibility was the runner-up with 23 percent. Working hours and other conditions of work (15 percent), unemployment insurance and other income support (15 percent), and wage determination (8 percent) were also used, but less frequently. Senegal's First and Second Poverty Reduction Support Credits are an example of conditions intended to enhance labor market flexibility measures. They did so by improving the labor market legal and regulatory framework, increasing available information on labor market opportunities, and establishing a job directory.

South Asia. Development policy loans for labor markets to South Asia have occurred only in the most recent years. Total lending to the region was US$65.7 million during fiscal years 2000 to 2007, but lending to the region occurred only in the last two years. In fiscal year 2006, development policy loans for labor markets amounted to US$15 million, increasing to US$50.7 million in fiscal year 2007. Average annual lending was US$8.2 million during the period, with large annual variations.

With only two years of lending and the level of lending being relatively low, the SAR applied just two types of labor market conditions—namely, enhancing labor market flexibility and promoting active labor market programs. Four out of five conditions were intended to increase labor market flexibility and one in five was on active labor market measures. Conditions intended to enhance labor market flexibility addressed such issues as legislation to facilitate greater flexibility in the use of contract labor; initiatives to raise the limit on the number of contract laborers that an employer could use without being subject to contract labor law regulations (India); and adoption of new involuntary separations procedures and revision of the industrial disputes legislation, factory ordinance, and legislation regarding termination of employment (Sri Lanka). For example, the active labor market policy condition applied in the First Poverty Reduction Support Credit for Sri Lanka aimed at better matching vocational training with labor market demands so as to increase employment opportunities for educated youth and university graduates.

Europe and Central Asia. Total development policy loans to Europe and Central Asia totaled US$535 million during the period. Conditions focused on wage determination mechanisms, labor market flexibility enhancement, and active labor market programs. Development policy loans in the region fluctuated significantly over the years, reaching a maximum in fiscal year 2002 (US$205 million) and a minimum in fiscal year 2005 (US$0), when there were no such loans for labor markets. Most conditions have been on wage determination mechanisms (30 percent), but also on labor market flexibility enhancement (26 percent) and on active labor market programs (22 percent).

The objective of improvements in wage determination mechanisms was to increase competitiveness in hiring. Wage determination mechanisms were found to be a condition mainly related to public administration reforms in countries such as Bosnia and Herzegovina, Bulgaria, the former Yugoslav Republic of Macedonia, Serbia and Montenegro, and Turkey. It was the most common condition in 2004. The wage determination mechanisms aimed to achieve competitiveness of civil service pay in these areas: recruitment and retention of staff, ceilings on new hiring of civil servants, laws on salaries, pay-grade reform for civil servants, job categories for civil servants to develop a pay-grade structure, new salary systems for civil servants, appointment and dismissal of civil servants, and performance assessment.

Conditions on enhancement of labor market flexibility focused on contracting, dismissals, and labor disputes. The condition for projects that enhanced labor market flexibility in the region dealt with contracting (fixed term, temporary, and part time), labor disputes (individual and collective), dismissals, contracted versus appointed personnel positions, recruiting, hiring, and employment law reform. This condition was, for example, part of loans to Bhutan, Bulgaria, and Romania (table 3.6).

Active labor market policy conditions focused on a variety of programs across countries. The active labor market policy measures in the ECA Region focused on labor redeployment programs (Serbia); counseling and job search assistance (Montenegro); prelayoff services (Romania); inclusion of more cost-effective active labor market interventions, job search and skill training programs, job clubs, assistance in self-employment, and job fairs (Serbia); and establishment of cantonal employment services and policy on active labor market programs (Bosnia and Herzegovina).

Latin America and the Caribbean. Total development policy lending in Latin America and the Caribbean amounted to US$751 million during the period, and the most frequently supported conditions were for unemployment insurance, active labor market programs, and wage determination. The LAC Region has the highest volume of development policy loans, with fiscal years 2000 and 2005 contributing significantly (more than US$200 million each year). In fiscal years 2002 and 2006, there were no development policy loans for labor markets in the region. The most frequently supported condition was unemployment insurance (40 percent). Active labor market policies (30 percent) and wage determination mechanisms (20 percent) were the next most important. Table 3.7 provides examples of unemployment insurance conditions.

In Latin America and the Caribbean, the active labor market policy measures focused on training programs, whereas wage determination mechanisms were part of a fiscal stabilization plan. The active labor market policies in Brazil focused on (a) deployment and retraining and (b) redesign of in-service teacher training programs, whereas in Colombia the focus was on job training and apprenticeship. A wage determination mechanisms condition in Paraguay and Guyana

Table 3.6: **Enhancing Labor Market Flexibility: Examples of Conditions**

Country and project	Objective or goal	Policy measures, condition, and action	Outcome
Bhutan: P104931 (2007), Second Development Policy Grant	Create better income-earning opportunities by improving investment climate, facilitating greater labor market flexibility, and increasing foreign direct investment.	Submit labor and employment act to national assembly. Simplify business registration, and reduce cost and time.	More flexible labor markets, leading to better business environment for potential investors and more job opportunities, improved foreign direct investment in country, and reduced cost of setting up business
Bulgaria: P094967 (2007), First Social Sectors Institutional Reform Development Policy Loan	Improve institutional framework in labor and social sectors to align their policies more closely with European Union standards. Improve efficiency of social protection system.	Continue government efforts to make labor market more flexible by folding seniority bonus into base wage. Introduce an impact evaluation system for main social assistance programs and monitor their effect not only on poverty and social indicators but also on job creation. Improve targeting of social assistance on the basis of comprehensive impact evaluation of the government.	At end of loan series, increase in employment rate to at least 60 percent (ages 15–64) and reduction in number of low-quality subsidized jobs by 25 percent from 2005 baseline
Romania: P008791 (2004), First Programmatic Adjustment Loan	Enhance flexibility of labor market to facilitate labor mobility, enterprise privatization and restructuring, and sectoral reforms.	Establish a multipartite consultative committee to assess effects of labor code on labor market. Enact amendments to labor code. Agree on strategy to improve labor market flexibility and reduce structural rigidities.	Marked and sustainable improvements in labor market indicators: labor participation rate, employment-to-population rate, share of long-term unemployed (over 12 months) to total unemployed, share of youth unemployed to total unemployed, and employment in services as a share of labor force

Source: Authors' compilation.

was part of the fiscal stabilization efforts aimed at fiscally sustainable public salary adjustments, maintenance of the nominal wage bill, a wage freeze for permanent employees, and reduction of the wage bill for contracted employees.

Distribution of Labor Market Lending by Sector Board

Among the sector boards, the Social Protection Sector Board leads in lending for improving labor market conditions, but other sectors also contribute. Half of all World Bank lending for labor markets is under the Social Protection Sector Board (table 3.8). Labor market support is also found under the Education (18 percent) and Economic Policy (7 percent) Sector Boards. The Social Protection Sector Board also has, on average, the largest labor market component for lending. The Social and Rural Development Sector Boards have much smaller components.

Analytical and Advisory Activities

The World Bank produced 93 analytical pieces on the labor market between 2005 and 2007, the majority of which were for economic and sector work. On average, 32 analytical pieces were produced per year for 2005, 2006, and 2007, with ESW being roughly two-thirds and TA about one-third (figure 3.7). The World Bank also demonstrated leadership in the analyses through its flagship publications: (a) the Middle East and North Africa 2004 flagship publication on the labor market (World Bank 2004a) and reports

Table 3.7: Unemployment Insurance or Other Income Support for the Unemployed: Examples of Conditions

Country and project	Objective or goal	Policy measures, condition, and action	Outcome
Colombia: P094097 (2006), Third Labor Reform and Social Development Policy Loan	Create effective authority to protect poor and vulnerable against threats and consequences of unemployment and economic volatility. Implement labor and training reforms.	Issue regulations to facilitate broader access to social security benefits. Create consolidated database of beneficiaries. Approve labor law.	Increased number of unemployment beneficiaries, access of independent workers to the social security system, protection of workers moving between informal and formal sector jobs, and increased number of courses and completing participants
Serbia: P078390 (2003), Social Sector Adjustment Credit	Improve benefits and programs for unemployed and dismissed workers.	Submit to parliament a new law on employment and insurance in case of unemployment: (a) revised unemployment benefit entitlements with respect to duration and level, (b) inclusion of more cost-effective active labor market interventions, (c) more appropriate definition of unemployment, and (d) revised rules on obligations of the unemployed to take work.	Implementation of new Serbian law on employment, including more cost-effective mix of active programs in force and unemployment benefits being paid in full and on time, and clearly defined social program budget within budget, with clear identification of eligible enterprises and triggers for access to social protection funds

Source: Authors' compilation.

Table 3.8: Investment Lending and Development Policy Lending Projects with Labor Market Components: Number of Projects and Percentage of Sector Lending, 2000–07

Sector board	Number of projects	Percentage of lending
Social Protection	68	49.6
Education	47	18.0
Economic Policy	12	7.2
Rural Development	19	5.5
Financial and Private Sector Development	14	4.5
Public Sector Governance	11	3.6
Transport	9	3.6
Energy, Mining, and Telecommunications	5	3.0
Social Development	10	1.3
Water and Sanitation	3	1.2
Poverty Reduction	2	1.2
Health	2	0.7
Urban Development	3	0.5
Global Information and Communications Technology	1	0.1
Total	206	100.0

Source: Authors' calculations based on sources discussed in the text.

on migration and education; (b) the Europe and Central Asia flagship publication, *Enhancing Jobs Opportunities* (World Bank 2005a) and another on migration (World Bank 2006a); (c) the Latin America and the Caribbean regional flagship report on labor market informality (World Bank 2007a); (d) the East Asia and the Pacific flagship publication on migration (World Bank 2006c), as well as an Africa project on job creation and core labor standards. In addition, the *World Development Reports* for 2005, 2006, and 2007 have all dedicated a chapter to labor markets.

The analytical work covers a broad geographic distribution. The ECA and MENA Regions are the two largest contributors, with 22 percent of the analytical pieces each (figure 3.8). The AFR and EAP Regions are in second place, each contributing 14 percent of the analytical and advisory activities. The South Asia and LAC Regions also produced

FIGURE 3.7: NUMBER OF ANALYTICAL PIECES BY TYPE OF PRODUCT, 2005–07

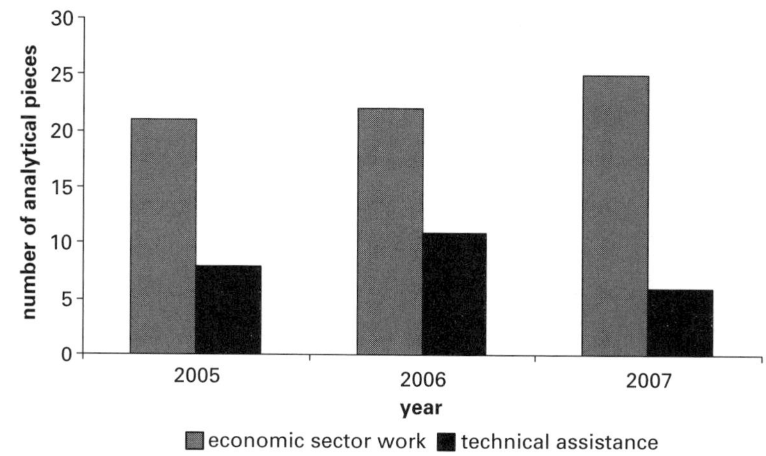

Source: Authors' calculations based on sources discussed in the text.

FIGURE 3.8: PERCENTAGE OF TOTAL ANALYTICAL PIECES BY REGION, 2005–07

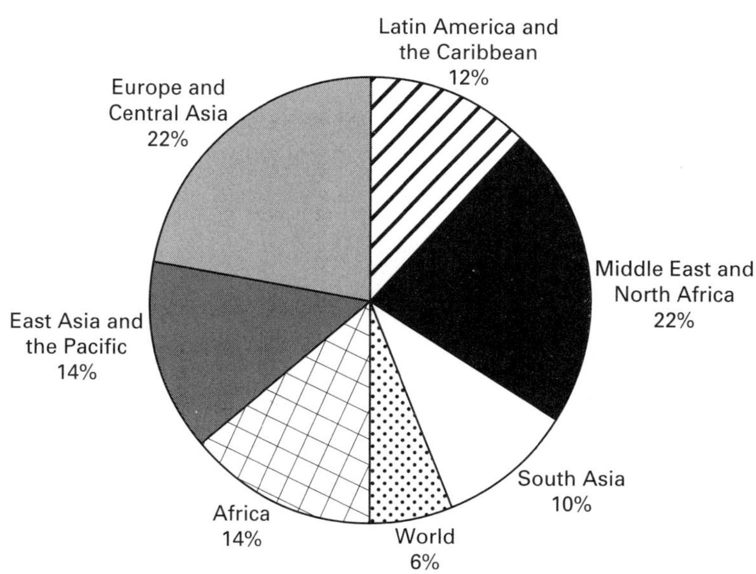

Source: Authors' calculations based on sources discussed in the text.

a significant number of analytical pieces, with 10 percent and 12 percent of the total, respectively. Thus, despite obtaining a relatively small loan volume, the MENA and EAP Regions produced substantial analytical work.[6] The LAC Region obtained the largest loans, but produced relatively fewer analytical and advisory activities. Clearly, analytical work has been spread across the regions much more equally than has lending.

The Social Protection Sector Board produced almost 60 percent of the labor market analytical pieces. The Social Development, Education, Economic Policy, and Poverty Reduction Sector Boards also produced a significant number of analytical and advisory activities (a combined 37 percent of the total—see table 3.9). Seven sectors produced analytical work over the three-year period. Analytical work tends to be focused more in specific sectors than are projects. Projects were distributed across 14 sectors over the longer time span of eight years.

Results of Lending and Knowledge Products, 2000–05

Table 3.10 provides a macropicture of the results achieved in labor markets during 2000 to 2005. These broad results depended on a wide variety of factors, only a portion of which can be attributed to Bank lending and knowledge products. Overall, with several outcomes diverging, it is difficult to say whether the global situation in labor markets improved and what the effect of the Bank's involvement has been. During the period, unemployment fell in all regions except South Asia and Southeast Asia and the Pacific. Generally, fewer people worked for less than US$1 or US$2 per day. The exception was the Africa region. Still, the results are mixed, with youth unemployment remaining high and the share of employed people in the population declining in most regions.

Results from a Review of Implementation Completion Reports

Although the global conditions in labor markets may not be uniformly improved, the World Bank's lending for labor market activities has produced positive results. Information from 88 implementation completion reports between 2002 and 2006,[7] showed that 5.3 million people were trained and 11 million benefited from employment or placement in labor market programs, such as job training or apprenticeships, for 67 of the projects reviewed (table 3.11). One success story of job creation for the poor and vulnerable in the LAC Region is the Jefes de Hogar project in Argentina, which was initiated in fiscal year 2003 (box 3.1). As many as 1.5 million people at a time participated in the project's workfare activities.

The private sector also benefits from World Bank lending in labor markets. The implementation completion report review showed that 3,540 enterprises received technical support and more than 300,000 were assisted in microenterprise development between 2002 and 2006. Likewise the scaling up of International Finance Corporation activities shows World Bank involvement in the area. The South Asia Region provides an example of a recently approved project for Bangladesh (fiscal year 2007) that will support microenterprises. The Additional Financing for the Second Poverty Alleviation Microfinance Project (US$15 million, of which US$3.75 million is for labor markets) will provide micro-

Table 3.9: Analytical Pieces by Sector Board, 2005–07

Sector board	Pieces	Percentage
Social Protection	55	59.1
Social Development	10	10.8
Education	9	9.7
Economic Policy	8	8.6
Poverty Reduction	7	7.5
Public Sector Governance	3	3.2
Financial and Private Sector Development	1	1.1
Total	93	100.0

Source: Authors' calculations based on sources discussed in the text.

Table 3.10: Intermediate Outcome Indicators: Improve Earnings Opportunities and Quality of Jobs

Region	Unemployment rate		Employment-to-population ratio		Working poor, US$1 per day			Working poor, US$2 per day			Annual labor force growth rate, 1995–2005	Youth-to-adult unemployment rate, 2004
	Level, 2005 (%)	Percent change, 2000–05	Level, 2005 (%)	Percent change, 1995–2005	Level, 2005 (millions)	Percent change (2000–05)	Share of total employment, 2005 (%)	Level, 2005 (millions)	Percent change (2000–05)	Share of total employment, 2005 (%)		
Sub-Saharan Africa	9.7	–0.3	66.7	–3.3	148.3	9.9	56.3	229.4	11.4	87.0	2.4	1.8
East Asia	3.8	–0.2	71.7	–4.7	104.0	–30.8	13.4	361.4	–14.5	46.5	1.0	2.1
Europe and Central Asia[a]	9.7	–0.4	52.1	–6.1	4.3	–63.2	2.6	21.1	–63.4	12.5	0.1	1.9
Latin America and the Caribbean	7.7	–0.5	60.9	2.9	28.0	3.7	11.8	75.6	6.6	31.8	2.5	2.0
Middle East and North Africa	13.2	–0.7	46.4	5.0	3.5	0.0	2.9	42.7	7.8	36.0	3.5	1.8
Southeast Asia and the Pacific	6.1	1.2	65.8	–2.1	29.7	–2.0	11.4	150.0	1.5	57.6	2.2	2.3
South Asia	4.7	0.2	57.2	–2.9	202.3	–9.8	35.8	494.3	9.6	87.3	2.2	2.3

Sources: Authors' calculations based on the World Bank's World Development Indicators database and ILO 2007a.
Note: 2005 data are preliminary estimates.
a. Excludes European Union members.

Table 3.11: Summary of Outcomes from Completed Labor Market Projects, Fiscal Years 2002–06

Beneficiaries	Institutional strengthening	Legal framework and policy reform	Physical outputs
67 operations out of 88 (76.1%) directly benefited targeted beneficiaries through different labor market measures: ■ 5.3 million beneficiaries (272,205 women) were trained. ■ 3,540 enterprises were technically supported. ■ 11 million beneficiaries (73,715 youth and 527 people with disabilities) were placed (including apprenticeships) and performed 3,169,649 person-days of public works. ■ 30,000 beneficiaries received job search assistance or counseling. ■ 156,000 beneficiaries received severance pay. ■ 1,305 enterprises were created or assisted. ■ 300,617 beneficiaries (144,081 women) benefited from microenterprise development.	Out of 85 fully or partially labor market–oriented operations, 42 (49%) contained elements of capacity building and institutional strengthening through one or several interventions: ■ 17 projects included hiring and training of agents and trainers. ■ 10 projects implemented a labor market information system to monitor, evaluate, and control labor market initiatives by identifying the characteristics of the labor market. ■ 3 projects established or enhanced a monitoring and evaluation system, for example, to evaluate projects for the poor.	20 projects (24%) affected the legal framework or helped develop a strategy or policy: ■ 16 projects supported new legislation or decrees, such as introducing a new labor law or amending a social assistance decree. ■ 8 projects helped develop a new strategy, including advancement of a national employment strategy, a comprehensive training strategy, and a national strategy for children and youth.	14 projects (16%) contributed to building or rehabilitating training centers to be used for training and upgrading workers for the labor market.

Source: Implementation completion reports.

credit for the urban poor—specifically, poor rickshaw pullers. The reason for targeting poor rickshaw pullers is that they were affected by a ban against nonmotorized transport on certain Dhaka roads, thus leaving them without a source of income. Funds added to the urban microcredit component will be used to create a revolving fund for financing the microcredit loans to the target borrowers, and ultimately to benefit more than 40,000 people. Apart from direct microcredit loans, the borrowers will also receive training in technical skills to facilitate a career change.

Labor market effects of lending go beyond immediate beneficiaries and achieve institutional strengthening and capacity building. Close to half the projects reviewed contained capacity building and institutional strengthening. These components sought to enhance monitoring and evaluation systems to help strengthen social protection programs, improve labor market information systems, and train trainers. For example, the Technical and Vocational Education and Training Project in Mozambique (fiscal year 2006) supported labor market monitoring, built information capacity, and improved labor administration (of the US$30 million loan, US$8.7 million, or 29 percent, was assigned to labor markets).

Improvement of the Legal Framework

Nearly one-fourth of the projects reviewed had a direct effect on the legal framework or helped develop a strategy or policy. For example, projects supported the introduction of new labor laws and helped develop a national strategy for children and youth. The adoption of core labor standards in many countries is another area of positive results. For example, in fiscal year 2002, Serbia obtained a development policy loan that, among other issues, addressed the labor market law. As a result, a new labor law was approved, which improved labor mobility by reducing lump-sum payments to workers who lost their jobs to levels observed in most other countries in the region. Similarly, in fiscal year 2005, Macedonia obtained a development policy loan that led to

BOX 3.1

JEFES DE HOGAR, FISCAL YEAR 2003

The Jefes de Hogar (Heads of Household) project is the workfare part of a social safety net launched by Argentina to alleviate the impact of rising unemployment caused by the worsening economic crisis. The project builds on the earlier Bank-funded project, Trabajar, which was very effective in targeting the poor. A stipend of Arg$150 per month (around US$40) is provided to an unemployed head of household in exchange for four hours of work in a workfare subproject. The project comprises workfare subprojects in community services, minor construction, repair, expansion, maintenance or remodeling of schools, health facilities, basic sanitation facilities, small roads and bridges, culverts and canals, community kitchens and centers, tourist centers, low-cost housing, and other productive activities. There are two types of subprojects. In the first type, the program finances a share of the cost of materials as well as beneficiary payments. In the second type, the program finances only the payment to the beneficiaries.

The number of participants in the workfare activities was estimated to be 1.5 million at the project's peak, with a slow decline during the two years of project implementation. The World Bank is to finance an estimated 60 percent of the workfare participants over the life of the project. The project also provides partial financing of materials for 8,000 to 10,000 workfare subprojects. Out of the total loan of US$600 million, US$582 million (97 percent) is assigned to labor markets. The project's total value is an estimated US$1.987 billion.

Source: World Bank 2003.

a change in the law on civil servants. Key provisions of the law and its subsidiary legislation included (a) a uniform, rule-based, and less compressed salary structure for all civil servants; (b) uniform definitions of the types of positions encompassed by the civil service; (c) competitive and transparent recruitment procedures; and (d) establishment of an independent agency, the Agency for Civil Servants, to enforce these provisions.

Still, the effect of development policy lending is more difficult to pinpoint. Given the scope of development policy lending and the built-in triggers to implement labor market reforms, this lending probably does have a significant effect. However, that effect needs to be evaluated. Labor market outcomes have become important topics in the Bank's policy dialogue with client countries. Development policy loans to several countries have included triggers and performance requirements related to labor market reforms. The Bank has also explicitly introduced labor market indicators as important tools to benchmark countries and to measure the quality of their investment climates.

Results from Analytical Work

Data and findings from the Bank's analytical work on labor markets are essential to the Country Assistance Partnership Strategy, and they inform lending operations, especially policy-based operations and TA projects. For example, the urban labor market study for Ethiopia has provided essential information for the government's new Poverty Reduction Strategy Paper (PRSP). This study led to a greater emphasis on urban development than the previous PRSP. In addition, the World Bank conducted analytical work in 5 of the 17 countries cited in the Doing Business database as later reforming their labor regulations (during 2004 to 2006). For example, the 2003 Country Economic Memorandum for the former Yugoslav Republic of Macedonia provided a comprehensive analysis of labor market performance and emphasized the importance of reviewing labor regulations. It informed the debate for the revision of the labor code that took place in the subsequent year. Similarly, the structural adjustment credits in Serbia and in Montenegro (2001 and 2002, respectively) included conditions to enhance the flexibility of the labor market while providing protection to workers. This work directly influenced the reform of the labor code that took place in subsequent years.

CONCLUSIONS AND STRATEGIES FOR THE FUTURE

Recent decades have witnessed the mixed success of developing countries' efforts to improve their labor market outcomes through structural and other economic reforms. Although the World Bank, as well as other international and bilateral organizations, has undertaken a number of initiatives to better integrate employment into a development agenda, further efforts on both the research front and the policy front are needed to successfully place employment at the center of countries' development strategies. To help achieve that goal, the World Bank took stock of the emerging labor market issues by performing regional labor market reviews and, on the basis of that exercise, recently launched an ambitious, in-depth, policy-oriented labor market research that leverages the international research community and is financed by a multidonor trust fund. Other important components include developing a policy-relevant, multisector framework—MILES—and other policy tools to help countries design a comprehensive labor market strategy and foster partnerships with numerous bilateral and multilateral agencies. These initiatives are described in this section.

Results and Directions from the 2003 Stocktaking Exercise

The Human Development Network, Social Protection (HDNSP), initiated a stocktaking exercise in 2003 to (a) consolidate existing knowledge on labor markets, (b) diffuse this knowledge across regions and sectors in an accessible manner, and (c) identify areas where important knowledge gaps remain and where further research is needed. The main messages that emerged from the exercise are as follows:[8]

1. *The objective of employment creation and better jobs is an important but underfocused dimension of the development agenda.* Because labor is often the only asset of the poor, providing jobs and making the market where this asset is exchanged more efficient are crucial to poverty reduction. Yet improving access to jobs is not sufficient for poverty reduction; jobs must have decent wages and, hence, higher productivity levels. The objective of more and better jobs will not be achieved by simply replacing growth with employment at the center of the development debate; rather, practitioners need to think differently about the labor market and development and how they contribute to employment, poverty reduction, and economic growth.
2. *The importance of labor market institutions for employment and growth differs substantially across regions and countries.* These institutions—comprising labor market regulations, active and passive labor market policies, and wage-setting rules—seem to have relatively little effect on the labor markets of some regions—particularly regions where most employment is in the informal economy (although regulations and institutions may be causing some informality). Nevertheless, such institutions are perceived as a binding constraint in other regions.
3. *The labor market discussion seems to lack a conceptual framework for analyzing labor market outcomes, partly because of a lack of diagnostic tools and agreed-on labor market models.* The diagnostic tools must be improved to assess labor market conditions in a given country, to identify vulnerable groups, and ultimately to provide better policy advice. Standard labor market indicators may not be appropriate in low-income countries, where vulnerability often takes different forms than in middle- or high-income countries. There is also a shared view that no labor market model that fits all countries exists. This model uncertainty may have consequences in the real world, because it is not conducive to a rational policy discourse and may explain the lack of a clear-cut concept on the political economy of labor market reforms.

Initiatives by the Bank to Respond to These Messages

Carrying Out the Labor Market Research Strategy. Developed jointly by the HDNSP, the Poverty Reduction and Economic Management Program, and colleagues from the regions and other networks and based on wide consultation and continual feedback from counterparts and partners, a new labor market research strategy emerged that reflects regional priorities (see World Bank 2007b). The strategy identifies seven key research topics (see annex 3.A for details):

1. Diagnosis of labor market conditions and vulnerability in middle- and low-income countries
2. Links between the business environment, labor demand, and poverty reduction
3. Benefits and costs of structural reforms and globalization for workers
4. Causes and consequences of formality and informality
5. Effects of labor market policy and institutions
6. Best practices in skills development and skills upgrading
7. International migration and labor markets in origin and host countries.

The research agenda outlined above is ambitious and requires a commitment and joint action of the World Bank, other multilateral agencies, and the international research community. The World Bank is implementing this research strategy through its regular work consisting of analytical and advisory activities, economic sector work, technical assistance, and knowledge products. In October 2007, the World Bank also obtained support from donors to launch a multidonor trust fund called Labor Markets, Job Creation, and Economic Growth: Scaling Up Research, Capacity Building, and Action on the Ground. Current donor commitments exceed US$5 million, with several other donors likely to join in 2008.

The objective of the multidonor trust fund is to improve understanding of how labor markets in developing countries function, to offer new evidence about policies that create good jobs as well as reduce inequality and social exclusion, and to promote effective labor market policy making in developing countries. Its main activities will consist of

- *Filling the knowledge gaps.* The fund will support cutting-edge research by the global academic and research community on key policy issues related to the creation of better jobs, as well as the reduction of inequality and social exclusion.
- *Overcoming the capacity gaps.* The fund will build the capacity of developing country's policy makers and researchers on labor market analysis, evaluation techniques, and good practices in labor market policy.
- *Bridging the experience gaps.* The fund will catalyze country-level activities aimed at analyzing local labor market conditions and piloting promising approaches.

Implementing the MILES framework. The Bank has developed an operational policy framework called MILES to help countries design a comprehensive labor market strategy to create more and better jobs (World Bank 2008a). *MILES* stands for the five areas emphasized by the framework: macroeconomic conditions, investment climate and infrastructure, labor market regulations and institutions, education and skill development, and social protection. Strategies designed using the MILES framework will help reduce poverty, stimulate economic growth, and contribute to sustainable development. Building on various diagnostic tools in areas central for job growth, the framework identifies key constraints for job creation in an individual country, proposes policy priorities and required reforms, and helps to implement them. The framework rests on intensive policy dialogue with key stakeholders and results in a comprehensive labor market strategy that helps client countries to combat poverty and stimulate economic growth.

The MILES framework recognizes that successful policies must concentrate on key binding constraints to growth and job creation in each sector. Attempting to address all reform needs simultaneously is not politically feasible. The framework relies on the following instruments to identify the most binding constraints:

- Reviews of existing studies on constraints to growth and job creation (such as effects of institutions on labor market outcomes)
- Opinion polls across the various economic agents (for example, employers, workers, and governments)
- Growth diagnostics—a new approach to economic reforms that focuses on binding constraints and limited political capital
- Scorecards that prioritize reforms in each of the five MILES areas on the basis of diagnostic tools developed by the Bank and other institutions.

Development and implementation of the MILES framework on the country level involve three steps:

1. Review of the policy and institutional framework to identify the most binding constraints in the MILES areas. Various types of analysis could be used, including existing diagnostic tools developed by the Bank and other institutions for each of the MILES areas;[9]
2. Formulation of reforms in priority sectors, ensuring their internal consistency;
3. Implementation of reforms to overcome the binding constraints and to create a critical policy constituency.

Implementation of the MILES framework requires obtaining support from key stakeholders and close cooperation across different ministries, institutions, and social partners. The Bank is well placed to carry out this task by using its analytical and advisory activities and economic and sector work to provide analytical content and by providing the multisector development policy loans and investment loans to ensure the necessary funding. The MILES framework is being successfully piloted in a number of countries, including Armenia, the Baltic countries, Bangladesh, Bolivia, Brazil, Cambodia, Egypt, India, Madagascar, Morocco, Serbia, Tanzania, Thailand, Tunisia, and Turkey.

Developing Toolkits. As the Bank deepens its knowledge, it is also developing instruments and tools that benefit from the new knowledge, support operations, and policy dialogue. Efforts include the following:

- *Further developing and implementing labor market diagnostic tools.* What are the relevant labor market indicators for low-income countries? A move is being made from straight incidence measures to quality indicators.
- *Piloting MILES.* Efforts are being made to strengthen this framework to help in country work.
- *Piloting the Unemployment Insurance Simulation Model (UISIM).*[10] Other toolkits are also being developed to support activation policies.
- *Updating inventories of active labor market programs and youth employment interventions.* These programs are being made accessible to large audiences.
- *Developing in-country capacity.* Areas of focus include statistical offices, employment offices, and ministries of labor.

How to Build Partnerships

The World Bank cannot carry this agenda forward alone. Within the Bank, the Human Development Network, Poverty Reduction and Economic Management Unit, Social

Development Unit, International Finance Corporation, and Private Sector Development Unit are all key to making progress in this area. Externally, the Bank has built close relationships with the International Labour Organization (ILO) and with the bilateral agencies that have been most active in this area (such as the German Agency for Technical Cooperation; the Swedish International Development Cooperation Agency; and similar agencies in Austria, Italy, and Norway). New collaboration with the international research community, particularly in developing countries, using the Institute for the Study of Labor network has been pursued since 2006. The World Bank, the International Monetary Fund, the International Confederation of Free Trade Unions, and World Confederation of Labour (now the International Trade Union Confederation) adopted a protocol to formalize and intensify this engagement process.

Other partnerships include the following:

- Better Work, a partnership between the International Finance Corporation and the ILO, is now under way. It aims at improving labor practices and competitiveness in global supply chains. The World Bank seconded an HDNSP staff to work on the program at the ILO. The Better Factories Cambodia project serves as a model for this new global program, with projects under development in Jordan, Lesotho, and Vietnam (apparel industry) and in Africa (agribusiness).
- The Youth Employment Network (World Bank, ILO, and United Nations) was created in 2000 and has focused on four global priority policy areas to improve youth employment. The four *E*'s are employability, equal opportunities, entrepreneurship, and employment creation. Early difficulties related to its governance structure and the role of different partners limited the effectiveness of the network. The Bank and the ILO are working together to redefine the role of the Youth Employment Network and to recruit a new director-coordinator better suited to move this partnership forward.
- Understanding Children's Work (World Bank, ILO, and United Nations Children's Fund) was founded in 2000 and has developed innovative technical tools used to measure, monitor, and analyze child labor.
- A recently concluded partnership called Job Creation, Core Labor Standards, and Poverty Reduction in Africa was funded by the German government (World Bank, ILO, and German Agency for Technical Cooperation). Objectives of the project were to (a) improve understanding of the poor labor market outcomes in the region, (b) build analytical capacity of the governments and social partners in this field, and (c) test promising approaches in selected countries (Burkina Faso, Ethiopia, and Ghana).
- The World Bank and the ILO are engaged in discussions about additional partnership opportunities under the World Bank's Justice and Human Rights Trust Fund. Such partnerships could improve practitioners' understanding and strengthen operations related to international core labor standards.

Informal Collaboration

- In keeping with the recommendation of the World Commission on the Social Dimension of Globalization report (2004) regarding the creation of policy coherence initiatives, the World Bank holds quarterly meetings with ILO technical staff members and individuals from other international organizations, including the International Monetary Fund, to share relevant research findings in the areas of employment, growth, and poverty reduction. The World Bank and the ILO are jointly driving an annual show-and-tell seminar series with a number of development agencies. The last meeting, in February 2007, focused on data and development. The World Bank looks forward to working with the ILO to implement recommendations emerging from the complementary research agendas, at both the global and the country levels.
- The World Bank seconded a staff to the Secretariat of the World Commission on the Social Dimension of Globalization to assist in drafting and reviewing the report. The Bank also hosted meetings for the report's authors with various World Bank experts.
- As the PRSP effort was getting under way, Bank staff members regularly met with personnel from the ILO and agreed to coordinate activities in five pilot PRSP countries to integrate social dialogue into the process of PRSP formation and employment-related topics into the content of strategies.

ANNEX 3.A: RESEARCH TOPICS IDENTIFIED UNDER LABOR MARKET, JOB CREATION, AND GROWTH: AN OPERATIONALLY RELEVANT RESEARCH STRATEGY

This annex presents seven key research priorities in the area of labor markets that were identified by the 2003 stocktaking initiative described under "Conclusions and Strategies for the Future." For a complete exposition of these areas, see *Labor Market, Job Creation, and Growth: An Operationally Relevant Research Strategy* (World Bank 2007b).

Diagnosis of Labor Market Conditions and Vulnerability in Middle- and Low-Income Countries

Improving development practitioners' assessment of labor market conditions and policy challenges requires more and better information. In many low-income countries, standard labor market indicators are inappropriate. Most workers cannot afford to be unemployed and may well be engaged in full-time employment while remaining in poverty. Better diagnosis is particularly needed to identify vulnerability in the labor market. In many countries, the traditional dichotomy of formal and informal employment may not characterize well the vulnerability of workers (as will be discussed later). Vulnerability may also be the result of misguided policies or social norms that lead to social exclusion and discrimination. Although social exclusion is entrenched in some countries, only rough and incomplete measures are available to identify this phenomenon. A more complete set of labor market diagnostics needs to be developed to assess labor market performance and to identify vulnerable groups and design effective policies to improve their welfare. Further research is needed in a number of specific areas:

- Reviewing diagnostic tools to assess labor market conditions in countries at different stages of development and with different economic and social structures
- Improving identification of vulnerability in the labor market
- Improving identification of vulnerability among children and the youth
- Understanding the gender dimensions of vulnerability in employment
- Identifying and facing up to social exclusion.

Links Among the Business Environment, Labor Demand, and Poverty Reduction

The challenge of creating more and better jobs largely relies on improvements in the investment climate in which firms find the incentives and opportunity to invest productively, grow, and hire workers. Existing bottlenecks in the investment climate affect the three main channels through which growth can affect poverty reduction: (a) the sustainable growth path; (b) the employment content of growth (that is, the elasticity of employment to output growth); and (c) the poverty reduction effect of employment growth (the poverty elasticity to employment). Moreover, different reforms of the investment climate may affect these three channels in ways that may influence the short-term and long-term effect of growth on poverty reduction. In many developing countries dominated by traditional economic production, two other important issues relating to labor demand concern rural, nonagricultural activity and the efficient migration of rural workers to urban areas where employment opportunities are growing. These issues have direct and potentially powerful implications for poverty reduction. Further research is needed in a number of specific areas, including

- Assessing labor demand in countries at different levels of development and with different investment climates
- Understanding the role of labor in the link between growth and poverty, especially in low-income countries.

Benefits and Costs of Structural Reforms and Globalization for Workers

This topic is closely related to the previous one. The international evidence suggests that macro, trade, and structural reforms can involve large reallocations of resources—including labor—across firms, sectors, and locations, often with adverse effects on labor markets. In Equatorial and Central Africa, these reforms were accompanied by persistent open unemployment, by declining participation, and sometimes by stagnating real wages. In Latin American and Caribbean countries, the adverse effect of reforms on jobs has been much smaller but often at a cost of substantial wage losses. Increased trade openness is exposing many low-income countries to greater opportunities, but they are also being more exposed to fluctuations of international markets. Further research is needed in a number of specific areas, including

- Identifying the channels by which different types of reforms affect labor market outcomes
- Identifying the medium-term job growth prospects of structural reforms
- Identifying the optimal sequencing of reforms for job creation
- Identifying the best mechanisms of income support and reemployment for affected firms and workers.

Causes and Consequences of Formality and Informality

All labor markets include diverse types of employment with regard to "formal" jobs, "informal" jobs, and variations in between. In many developing and transition countries, informal employment has been growing more rapidly than more formal employment. This situation has raised many questions for labor market analysis and also for policy making. It also has close links with the earlier theme on diagnosis and vulnerability. It is obvious that the reality is more complex than the traditional view of an informal "sector" where the poor, unable to find formal jobs, eke out a subsistence living through very-low-productivity labor. Although this characterization applies in some cases, empirical studies in Latin America have shown that some workers seem to be voluntarily moving to the informal sector to improve their lot. Moreover, workers in sectors traditionally considered formal are increasingly employed in temporal, precarious jobs—a trend that blurs the line between formal and informal employment. Little is known about informality, its drivers, and its links to formal labor markets. Further research is needed in a number of specific areas, including

- Investigating the dynamics of the formal and informal economy
- Rethinking social protection for informal workers
- Identifying the effects of labor regulations and social protection programs on informality.

Effects of Labor Market Policy and Institutions

Research suggests that economic growth requires the capacity to reallocate resources—including human resources—from declining to expanding sectors, and from low-productivity to high-productivity activities. However, in many countries, labor regulations appear to be ill suited to facilitate this process. In many developing countries, hiring and firing regulations are much stricter than those in high-income countries, thereby hindering the reallocation of labor across uses, and yet few of these countries have adequate programs to support the unemployed. Nevertheless, it should be recognized that labor market regulations, albeit imperfect, constitute a form of social protection and cannot simply be dismissed. Moving beyond a trade-off between labor market flexibility and worker security is necessary to identify (a) the benefit and costs of existing regulations and social protection mechanisms and (b) potential alternatives that could yield higher benefits at a lower social and economic cost. Further research is needed in a number of specific areas, including

- Identifying the effects of labor regulations on total employment levels and growth, formal sector employment growth, informal-formal decisions, productivity growth, consumption smoothing, and risk management strategies
- Identifying the effects of labor market regulations on particular groups of the labor force
- Assessing the role of international labor standards in trade and development (such as on child labor)
- Understanding the political economy of labor reforms
- Identifying alternative protection mechanisms with lower economic costs
- Understanding how to promote social dialogue.

Best Practices in Skills Development and Skills Upgrading

Important skill shortages are identified in most developing countries. In many countries of South Asia and Sub-Saharan Africa, illiteracy rates are still very high, and enrollment in secondary education is still fairly low in many low- and middle-income countries. Not surprisingly, many employers in these countries consider skill shortage as one of their main constraints in the operation of their business and potential for growth. Increasing the quality of the labor force is essential to increase the productivity and the earnings of workers. Yet in many countries, state-provided training services have been inadequate and disconnected from the requirements of employers. Interventions in skill formation should take into account that (a) most training takes place on the job, (b) medium- and high-skilled workers are more likely to be trained by firms than low-skilled workers, (c) many workers in developing countries are self-employed, and (d) economic analysis has often shown that the returns to human capital investments in workers are highest when workers are supported in furthering their general (school-provided) education. With all these considerations, it remains unclear what the best models are for skills development and skills upgrading in the labor force. Further research is needed in a number of specific areas, including

- Identifying efficient government interventions in training programs and policies
- Identifying the role of labor force skills in determining economic outcomes in a context of globalization
- Attempting to answer several crucial questions:
  - What are the best training models for building a skilled labor force?
  - What are the appropriate public and private roles?
  - How should the training system interact with the education system, facilitating the entry of young people into the labor market?

International Migration and Labor Markets in Origin and Host Countries

The demographic development between the main regions of the world is characterized by large disequilibriums as a result of differences in the timing and scope of fertility and mortality trends. Because some of these differences will become more pronounced in the decades to come, these disequilibriums will accentuate the divergence in labor force growth between regions. Europe and Japan will have low or even negative growth, and other regions, such as the Middle East and North Africa or India, will have continued high growth. For the rich countries in the developed world, a constant or declining labor force implies lower gross domestic product per capita growth, unless a declining labor supply is fully compensated by higher growth in productivity. Such countries risk being negatively affected by an older and less entrepreneurial population. Labor force stagnation also implies a higher burden through social security programs, such as pension and health programs, which is largely independent of how these programs are funded.

Meanwhile, developing countries that have continued strong labor force growth will be extremely hard-pressed to create the millions of additional jobs needed to accommodate the new entrants. This disequilibrium calls for demographic arbitrage and ideas on how to structure capital as well as labor flows as a win-win-win situation (for sending country, receiving country, and migrants). Such efforts include managed temporary or permanent migration, better use of remittances in labor-sending countries, and appropriate social policy programs that make return migration individually attractive and fiscally sustainable for the sending country. Further research is needed in a number of specific areas, including

- Understanding demographic disequilibriums and skill gaps
- Assessing migration policies in receiving countries
- Assessing migration policies in sending countries
- Understanding the role of portability of social benefits.

NOTES

[1] All projects coded BE were eventually dropped to avoid double-counting loans, because the pensions team claimed them.

[2] ImageBank is a repository of more than 46,000 reports produced by the World Bank since 1946, including analytical and advisory work and project documents. IRIS is the World Bank's institutional electronic repository for business unit documents, general correspondence, and project files.

[3] Whenever possible, documents with thematic code 51 were obtained (from ImageBank, IRIS, or the team task leader) and labor market components were identified. When a document was incomplete, missing, or had a top-ranked secondary code (EV, JB, or BE), information on the contents was found in the operations portal.

[4] Only ESW and TA pieces are identified in the BW, which excludes some labor market–related analytical work done by the World Bank. For example, the search excluded labor-focused books and *World Development Reports* published by the World Bank. The 2005 *World Development Report* (World Bank 2004b) focused on the investment climate and devoted one chapter to the interactions between growth, job creation, and functioning of the labor market. The 2006 *World Development Report* (World Bank 2005b) addressed equity and development and discussed at length how better-functioning labor markets can help to reduce inequalities and promote a better sharing of the fruits of growth. Finally, the 2007 *World Development Report* (World Bank 2006b) discussed the challenges for policy makers in facilitating the transition from school to work and in improving employment outcomes for youth in different countries.

[5] Just US$9.9 million (less than 1 percent) over the eight years was a blend of IBRD and IDA lending, with the US$9.5 million occurring in 2007.

[6] Keep in mind that projects are analyzed for 2000 to 2007 and analytical work covers only 2005 to 2007.

[7] Because implementation completion reports account for only closed projects, more recent projects are not included in the review. Not all implementation completion reports have specific information on the number of workers assisted or classrooms built, which means the results are likely to be significantly underestimated.

[8] See the summary of the conference by Robert Holzmann at http://www.worldbank.org/sp.

[9] The essential phase in applying the MILES framework is the identification of binding constraints to job creation. Possible methods include surveys of existing studies on such constraints in a country (such as effects of institutions on labor market outcomes) or opinion polls about binding constraints among various actors (businesses, workers, and social partners). HDNSP is also in the process of refining the methods to identify such binding constraints, such as the use of scorecards in areas crucial to job creation, structural models, and experimental approaches.

[10] UISIM is a simulation model developed to project incomes and expenditures of unemployment insurance programs under various scenarios. For its description, see World Bank (2008b).

REFERENCES

Barwell, Ian. 1996. "Transport and the Village: Findings from African Village-Level Travel and Transport Surveys and Related Studies." Africa Region Discussion Paper 344, World Bank, Washington, DC.

International Labour Office. 2006. *The End of Child Labour: Within Reach.* Geneva: International Labour Office.

ILO (International Labour Organization). 2007a. *Global Employment Trends.* Geneva: ILO.

———. 2007b. *Key Indicators of the Labour Market.* Geneva: ILO.

———. 2008. *Global Employment Trends.* Geneva: ILO.

World Bank. 2001. *Social Protection Sector Strategy: From Safety Net to Springboard.* Washington, DC: World Bank. http://go.worldbank.org/97LBYDY3U0.

———. 2003. "Jefes de Hogar (Heads of Household) Program." Project appraisal document, World Bank, Washington DC.

———. 2004a. *Unlocking the Employment Potential in the Middle East and North Africa: Toward a New Social Contract.* Middle East and North Africa Development Report. Washington DC: World Bank.

———. 2004b. *World Development Report 2005: A Better Investment Climate for Everyone.* Washington, DC: World Bank.

———. 2005a. *Enhancing Job Opportunities: Eastern Europe and the Former Soviet Union.* Washington, DC: World Bank.

———. 2005b. *World Development Report 2006: Equity and Development.* Washington, DC: World Bank.

———. 2006a. *Migration and Remittances: Eastern Europe and the Former Soviet Union.* Washington, DC: World Bank.

———. 2006b. *World Development Report 2007: Development and the Next Generation.* Washington, DC: World Bank.

———. 2006c. *At Home and Away: Expanding Job Opportunities for Pacific Islanders through Labor Mobility.* Washington, DC: World Bank.

———. 2007a. *Informality: Exit and Exclusion.* Washington, DC: World Bank.

———. 2007b. *Labor Market, Job Creation, and Growth: An Operationally Relevant Research Strategy.* Washington, DC: World Bank.

———. 2007c. *World Development Report 2008: Agriculture for Development.* Washington, DC: World Bank.

———. 2008a. *MILES to Go: A Quest for an Operational Labor Market Paradigm for Developing Countries.* Washington, DC: Human Development Network, World Bank.

———. 2008b. "Unemployment Insurance Simulation Model." Employment Primer Note, Human Development Network, World Bank, Washington, DC.

World Commission on the Social Dimension of Globalization. 2004. *A Fair Globalization: Creating Opportunities for All.* Geneva: International Labour Office.

CHAPTER 4 four

PENSIONS IN WORLD BANK LENDING AND ANALYTICAL WORK, 1984–2007

Richard Hinz, Melike Egilmezler, and Sergiy Biletsky

INTRODUCTION

This chapter presents an overview of the World Bank's lending and knowledge-building activities that have improved pension systems in client countries during the past two decades.

Objectives

The objectives of this report are (a) to describe the policy framework that has guided the Bank's work on pension-related issues, (b) to present relevant information about the nature and extent of the Bank's lending and policy advisory work in this area, and (c) to discuss some of the results that have been achieved through this work, as well as future policy directions.

The chapter covers the level and characteristics of all the Bank's lending operations that included a component related to pensions during fiscal years 2002 to 2007, as well as over a longer time period going back to 1984, when the Bank initiated a meaningful level of pension work. Thus, this report updates a portfolio review that was a central element of the evaluation of pension work carried out by the Bank's Independent Evaluation Group (IEG) for the period from 1984 through early 2004 (IEG 2006). The update provides an overview of the World Bank's pension lending trends by region, type of intervention, sector board, and type of lending instrument. It also contains a more general review of the analytical and advisory activities (AAA) related to pensions in the period following the IEG review. The chapter concludes with observations about the results of the pension work and the priorities for the future.

The Bank's Social Risk Management Framework and Pensions

The World Bank's approach to pensions and, more broadly, to old-age income security has developed in parallel with its thinking about the Social Risk Management framework. This framework evaluates social protection systems in relation to their capacity to provide risk management capabilities that can best address the diverse risks to which individuals or households are exposed in an environment characterized by asymmetric information and malfunctioning or nonexistent markets.

Pension and old-age income systems assist individuals in addressing the risk of poverty in old age and provide formal means for consumption smoothing and for transferring income from periods of economic activity to periods of old age in which the capacity for earnings and economic support is significantly diminished. They provide risk management capabilities to three main groups: lifetime poor people, nonpoor informal sector workers, and formal sector workers.

Richard Hinz is adviser and head of the Pension Team of the World Bank's Social Protection and Labor Department. Sergiy Biletsky is social protection specialist on this team. Melike Egilmezler was a consultant at the World Bank; she is now working as an expert at the Undersecretariat of Treasury in Turkey.

Those groups require differentiated risk management instruments that can function as a cohesive system.

Some individuals have little capacity to participate in formal pension systems that are based on savings and earnings. Such people face a high risk of poverty in old age when they can no longer earn income. Others with greater participation in the formal economy require instruments that enable deferred consumption and income smoothing. These people require instruments that can create sustainable systems of intergenerational transfers. Such systems can be in the form of traditional pay-as-you-go public pension systems or can be a means of accumulating financial resources over extended periods and efficiently translating such resources into sources of old-age income. The risks faced by these groups are related to the fiscal sustainability of public systems, the efficiency and security of financial markets and institutions, and the consequences of macroeconomic shocks.

The consideration of these and a variety of other risks that need to be managed to provide effective old-age income systems has resulted in the development of the World Bank's multipillar policy framework to guide its work on the development of the reform of pension systems. This framework evaluates pension systems in the context of their ability to align their various elements with the needs of the relevant population groups and the capacity of the country environment. Specific risk management characteristics and the overall ability to manage the range of relevant risks through the diversification of the instruments are central to this approach. The resulting overall policy framework emphasizes the reform of existing elements of pension systems to better align those systems with the specific risk toward which they are directed and to ensure their long-term stability and sustainability. It also focuses on managing overall systemic risks through diversification among as many elements of a pension system as are deemed feasible within the specific country.

Evolution of the Bank's Pension Work and Policy Framework

Since the early 1980s, the World Bank has been engaged in policy analysis, advice, and a range of lending activities directed toward pension systems and pension reforms. This work has occurred in an increasingly diverse range of country settings. It includes assessments of the structure, sustainability, and outcomes of pension systems; specific technical assistance and policy analysis for elements of pension systems; and support in the drafting of legislation and actual implementation of reforms. The World Bank has worked on pension reforms in more than 80 countries, and the demand for its support continues to grow.

Over the course of the two decades of this work, the Bank has developed a policy framework based on its extensive country experience with reform, an ongoing dialogue with academics and partner organizations, and an evaluation of pension reforms worldwide.

The Bank has developed a conceptual framework that takes into account the importance of individual country conditions and the need for flexible application of a diversified multipillar model for pension systems in formulating its analysis and policy recommendations. The framework starts with the initial conditions, which establish both the motivation for reform and the constraints on feasible reform options. Initial conditions include inherited systems, the reform needs of such systems, and the enabling environment, which may or may not be conducive to a reform process. Once the initial conditions are determined, the framework identifies the core objectives of country pension systems: protection against the risk of poverty in old age and consumption smoothing during one's working lifetime and into retirement. In setting out the objectives of pension systems, policy makers also need to consider broader questions of social protection and social policy toward the poor in the society as a whole.

The past decade of experience has reinforced the need in nearly every circumstance to move away from the single-pillar design. Experience has demonstrated that the multipillar design can better deal with the many objectives of pension systems—the most important being poverty reduction and income smoothing—and more effectively address the kinds of economic, political, and demographic risks facing any pension system. The proposed multipillar design is much more flexible and better addresses the main target groups in the population. Advanced funding is still considered useful, but the limits of funding in some circumstances are also seen much more sharply. The Bank's main motivation for supporting pension reform has not changed. The need for reform is still strong. Most countries' pension systems still do not deliver on their social objectives. They create significant distortions in the operation of market economies, and they are not financially sustainable when faced with an aging population.

The Bank's framework has five pillars:

- The noncontributory "zero pillar" extends some level of old-age income security to all the elderly where social conditions warrant and fiscal circumstances can sustain such a system.
- An appropriately sized "first pillar" has the objective of replacing some portion of lifetime preretirement income through contributions linked to earnings. This mandatory

pillar is either partially funded or financed on a pay-as-you-go basis.

- A funded defined-contribution "second pillar" typically provides privately managed individual savings accounts and establishes a clear link between contributions, investment performance, and benefits. This mandatory pillar is supported by enforceable property rights and may support financial market development.
- A funded voluntary "third pillar" takes many forms, such as individual savings and occupational pension funds.
- A nonfinancial "fourth pillar" includes access to informal support (such as assistance from families), to formal social programs (such as health and housing programs), and to individual assets.

The Bank continues to support pension reforms in client countries through a wide range of mechanisms. These mechanisms include direct financial support through lending operations, as well as analytical and advisory services through a number of different studies, including economic and sector work, working papers, and sector reports.

METHODOLOGY

The foundation for this review is the database of World Bank pension-related projects developed for the IEG's "Pension Reform and the Development of Pension Systems: An Evaluation of the World Bank Assistance," which was published in January 2006. This publication was based on a comprehensive data set of Bank projects covering fiscal year 1984 through early fiscal year 2004. This data set was supplemented by a review of Bank pension-related projects carried out from late fiscal year 2004 through the end of fiscal year 2007 (June 30, 2007). Hence, the database used for this review provides a comprehensive set of information on Bank activities over the extended period (see annex 4.A).

The information on Bank lending activities is discussed for two time periods. The focus of the discussion is on the most recent six-year period, fiscal years 2002 through 2007, and provides information on a common basis with the presentation for the other major areas of social protection. The discussion of Bank lending is supplemented with comparable data from the IEG review.

The information is presented for two groups of activities. The main presentation for which it is possible to compile relatively comprehensive data addresses the Bank's lending activities. This presentation is then supplemented with information on and analysis of some of the extensive AAA and other research work that have been completed in recent years. Because analytical and research work on pensions is often included within a variety of other activities, and because there has been no consistently applied means of coding this work for later identification, it is challenging to develop a comprehensive inventory of these activities. This limitation of the analysis exists even though the work that can be identified through coding is substantial, is representative of the Bank's activities in this area, and is a useful addition to the analysis. Additional listings of the major types of analytical and research work by the Bank are contained in the annexes.

Updating the Database on Bank Lending Operations through Fiscal Year 2007

Updating the database involved two tasks: identifying the inventory of Bank operations and analyzing the value of the project attributed to the pension components.

Identifying the Inventory of Bank Operations. As with the IEG study, information to identify the projects was taken from the Bank's Business Warehouse (BW) system. All the projects that were approved by the Board of Directors during the period were screened on the basis of the sector and thematic codes assigned to projects in this system. The sector codes used to identify potential pension-related lending projects were BE (*Compulsory Pension and Unemployment Insurance*) and FD (*Noncompulsory Pensions, Insurance, and Contractual Savings*). The Bank's project coding system requires that the BE code be used for family benefits; other social insurance benefits (except health insurance); pensions (social security) and old-age, disability, and survivors' insurance; sick-pay benefits; and unemployment benefits. The FD code is assigned to operations related to contractual savings; insurance (including reinsurance) of nonlife business, except health insurance (such as accident, fire, property, motor, marine, aviation, transport, pecuniary loss, and liability insurance); life insurance; and noncompulsory private pensions.

Thematic code 87 (*Social Risk Mitigation*) was also used to capture projects that might have a pension-related component. Code 87 is defined as activities aimed at mitigating the impact of risks that individuals and households are likely to face in the future, including diversification, insurance, and risk exchange. It includes income support for elderly people, people with disabilities, and survivors, as well as other risk mitigation activities.

It was also necessary to identify possible errors of exclusion—where pension-related activities were not reflected in the Bank's coding system—so that a more accurate and complete representation of the portfolio could be achieved.

Hence, all projects mapped to the Social Protection Sector Board were also reviewed for a possible pension component that should be included in the review. In addition, a word search for *pension* was conducted on the World Bank's ImageBank Web site for project appraisal documents (PADs), program documents, implementation status reports, and implementation completion reports (ICRs) to find any other pension-related work.

This process identified 175 projects for fiscal years 2004 to 2007 that had some indication of containing pension-related elements and were thus potential candidates to be added to the previous IEG-developed database to provide the complete inventory of pension lending work for fiscal years 1984 through 2007.

The project documents for these 175 loans and credits were then reviewed manually to determine whether they included any meaningful pension elements. For investment lending, the detailed project description section of the PADs was reviewed to identify any pension-related components. For adjustment lending, the policy matrices of the program documents were reviewed for pension-related conditionalities. This manual review concluded that from the overall sample of 175 projects, slightly more than one-third (61) had a pension-related component The characteristics of these lending projects were then mapped into the framework of the existing database to provide a comprehensive set of data on pension lending covering fiscal years 1984 through 2007.

Analyzing the Value of Project Attributed to the Pension Components. For investment lending, the U.S. dollar amounts allocated to pension-specific components are given in the detailed project description in the PADs. For adjustment lending, the pension lending amount for each project was estimated by calculating the percentage of reform actions or conditions that were pension specific. For instance, if the policy matrix of a program document has 2 pension-related prior actions out of a total of 10 prior actions, the pension component cost as a percentage of the Bank's commitment is calculated to be 20 percent, and that percentage of the loan amount is allocated to the pension component cost in the database.

Analytical and Advisory Activities and Research Work

Because of the inherent difficulty and complexity of developing a comprehensive database of information on the Bank's pension-related AAA work, no attempt was made to address this work in a similar depth to the lending operations. This review was limited to providing a representative sample of the work that has been completed since the IEG review.

Similar to the methodology used for the lending analysis, the BW was used to provide a list of all Bank-generated official economic and sector work (ESW) with sector code BE. Two separate lists were created for the ESW with sector code FD and thematic code 87. This review yielded the following numbers of reports for fiscal years 2004 to 2007:

- ESW coded as sector BE: 87 reports
- ESW coded as sector FD: 37 reports (only 23 of these reports were not on the list generated by sector code BE)
- ESW with theme code 87: 73 reports (all the reports concerning pensions were already included in the list generated by sector code BE).

The list of ESW with the BE sector code was used as the main list and was compared with the other two lists to identify and capture other reports on pensions. As a result, 110 reports were identified. However, only 34 of these reports were available in ImageBank for further analysis. This subset of the identified ESW was then used to formulate this element of the review.

ImageBank was also used to search for relevant ESW documents on pensions. A search was conducted for *pensions* and *social security* for fiscal years 2004 to 2007 for the following report types:

- Economic reports
- Sector reports
- World Bank Institute working papers
- Policy notes
- Country Economic Memorandums
- Public Expenditure Reviews
- Other social protection studies.

This exercise produced an additional 341 documents for potential inclusion in the inventory. The 341 reports were reviewed manually to determine if they included meaningful treatment of pension issues. The reports that are part of the final database were selected because of the presence of pension-related analytical work. The reports that mentioned pensions in only a few instances or in only a tangential manner were excluded from the database.

The combination of the list derived from BW (34 reports) and the review of reports from the word search in ImageBank (112 reports) resulted in 146 reports for fiscal years 2004 to 2007. Of these 146 reports, 126 focus on specific countries and 20 deal with general or regional pension reform issues. This distribution of topics is comparable to the data set for the 1984 to 2003 period, which includes 335 reports, of which 237 were country specific and the rest were regional or thematic in scope.

REVIEW OF PENSIONS PORTFOLIO, 1984–2007

This section provides an overview of the World Bank's pension lending operations since 1984. The overview is based on the overall database created by combining the earlier IEG-developed information with that from the subsequent time period. The section first provides an analysis of the more recent period (fiscal years 2002–07) and then combines that data set with the data from the earlier period (fiscal years 1984–2001) for a longer-term overview of lending. The presentation includes a broad overview of lending, as well as a more detailed breakdown of lending by region, sector board, country income level, and type of lending instrument (see annex 4.B.1).

Pension Lending in the Most Recent Period (Fiscal Years 2002–07)

From July 1, 2001 (the beginning of fiscal year 2002), through June 30, 2007, the World Bank conducted 112 projects in 56 countries in which some aspect of lending was associated with pensions. The total value of those loans was US$13.2 billion, representing 10.3 percent of the total of US$128.1 billion of World Bank lending approved during that six-year period. Of those loans, which cover a range of sectors and issues, an estimated US$2.04 billion (15.4 percent) were directly related to pensions. Thus, about 1.6 percent of overall World Bank lending during the period was directly related to pensions.

Pension lending was widely distributed among Bank client countries during the recent period. Among the 56 countries receiving loans that involved pensions in fiscal years 2002 to 2007, the majority (63 percent) had only one loan with a pension component. Among those with multiple pension-related loans, Colombia had the highest number at six, followed by India and Turkey with three loans each. The aggregate figures for this period are shown in table 4.1.

There is considerable variation in the level and proportion of the Bank's pension-related lending during these years. The peak was US$691 million (3.2 percent of the overall value of lending) in fiscal year 2005 (figure 4.1). The lowest level of lending was US$91.4 million in fiscal year 2007, representing only about 0.4 percent of lending. The relative level of the pension-related proportion of the loans also has a high degree of variation, ranging from 24.8 percent of loans in fiscal year 2005 to 9.5 percent in fiscal year 2007.

This year-to-year variation is very similar to the pattern observed over the longer period, as discussed in the next subsection. It likely occurred because in some years there were large loans with pension components, whereas in other years, operations were smaller. There is also a pipeline effect, which creates considerable "lumpiness" in the year-to-year distribution when the total loan amount is recorded on the Board approval date. A notable example of this pipeline effect is the Brazil Programmatic Fiscal Reform Loan, which was approved in June at the very end of fiscal year 2005. With a total value of US$658 million, 80 percent of which was allocated to the reform of the pension system, this loan represents a very large share of pension lending for that year.[1] Unfortunately, allocating the total loan amount by the loan approval date is the only feasible way to categorize lending. The available data on lending do not readily facilitate an analysis of disbursals that could be assigned to specific loan themes. If such a loan disbursement method were feasible, year-to-year variations in lending might be smaller.

Pension Lending over the Longer Term (Fiscal Years 1984–2007)

In the earlier period (fiscal years 1984–2001) included in the IEG database of pension lending (which, as noted, also includes lending for fiscal year 2002 through most of fiscal year 2004), 154 loans were determined to have some pension-related component. These loans had an aggregate value of US$29.9 billion, of which the pension components were determined to be US$5.5 billion, or about 18.3 percent of the value of these loans (see table 4.2). Although the mid 1980s saw some pension activity, this analysis indicates that pension lending by the Bank did not begin in earnest until 1990, before which there had been only US$28.5 million in pension-related loans. By the mid 1990s, the Bank had significantly increased its pension work, reaching a peak in fiscal years 1997 to 2000, when pension lending averaged over US$1 billion annually and ranged from 4.5 to 7.0 percent of overall Bank lending. In the more recent period (fiscal years 2002–07), pension lending was typically combined into larger loan packages, with the pension components averaging 15.4 percent of the value of the relevant loans (table 4.3). However, a somewhat different pattern is seen in the peak years, in which pension components were a much larger part of the relevant loans. In 1997, for example, pension lending represented nearly one-half of the lending in the projects in which pensions were included and reached the highest overall share of Bank lending at 7.0 percent.

Table 4.1: **World Bank Lending with Pension Components, Fiscal Years 2002–07**

Fiscal year	Number of loans with pension component	Value of pension component (US$ millions)	Total Bank lending with pension component (US$ millions)	Total Bank lending (US$ millions)	Pension component (as % of total Bank lending)	Pension component (as % of loans with pension component)
2002	23	214.3	2,687.7	19,519	1.1	8.0
2003	18	158.1	1,158.9	18,513	0.9	13.6
2004	23	540.0	2,793.8	20,080	2.7	19.3
2005	20	691.0	2,784.1	21,893	3.2	24.8
2006	16	342.2	2,826.7	23,581	1.5	12.1
2007	12	91.4	958.0	24,536	0.4	9.5
Total	112	2,036.9	13,209.1	128,123	1.6	15.4

Source: Authors' calculations, based on the Business Warehouse data and World Bank documents.
Note: Because of rounding, totals may deviate slightly from the sum of the parts.

FIGURE 4.1: **PENSION-RELATED LENDING, FISCAL YEARS 2002–07**

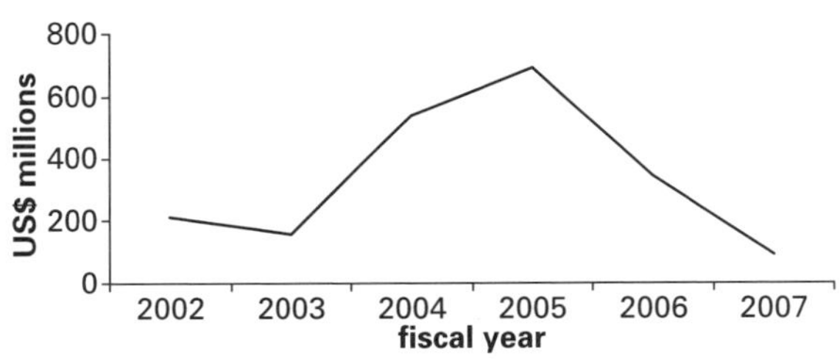

Source: Authors' calculations, based on the Business Warehouse data and World Bank documents.

Combining these earlier data with data from the most recent period shows that World Bank pension-related lending totaled US$7.5 billion for the 24-year period (1984–2007), averaging US$310 million per year. This amount represents 1.5 percent of the value of all World Bank loans that have been approved since 1984. The wide variation in lending levels is shown in figure 4.2.

There have been three distinct periods of Bank pension lending (see figure 4.2 and table 4.3). During the 1980s and early 1990s, the level of pension lending was low. Negligible lending for pensions occurred through 1990, with no loans approved in three of the seven years. In the three years when there was activity, the amounts involved were no more than US$17 million during any year. The total amount of pension lending during the entire decade was only US$454 million, representing, on average, 0.2 percent of overall Bank lending in the period.

Pension-related lending began to accelerate in 1991, when a number of countries in Latin America initiated reforms. As countries in Eastern Europe and Central Asia sought to undertake major reforms of their pension systems, this acceleration was strongly reinforced. The pension reforms occurred in conjunction with the major structural transitions during this era and, later, in response to the financial crises of the late 1990s. During fiscal years 1995 through 2001, the level of pension-related lending increased to US$5.0 billion, representing 3.3 percent of total Bank lending.

This surge in activity began to abate in 2001, with recent years characterized by a lower but relatively constant level of pension lending. Over this later period, the aggregate value of pension-related loans was US$2.04 billion, less than half the annual average level of the preceding period.

Distribution of Lending by Region

During fiscal years 2002 to 2007, pension lending continued to be concentrated in the Latin America and Caribbean (LAC) and Europe and Central Asia (ECA) Regions in both the number of operations and the value of lending (see table 4.4).

Table 4.2: **World Bank Lending with Pension Components, Fiscal Years 1984–2001**

Fiscal year	Total Bank lending (US$ millions)	Total Bank lending with pension component (US$ millions)	Value of pension component (US$ millions)	Pension component (as % of total Bank lending)	Pension component (as % of loans with pension component)
1984	15,484	5.0	0.4	0.0	7.2
1985	14,337	0.0	0.0	0.0	n.a.
1986	16,347	0.0	0.0	0.0	n.a.
1987	17,621	80.0	11.4	0.1	14.3
1988	19,171	0.0	0.0	0.0	n.a.
1989	21,337	181.1	16.7	0.1	9.2
1990	20,702	295.2	14.2	0.1	4.8
1991	22,622	654.3	36.9	0.2	5.6
1992	21,703	1,777.2	163.6	0.8	9.2
1993	23,524	1,003.1	169.9	0.7	16.9
1994	20,792	929.0	41.0	0.2	4.4
1995	22,522	2,237.0	172.7	0.8	7.7
1996	21,326	947.4	50.8	0.2	5.4
1997	19,147	2,731.2	1,336.9	7.0	49.0
1998	28,592	8,500.8	1,316.8	4.6	15.5
1999	29,147	7,013.0	1,310.8	4.5	18.7
2000	15,276	2,342.5	789.9	5.2	33.7
2001	17,251	1,184.5	50.1	0.3	4.2
Total	366,899	29,881.3	5,482.2	1.5	18.3

Source: Authors' calculations, based on the Business Warehouse data and World Bank documents.
Note: n.a. = not applicable. Because of rounding, totals may deviate slightly from the sum of the parts.

Table 4.3: **World Bank Lending with Pension Components, Fiscal Years 1984–2007**

Time period	Total Bank lending (US$ millions)	Total Bank lending with pension component (US$ millions)	Value of pension component (US$ millions)	Pension component (as % of total Bank lending)	Pension component (as % of loans with pension component)
1984–94	213,638	4,924.9	454.2	0.2	9.2
1995–2001	153,261	24,956.4	5,028.1	3.3	20.1
2002–07	128,123	13,209.1	2,036.9	1.6	15.4
Total	495,021	43,090.4	7,519.1	1.5	17.4

Source: Authors' calculations, based on the Business Warehouse data and World Bank documents.
Note: Because of rounding, totals may deviate slightly from the sum of the parts.

FIGURE 4.2: **WORLD BANK LENDING WITH PENSION COMPONENTS, FISCAL YEARS 1984–2007**

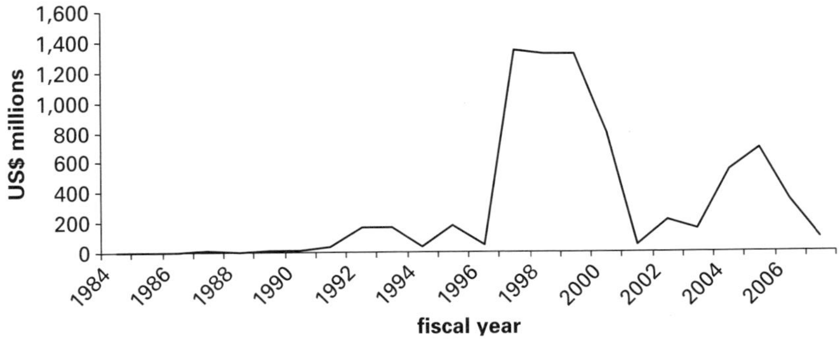

Source: Authors' calculations, based on the Business Warehouse data and World Bank documents.

Table 4.4: **Regional Distribution of World Bank Pension Lending Activities, Fiscal Years 2002–07**

Region	Number of countries with pension-related loans	Number of pension-related loans	Total Bank lending with pension component (US$ millions)	Value of pension component (US$ millions)	Pension component (as % of loans with pension component)
Africa	10	19	796.3	55.7	7.0
Europe and Central Asia	19	45	5,004.1	690.5	13.8
Latin America and the Caribbean	16	32	4,411.2	993.1	22.5
Middle East and North Africa	6	6	902.5	65.3	7.2
South Asia	5	10	2,095.0	232.3	11.1
Total	56	112	13,209.1	2,036.9	15.4

Source: Authors' calculations, based on the Business Warehouse data and World Bank documents.

The ECA Region had the most pension-related lending operations, with 45 projects in 19 countries, accounting for more than a third of all pension lending operations during this period. The LAC Region had a similar proportion of the projects, with 32 loans in 16 countries. Together these two regions account for two-thirds of the loans with pension components. Other regions, however, continued to emerge within the pensions lending portfolio. The Sub-Saharan Africa (AFR) Region had a significant number of operations, with 19 loans in 10 countries, followed by the South Asia Region (SAR) with 10 loans in 5 countries. Pension-related lending remained at very low levels in the Middle East and North Africa (MENA) Region with only six loans in six countries and the East Asia and the Pacific (EAP) Region, which had no pension-related lending during the period.

The LAC Region received the largest proportion of pension lending, with US$993.1 million—nearly half the total amount in the period. As noted earlier, this difference is the result of a single large loan to Brazil approved in late 2005 that accounts for the majority of the region's pension-related lending. The ECA Region received US$690.5 million in loans. Together these two regions accounted for 82.6 percent of the value of the pension lending during the period. Among the other regions, pension lending was US$65.3 million in the MENA, US$55.7 million in the AFR Region, and US$232.3 million in the SAR. The proportion of operations and lending values for the various regions and the distribution over the four-year period are shown in figure 4.3.

An analysis of the regional distribution of lending during the six-year period indicates considerable year-to-year variation. In fiscal years 2002 and 2003, when overall pension lending had fallen to comparatively low levels, the ECA and LAC Regions experienced similarly modest (by comparison to many other years) levels of pension lending. The other regions had minimal levels of lending activity during those two years.

More recently, there has been far greater fluctuation in relative lending levels between the ECA and LAC Regions. In fiscal year 2004, the ECA Region accounted for both the largest number and the highest value of pension operations, with more than half of all the relevant operations and a similar proportion of the value of the loans (tables 4.5 and 4.6). Turkey's Third Programmatic Financial and Public Sector Adjustment Loan contributed significantly to this high share of pension commitments, with a pension-related value of US$200 million, which is 80 percent of the ECA pension lending for the year and 37 percent of overall pension lending in fiscal year 2004. The LAC Region accounts for most of the remaining pension portfolio (26 percent), followed by the SAR and the MENA Region, respectively. All fiscal year 2004 projects in the LAC Region that have a pension component are adjustment lending

FIGURE 4.3: PROJECTS WITH A PENSION COMPONENT BY REGION, FISCAL YEARS 2002–07

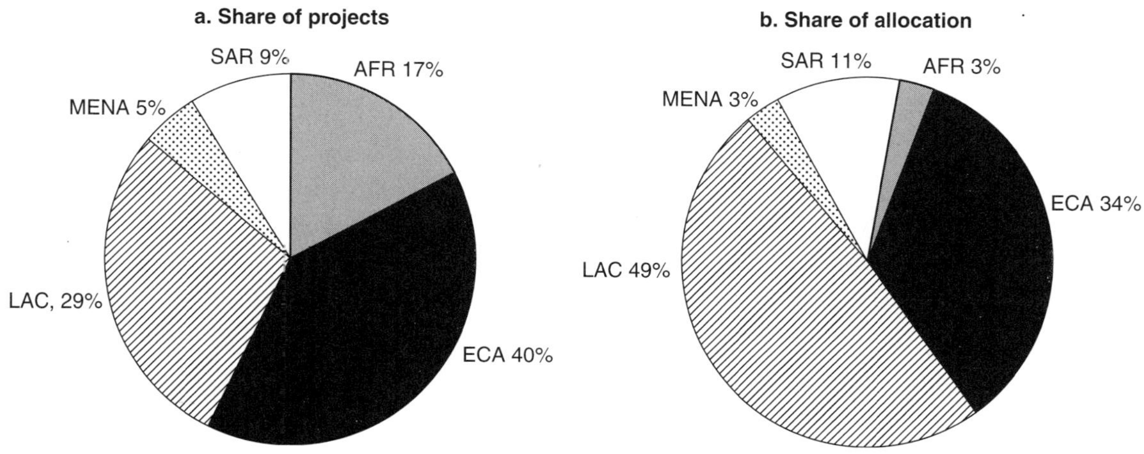

Source: Authors' calculations, based on the Business Warehouse data and World Bank documents.
Note: AFR = Africa; ECA = Europe and Central Asia; LAC = Latin America and the Caribbean; MENA = Middle East and North Africa; SAR = South Asia Region. Figure reflects a total of 112 projects and a pension portfolio of US$2.037 billion.

Table 4.5: Number of Projects with Pension Components by Region, Fiscal Years 2002–07

	Fiscal year						
Region	**2002**	**2003**	**2004**	**2005**	**2006**	**2007**	**Total**
Africa	2	3	2	4	6	2	19
East Asia and Pacific	0	0	0	0	0	0	0
Europe and Central Asia	10	7	12	7	6	3	45
Latin America and the Caribbean	6	6	6	7	2	5	32
Middle East and North Africa	2	1	1	0	1	1	6
South Asia	3	1	2	2	1	1	10
Total	23	18	23	20	16	12	112

Source: Authors' calculations, based on the Business Warehouse data and World Bank documents.

Table 4.6: **Lending Commitments for Pensions by Region, Fiscal Years 2002–07**

Region	Fiscal year (US$ millions)						Total
	2002	2003	2004	2005	2006	2007	
Africa	5	6	18	17	9	0	56
East Asia and Pacific	0	0	0	0	0	0	0
Europe and Central Asia	101	85	252	62	173	16	691
Latin America and the Caribbean	86	62	82	601	100	62	993
Middle East and North Africa	7	4	3	0	50	1	65
South Asia	14	0	185	11	10	12	232
Total	214	158	540	691	342	91	2,037

Source: Authors' calculations, based on the Business Warehouse data and World Bank documents.
Note: Because of rounding, totals may deviate slightly from the sum of the parts.

operations with an emphasis on improving fiscal sustainability and efficiency of social protection programs and pension systems through parametric reforms or institutional and supervisory capacity building.

Fiscal year 2005 sees a shift in trends with the LAC Region dominating more than 85 percent of the portfolio, mainly because of a large social security reform loan to Brazil. There is a decrease in the share of ECA lending for this period; however, AFR picks up in this period, mostly because poverty reduction support credits and an economic growth and management credit were extended to countries such as Cape Verde, Uganda, and Zambia, and these credits contain modest pension reform components.

Despite the comparatively large number of projects in the AFR Region in fiscal year 2006, most were investment lending projects that focused on public service and financial sector support. Only small components could be attributed to pensions, and they accounted for only 3 percent of pension lending in fiscal year 2006. The relatively larger pension proportions in the ECA Region are because of the region's strong emphasis during this period on strengthening administrative capacity building in the relevant institutions and ministries. This capacity was necessary to implement major structural reforms that were undertaken in the preceding decade.

The LAC Region dominates the small pension portfolio in fiscal year 2007. Highlights for this year include India's Third Andhra Pradesh Economic Reform Credit, which introduced a defined-contribution (fully funded) pension scheme as part of the pension reform. In fiscal year 2007 in the MENA Region, a project in Iraq was implemented to strengthen the policy, management, and administrative capacity in the Ministry of Labor and Social Affairs, and to assist in developing, managing, and monitoring pension reforms in the Ministry of Finance.

The longer-term distribution by region of pension lending is shown in table 4.7. The experience of the most recent six-year period is essentially a continuation of the lending pattern over the longer term, although at lower overall levels (than in the peak years). The longer-term trend also indicates that the other regions—notably the EAP Region in fiscal years 1998 and 1999, the SAR in fiscal year 2004, and to a lesser extent the MENA Region in fiscal year 2006—had substantial lending in some years through a few large operations.

Distribution of Lending by Country Income Level

The analysis of lending in relation to the characteristics of the recipient countries indicates that the Bank's pension operations have been highly concentrated among middle-income countries. This finding is consistent with the nature of pension reforms, which tend to primarily occur in countries that have achieved sufficient income levels to have been able to afford to establish a formal pension system. This explains the high lending shares in the ECA and LAC Regions, which are composed mainly of middle-income countries. During the 2002 to 2007 period, the largest number of lending operations (42 percent) occurred in countries that were classified as lower-middle income, with a similar proportion (37 percent) in upper-middle-income countries. A relatively small proportion (21 percent) of lending operations occurred in low-income

Table 4.7: **Regional Distribution of Pension Lending, Fiscal Years 1984–2007**

Fiscal year	Africa	East Asia and Pacific	Europe and Central Asia	Latin America and the Caribbean	Middle East and North Africa	South Asia
1984	0.0	0.0	0.0	0.4	0.0	0.0
1987	0.0	0.0	0.0	11.4	0.0	0.0
1989	0.2	0.0	0.0	16.6	0.0	0.0
1990	0.0	0.0	5.6	0.0	0.0	8.7
1991	1.6	0.0	35.0	0.3	0.0	0.0
1992	2.4	0.0	16.7	119.5	25.0	0.0
1993	2.9	0.0	154.5	3.1	0.0	9.4
1994	0.0	0.0	26.4	14.7	0.0	0.0
1995	0.0	13.5	156.1	1.9	0.1	0.0
1996	24.0	5.7	6.7	14.4	0.0	0.0
1997	5.3	0.0	370.3	944.4	13.0	4.1
1998	2.0	301.9	453.4	527.2	25.0	7.2
1999	6.1	206.3	76.9	1,021.5	0.0	0.0
2000	56.5	0.8	192.1	533.9	0.0	6.3
2001	0.0	0.0	26.6	14.8	0.0	8.6
2002	4.9	0.0	101.4	86.3	0.7	14.3
2003	6.0	0.0	85.4	62.0	0.4	0.3
2004	18.3	0.0	252.3	81.8	0.3	184.8
2005	16.8	0.0	61.9	601.4	0.0	10.9
2006	9.2	0.0	173.3	99.5	50.0	10.2
2007	0.5	0.0	16.2	62.1	0.1	11.8

Source: Authors' calculations, based on the Business Warehouse data and World Bank documents.
Note: There were no programs in 1985, 1986, and 1988.

countries. Overall, middle-income countries account for three of every four lending operations. With regard to the pensions lending commitments, the concentration in the higher-income groups is even greater, with upper-middle-income countries receiving by far the greatest share of lending at 66 percent of the value of loans, compared with 20 percent for the lower-middle-income group. Low-income countries receive 14 percent (see figures 4.4 and 4.5).

As with many of the other characteristics of lending recipients, this pattern is consistent with that of the previous decades (see figures 4.6 and 4.7). The only fiscal years when the amount of pension lending extended to lower-middle-income countries was higher than to upper-middle-income countries were 1992, 1995, 1996, and 2007. For all the other years, upper-middle-income countries received the highest levels of pension-related lending.

Distribution of Lending by Type of Lending Instrument

Lending activities can be distinguished by the type of instrument and in relation to the eligibility of the country for subsidized lending through the International Development Association (IDA).

Types of Lending Instruments. Lending for pensions generally involves three basic types of operations: development policy loans, investment loans, and technical assistance loans. The most prevalent are the development

FIGURE 4.4: **SHARE OF LOANS BY INCOME LEVEL, FISCAL YEARS 2002–07**

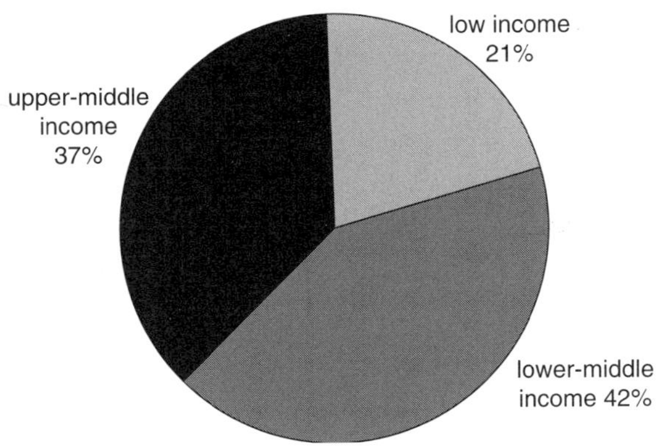

Source: Authors' calculations, based on the Business Warehouse data and World Bank documents.

FIGURE 4.5: **SHARE OF ALLOCATION BY INCOME LEVEL, FISCAL YEARS 2002–07**

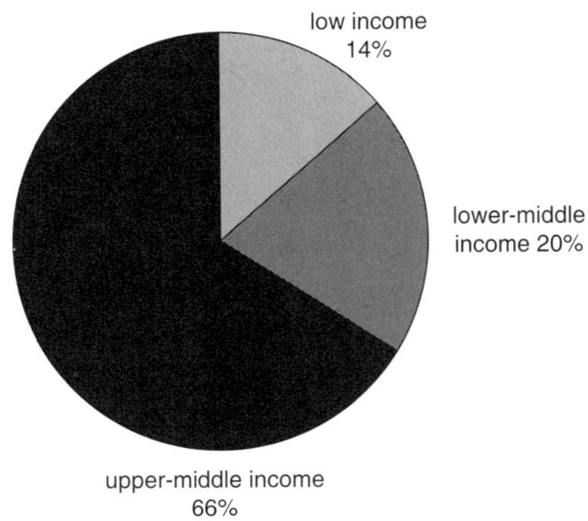

Source: Authors' calculations, based on the Business Warehouse data and World Bank documents.

FIGURE 4.6: **NUMBER OF PENSION-RELATED OPERATIONS BY INCOME LEVEL, FISCAL YEARS 1984–2007**

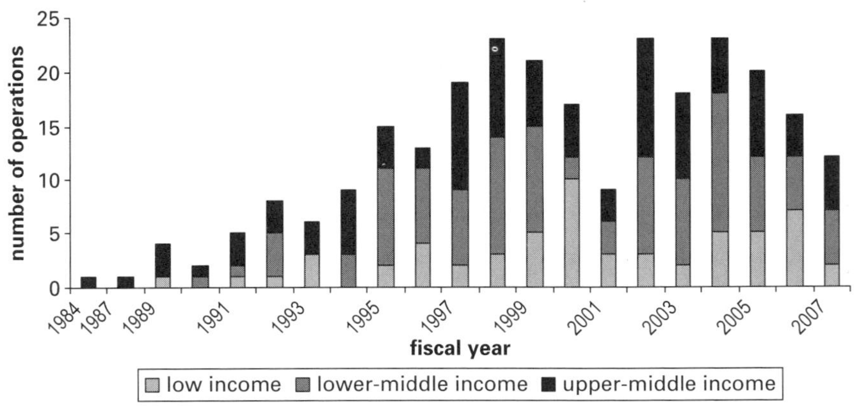

Source: Authors' calculations, based on the Business Warehouse data and World Bank documents.

FIGURE 4.7: **PENSION-RELATED LENDING COMMITMENTS BY INCOME LEVEL, FISCAL YEARS 1984–2007**

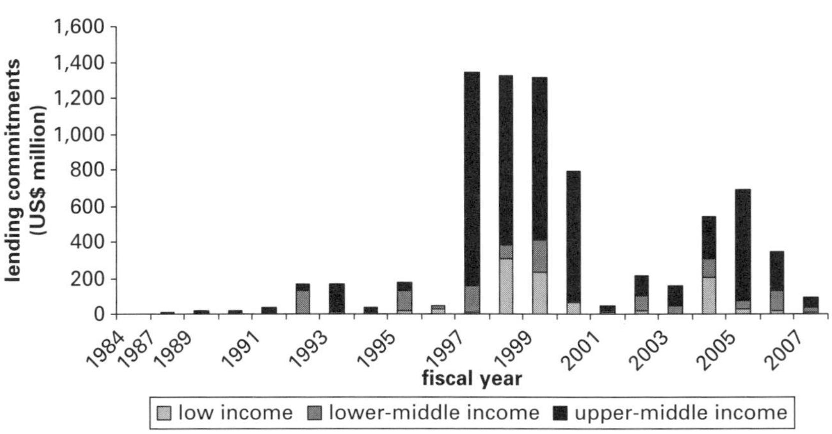

Source: Authors' calculations, based on the Business Warehouse data and World Bank documents.

policy loans, previously called *adjustment lending*. These loans provide general revenue support on the basis of a commitment to meet certain conditions or to undertake specified reforms. In the context of pensions, they usually support basic structural reform of pension systems—typically a major redesign of the system or major changes to the parameters of an established pay-as-you-go public system to enable it to remain fiscally viable over the longer term. Reforms involving major design changes have usually involved a transition to a multipillar structure either to diversify risks and better align the country's pension system with a market-oriented economy or to improve the capacity of the system to accommodate significant demographic change. This approach often involves introducing fully funded second pillars or moving toward a notional defined-contribution design.

The second, less prevalent type of loan is an investment loan that typically involves support for institutional reform. Such loans often include a significant focus on capacity building to enhance a country's ability to implement reforms. Investment lending may build capacity to support reforms either before or after the introduction of the reform. Technical assistance loans that provide specific technical support for a reform are a subset of investment lending.

Among the 112 loans approved during fiscal years 2002 to 2007 that had a pension component, approximately two-thirds were development policy or adjustment loans and one-third were investment loans, including technical assistance loans (table 4.8). Although there are wide differences in the lending level within the regions, policy lending was most prevalent in all the regions except the AFR Region, which had eight adjustment-type loans and nine investment loans (table 4.8). Policy and adjustment lending was even more dominant when considered in relation to the dollar value, with approximately three-fourths of the lending during the period within this category (table 4.9).

The notable exception to the greater use of investment lending was a single large loan in the SAR that represented the majority of the lending in that region. This loan, however, was atypical for pension lending because it was used to fund severance pay to settle some pension liabilities associated with an Enterprise Growth and Bank Modernization Loan in Bangladesh. Although coded as a pension-related activity, this type of lending is not directed toward broader pension reforms. As discussed previously, the smaller size and greater fragmentation of investment and technical assistance lending are likely related to the characteristic of many investment loans to combine many different aspects related to pensions and other social protection and financial sector development issues.

Review of pension lending over the longer term reveals that the more recent period is consistent with the pattern that has prevailed over the full period in which the majority of pension lending has been in the form of policy-type loans. The aggregate values of the different types of loans during fiscal years 1984 to 2007 are shown in table 4.10. This table shows that in the peak period of lending in the late 1990s, more than 90 percent of the lending was policy based. The pattern by loan type over the period is illustrated in figure 4.8.

International Bank for Reconstruction and Development Versus International Development Association Lending. The analysis of World Bank pension lending by category in relation to the eligibility of the borrower for IDA, International

Table 4.8: Distribution of Pension-Related Lending by Lending Instrument and Region: Number of Loans, Fiscal Years 2002–07

	Number of loans			
Region	Investment loans	Technical assistance	Policy or adjustment loans	Total
Africa	9	2	8	19
Europe and Central Asia	15	2	28	45
Latin America and the Caribbean	4	5	23	32
Middle East and North Africa	1	0	5	6
South Asia	2	1	7	10
Total	31	10	71	112

Source: Authors' calculations, based on the Business Warehouse data and World Bank documents.

Table 4.9: **Distribution of Pension-Related Lending by Lending Instrument and Region: Amount of Lending, Fiscal Years 2002–07**

Region	Amount (US$ millions)			
	Investment loans	Technical assistance	Policy or adjustment loans	Total
Africa	15.1	8.6	32.0	55.7
Europe and Central Asia	193.5	7.2	489.8	690.5
Latin America and the Caribbean	11.8	51.9	929.4	993.1
Middle East and North Africa	0.8	0.0	64.5	65.3
South Asia	180.1	0.3	51.9	232.3
Total	401.3	68.0	1,567.6	2,036.9

Source: Authors' calculations, based on the Business Warehouse data and World Bank documents.
Note: There were no programs in 1985, 1986, and 1988.

Table 4.10: **Pension Portfolio by Lending Instrument, Fiscal Years 1984–2007**

Fiscal year	Investment loans (US$ millions)	Technical assistance (US$ millions)	Adjustment loans (US$ millions)
1984	0.0	0.4	0.0
1987	0.0	0.0	11.4
1989	0.0	4.9	11.8
1990	0.0	0.0	14.2
1991	1.9	1.6	33.4
1992	0.0	2.0	161.6
1993	154.5	0.0	15.4
1994	17.6	8.8	14.6
1995	38.0	2.5	132.2
1996	3.2	8.7	38.9
1997	78.4	24.4	1,234.1
1998	28.4	14.8	1,273.6
1999	12.6	8.0	1,290.2
2000	4.2	16.2	769.5
2001	11.1	0.0	38.9
2002	54.2	0.0	160.1
2003	41.6	14.4	102.0
2004	203.2	3.4	333.4
2005	49.4	45.2	596.4
2006	52.0	0.0	290.2
2007	0.8	5.0	85.6

Source: Authors' calculations, based on the Business Warehouse data and World Bank documents.

Bank for Reconstruction and Development (IBRD), or blended-rate lending is consistent with the fact that the pension reform work has remained concentrated in middle-income countries. During fiscal years 2002 to 2007, about 60 percent of pension lending operations took place in IBRD countries, whereas IDA countries constituted 26 percent of these loans. However, the majority (14 percent of this 26 percent) were in heavily indebted poor countries (HIPC). IBRD countries received a higher average value of loans, accounting for 85 percent of the dollar commitments. In contrast, IDA countries received only 12 percent of the value of the pension lending. The number of operations in blend countries constituted 14 percent of all operations with a pension component, but only 3 percent of the lending amount (see figures 4.9 and 4.10).

Pension-related lending commitments over the longer period indicate a pattern consistent with recent years, with the majority of the value of loans going to IBRD countries, although there are some exceptions (table 4.11). In fiscal year 1990, when IBRD countries received no pension lending, pension loans were divided between IDA and "not assigned" (Hungary was the exception as part of a structural adjustment loan). Similarly in 1993 and 1994, the "not assigned" category had a larger share of pension-related commitments than in the previous period. Hungary and Slovenia were the reason: Hungary constituted a large portion of the total pension lending commitments, with 78 percent in 1993 through the Pensions Administration and Health Insurance Project, and Slovenia with 19 percent in 1994 through an Enterprise and Financial Sector Adjustment Loan. The "not assigned" category increased during the later period (especially in 1998 and 1999) because of three structural adjustment loans extended to the

FIGURE 4.8: PENSION PORTFOLIO BY LENDING INSTRUMENT, FISCAL YEARS 1984–2007

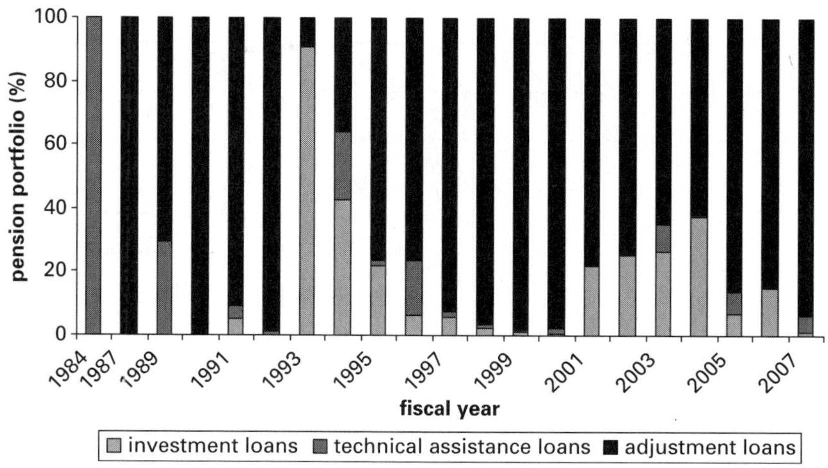

Source: Authors' calculations, based on the Business Warehouse data and World Bank documents.

FIGURE 4.9: SHARE OF LOANS BY LENDING CATEGORY, FISCAL YEARS 2002–07

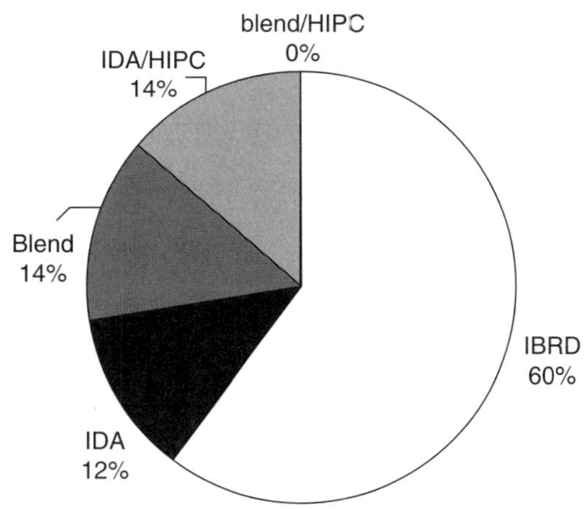

Source: Authors' calculations, based on the Business Warehouse data and World Bank documents.
Note: HIPC = heavily indebted poor countries; IBRD = International Bank for Reconstruction and Development; IDA = International Development Association.

FIGURE 4.10: SHARE OF ALLOCATION BY LENDING CATEGORY, FISCAL YEARS 2002–07

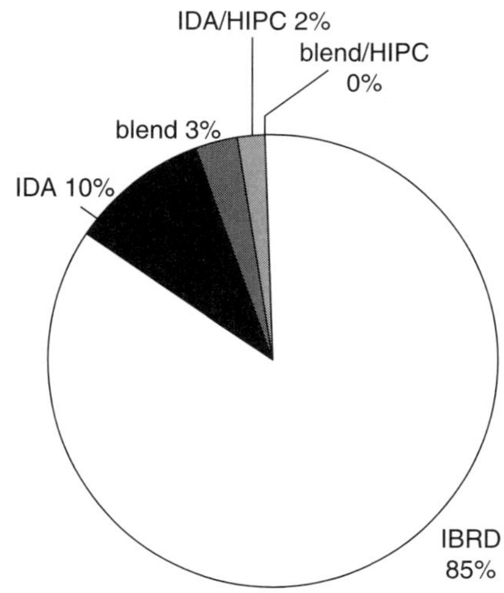

Source: Authors' calculations, based on the Business Warehouse data and World Bank documents.
Note: HIPC = heavily indebted poor countries; IBRD = International Bank for Reconstruction and Development; IDA = International Development Association.

Republic of Korea (with total loan amounts of US$7 billion) during the Asian financial crisis.

Distribution of Lending by Sector Board

The pension work within the Bank is distributed among several sector boards. The sector boards serve as the basic governance and authorizing bodies for the lending projects. Review of the mapping of pension lending among the various boards indicates that the pension work has been primarily distributed among four sectors within the Bank: social protection, economic policy, financial sector, and public sector governance.

For fiscal years 2002 to 2007, the distribution of the pension lending portfolio by sector board indicates that the Economic Policy and Social Protection Sector Boards account for the highest number of projects involving

Table 4.11: Pension-Related Lending by Country Category, Fiscal Years 1984–2007

Fiscal year	IBRD	IDA	Blend	IDA/HIPC	Blend/HIPC	Not assigned
1984	0.4	0.0	0.0	0.0	0.0	0.0
1987	11.4	0.0	0.0	0.0	0.0	0.0
1989	16.6	0.0	0.0	0.2	0.0	0.0
1990	0.0	8.7	0.0	0.0	0.0	5.6
1991	24.7	0.0	0.0	1.6	0.0	10.3
1992	160.0	0.0	0.0	2.4	0.1	0.0
1993	25.6	0.0	9.4	2.9	0.0	132.0
1994	29.0	0.0	4.2	0.1	0.0	7.7
1995	143.0	8.4	13.8	7.5	0.0	0.0
1996	2.8	10.6	0.0	24.1	13.0	0.0
1997	1,269.4	0.0	19.8	0.0	0.0	47.8
1998	867.8	26.5	24.3	2.3	0.1	394.8
1999	1,048.6	15.6	13.7	31.9	0.1	200.0
2000	715.8	1.1	6.3	64.5	0.0	2.2
2001	25.7	0.0	11.2	0.0	0.0	13.1
2002	190.5	8.0	15.8	0.0	0.0	0.0
2003	141.1	2.6	9.1	3.7	0.0	1.6
2004	318.6	180.0	12.9	25.6	0.0	2.9
2005	661.6	11.3	8.3	9.8	0.0	0.0
2006	320.8	0.4	10.2	10.8	0.0	0.0
2007	77.9	1.6	11.8	0.0	0.0	0.0

Source: Authors' calculations, based on the Business Warehouse data and World Bank documents.
Note: There were no programs in 1985, 1986, and 1988.

pensions, with 21 percent each. All projects mapped to the Economic Protection Sector Board are development policy lending and poverty reduction support credits. The pension component of most adjustment loans mapped to that sector board aim to (a) improve the efficiency of social security administration, (b) redesign the financing structure, and (c) implement parametric reforms to ensure long-term financial sustainability of pension systems.

The operations mapped to the Social Protection Sector Board are divided equally between investment and adjustment lending. They focus mainly on improving the efficiency and transparency of social security systems through institutional modernization. This modernization consists of (a) developing unified contribution collection and reporting systems, (b) establishing central registries that are based on modem information technology and processes, and (c) developing capacity for better policy analysis and evaluation of the pension systems. Although the number of projects mapped to each of these sector boards is nearly the same, spending on pension activities according to the sector board to which loans are mapped varies (see figure 4.11, panel b). With regard to allocation, projects mapped to the Social Protection Section Board account for 39 percent of the portfolio, whereas projects mapped to the Economic Protection Sector Board cover only 25 percent. Other sector boards that have pension-related projects are the Public Sector Governance Sector Board and Financial and Private Sector Development Sector Board, where the pension-related projects amount to 20 percent and 11 percent, respectively. The amount of allocation to pensions is

FIGURE 4.11: **PROJECTS INVOLVING PENSIONS BY SECTOR BOARD OF APPROVAL, FISCAL YEARS 2002–07**

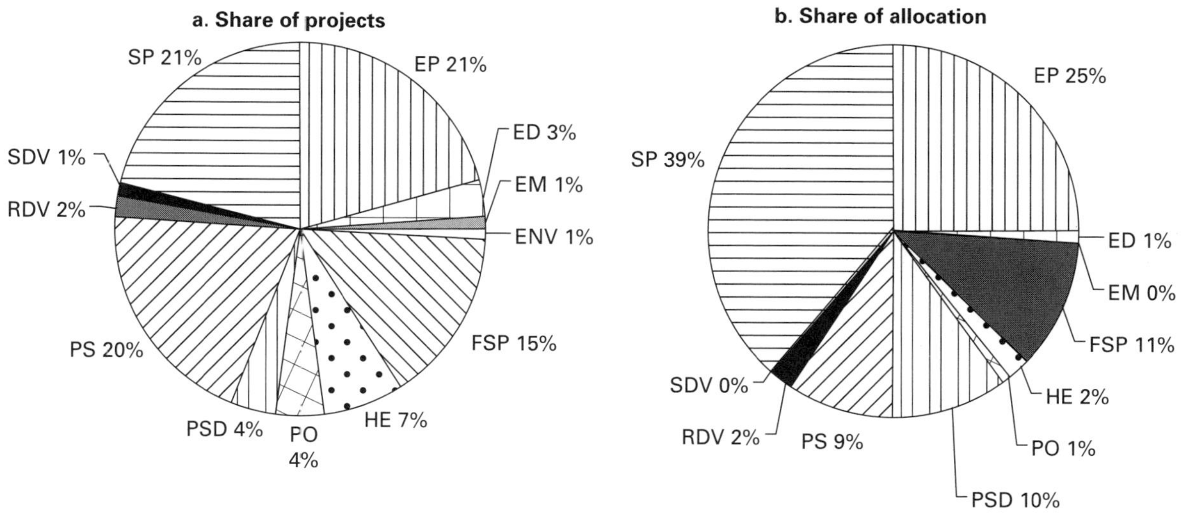

Source: Authors' calculations, based on the Business Warehouse data and World Bank documents.
Note: ED = Education; EM = Energy and Mining; EP = Economic Policy; FSP = Financial Sector; HE = Health, Nutrition, and Population; PO = Poverty Reduction; PS = Public Sector Governance; PSD = Private Sector Development; RDV = Rural Development; SDV = Social Development; SP = Social Protection. Figure reflects a total of 112 projects and a pension portfolio of US$2.037 billion.

11 percent in the Financial and Private Sector Development Sector Board and 9 percent in the Public Sector Governance Sector Board.

The projects mapped to the Public Sector Governance Sector Board include more (a) second- and third-pillar reform design and implementation and (b) development of a regulatory and supervisory framework than do the other sector boards. Development of policies and establishment of mechanisms to eliminate pension arrears and actuarial deficits are also among the main issues tackled in projects mapped to that sector board. In contrast, most projects mapped to the Financial and Private Sector Development Sector Board are financial and banking sector development support or reform credits or technical assistance projects, where pension issues are part of the larger financial sector reform agenda. Some issues are the development of legislation for establishing private pension funds, provision of capacity building to ministries to strengthen the regulatory and supervisory frameworks, and improvement of the capacity of pension funds to undertake actuarial analysis and investment decisions to ensure risk diversification.

For the earlier period, 1984 to 2001, the operations that focus on pension issues by sector board are as follows: the Economic Policy Sector Board has the highest percentage of operations with a pension component (34 percent), followed by the Social Protection Sector Board (19 percent). The other sector boards that manage operations with pension components are Public Sector Governance Sector Board and Financial and Private Sector Development Sector Board. With regard to the lending commitments by sector board, the Social Protection Sector Board has the highest share with 50 percent, despite a relatively low share of operations (20 percent) for the same period. The Economic Protection Sector Board, in contrast, has a higher share of operations, yet lower lending commitments for the pension cost of the projects (19 percent). Pension lending commitments of the Public Sector Governance Sector Board and Financial and Private Sector Development Sector Board are more or less consistent with the number of operations managed by each sector board.

Distribution of Lending by Pension Pillar

A key issue in assessing the nature of the Bank's pension work and the degree to which the multipillar policy framework has guided the lending operations is an assessment of the architecture of the pension systems for which lending was provided. In constructing the database of pension lending, the IEG reviewed the relevant documents and assigned each operation to one of several categories of pension systems, depending on the number of pillars. Originally, a three-pillar framework was used, assigning mandatory public systems operating on a pay-as-you-go basis to the first pillar, mandatory funded defined-contribution systems to the second, and complementary private systems to the third. This system was essentially the same as the later five-pillar framework, minus the zero and fourth pillars. For comparability to the earlier work, the subsequent operations have, therefore, been categorized within the three-pillar framework.

Table 4.12 summarizes the distribution of Bank lending during fiscal years 2002 to 2007 among three of the five pillars within the multipillar model; these three pillars represent most of the work over the past two decades. The data show the continuing Bank support for a wide range of pension system designs in different countries. The majority of the loans (60 out of 112) and of the value of lending operations (55.5 percent) supported system designs with more than one pillar. About 40 percent of the lending value supported three pillars of pension systems. Only 24 percent of pension loans were associated with a single pillar. The projects not associated with any pillar supported mainly institutional reforms related to social security systems.

A similar analysis of pension lending for fiscal years 1984 to 2001, as shown in table 4.13, indicates that loans associated with a single pillar constituted a much higher proportion (46 percent) of pension-related lending than in the later period, indicating the shift of the Bank's pension work away from single-pillar reforms. The focus of the early work was on parametric reforms of mature single-pillar systems facing severe solvency issues. The Bank's work now focuses more on system reforms and a broader restructuring of pension systems.

Types of Interventions. The nature of pension lending can be further delineated into three main categories of interventions: institutional capacity building, general analytical support, and actual reform measures. The Bank's pension-related lending (figure 4.12) has been roughly equally divided among these three categories.

Quality of Pension Portfolio, Fiscal Years 2002–07

An indication of the quality of the pension lending can be derived from the Bank's regular review in which operations are rated in terms of several types of quality measures.

Implementation Status Report and Project Status Report. Ninety-four of the 112 loans and credits for pension reform, approved between fiscal years 2002 and 2007, were rated in implementation status reports (ISRs) on their achievement of development objectives (DOs) and implementation progress (IP). Seventy-seven projects out of 94 (82 percent) were rated satisfactory for DOs, and 74 (79 percent) projects

Table 4.12: **World Bank Pension-Related Lending Classified by Pillar, Fiscal Years 2002–07**

Type of pension project	Number of loans	Total Bank lending with pension component (US$ millions)	Value of pension component (US$ millions)	Pension-related lending (as % of total lending)
Loans associated with a single pillar	46	4,945	488	24.0
First pillar	37	3,884	440	21.6
Second pillar	4	323	13	0.6
Third pillar	5	739	36	1.8
Loans associated with more than one pillar	60	5,988	1,130	55.5
First and second pillars	13	1,635	146	7.2
First and third pillars	10	493	65	3.2
Second and third pillars	7	1,003	94	4.6
All three pillars	30	2,858	824	40.5
Loans not associated with any pillar	6	2,275	419	20.6
Total	112	13,209	2,037	100.0

Source: Authors' calculations, based on the Business Warehouse data and World Bank documents.
Note: Because of rounding, totals may deviate slightly from the sum of the parts.

Table 4.13: World Bank Pension-Related Lending Classified by Pillar, Fiscal Years 1984–2001

Type of pension project	Number of loans	Total Bank lending with pension component (US$ millions)	Value of pension component (US$ millions)	Pension-related lending (as % of total lending)
Loans associated with a single pillar	92	15,926	2,545	46.4
First pillar	71	11,135	2,260	41.2
Second pillar	7	263	127	2.3
Third pillar	14	4,528	158	2.9
Loans associated with more than one pillar	57	12,263	2,936	53.6
First and second pillars	15	3,142	1,358	24.8
First and third pillars	29	7,982	1,486	27.1
Second and third pillars	0	0	0	0.0
All three pillars	13	1,139	93	1.7
Loans not associated with any pillar	5	1,692	1	0.0
Total	154	29,881	5,482	100.0

Source: Authors' calculations, based on the Business Warehouse data and World Bank documents.
Note: Because of rounding, totals may deviate slightly from the sum of the parts.

FIGURE 4.12: FREQUENCY OF PENSION-RELATED ACTIVITIES BY TYPE OF INTERVENTION, FISCAL YEARS 1984–2007

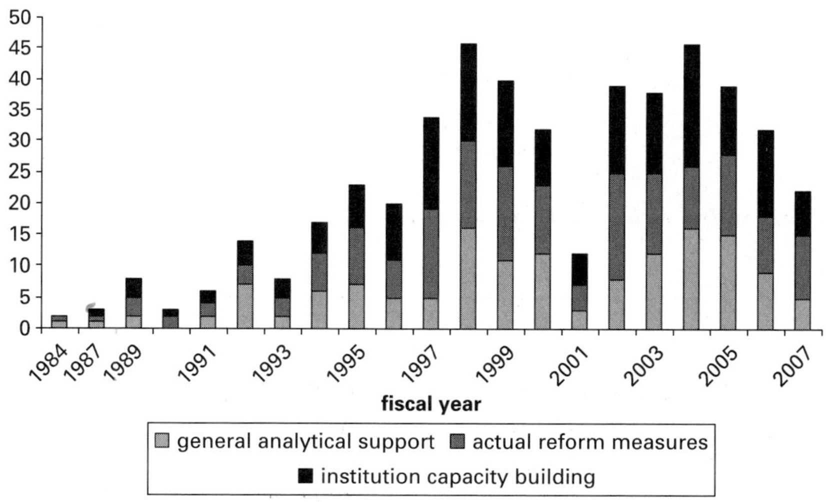

Source: Authors' calculations, based on the Business Warehouse data and World Bank documents.

were rated satisfactory for IP (figure 4.13). Only two projects were rated marginally unsatisfactory for both DOs and IP, whereas two were rated unsatisfactory for DOs and four were rated unsatisfactory for development outcome.

During the earlier period (1984–2001), 143 out of 154 loans and credits related to pension issues were rated in the project status report (PSR). Of the 143, 113 (79 percent) were rated satisfactory for DOs and 110 (77 percent) were rated satisfactory for IP (figure 4.14). Eighteen were rated as highly satisfactory for development outcome (13 percent) and 17 were rated as highly satisfactory for IP (12 percent). Only 8 percent (11 projects) were rated unsatisfactory for DOs and 10 percent (16 projects) were rated unsatisfactory for IP.

FIGURE 4.13: **PENSION PROJECT QUALITY RATINGS FROM IMPLEMENTATION STATUS REPORTS, FISCAL YEARS 2002–07**

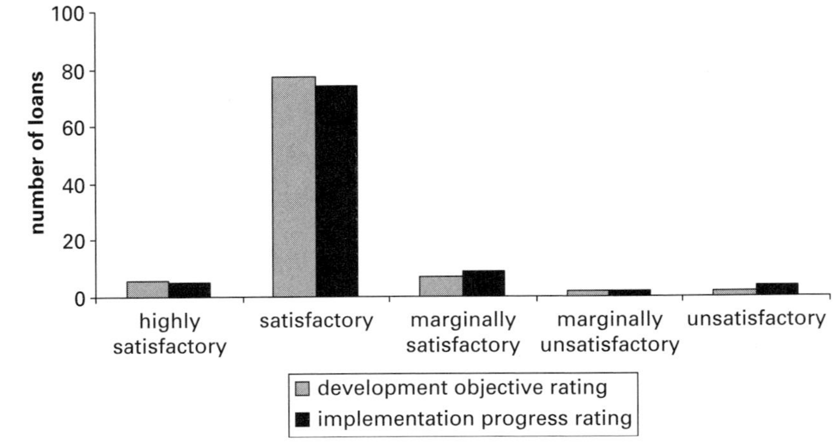

Source: Authors' calculations, based on the Business Warehouse data and World Bank documents.

FIGURE 4.14: **PENSION PROJECT QUALITY RATINGS FROM PROJECT STATUS REPORTS, FISCAL YEARS 2002–07**

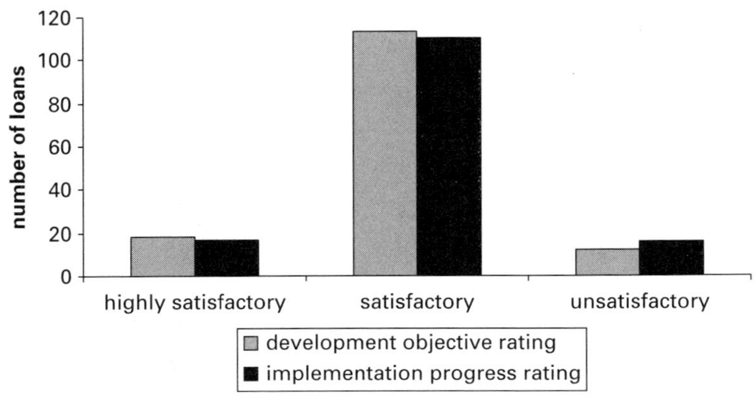

Source: Authors' calculations, based on the Business Warehouse data and World Bank documents.

Implementation Completion Report Review. ICRs were available for only 21 of the 112 loans and credits in the recent period at the time of the review. The pension component was rated satisfactory by all the ICRs. Only one ICR stated that the sustainability of the pension reform effort was in doubt because of several measures taken after the closing of the operation.[2] The overall outcome ratings for these 21 projects are as follows: 18 projects (86 percent) were rated satisfactory, 2 projects marginally satisfactory (10 percent), and 1 project highly satisfactory. The sustainability rating was "highly likely" for six (29 percent) and "likely" for the rest. Institutional development impact was evaluated as "substantial" for all projects except two, which were evaluated as having "modest" institutional development impact.

Analytical and Advisory Work and Research-Related Pensions

In addition to its lending activities, the World Bank undertakes a variety of AAA work that has a direct influence on pension reforms in client countries. The analytical work that is directly related to client requests or specific projects is coded as economic and sector work. The inventory of ESW can be identified through a review of projects maintained in the Bank's Business Warehouse. However, unlike lending, the documentation for this work is less structured and therefore less amenable to a comprehensive review. In addition to ESW, there is a range of other analytical and research products that provide general analysis or specific policy advice on pension issues. The IEG review developed a database of this body of work, which was based on more than 1,000 documents available in the Bank's ImageBank document system.

An attempt was made to replicate this data set for the subsequent period through the end of fiscal year 2007. Although it is possible to identify the ESW projects through the BW, the relevant documents are in some cases not readily available for review. As in the IEG review, this effort was supplemented with a search for other relevant work using the key word *pensions* in the ImageBank system. This process yielded several hundred additional documents that were reviewed for a significant pension element. A substantial portion of the large inventory of potential pension-related AAA work was obtainable through the ImageBank system. Because there was no indication of any pattern of documents that were unavailable, this sample was assumed to be representative and was used to represent the AAA work in the ensuing period on a comparable basis to the earlier IEG review.

AAA and research work for fiscal years 2004 to 2007 for which the documents were readily accessible in ImageBank included 146 reports. Of these reports, 126 focus on specific countries and the rest deal with general or regional pension reform issues. The IEG review of the earlier period included 335 reports, of which 237 were country specific; the rest were either regional or thematic. Review of the documents from the sample of work in the latest period indicates that they addressed pension issues in 60 countries. Of those 60 countries, 9 account for about one-third of the studies that focus on specific countries. The most studies concerning pensions were directed toward Chile (nine reports), followed by China, Mexico, and Serbia with five reports each. Colombia, Peru, Poland, and Ukraine, have four reports each. Some of the work focused exclusively on pensions and social security systems, whereas pension issues were covered in other, more comprehensive reports focusing on social protection policy, fiscal sustainability, economic growth and poverty alleviation, public governance and public expenditure, and labor reform.

Regional Distribution. World Bank analytical and research work on pensions mirrors the high level of lending in the Europe and Central Asia and Latin America and Caribbean Regions (figure 4.15). They are the only two regions that have undertaken multipillar pension reforms. They also have the most studies, including technical advice on pension reform. The ECA Region has the most analytical products (34 percent of all the work) in this period, followed by the LAC Region (30 percent). Twenty-one countries in the ECA Region and 13 countries in the LAC Region were covered. There was also a considerable volume of work undertaken in the MENA Region (11 percent of the pension analytical work); this finding is notably out of proportion to the lending levels for fiscal years 2004 to 2007. The MENA sample that addresses pension issues in nine countries includes Afghanistan, Djibouti, the Arab Republic of Egypt, Iran, Iraq, and Jordan. The MENA Region has therefore made a strong effort to engage in the pension reform policy dialogue in the regions, which may lead to increased lending in the future. The EAP Region has also undertaken a level of analytical work. The region had no pension-related lending during the period.

Figure 4.16 represents the distribution of analytical products according to region and fiscal year. World Bank analytical work reached a high in fiscal years 2006 and 2007 (42 studies in each year). The increase in the number of

FIGURE 4.15: SHARE OF ANALYTICAL PRODUCTS DEALING WITH PENSIONS BY REGION, FISCAL YEARS 2004–07

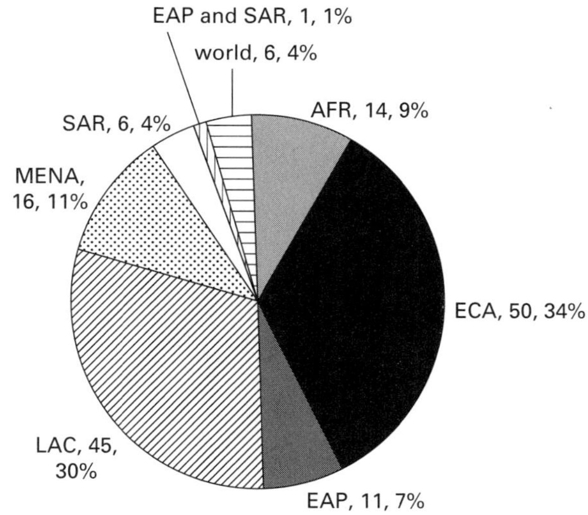

Source: Authors' calculations, based on the Business Warehouse data and World Bank documents.
Note: AFR = Africa; EAP = East Asia and the Pacific; ECA = Europe and Central Asia; LAC = Latin America and the Caribbean; MENA = Middle East and North Africa; SAR = South Asia Region. Figure shows number and share of total analytical products. The total number of products is 146.

FIGURE 4.16: **NUMBER OF ANALYTICAL PRODUCTS DEALING WITH PENSIONS BY REGION, FISCAL YEARS 2004–07**

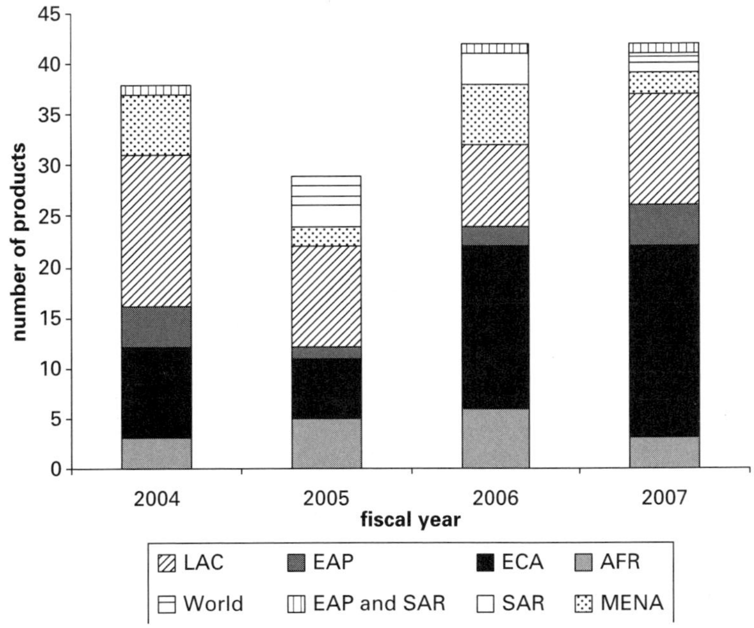

Source: Authors' calculations, based on the Business Warehouse data and World Bank documents.
Note: AFR = Africa; EAP = East Asia and the Pacific; ECA = Europe and Central Asia; LAC = Latin America and the Caribbean; MENA = Middle East and North Africa; SAR = South Asia Region.

studies on the ECA Region in those years was the main reason. This total, however, includes several studies commissioned in conjunction with the IEG review.

Distribution by Type of Product. Analytical work on pensions takes many different forms. Figure 4.17 provides a snapshot of the share of different types of analytical products that dealt with pension issues in 2004 to 2007. The largest category is working papers, with 28 percent, followed by sector reports and economic reports with 25 percent each. If combined with policy research working papers and World Bank Institute working papers, the share of working papers in pension analytical work increases to 40 percent.

Diversity of Pension Reform Issues in Bank Analytical work. World Bank AAA for fiscal years 2004 to 2007 includes analysis of specific issues pertaining to pensions, descriptions of pension systems, and advice on improving the functioning and sustainability of pension systems and reform options. Of the 146 documents mentioned, 51 (35 percent) specifically focus on pensions and social security systems. The majority of the remaining studies concern poverty reduction, public expenditure and institutional reviews, financial systems development and reform studies,

FIGURE 4.17: **TYPES OF PENSION-RELATED ECONOMIC SECTOR WORK, FISCAL YEARS 2004–07**

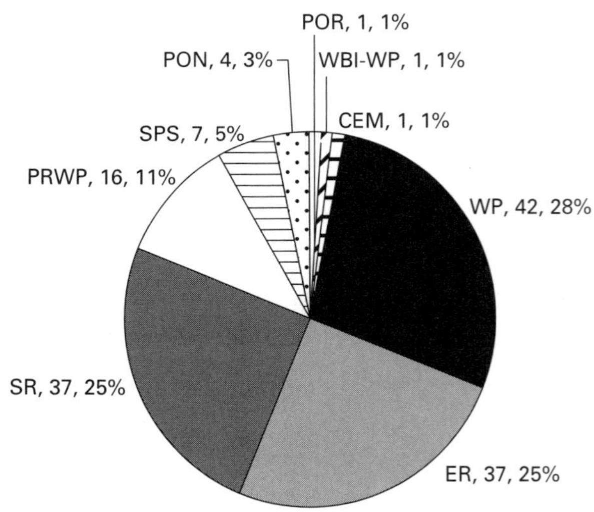

Source: Authors' calculations, based on the Business Warehouse data and World Bank documents.
Note: CEM = Country Economic Memorandum; ER = economic report; PON = Policy Note; POR = poverty assessment; PRWP = Policy Research Working Paper; SPS = other social protection study; SR = sector report; WBI-WP = World Bank Institute working paper; WP = working paper. Figure shows number and share of pension-related documents. The total number of documents is 146.

corporate governance country assessments, and other issues. These reports incorporate analyses of pensions and are therefore included.

Figure 4.18 shows the frequency of pension topics in World Bank analytical support for fiscal years 2004 to 2007. The most frequent topics include fiscal sustainability; targeting, coverage, and eligibility of pension systems; old-age income; and poverty. Those issues are covered by 50 to 60 percent of all pension-related AAA work. Because one of the purposes of pension policy reforms is poverty reduction among the elderly and improved consumption smoothing for old age, there is considerable overlap with nearly all analytical work. The gender dimension of poverty or social security is not an issue commonly dealt with in Bank AAA (7 percent) on pensions.

Income Level and Lending Category. IBRD countries were the subject of 64 percent of the analytical work reviewed, whereas IDA countries accounted for 19 percent, with 8 percent directed to IDA countries and HIPC (figure 4.19). Blend countries and those "not assigned" share the rest of the analytical work, with 10 percent and 7 percent, respectively. The distribution of analytical work in relation to the income level of its focus is similar to that of lending, with the largest share, 42 percent, addressing lower-middle-income countries and a similar proportion, 40 percent, directed to upper-middle-income countries (figure 4.20).

The Bank's Pension Primer Series. The Bank's Social Protection Unit has also produced policy advice and research work essential for countries that are establishing or reforming a pension system. This information is maintained in the Pension Primer Series, which is available in hard copy and through the Bank's Pensions Web site. This series includes Primer Notes that provide short summaries of key topics and Primer Papers that provide a more in-depth treatment of a broader range of relevant issues.

At the end of fiscal year 2007, the series now contained 16 Primer Notes and 47 Primer Papers; 5 of the Primer Notes and 16 of the Primer Papers have been added to the series since the beginning of fiscal year 2002. The new Primer Notes and Primer Papers address a range of emerging issues,

FIGURE 4.19: ANALYTICAL PRODUCTS BY LENDING CATEGORY, FISCAL YEARS 2004–07

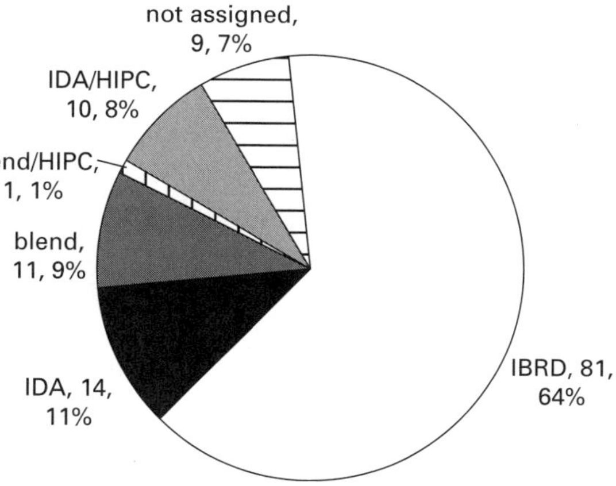

Source: Authors' calculations, based on the Business Warehouse data and World Bank documents.
Note: HIPC = heavily indebted poor countries; IBRD = International Bank for Reconstruction and Development; IDA = International Development Association. Figure shows number and share of total analytical products. The total number of products is 126.

FIGURE 4.18: PENSION-RELATED TOPICS ADDRESSED IN WORLD BANK ANALYTICAL WORK, FISCAL YEARS 2004–07

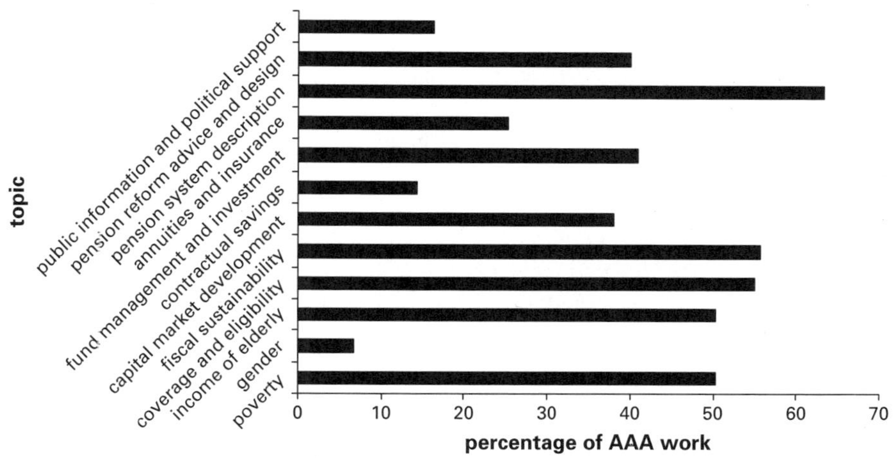

Source: Authors' calculations, based on the Business Warehouse data and World Bank documents.

FIGURE 4.20: **ANALYTICAL PRODUCTS BY INCOME LEVEL, FISCAL YEARS 2004–07**

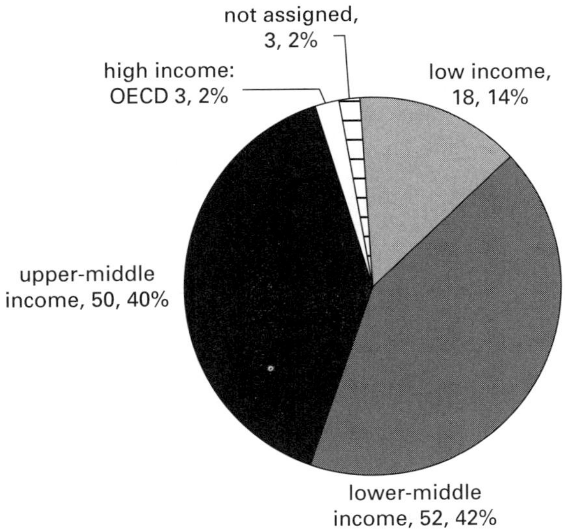

Source: Authors' calculations, based on the Business Warehouse data and World Bank documents.
Note: OECD = Organisation for Economic Co-operation and Development. Figure shows number and share of total analytical products. The total number of products is 126.

including those related to notional defined-contribution systems, pensions for veterans, reform of civil service pensions, life-course planning and financial literacy, measurement of pension debt, and management of public pension reserves. In addition, the Primer Notes and Primer Papers provide in-depth case study reviews of a broad range of pension reforms throughout the world.

Supplementing the Pension Primer Series are publications within the Bank's Social Protection Discussion Paper Series. In addition to the Primer Papers that are also included in this series, 23 pension-related papers are included, 15 of which have been added since 2002. The Bank's Policy Research Working Paper Series also contains a number of pension-related papers.

Major Publications on Pensions. In addition to the analytical products, research reports, and working papers, the Bank published 13 books during fiscal years 2002 to 2007. These books were published by the social protection sector staff and the private and financial sector development staff. They represent an important and highly visible element of the Bank's pension-related work. Some of these publications are compilations of papers that provided the basis for major conferences sponsored by the Bank. Others are major country-specific work on topics such as the development of annuity systems or the evaluation of the performance of funded pension systems in specific countries. Another major publication is a book developed by a cross-sectoral team of Bank staff members working on pensions. Published in mid 2005, it provides an overview of the Bank's current policy framework on pension systems and reform and reviews the key issues that will guide the work going forward. A listing and short summary of these publications are contained in annex 4.C.

Results of the Bank's Pension Work

The Bank's typical engagement in pension reforms has been characterized by developing the policy and analytical capacity of staff members engaged in the reform effort through the provision of background materials, training, and analytical tools, followed by participation and support for a diagnostic study to identify key problems and reform options. Because of the highly sensitive nature of the political process associated with a reform, Bank lending has typically not been directly involved in the reform process, although in some cases follow-up investment lending has supported some of the capacity building required for reform implementation.

The nature of this policy-oriented engagement and the preponderance of policy and adjustment lending that is linked to the commitment to undertake a reform rather than the results achieved by the reform make it very challenging to explicitly link specific results with the Bank's work. In addition, many results of the Bank's efforts in this area are exerted rather indirectly, through increased understanding and acceptance of the issues and options for pension reform derived from the considerable body of policy analysis and research and the increased use of the multipillar policy framework.

Because the key outcomes for pension systems are significantly intertwined in a wide range of other macroeconomic and developmental factors, the attribution process becomes even more problematic for pensions. Key outcomes, such as improvements in the fiscal sustainability of systems or the contribution of pension systems to the development of financial systems and overall capacity for growth, are virtually impossible to distinguish from the many other factors that affect the results. Moreover, the discrete effects of a pension reform that could possibly be directly measured, such as improvements in the economic status or poverty rates of the elderly or the long-term fiscal effects of a reform, are not realized until many years later, making outcomes virtually impossible to measure in a timely or accurate manner.

Therefore, one of the most significant challenges facing the Bank in relation to its pension work is to establish a framework that can overcome these formidable limitations by considering and measuring the projected and actual results of its work in this area. Developing a reasonable and measurable set of indicators to monitor and evaluate the intended outcomes and results of the Bank's continuing engagement on pension issues will need to be a primary focus for the Bank if it is to effectively incorporate pension work into the results-based framework. However, at present, although some indicative information of results can be derived from the review of recently completed lending operations, outcomes are likely best considered from a broader policy perspective and in the context of the discussion of the experience of several countries in which the Bank has been significantly involved in the pension reform process.

Outcomes from Recent Operations. In a review of the implementation completion reports from pension-related lending operations that were completed during fiscal years 2002 to 2006, the following types of results were reported:

- Thirty-three pension projects were completed in 22 countries. Twelve of these countries indicated improvement in their implicit pension debt; 13 have increased their financial sustainability through improvements in the ratio of the net present value of financing flows, and 7 have added pillars to their public pension systems.
- Seventeen of the projects focused on institutional strengthening either by establishing new institutions or by building capacity in existing ones. Twelve of these operations supported the establishment, restructuring, or modernization of institutions responsible for social security and pensions to complement ongoing reform efforts, increase operational efficiency, or improve governance and supervision. Eight of the projects provided training programs to staff members of various ministries and institutions through seminars and workshops, and three provided training related to pension system development and modeling and information management.
- Nineteen projects supported changes in the legal framework through new legislation or a decree. New legislation—as well as amendments to the existing legal framework—mainly aimed to reform or consolidate existing pension systems, regulate the additional pillars, or establish transparent and financially viable indexation rules to contribute to fiscal sustainability. Five projects financed technical assistance that entailed advisory services on proposed pension reforms and outlined reform implementation steps. Some included design of processes for the restructuring of the pension system or preparation of the draft legal framework for the introduction of new pillars. Seven projects produced studies, strategic planning materials, and statistical and actuarial reports reviewing various aspects of pension reform.
- Ten projects enhanced the centralized record-keeping merger of decentralized pension funds into a national system, the installation of new management information systems, the compilation of databases, or the upgrading of information technology systems. Five contributed to increasing timeliness or accuracy of benefit determinations by developing single registry systems for pension funds and establishing mechanisms to incorporate information about beneficiaries, and five supported the design and implementation of an automated administrative system.

THE EXPERIENCE OF THREE ILLUSTRATIVE COUNTRIES' PENSION REFORMS

Understanding the nature of the outcomes of the Bank's engagement with clients on pensions is best illustrated through some important country cases.

A typical pension reform engagement by the Bank is triggered by major problems with the financial sustainability of a country's pension system that lead to lending for general budget support. This lending is closely followed by some combination of technical assistance lending and advisory work by the Bank to help improve the capacity within the country to evaluate the pension system and develop feasible reform options. The analytical work is then used to support an internal reform process that often has no direct Bank involvement or lending because of political sensitivities and other related factors. To support the transition following reform, additional lending often takes place in the form of policy and adjustment operations or through investment loans that support implementation. In some cases, the reform is a multistage process in which the initial reform is followed by further Bank policy work that leads to extensions or refinements of the reformed system.

Case Study 1: Brazil

The Bank's recent engagement in the pension reform in Brazil over the past decade provides a good example of this process and the kinds of outcomes that pension reform has achieved. In 1988, amendments to Brazil's constitution created large new pension entitlements for broad groups of the population. Within a decade, it had become apparent that the anticipated financing would be insufficient to support the entitlements, and the pension system had become a major contributor to large fiscal deficits that had created a macroeconomic crisis. A reform was undertaken to adjust the benefit formulas and retirement ages and to constrain some of the special pension regimes to lay the foundations for a broader reform effort in 1998. The Bank supported this reform through a major policy lending operation in 1998.

Building on this initial engagement, the Bank provided two technical assistance loans in 1999 to strengthen the administration of pensions at the state and municipal level. It also undertook a major ESW project to provide an overall evaluation of the pension systems and the analytical basis for further reforms. Those measures helped support a second stage of reform in 1999 in which benefits were adjusted in a major part of the pension system to provide a more direct link to contributions. The Bank's analytical work contributed to the analysis of options and provided the analytical tools to reliably project the fiscal effects of the reform. The 1999 reforms resulted in substantial savings, which are projected to be as great as 6.5 percent of gross domestic product (GDP) by 2050 (see table 4.14).

The pension reform process continued in the ensuing years with active World Bank involvement. In 2003, a major reform of civil servant pensions was undertaken, for which the Bank continued to provide analysis and policy advice. The Bank continued to provide support for the evaluation of outcomes of this reform, which is projected to result in an additional 3.3 percent of GDP reduction in the deficits of the pension system by 2050 (see table 4.15).

The Bank's engagement continued after the 2003 reforms with a major development policy loan linked to the pension reform process and approved in late 2005. Another major ESW effort to define further reform options and a technical assistance loan was completed in fiscal year 2007. With significant support from the Bank, the pension reform effort has now extended to the subnational level in Brazil with direct policy work and the consideration of future lending at the state level. Overall, the Bank has provided significant lending and policy development support and continues to perform that role today. This support has been an integral part of a sequence of major reforms that have significantly improved the long-term fiscal sustainability of the pension systems in the country.

Table 4.14: Projected Savings from 1998–99 Brazil Pension Reforms

Year	2004	2010	2020	2030	2040	2050
Savings (% of GDP)	−0.6	0.1	2.0	4.3	5.9	6.5

Source: Authors' calculations, based on the Business Warehouse data and World Bank documents.

Table 4.15: Projected Savings from 2003 Brazil Pension Reforms

Year	2004	2010	2020	2030	2040	2050
Savings (% of GDP)	0.3	0.9	1.3	1.6	2.4	3.3

Source: World Bank staff analysis contained in loan and AAA documents.

Case Study 2: Turkey

The Turkish government passed a significant pension reform in 1999 that instituted a minimum retirement age for all Turkish workers. However, given the previous lack of a minimum age and the prevalence of very early retirement in Turkey, the minimum age was phased in very slowly. It began with age 38 for women and age 43 for men for the first cohorts retiring under the new law, and it culminated with age 58 for women and age 60 for men, effective only for those entering the labor force after the new law took effect. The law also changed the benefit structure for private sector workers and the self-employed and raised the contribution ceiling applicable to private sector workers. The Emergency Reform Loan the Bank provided the government in 1999 supported these changes in the pension system, but a Country Economic Memorandum produced shortly after the reform suggested that the reforms, while significant, were insufficient to lead to fiscal sustainability. The government agreed with the assessment but felt that there were political constraints to making additional short-term changes.

By 2002, the initial revenue increase, which came from the rise in the contribution ceiling, had leveled off, and the pension system again began running deficits. At this point, the Bank again began working with the government on policy reforms that would move the system to fiscal sustainability. The proposed reforms maintained a single public pillar and included the following:

1. A long-term rise in the retirement age from 58 for women and 60 for men to 65 for both men and women
2. A lowering and flattening of the accrual rate so that the pension system would no longer reward the first 10 years of contribution at a much higher rate than later years and thus would provide incentives for shorter working careers
3. A move away from revaluing wages used for pension calculation by growth in nominal GDP

4. Most importantly, a unification of the pension system for all Turkish workers, which substantially reduced the indexation after retirement for civil servants.

These reforms were passed in May 2006, but they were then rejected by the Constitutional Court in December 2006. The government has now presented a variant of the 2006 law to the parliament, but it maintains most of the fiscal savings of the original law. The passage of the May 2006 law was supported by the Programmatic Public Sector Development Policy Loan, and the implementation was to be supported by a second development policy loan in the same series. The restructuring of the law has been supported both by preparation work on this second development policy loan and by formal technical assistance provided to the Turkish government.

The savings in the pension system from undertaking these reforms can be measured in two ways: by the projected drop in the fiscal deficit and by the drop in pension system liabilities. The benefits can be seen in figures 4.21 and 4.22. The pension system reaches fiscal sustainability in the long term, with sustainability defined as a deficit less than 1 percent of GDP. Further increases in the retirement age that keep pace with higher life expectancies would be completely sufficient to reduce the deficit further, if required. It will take a long time for the reform to reach sustainability because current workers' rights have been grandfathered. With regard to implicit pension liabilities, given that the future rights of current workers are being accrued under the new system, there will be an immediate drop of almost 25 percent in the implicit pension debt, to be followed by a

FIGURE 4.21: PENSION SYSTEM LONG-TERM SUSTAINABILITY IN TURKEY

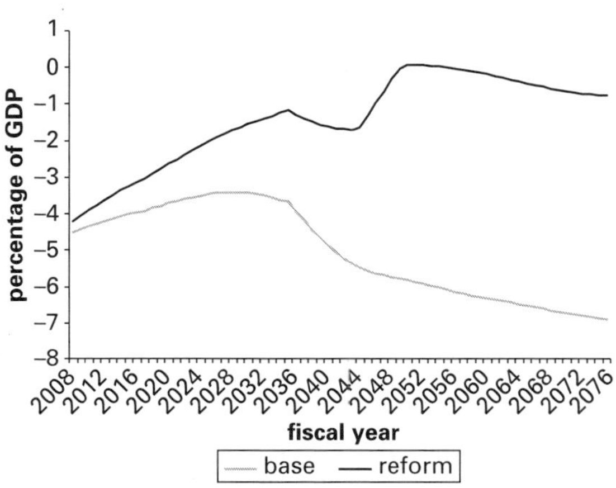

Source: World Bank staff analysis contained in loan and AAA documents.

FIGURE 4.22: INITIAL AND LONG-TERM DECLINE OF IMPLICIT PENSION DEBT IN TURKEY

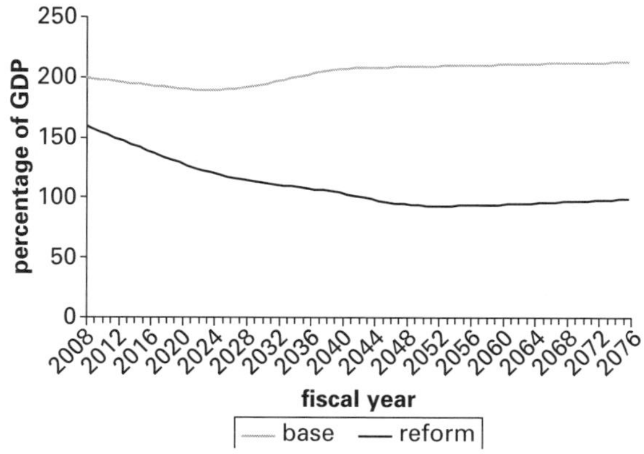

Source: World Bank staff analysis contained in loan and AAA documents.

longer-term drop of more than 50 percent as the new retirement ages become applicable.

Case Study 3: Slovak Republic

The Slovak Republic undertook an ambitious pension reform agenda, which was supported by the World Bank Social Benefits Reform Administration Loan. In 2003, a comprehensive reform of the public pay-as-you-go pillar was enacted. Implementation began in January 2004. The pension system was transformed from a highly redistributive, conventional, defined-benefit system into a point system in which contributions were tightly linked to benefits and all social assistance components were consolidated into a separate social assistance benefit. This reform was followed by legislation enacting a second pillar beginning in January 2005. Current workers were given a choice of remaining with their public pension system only or of splitting their contribution between the public system and their own private accounts. New workers were automatically enrolled in the split-contribution system.

Figure 4.23 shows the change in the deficit of the pension system following the reform. In the absence of reform, the deficit would have peaked at over 10 percent of GDP, with a long-run deficit of about 8 percent of GDP. The parametric reform of the first pillar, by itself, halved the projected deficits, both at the peak and in the long term. The introduction of a second pillar initially raises the deficit by as much as 1 percent of GDP, but it ultimately lowers the deficit to less than half of what the parametric reform alone could achieve, thus resulting in a reduction of more than

FIGURE 4.23: **PENSION DEFICITS WITH AND WITHOUT REFORM IN THE SLOVAK REPUBLIC**

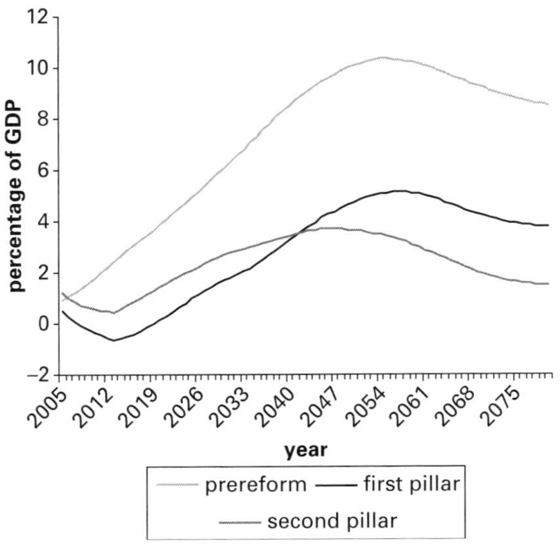

Source: World Bank staff analysis contained in loan and AAA documents.

75 percent of the deficit. The remaining deficit is still close to 2 percent of GDP even in the long run, which is not financially sustainable. However, small parametric changes, such as a rise in the long-run retirement age from the legislated age of 62 for men and women, and a move to inflation indexation from the current practice of indexing to 50 percent of nominal wage growth and 50 percent of inflation would be sufficient to make the system fiscally sustainable in the long run. Both long-run changes are in line with international best practices and are being considered by the government as future changes.

Policy makers understand that pension reform is typically extremely difficult and politically sensitive. Governments often find it difficult to move to a fiscally sustainable position with parameters at international best-practice levels in one pass, particularly if the current system deviates significantly from the optimal. Even when the government agrees in principle on the measures that need to be taken, the implementation of reform still faces political constraints and requires settling time before the next phase of the reform can be legislated. The realization of results from reforms is correspondingly slowed.

CONCLUSIONS AND STRATEGIES FOR THE FUTURE

The Bank's approach to work on pensions and the associated strategy has evolved considerably since the inception of this work in the mid 1980s. The evolution of the Bank's work is driven by the experience and lessons learned through diverse country engagements and by considerable research and policy analysis undertaken over this period on both a cross-country and an individual country basis. The Bank has made a concerted effort to coordinate its approach at a country level and to leverage its strengths with those of other development partners. The 2001 *Social Protection Sector Strategy* (World Bank 2001) has been supplemented by the framework presented in the report *Old-Age Income Support in the 21st Century* (Holzmann and Hinz with others 2005).[3] The Bank's thinking about pensions and old-age income security has moved in parallel with the development of the Social Risk Management framework developed in the 2001 strategy. The strategy provides the conceptual underpinnings for dealing with the diverse risks to which individuals and households are exposed and with asymmetric information and malfunctioning or nonexistent markets.

The approach taken in the 2001 strategy is differentiated according to country characteristics and depends on assessments of prospective vulnerability of the elderly population in relation to other vulnerable groups. The Social Risk Management framework in the strategy spells out how public policies can create an enabling environment in which communities, businesses, and individuals can cope, mitigate, or prevent the risks that increase a population's vulnerability to poverty. It supports flexible multipillar pension reform while ensuring adequate retirement income for informal sector workers and the lifetime poor. Moreover, it has weighed the fiscal resources and institutional capacity necessary to provide additional support for vulnerable populations.

Since 1984, the World Bank has made 266 loans that have had components that were directed to the establishment or reform of a pension system. The aggregate value of the elements of these loans that can be attributed to pension-related projects was more than US$7.5 billion and represents about 1.5 percent of total World Bank lending during this period.

The lending for pensions began slowly during the 1980s and then exhibited two major peaks of activity during which pension lending represented about 5 to 7 percent of overall Bank lending from 1995 to 2001 and 3 to 5 percent of lending from 2004 to 2005. Lending for pensions can be viewed as essentially divided into three distinct periods. In the Bank's engagement on pensions from 1984 through 1995, lending for pensions was in the early stages of development and acceptance by clients. This period was characterized largely by policy development within the Bank and advisory work with clients. By the mid 1990s, the Bank had formulated an approach to pensions and developed an internal capacity and expertise. This achievement coincided with a rapid spike in demand as the countries of Central and Eastern Europe faced immediate fiscal crises during the early years of the transition. These fiscal crises involved unfunded and unsustainable liabilities from their inherited pension systems and rapidly aging populations.

This situation led to considerable lending activity through the inclusion of pension reforms in a number of the large policy and adjustment lending operations during this period. At the same time, many Latin American systems faced similar crises as they began to mature and their unsustainable liabilities began to come due. This fiscal stress was exacerbated by the financial crisis of the late 1990s and led to the Bank's period of peak lending, which was concentrated in the LAC and ECA Regions, as well as in East Asia. Following this period, pension work became more diverse as it evolved to address implementation issues in the countries that had enacted reforms and the initiation of policy development and reform in other regions. This latest period has been characterized by more geographical dispersion of the work and a greater focus on investment lending and capacity building. During fiscal years 2002 to 2007, pension lending remained at roughly the long-term average of about 1.5 percent of overall Bank lending.

Consistent with the characteristics described here, over the several decades in which the Bank has been engaged in pension work the majority of lending has been to middle-income and IBRD countries. Pension lending continues primarily as components of much larger policy loans. In recent years, the level of investment lending for pensions has been increasing. Pension-related work has been broadly distributed among the sectors, with most of the lending mapped to the Social Protection, Economic Policy, and Financial and Private Sector Development Sector Boards, which reflects the cross-sector nature of pension issues. These patterns are likely to continue in the near future, although pension work in other regions is gradually evolving.

Since the mid 1980s, the Bank has undertaken hundreds of AAA related to pensions. They represent an important contribution to the global knowledge base on pension reform and have been the foundation for much of the Bank's work in this area. The Bank continues to play a key leadership role in the development of pension policy and contributes to global knowledge through the publication of its research work and the provision of specific analytical work that has guided pension reform efforts in many countries. In many respects, the Bank's research, policy development, and analysis of reform options in specific countries represent its most significant contribution to pension reforms during the period. The AAA address many key issues in the development of social protections systems, the role of pensions in economic and fiscal stability, and the many issues related to the development and operation of financial services and markets that are associated with the development of funded pension systems.

Future Activities

The nature of the Bank's engagement on pension issues continues to evolve as pension work moves beyond the initial focus on unsustainable systems in several regions toward supporting the establishment of multipillar systems in a much wider range of settings. In considering the priorities and challenges of this expansion, the Bank's approach to pensions and its assessment of future directions were recently discussed with the Bank's Board of Directors. This discussion focused on the following issues:

- *The issue of fiscal affordability and sustainability remains of primary importance for the Bank and client countries.* Civil service pension schemes often pose important and specific challenges for ensuring fiscal sustainability while maintaining strong incentives to employ and retain public servants. Additional reform measures are needed in many client countries where employment in the civil service and in parastatal authorities has been a significant proportion of the formal labor force.[4] A medium- and longer-term fiscal framework that recognizes the implicit pension liabilities associated with civil service and other mandatory pension schemes is an important ingredient for moving forward with a pension reform program that is consistent with a balanced fiscal position. Where reforms have included the introduction of a privately managed, funded pillar, returns have been higher than the implicit returns in existing pay-as-you-go schemes.[5]
- *The Bank has partnered with academics and practitioners to develop innovative ways to reform and operate a first pillar in the form of nonfinancial defined-contribution schemes.*[6] This design offers a promising alternative approach to parametric pension reforms. It substantially improves the relationship between contributions and benefits while avoiding the need for financing the transition costs associated with moving from unfunded to funded schemes that arise when the contributions of younger workers are directed toward funded accounts while the benefits

accrued by retirees still need to be paid. This innovation comes at a time when many developing countries are wondering how to relieve the demographic and economic pressures on their pension systems, while avoiding the creation of additional burdens for future workers.

- *The measurement of poverty prevalence, trends, and vulnerability among the elderly is an important element for determining pension policies and instruments and a primary means of benchmarking performance.* Informal support systems have been breaking down and cannot meet the challenge of poverty among the elderly in many developing countries. In some countries, the burden on the elderly has risen enormously as a result of rural-to-urban migration, the dissolution of traditional extended family structures, and mortality among working-age adults resulting from the HIV/AIDS pandemic. Moreover, traditional family support systems, while reasonably reliable during normal times, can break down when families are faced with the covariate shocks experienced in developing countries. Country-level evaluations of the prevalence of poverty and vulnerability among the elderly are needed to help measure the potential effect of different pension policies and instruments. Focused poverty assessments will therefore be an essential part of the Bank's work in pension reform going forward.
- *The Bank and client countries have also increasingly recognized the effect of the pension governance framework on sustainability and benefit adequacy.* Governance not only affects the returns on reserves of pension schemes; it can also affect the size of real and contingent fiscal liabilities, adequate and efficient provision of benefits, and—most significantly—public credibility. The latter is important for achieving compliance and meaningful coverage for mandatory schemes, as well as voluntary participation in occupational and individual savings schemes. More work is needed to develop a methodology for a baseline assessment of the governance of publicly managed pension schemes, to create a toolkit of best practices for such governance, and to provide guidance on reform measures for achieving those best practices. Similarly, principles are needed for more effective pension regulation. Financial markets need adequate supervision to prevent possible fraud or excessive risk taking—a need that is heightened in mandatory schemes and those with the provision of public guarantees. Pension administration systems are a necessary condition for most pension reform efforts, so increasing attention has been given to collection, reconciliation, benefit payments, and information technology systems when providing advice on pension reforms.
- *The effect of management and administrative costs on sustainability and benefit adequacy has also been recognized as being critical to the performance of pension systems.* Recognizing that many public and privately managed mandatory pension schemes have relatively high management and administrative costs, a number of countries are reviewing their design and supervision to strengthen administration and improve efficiency and risk management. Greater attention is needed by the Bank and its counterparts in designing competitively managed schemes that reduce costs while reasonably managing risks. Further work on approaches appropriate to the need of small states is required to address the large economies of scale and therefore high costs of administration, as well as the investment risks arising from volatility.
- *The level of coverage of mandatory and voluntary pension schemes in many settings must be expanded to achieve overall pension adequacy so that the vast majority of the population receives benefits sufficient to prevent old-age poverty and has a reliable means to smooth lifetime consumption.* Even countries that have introduced reforms since the 1980s are believed to have had limited success in expanding coverage of the labor force under formal pension schemes. More analysis is needed of poverty mitigation provided by informal support and risk management systems and options for strengthening such systems. The Bank is working to identify the best-practice characteristics of voluntary savings schemes to develop policy options that better use informal channels to mobilize savings. The Social Protection Anchor has placed substantial importance on developing further guidance on mechanisms for increasing coverage and, with support solicited from other development partners, aims to provide guidance to staff members and country policy makers.
- *Additional efforts are needed by the Bank to help developing countries improve the performance of funded pension pillars, including remedying weaknesses in the financial sector that have constrained reform efforts.* The mixed savings and capital market effects of pension reforms suggest additional efforts by the Bank to assist developing countries in their attempts to improve the structure and performance of funded pension pillars, through Financial Sector Assessment Programs and focused sector work. Recent and more focused Financial Sector Assessment Programs and AAA made on request have involved an in-depth review of the performance of recently established second and third pillars and the broader relationship between pension reform and financial market development.

Strategies

The following strategies were considered in formulating the Bank's approach to future pension-related work:

- *The Bank recognizes that design options suitable to the enabling environment and inherited systems may be limited in many, particularly low-income, countries.* The Bank is therefore developing diagnostic criteria for assessing the conduciveness of country conditions to funded pension schemes, including second-pillar reforms. These criteria include macroeconomic and fiscal conditions, the capacity and oversight of financial markets, systems for data management and disclosure, and other systems of oversight to ensure consumer protection and the accountability of participating public and private institutions not regulated under financial markets. Greater attention is needed to develop reform options for those countries facing substantial reform needs where macroeconomic and fiscal conditions and institutional capacity limit the range of options. Equally important are related initiatives to improve the enabling environment and to increase the range of viable reform options.
- *The Bank has undertaken substantial recent analysis of the withdrawal phase of funded pension systems—including annuity markets—that is designed to identify best regulatory practices and institutional arrangements.* This analysis includes the examination of several countries with large pension systems that have developed markets for annuities. Filling this knowledge gap will enable Bank staff members to provide sound advice in this area, thereby helping these countries build efficient and transparent annuity markets and institutions capable of effectively managing the risks of the withdrawal phase.
- *The experience in many countries suggests that the Bank needs to tailor the pace of pension policy reforms to the development of the management and administrative aspects of pension systems, including institution and capacity building, and to provide additional support in these essential areas.* These areas are an increasingly important source of demand for Bank advice and support. As a result, the Bank will need to continue to focus its attention on implementation issues in order to maintain its intellectual and operational usefulness to its clients.

Proposed Approach

The unifying objective of the Bank's pension strategy for the future is to work with client countries to establish pension systems that manage the risk of old-age poverty and efficiently provide lifetime consumption smoothing in a manner that is supportive of growth and development. Country-specific objectives for pension systems should be jointly determined by applying the Bank's multipillar framework and evaluation criteria to country needs and priorities and should reflect a joint assessment of realistic outcomes. Achieving this objective requires a focused effort on the key substantive issues in conjunction with an effective organization and management process through which the work is undertaken. The following approach will help to accomplish this goal:

- Central anchors should be responsible for providing regional and counterpart staff members with
  - —The analytical framework and toolkits for pension policy analysis
  - —Common measurement methods that are linked to outcome and results indicators and are supported by global benchmarks and a database of cross-country information
  - —Metrics for determining the efficacy of policy and institutional development approaches pursued
  - —Relevant research and knowledge management products that support the policy agenda
  - —Training of regional staff members, counterparts, and other development partners in the techniques and policy frameworks developed
  - —Intersectoral and interinstitutional coordination at a Bank-wide level
  - —Assurance of the consistency of the Bank's approach with international best practices.
- Core substantive issue areas where central anchors should concentrate would be those that are relevant to the largest number of Bank clients and where the Bank can have the most effect:
  - —Fiscal affordability and sustainability, including the reform needs of public service pension schemes
  - —Measurement of poverty prevalence, trends, and vulnerability among the elderly population as a means of establishing core objectives for policy makers and for determining pension policies and instruments
  - —The governance framework for public and privately managed schemes, including the regulatory and oversight framework
  - —Modalities for improving efficiency and risk management in an effort to reduce costs and therefore improve sustainability and adequacy
  - —Approaches to increasing coverage to better insulate a broader proportion of the lifetime poor and vulnerable elderly populations

— Complementary reform programs in fiscal management and capital markets development to improve the environment for funded mandatory and voluntary savings.

- Central anchors will work closely with regional staff members to refine these priorities in accordance with changes in the needs and demands of country clients.
- Regional staff should be responsible for
  — Identifying and organizing country-driven engagements consistent with results-based country assistance strategies according to the priorities set out in country-owned plans, such as Poverty Reduction Strategy Papers
  — Drawing on the analytical framework, toolkits, indicators, benchmarks, and metrics provided by central anchors to undertake the assessment process to formulate an appropriate policy framework that will guide the Bank's provision of advice, lending, and technical support to the pension reform
  — Developing and carrying out country and regional knowledge management functions, including disseminating country, regional, and Bank-wide insights to counterparts and other development partners
  — Ensuring an internal coordination process that draws on the best staff expertise appropriate to country needs and external coordination with other development partners on a country and regional basis.
- As the Bank's policy advice on pensions is generally highly regarded internationally, regional staff members will continue to strengthen many forms of client engagement, including providing reimbursable technical assistance; providing subsovereign lending where applicable; and leveraging external financial support at a central and a regional level from trust funds, partnerships, and so forth for capacity building, knowledge generation, and dissemination.

Pension reforms supported by the Bank through this process should continue to emphasize fiscal sustainability; broad participation to improve the adequacy and equity of outcomes; risk management through diversification of instruments, advance funding, and market-based products; financial sector development; and the strengthening of poverty alleviation through appropriately designed arrangements that can reach the lifetime poor and the informal sector.

ANNEX 4.A: INFORMATION CONTENTS OF THE IEG DATABASE

The IEG database contains information on bank pension lending and AAA related to pensions.

Lending

IEG Database Headings. Data on Bank lending in the IEG database is compiled under the following main headings:

- *Project information* consists of project ID and name, region, and country, followed by lending instrument type (investment, adjustment, technical assistance) and loan type.
- *Lending commitment* provides information on the commitment, cancellation, disbursement, and project cost amounts in millions of U.S. dollars.
- *Loan dates* specify the approval date, approval fiscal year, and approval exit fiscal year.
- *Project status* indicates whether the operation is closed or still active. The Quality Assurance Group section indicates ratings for the operation at entry and at supervision.
- *Pension component cost information* presents data on pension cost (in millions of U.S. dollars), pension cost as a percentage of Bank commitment, and size of the pension component (on a scale indicating less than 30 percent, 30 percent to 80 percent, and 80 percent to 100 percent of the total loan commitment).
- *Sector and subsector classification* indicates the sector board to which the project is assigned and the five sectors that the operation aims to support.
- *Status report (PSR and ISR) section* covers the latest evaluation date, development objective rating, implementation progress, and risk ratings.
- *Operations Evaluation Department (OED) evaluations* include evaluation type, ratings on outcome, sustainability, institutional development impact, overall Bank performance, overall borrower performance, and evaluation of the pension component.
- *Objectives and outcomes* presents information on pension-related objectives and actions and, when available, information on the outcomes achieved through the operation.
- *Classification by type of activity and pillar within the pension system* delineates each operation according to three groupings of activities (general analytical support, reform measures, and institution building) and indicates which of the three main pillars of the pension system are addressed for each type of activity.

Characteristics of Individual Lending Operations. The classification methods developed by the IEG for the earlier study were used to provide descriptive information on each of the additional operations in the subsequent period.

- *Project identification information,* including project ID numbers, relevant dates, lending categories, and the country and region involved, was derived directly from the loan documents.
- *Country classification* by lending category (IBRD, IDA, and blend) and by country income level was derived by comparing the countries involved against the categorizations contained in the World Bank List of Economies in the July 2007 *World Development Indicators* database.
- *The value of the project attributed to the pension components.* For investment lending, the U.S. dollar amounts allocated to pension-specific components are given in the detailed project description in the PADs. For adjustment lending, the pension-specific reform actions and conditions as a percentage of total number of reform actions and conditions were used to calculate the pension lending amounts for each project. For instance, if the policy matrix of a program document has 2 pension-related prior actions out of 10 total prior actions, the pension component cost as a percentage of Bank commitment is 20 percent, and that percentage of the loan amount is allocated to the pension component cost in the database.
- *Project status,* including information on any quality assessment, is derived from the review of ISRs and ICRs taken from both the Bank's Operations Web site and others found in ImageBank. With regard to portfolio monitoring and quality, of the 65 projects covering the years 2004 to 2007, 58 of them had ISRs available, and they contained ratings for the projects. In contrast, only 16 of these projects had completed ICRs available, and 14 of them were rated by the OED. The performance ratings in the ISRs, ICRs, and OED documents are used in this review to measure the portfolio quality.
- *Summary descriptions of project objectives* are taken from the relevant narrative sections of the PAD, in particular annex 4, the detailed project descriptions. The full PADs were searched for key words, and decisions were made on the most relevant sections.
- *Classification of the activity* into three major categories—analytical support, actual reform measures, and institutional capacity building—was done through manual review of the PADs and other loan documents. This examination usually involved a review of the detailed project description contained in annex 4 of the PAD and decisions regarding the nature of the objectives described in the loan documents.

- *Delineation of the element of the pension system* within the World Bank multipillar pension taxonomy[7] was also done through review of the project descriptions contained in the PADs and other documents. The first pillar is identified as a public pension plan, publicly managed (defined benefit or notional defined contribution) with mandated participation and funded through contributions, perhaps with some financial reserves. The second pillar is defined as occupational or personal pension plans (fully funded defined benefit or fully funded defined contribution), where participation is voluntary and funding is through financial assets. The third pillar's characteristics are similar to the second pillar's—that is, occupational or personal pension plans (partially or fully funded defined benefit or funded defined contribution) and funded by financial assets. However, participation in this pillar is voluntary, not mandated.

Analytical and Advisory Activities

IEG Database Headings. Data on Bank AAA in the IEG database is compiled under the following main headings:

- *General AAA information* consists of report number, specific region, and specific country, document title, date, fiscal year, report type, and author or task manager name.
- *Classification by issues addressed* is made according to the type of areas in which the report provides analytical support. The headings of classification include common pension-related topics, including:
  - — Poverty
  - — Gender effect
  - — Income of the aged
  - — Targeting, coverage, and eligibility
  - — Fiscal sustainability
  - — Capital market development
  - — Contractual savings
  - — Fund management and investment
  - — Annuities and insurance
  - — Pension system description
  - — Pension reform design
  - — Public information and political support
  - — Public administration and costs
  - — Transition costs.
- *Classification by pillar* is divided into two parts that determine whether the AAA work has any component related to three different pillars. The two parts—"mention of the pillar" and "recommendation of pillar"—aim to clarify the scope of the analytical program.

Characteristics of Each Analytical or Advisory Activity. In addition to the classification developed by IEG, the recent list has been extended to include a column titled "Summary/Explanations" to give a brief overview of the pension component in the report. The classification is as follows:

- *Regional analysis.* The reports that specifically identified the region or country were classified as regional analyses, whereas solely thematic reports were classified as covering the world.
- *Analysis by instrument type.* The reports were classified according to the document type listed next to them under ImageBank.
- *Classification by issues or topics.* The pension agenda addressed in each report was reflected in the database through a classification system used for the IEG review and listed in the previous subsection. The documents identified were manually reviewed to determine whether each specific issue (such as poverty, gender, or income of the aged) was part of the discussion.
- *Income level and lending category.* Two additional columns were inserted in the IEG database to facilitate an analysis of AAA work by income level and lending category. The same list used for the lending categorization (World Bank List of Economies in the July 2007 *World Development Indicators* database) was used for this classification.

ANNEX 4.B: WORLD BANK PENSION LENDING AND ECONOMIC AND SECTOR WORK

The tables in this annex show the pension lending and economic sector work conducted by the Bank during the period under study. Annex 4.B.1 shows pension lending projects for fiscal years 2002 to 2007. Pension lending projects for fiscal years 1983 to 2001 are listed in annex 4.B.2. Annex 4.B.3 shows the Bank's economic and sector work for 2004 to 2007.

ANNEX 4.C: WORLD BANK PUBLICATIONS SUBSTANTIALLY DIRECTED TO PENSIONS, FISCAL YEARS 2002–07

Title: "Competition and Performance in the Polish Second Pillar"

Authors: Heinz Rudolph and Roberto Rocha

Type of publication: World Bank Working Paper 107

Year of publication: 2007

Abstract: This working paper provides an assessment of the Polish funded pension system and the quality of the regulatory framework for the accumulation phase. Two elements distinguish the Polish pension fund portfolios from those of other reforming countries: the relatively high component of domestic equity and the negligible component on international securities. The paper provides several recommendations for expanding the opportunities for investments to pension funds. It finds that pension fund management companies have been able to exploit scale economies in certain areas of the business, such as revenue collection, and proposes to study mechanisms to enhance them even more by centralizing the account management system, which may also help increase portfolio efficiency and competition. The paper suggests that with the payout phase starting in 2009, broad definitions in areas such as the roles of the public and private sector need to be established. It examines products and options that authorities may consider for the design of the payout phase.

Title: "Financial Sector Dimensions of the Colombian Pension System"

Authors: Heinz Rudolph, Hela Cheikrouhou, Roberto Rocha, and Craig Thorburn

Type of publication: World Bank Working Paper 106

Year of publication: 2007

Abstract: This working paper provides an assessment of the funded pension system and the quality of the regulatory framework for both the accumulation phase and the payout phase. It suggests that the lack of portfolio diversification may contribute to low returns and poor pensions in the future and provides a number of recommendations to expand the opportunities for investments to pension funds. The paper also finds that pension fund administrators are not exploiting the scale economies in certain areas of the business, such as revenue collection and account management, and proposes mechanisms to reduce costs and increase efficiency through greater competition. The paper examines the products and options offered at retirement. It finds a bias toward the payment of pensions in the form of lump sums and suggests alternatives for improving the availability of other instruments. Enhancements in the regulatory framework of insurance companies are also proposed.

Title: *From Red to Gray: The "Third Transition" of Aging Populations in Eastern Europe and the Former Soviet Union*

Authors: Mukesh Chawla, Gordon Betcherman, and Arup Banerji, with Anne M. Bakilana, Csaba Feher, Michael Mertaugh, Maria Laura Sanchez Puerta, Anita M. Schwartz, and Lars Sondergaard

Type of publication: Book

Year of publication: 2007

Abstract: By 2025, many countries in Eastern Europe and the former Soviet Union will have among the oldest populations in the world. This demographic transition is unique, with two key differences with other aging economies in Western Europe and East Asia. First, this third transition is uniquely overlaid on the first two transitions in the region—the still-unfinished postsocialist political and economic transformations. Second, most of these countries must cope with the challenges of aging while still relatively poor and with economic and political institutions that are still developing. This book looks at the distinctive challenges of aging that the transition countries face.

Title: *Developing Annuities Markets: The Experience of Chile*

Authors: Roberto Rocha and Craig Thorburn

Type of publication: Book, *Directions in Development* series

Year of publication: 2007

Abstract: Demographic aging strains pension systems around the world, frequently leading to large pension expenditures and deficits. The increasing awareness of a looming pension crisis has led to a wave of pension reforms, particularly in the past decade. The purpose of this report is to examine the Chilean experience in developing the market for retirement products, including programmed or phased withdrawals and annuities, and to draw lessons for other countries that are also making efforts to develop such markets or that anticipate the need to do so. The book examines the performance of the market and the evolution of the regulatory framework since the implementation of the pension reform of 1981, but with a focus on the past 10 years.

Title: *Pension Reform: Issues and Prospects for Non-Financial Defined Contribution (NDC) Schemes*

Editors: Robert Holzmann and Edward Palmer

Authors: Juha M. Alho, Nicholas Barr, Axel H. Börsch-Supan, Sarah M. Brooks, Agnieszka Chłoń-Domińczak, Peter Diamond, Inmaculada Domínguez-Fabián, Bernhard Felderer, Daniele Franco, Marek Góra, Sandro Gronchi, Anna Hedborg, Robert Holzmann, Reinhard Koman, Bo Könberg, Jukka Lassila, Florence Legros, Assar Lindbeck,

Table 4.B.1: **Pensions Lending, Fiscal Years 2002–07**

Number	Project name	Country	Approval year	Project ID	Loan type	Total commitment (US$ millions)	Pension cost (US$ millions)
1	**Andhra Pradesh Economic Reform Program Project**	India	2002	P073113	Adjustment	250.0	6.1
2	**Second Private Sector Adjustment Loan Project**	Romania	2002	P067575	Adjustment	300.0	24.0
3	**Third Structural Adjustment Credit Project**	Moldova	2002	P065163	Adjustment	30.0	1.8
4	**Second Programmatic Structural Adjustment Loan Project**	Latvia	2002	P069890	Adjustment	20.2	1.6
5	**Second Programmatic Social Reform Loan Project**	Peru	2002	P073817	Adjustment	100.0	8.9
6	**Municipal Pension Reform Project**	Brazil	2002	P074777	Technical assistance	5.0	5.0
7	**Health System Reform Project**	Honduras	2002	P053575	Investment	27.1	3.6
8	**Structural Adjustment Credit Project**	Serbia and Montenegro	2002	P076764	Adjustment	15.0	1.8
9	**Structural Adjustment Loan Project**	Uruguay	2002	P077172	Adjustment	151.5	25.3
10	**Mexico Technical Assistance for Public Sector Social Security Reform**	Mexico	2002	P074795	Technical assistance	8.7	2.9
11	**Social Benefits Reform Administration Project**	Slovak Republic	2002	P038090	Investment	23.5	40.3
12	**Second Structural Adjustment Credit Project**	Pakistan	2002	P074968	Adjustment	500.0	8.1
13	**Economic Reform Technical Assistance Project**	Sri Lanka	2002	P077586	Technical assistance	15.0	0.3
14	**Poverty Reduction Strategy Credit Project**	Albania	2002	P069935	Adjustment	20.0	1.6
15	**Public Expenditures Reform Loan Project**	Mauritius	2002	P075070	Adjustment	40.0	4.7
16	**Public Sector Management Adjustment Credit Project**	Former Yugoslav Republic of Macedonia	2002	P066154	Adjustment	15.0	0.8
17	**Emergency Public Administration Project**	Afghanistan	2002	P077417	Investment	10.0	0.1
18	**Pensions System Investment Project**	Croatia	2002	P063546	Investment	27.3	35.6
19	**Structural Adjustment Credit Project**	Serbia and Montenegro	2002	P074586	Adjustment	70.0	8.3

20	**Financial Sector Strengthening**	Uganda	2002	P074649	Investment	11.7	0.7
21	**Second Public Sector Reform Loan Project**	Jordan	2002	P066826	Adjustment	120.0	4.3
22	**Growth and Competitiveness Project**	Cape Verde	2003	P074055	Investment	11.5	2.3
23	**Paraguay Economic Recovery Loan**	Paraguay	2003	P086543	Adjustment	30.0	5.3
24	**Second Programmatic Adjustment Loan Project**	Ukraine	2003	P074972	Adjustment	250.0	21.7
25	**Programmatic Human Development Reform Loan Project**	Ecuador	2003	P082395	Adjustment	50.0	10.0
26	**Fifth Structural Adjustment Credit Project**	Armenia	2003	P075758	Adjustment	40.0	2.9
27	**Social Sector Adjustment Credit Project**	Serbia and Montenegro	2003	P078390	Adjustment	80.0	13.3
28	**Private Investment Promotion Project**	Senegal	2003	P051609	Investment	46.0	3.0
29	**Programmatic Social Reform III**	Peru	2003	P078951	Adjustment	150.0	20.0
30	**Second Poverty Reduction Support Credit Project**	Albania	2003	P077739	Adjustment	18.0	0.7
31	**Chile Social Protection Sector Adjustment Loan Drawdown Option**	Chile	2003	P078088	Adjustment	200.0	26.0
32	**Social Insurance Technical Assistance Credit Project**	Bosnia and Herzegovina	2003	P071004	Technical assistance	7.0	6.2
33	**Colombia Programmatic Financial Sector Adjustment Loan I**	Colombia	2003	P078869	Adjustment	150.0	10.0
34	**Colombia First Labor Reform and Social Structural Adjustment Loan**	Colombia	2003	P079060	Adjustment	200.0	22.0
35	**Social Protection Administration Project**	Armenia	2004	P087620	Investment	5.2	1.3
36	**Pension System Administration Investment Project**	Montenegro	2004	P087470	Investment	5.0	2.6
37	**Enterprise Growth and Bank Modernization**	Bangladesh	2004	P081969	Investment	250.0	180.0
38	**Public Sector Management Adjustment Loan Project**	Former Yugoslav Republic of Macedonia	2004	P074893	Adjustment	30.0	1.7
39	**Financial Sector Program Project**	Niger	2004	P074316	Technical assistance	14.8	1.9
40	**Andhra Pradesh Economic Reform Program II**	India	2004	P075191	Adjustment	220.0	4.8
41	**Financial Sector Technical Assistance**	Dominican Republic	2004	P078838	Technical assistance	12.5	1.5

(continued)

Table 4.B.1: **Pensions Lending, Fiscal Years 2002–07** (*continued*)

Number	Project name	Country	Approval year	Project ID	Loan type	Total commitment (US$ millions)	Pension cost (US$ millions)
42	**Public Financial Management Reform Structural Adjustment Operation Project**	West Bank and Gaza	2004	P088754	Adjustment	20.0	2.9
43	**Fourth Poverty Reduction Support Operation Project**	Uganda	2004	P074082	Adjustment	150.0	3.0
44	**Zambia Economic Management and Growth Credit**	Zambia	2004	P040631	Adjustment	40.0	6.8
45	**Private Sector Adjustment Credit**	Senegal	2004	P080013	Adjustment	45.0	16.4
46	**Structural Adjustment Credit 2**	Montenegro	2004	P074908	Adjustment	18.0	1.3
47	**First Programmatic Adjustment Loan Project**	Romania	2004	P008791	Adjustment	150.0	5.0
48	**Payments and Banking System Modernization Project**	Kyrgyz Republic	2004	P074881	Investment	9.0	0.4
49	**Social Protection Project**	Former Yugoslav Republic of Macedonia	2004	P074358	Investment	9.7	8.6
50	**Third Programmatic Financial and Public Sector Adjustment Loan Project**	Turkey	2004	P082996	Adjustment	10,000.00	200.0
51	**Second Programmatic Adjustment Loan Project**	Bulgaria	2004	P081637	Adjustment	150.0	1.6
52	**Nigeria Economic Reform and Governance Project**	Nigeria	2004	P088150	Technical assistance	140.0	6.7
53	**Peru Programmatic Social Reform Loan IV**	Peru	2004	P083968	Adjustment	100.0	13.0
54	**Education Sector Development Support Credit**	Bangladesh	2004	P077789	Adjustment	100.0	4.3
55	**Economic Management Structural Adjustment Credit Project**	Bosnia and Herzegovina	2004	P071039	Adjustment	34.0	3.4
56	**Health Transition Project**	Turkey	2004	P074053	Investment	60.6	2.8
57	**Colombia Programmatic Financial Sector Loan II**	Colombia	2004	P082597	Adjustment	100.0	11.0
58	**Pension and Social Assistance**	Azerbaijan	2004	P049892	Investment	10.0	7.6
59	**Poverty Reduction Support Credit Project**	Nicaragua	2004	P082885	Adjustment	70.0	7.0
60	**Development Policy Loan**	Ukraine	2005	P079316	Adjustment	251.3	23.8

61	**Consolidated Collection and Pension Administration Reform Project**	Serbia	2005	P090418	Investment	25.0	25.0
62	**Mozambique Financial Sector Technical Assistance Project**	Mozambique	2005	P086169	Investment	10.5	3.9
63	**Brazil First Programmatic Fiscal Reform—Social Security Reform**	Brazil	2005	P086525	Adjustment	658.3	519.0
64	**Programmatic Development Policy Loan for Sustainable Development Project**	Colombia	2005	P081397	Adjustment	150.0	0.0
65	**Uruguay Social Program Support Loan**	Uruguay	2005	P095028	Adjustment	75.4	4.2
66	**Economic Management Capacity-Building Project**	Ghana	2005	P092986	Investment	25.0	0.5
67	**Social Insurance Technical Assistance Supplement**	Bosnia and Herzegovina	2005	P095596	Technical assistance	2.0	1.0
68	**Programmatic Adjustment Loan Project**	Croatia	2005	P082278	Adjustment	184.9	6.3
69	**First Poverty Reduction Support Credit**	Cape Verde	2005	P078860	Adjustment	15.0	0.3
70	**Business Productivity and Efficiency Loan**	Colombia	2005	P094301	Adjustment	250.0	28.0
71	**Health and Social Protection Project**	Kyrgyz Republic	2005	P084977	Investment	15.0	2.0
72	**Programmatic Broad-Based Growth Development Support Loan**	El Salvador	2005	P093133	Adjustment	100.0	16.7
73	**Banking Sector Development Policy Support Credit**	Pakistan	2005	P083079	Adjustment	300.0	6.6
74	**Privatization Social Support Program 2**	Turkey	2005	P094167	Investment	465.4	24.4
75	**Programmatic Adjustment Loan 3**	Bulgaria	2005	P078675	Adjustment	150.0	4.5
76	**Second Institutional Strengthening of the National Social Security Administration Technical Assistance Loan Project**	Argentina	2005	P092836	Technical assistance	25.0	37.5
77	**Poverty Reduction Support Credit**	Azerbaijan	2005	P074938	Adjustment	20.0	0.7
78	**Financial Sector Support Project**	Tanzania	2006	P099231	Investment	15.0	2.5
79	**Second Public Service Management Program Support Project**	Zambia	2006	P082452	Investment	30.0	1.6
80	**Access to Financial Services Project (Adaptable Program Loan 1)**	Ukraine	2006	P076553	Investment	150.0	8.0
81	**Financial Sector Development Policy Loan**	Arab Republic of Egypt	2006	P088877	Adjustment	500.0	50.0
82	**Second Orissa Socio-Economic Development Program Credit Project**	India	2006	P097036	Adjustment	225.0	10.2

(continued)

Table 4.B.1: **Pensions Lending, Fiscal Years 2002–07** *(continued)*

Number	Project name	Country	Approval year	Project ID	Loan type	Total commitment (US$ million)	Pension cost (US$ million)
83	**First Programmatic Reform Implementation Development Policy Loan**	Uruguay	2006	P083927	Adjustment	100.0	20.0
84	**Public Service Performance Enhancement Project**	Uganda	2006	P050440	Investment	70.0	0.3
85	**Poverty Reduction Support Credit 2**	Cape Verde	2006	P090875	Adjustment	10.0	0.4
86	**Post-Accession Rural Support Project**	Poland	2006	P065270	Investment	88.8	33.2
87	**Emergency Social Protection Project**	Iraq	2006	P099295	Investment	0.0	0.8
88	**Panama Development Policy Loan**	Panama	2006	P098376	Adjustment	60.0	8.5
89	**Panama Development Policy Loan**	Panama	2006	P098376	Adjustment	60.0	8.6
90	**Turkey Programmatic Public Sector Development Policy Loan**	Turkey	2006	P071052	Adjustment	500.0	100.0
91	**Mexico Finance and Growth Development Policy Loan I**	Mexico	2006	P097159	Adjustment	501.3	71.5
92	**Colombia Third Programmatic Labor Reform and Social Development Policy Loan**	Colombia	2006	P094097	Adjustment	200.0	20.0
93	**Second State Pension Reform Technical Assistance Project**	Moldova	2006	P099166	Adjustment	10.0	1.2
94	**Cape Verde Poverty Reduction Support Credit III (last of first series)**	Cape Verde	2007	P100807	Adjustment	10.0	0.5
95	**Andhra Pradesh Development Policy Loan III**	India	2007	P075174	Adjustment	225.0	11.8
96	**Second State Pension Reform Technical Assistance Project**	Brazil	2007	P089793	Technical assistance	5.0	5.0
97	**Fifth Poverty Reduction Support Credit Development Policy Loan**	Ghana	2007	P099287	Adjustment	110.0	0.0
98	**First Social Sectors Institutional Reform Development Policy Loan**	Bulgaria	2007	P094967	Adjustment	150.0	15.0
99	**Poverty Reduction Support Credit 3**	Armenia	2007	P093460	Adjustment	28.0	0.0

Source: Authors' calculations, based on the Business Warehouse data and World Bank documents.

Table 4.B.2: **Pensions Lending, Fiscal Years 1983–2001**

Number	Project name	Country	Approval year	Project ID	Loan type	Total commitment (US$ millions)	Pension cost (US$ millions)
1	**Technical Assistance Project**	Panama	1983	P007820	Technical assistance	5.0	0.4
2	**First Structural Adjustment Loan Project**	Uruguay	1987	P008142	Adjustment	80.0	11.4
3	**Social Sector Management Technical Assistance Project**	Argentina	1988	P005991	Technical assistance	28.0	3.5
4	**Second Structural Adjustment Loan**	Uruguay	1989	P008145	Adjustment	140.0	11.7
5	**Financial Sector Adjustment Project**	Ghana	1989	P000935	Adjustment	6.6	0.2
6	**Second Technical Assistance Project**	Uruguay	1989	P008157	Technical assistance	6.5	1.4
7	**Economic Restructuring Credit Project**	Sri Lanka	1990	P010347	Adjustment	95.2	8.7
8	**Structural Adjustment Loan**	Hungary	1990	P008476	Adjustment	200.0	5.6
9	**Structural Adjustment Loan Project**	Poland	1990	P008588	Adjustment	300.0	23.1
10	**Railways Restructuring Project**	Tanzania	1991	P002757	Investment	76.0	1.6
11	**Economic Management Structural Adjustment Credit Project**	Bulgaria	1991	P008307	Technical assistance	17.0	1.6
12	**Structural Adjustment Credit Project**	Bolivia	1991	P006184	Adjustment	40.0	1.1
13	**Second Structural Adjustment Loan Project**	Hungary	1991	P008492	Adjustment	250.0	10.3
14	**Second Public Sector Management Project**	Chile	1991	P006669	Technical assistance	17.2	2.0
15	**Second Financial Sector Adjustment Credit Project**	Ghana	1991	P000911	Adjustment	100.0	2.4
16	**Second Public Financial Management Operation Project**	Bolivia	1991	P006189	Investment	11.3	0.3
17	**Economic and Financial Reforms Support Loan Project**	Tunisia	1991	P005742	Adjustment	250.0	25.0
18	**Structural Adjustment Loan Project**	Romania	1992	P008779	Adjustment	400.0	16.7
19	**Structural Adjustment Loan Project**	Peru	1992	P008034	Adjustment	450.0	56.3
20	**Economic Recovery Loan Project**	Panama	1992	P007843	Adjustment	120.0	18.0

(continued)

Table 4.B.2: **Pensions Lending, Fiscal Years 1983–2001** (*continued*)

Number	Project name	Country	Approval year	Project ID	Loan type	Total commitment (US$ million)	Pension cost (US$ million)
21	**Social Safety Net Sector Adjustment Program Project**	India	1992	P009987	Adjustment	500.0	9.4
22	**Employment Services and Social Protection Project**	Russian Federation	1992	P008822	Investment	70.0	22.5
23	**Financial Sector Adjustment Loan Project**	Peru	1992	P008050	Adjustment	400.0	42.1
24	**Second Privatization and Industrial Reform Project**	Zambia	1993	P003226	Adjustment	100.0	2.9
25	**Technical Assistance for Social Safety Net Project**	Albania	1993	P008265	Investment	5.5	4.2
26	**Pension Administration and Health Insurance Project**	Hungary	1993	P008495	Investment	132.0	132.0
27	**Enterprise and Financial Sector Adjustment Loan Project**	Slovenia	1993	P008854	Adjustment	80.0	7.7
28	**Health Sector Reform Project**	Nicaragua	1993	P007778	Investment	15.0	0.1
29	**Third Structural Adjustment Loan Project**	Costa Rica	1993	P006952	Adjustment	100.0	3.1
30	**Technical Assistance Project**	Kazakhstan	1993	P008504	Investment	38.0	2.6
31	**Economic Recovery Loan Project**	Slovak Republic	1993	P008848	Adjustment	80.0	1.9
32	**Health Sector Reform: Social Security System Project**	Costa Rica	1993	P006954	Investment	22.0	1.5
33	**Financial Sector Adjustment Credit Project**	Uganda	1993	P002962	Adjustment	101.1	0.1
34	**Economic Recovery Loan Project**	Former Yugoslav Republic of Macedonia	1994	P008408	Adjustment	80.0	5.0
35	**Enterprise Housing and Social Security Reform Project**	China	1994	P003603	Investment	350.0	13.5
36	**Capital Market Development Technical Assistance Project**	Argentina	1994	P006062	Technical assistance	8.5	3.8
37	**Rehabilitation Loan Project**	Ukraine	1994	P009108	Adjustment	500.0	83.3
38	**Technical Assistance Project**	Turkmenistan	1994	P034092	Technical assistance	25.0	0.6
39	**Social Safety Net Project**	Kyrgyz Republic	1994	P008515	Investment	17.0	7.5

40	**Structural Adjustment Loan Project**	Moldova	1994	P008554	Adjustment	60.0	5.1
41	**Privatization Implementation Assistance and Social Safety Net Project**	Turkey	1994	P009102	Technical assistance	100.0	5.0
42	**Capital Market Development Project**	Argentina	1994	P005988	Investment	500.0	9.3
43	**Social Reform and Technical Assistance Project**	Former Yugoslav Republic of Macedonia	1995	P038092	Investment	14.0	0.5
44	**Rehabilitation Loan Project**	Uzbekistan	1995	P009129	Adjustment	160.0	10.0
45	**Economic Rehabilitation Support Loan Project**	Algeria	1995	P035704	Adjustment	150.0	1.2
46	**Financial and Enterprise Development Project**	Kazakhstan	1995	P008508	Investment	62.0	12.7
47	**Rehabilitation Credit Project**	Georgia	1995	P008410	Adjustment	75.0	3.3
48	**Capitalization Program Adjustment Credit Project**	Bolivia	1995	P006173	Adjustment	66.3	7.2
49	**Rehabilitation Credit Project**	Armenia	1995	P008275	Adjustment	60.0	3.8
50	**Financial and Enterprise Sector Adjustment Credit Project**	Macedonia	1995	P008409	Adjustment	85.0	5.5
51	**First Rehabilitation Loan Project**	Russian Federation	1995	P008816	Adjustment	600.0	20.0
52	**Nonbank Financial Institutions Assistance Project**	Ghana	1995	P000943	Technical assistance	23.9	1.3
53	**Economic Recovery and Investment Credit Project**	Zambia	1995	P003240	Adjustment	152.1	22.4
54	**Financial Markets and Pension Reform Technical Assistance Project**	Bolivia	1995	P034606	Technical assistance	9.0	6.1
55	**Financial Sector Technical Assistance Project**	Mexico	1995	P034161	Technical assistance	23.6	1.9
56	**Employment and Social Protection Project**	Romania	1995	P008776	Investment	55.4	3.8
57	**Coal Pilot Project**	Ukraine	1996	P044110	Investment	15.8	2.4
58	**Railway Restructuring Project**	Morocco	1996	P043725	Investment	85.0	9.4
59	**Structural Adjustment Project**	Lithuania	1996	P044056	Adjustment	80.0	13.3
60	**Social Insurance Administration Project**	Bulgaria	1996	P008323	Investment	24.3	32.3

(continued)

Table 4.B.2: **Pensions Lending, Fiscal Years 1983–2001** (*continued*)

Number	Project name	Country	Approval year	Project ID	Loan type	Total commitment (US$ millions)	Pension cost (US$ millions)
61	**Second Economic Reform and Development Loan Project**	Jordan	1996	P044139	Adjustment	120.0	3.5
62	**Coal Sector Adjustment Loan Project**	Russian Federation	1996	P038550	Adjustment	500.0	0.0
63	**Third Structural Adjustment Credit Project**	Lao People's Democratic Republic	1996	P004209	Adjustment	40.0	5.7
64	**Structural Adjustment Loan Project**	Latvia	1996	P044123	Adjustment	60.0	1.8
65	**Financial Sector Adjustment Project**	Kyrgyz Republic	1996	P034095	Adjustment	45.0	0.5
66	**Structural Adjustment Credit Project**	Georgia	1996	P034583	Adjustment	60.0	3.1
67	**Capacity-Building Project for Private Sector Promotion Project**	Cape Verde	1996	P000438	Investment	11.4	0.4
68	**Public Sector Modernization Technical Assistance Credit Project**	Honduras	1996	P034607	Technical assistance	9.6	1.1
69	**Contractual Savings Development Program Project**	Mexico	1996	P041820	Adjustment	400.0	200.0
70	**Provincial Pension Reform Adjustment Project**	Argentina	1996	P044445	Adjustment	300.0	620.0
71	**Structural Adjustment Technical Assistance Credit Project**	Georgia	1996	P044388	Technical assistance	4.8	0.3
72	**Coal Sector Adjustment Loan Project**	Ukraine	1996	P040564	Adjustment	300.0	20.0
73	**Capital Markets Development Project**	Croatia	1996	P040142	Investment	9.5	0.5
74	**Transition Assistance Credit**	Bosnia and Herzegovina	1996	P044033	Adjustment	90.0	10.4
75	**Improvement to Financial Reporting and Auditing Project**	Pakistan	1996	P036015	Investment	28.8	4.1
76	**Structural Adjustment Loan and Credit Project**	Former Yugoslav Republic of Macedonia	1997	P038393	Adjustment	60.0	0.0
77	**Second Structural Adjustment Credit Project**	Georgia	1997	P044797	Adjustment	60.0	6.0
78	**Rio de Janeiro State Reform Privatization Project**	Brazil	1997	P039197	Investment	250.0	20.8

79	**Second Structural Adjustment Technical Assistance Credit Project**	Armenia	1997	P051026	Technical assistance	5.0	0.3
80	**Critical Imports Rehabilitation Loan Project**	Bulgaria	1997	P050540	Adjustment	40.0	5.7
81	**Social Protection Implementation Loan Project**	Russian Federation	1997	P046496	Technical assistance	28.6	8.5
82	**Second Structural Adjustment Credit Project**	Armenia	1997	P044796	Adjustment	60.0	0.4
83	**Second Structural Adjustment Loan Project**	Moldova	1997	P044147	Adjustment	100.0	19.8
84	**Pension Reform Adjustment Loan Project**	Peru	1997	P008064	Adjustment	100.0	100.0
85	**Social Protection Adjustment Project**	Romania	1997	P050432	Adjustment	50.0	4.9
86	**Financial Markets Technical Assistance Loan Project**	Colombia	1997	P006884	Technical assistance	15.0	4.4
87	**Economic Reconstruction Loan Project**	Republic of Korea	1997	P055992	Adjustment	3,000.0	76.9
88	**Social Protection Adjustment Loan Project**	Russian Federation	1997	P038573	Adjustment	800.0	249.2
89	**Third Structural Adjustment Loan Project**	Zimbabwe	1997	P003334	Adjustment	140.0	5.3
90	**Structural Adjustment Credit Project**	Azerbaijan	1997	P041261	Adjustment	77.0	5.9
91	**Second Coal Sector Adjustment Loan Project**	Russian Federation	1997	P050486	Adjustment	800.0	0.0
92	**Second Structural Adjustment Technical Assistance Credit Project**	Georgia	1997	P051034	Adjustment	5.0	0.7
93	**National Pension Administration Technical Assistance Loan Project**	Argentina	1997	P046821	Technical assistance	20.0	20.0
94	**Public Sector Resource Management Adjustment Loan Project**	Kazakhstan	1997	P034093	Adjustment	230.0	8.5
95	**Welfare Reform Project**	Latvia	1997	P035807	Investment	18.1	32.6
96	**Second Structural Adjustment Loan Project**	Republic of Korea	1998	P056521	Adjustment	2,000.0	200.0
97	**State Pension Systems Reform Technical Assistance Project**	Brazil	1998	P057910	Technical assistance	5.0	5.0
98	**Pension Reform Structural Adjustment Loan Project**	Kazakhstan	1998	P050780	Adjustment	300.0	300.0
99	**Regulatory Reform and Privatization Technical Assistance Project**	Bolivia	1998	P057396	Technical assistance	20.0	1.1

(continued)

Table 4.B.2: **Pensions Lending, Fiscal Years 1983–2001** (*continued*)

Number	Project name	Country	Approval year	Project ID	Loan type	Total commitment (US$ millions)	Pension cost (US$ millions)
100	**Social Sector Adjustment Credit Project**	Kyrgyz Republic	1998	P038569	Adjustment	36.5	25.8
101	**Structural Adjustment Credit Project**	Tajikistan	1998	P047438	Adjustment	50.0	2.9
102	**Regulatory Reform Sector Adjustment Credit Project**	Bolivia	1998	P057030	Adjustment	40.0	1.0
103	**Special Repurchase Facility Support Loan Project**	Argentina	1998	P062992	Adjustment	505.1	19.4
104	**Special Structural Adjustment Loan Project**	Argentina	1998	P062991	Adjustment	2,525.3	101.0
105	**Second Contractual Savings Development Project**	Mexico	1998	P046006	Adjustment	400.0	400.0
106	**Social Sectors Adjustment Loan Project**	Former Yugoslav Republic of Macedonia	1998	P038392	Adjustment	29.0	4.8
107	**Public Policy Reform Adjustment Loan Project**	Panama	1998	P050608	Adjustment	61.0	6.1
108	**Third Structural Adjustment Credit Project**	Cameroon	1998	P054443	Adjustment	180.0	2.0
109	**Structural Adjustment Loan Project**	Republic of Korea	1998	P056235	Adjustment	2,000.0	225.0
110	**Public Sector Adjustment Loan Project**	Hungary	1998	P034082	Adjustment	150.0	92.9
111	**Contractual Savings Structural Adjustment Loan Project**	Uruguay	1998	P050717	Adjustment	100.0	100.0
112	**Third Structural Adjustment Credit Project**	Armenia	1998	P051171	Adjustment	65.0	1.5
113	**Andhra Pradesh Economic Restructuring Project**	India	1998	P049385	Investment	543.2	7.2
114	**Public Financial Structural Adjustment Credit Project**	Bosnia and Herzegovina	1998	P045546	Adjustment	63.0	10.5
115	**Contractual Savings Development Loan Project**	Morocco	1998	P047582	Adjustment	100.0	25.0
116	**Pension Reform Technical Assistance Project**	Macedonia	1998	P058056	Technical assistance	1.0	1.0
117	**Social Protection Adjustment Loan**	Bulgaria	1998	P051151	Adjustment	80.0	16.0
118	**Health Sector Modernization Project**	Nicaragua	1998	P035753	Investment	24.0	0.3
119	**Pension Reform Project**	China	1999	P058308	Technical assistance	5.0	6.3

120	**Social Protection Special Sector Adjustment Loan Project**	Brazil	1999	P063351	Adjustment	252.5	15.8
121	**Private Sector Adjustment Loan Project**	Romania	1999	P064853	Adjustment	300.0	0.0
122	**Second Financial Institutions Development Project**	Tanzania	1999	P057187	Investment	27.5	0.4
123	**Financial Markets Assistance Project**	Uganda	1999	P044213	Technical assistance	13.0	0.7
124	**Structural Reform Support Project**	Georgia	1999	P052154	Investment	16.5	1.5
125	**Second Public Financial Structural Adjustment Credit Project**	Bosnia and Herzegovina	1999	P055432	Adjustment	72.0	10.6
126	**Second Structural Adjustment Credit Project**	Madagascar	1999	P057378	Adjustment	100.0	5.4
127	**Social Protection Management Project**	Moldova	1999	P051173	Investment	11.1	11.1
128	**Second Financial Sector Adjustment Loan Project**	Peru	1999	P065596	Adjustment	300.0	136.4
129	**Railways and Ports Restructuring Project**	Mozambique	1999	P042039	Investment	100.0	1.5
130	**Social Security Special Sector Adjustment Loan Project**	Brazil	1999	P063340	Adjustment	757.6	757.6
131	**Structural Adjustment Credit Project**	Albania	1999	P055160	Adjustment	45.0	1.6
132	**Bank Restructuring and Debt Management Project**	Jamaica	2000	P071112	Adjustment	75.0	3.3
133	**Railway Restructuring Project**	Zambia	2000	P003227	Investment	27.0	0.0
134	**Financial Sector Development Project**	Mali	2000	P001748	Investment	21.0	1.7
135	**Pension and Financial Market Reform Technical Assistance Project**	Nicaragua	2000	P056087	Technical assistance	8.0	8.0
136	**Financial Sector Adjustment Credit Project**	Mongolia	2000	P068071	Adjustment	32.0	0.8
137	**Uttar Pradesh Fiscal Reform and Public Sector Restructuring Project**	India	2000	P065471	Adjustment	251.3	5.9
138	**Fiscal Sustainability Credit Project**	Zambia	2000	P039016	Adjustment	179.2	43.6
139	**Economic Rehabilitation and Recovery Credit Project**	Guinea-Bissau	2000	P065725	Adjustment	25.0	5.0
140	**Public/Private Partnership for Growth Project**	Cameroon	2000	P065927	Technical assistance	20.9	3.2
141	**Programmatic Structural Adjustment Loan Project**	Latvia	2000	P066153	Adjustment	40.4	2.2

(continued)

Table 4.B.2: **Pensions Lending, Fiscal Years 1983–2001** (*continued*)

Number	Project name	Country	Approval year	Project ID	Loan type	Total commit-ment (US$ millions)	Pension cost (US$ millions)
142	**Social Security Technical Assistance Project**	Brazil	2000	P062619	Technical assistance	5.1	5.1
143	**Economic Reform Loan Project**	Turkey	2000	P068792	Adjustment	759.6	189.9
144	**Civil Service Modernization Project**	Yemen	2000	P050706	Investment	30.0	0.3
145	**Second Social Security Special Sector Adjustment Loan Project**	Brazil	2000	P064901	Adjustment	505.1	505.1
146	**Technical Assistance for Economic Reform Project**	India	2000	P059501	Investment	55.0	0.4
147	**Economic Rehabilitation and Recovery Credit Project**	Sierra Leone	2000	P035637	Adjustment	30.0	1.2
148	**Second Structural Adjustment Loan Project**	Lithuania	2000	P068706	Adjustment	98.5	13.1
149	**Social Safety Net Project**	Jamaica	2001	P067774	Investment	40.0	5.6
150	**Structural Fiscal Adjustment Loan Project**	Colombia	2001	P073572	Adjustment	400.0	50.0
151	**Second Hard Coal Sector Restructuring Loan Project**	Poland	2001	P065351	Adjustment	100.0	2.6
152	**Structural Adjustment Loan Project**	Argentina	2001	P073591	Adjustment	400.0	24.5
153	**Social Sector Adjustment Credit Project**	Bosnia and Herzegovina	2001	P069058	Adjustment	20.0	2.4
154	**Social Sector Development Project**	Romania	2001	P008783	Investment	50.0	10.9

155	**Structural Adjustment Loan Project**	Croatia	2001	P067223	Adjustment	202.0	24.7
156	**Programmatic Financial Sector Adjustment Loan Project**	Brazil	2001	P070640	Adjustment	404.0	11.5
157	**Social Protection Project**	Serbia and Montenegro	2001	P072405	Investment	4.2	0.2
158	**Social Service Delivery Project**	Albania	2001	P055383	Investment	10.0	0.2
159	**Financial Sector Technical Assistance Loan Project**	Brazil	2001	P073192	Investment	14.5	0.5
160	**Economic Assistance Grant to Support Social Protection**	Serbia and Montenegro	2001	P074124	Investment	10.0	1.6
161	**Second Health Sector Strengthening and Modernization Project**	Costa Rica	2001	P073892	Investment	17.0	2.1
162	**Third Economic Competitiveness Adjustment Loan Project**	Tunisia	2001	P055815	Adjustment	252.5	4.9
163	**Financial Sector Supervisory Authority Project**	Mauritius	2001	P073594	Investment	1.8	0.2
164	**Programmatic Adjustment Loan Project**	Ukraine	2001	P070693	Adjustment	250.0	19.5
165	**Fiscal Consolidation Credit Project**	Djibouti	2001	P065790	Adjustment	10.0	2.5
166	**Structural Adjustment Credit Project**	Pakistan	2001	P071463	Adjustment	350.0	5.2
167	**First Karnataka Economic Restructuring Loan/Credit Project**	India	2001	P055490	Adjustment	150.0	3.4

Source: Authors' calculations, based on the Business Warehouse data and World Bank documents.

Table 4.B.3: **Economic and Sector Work, Fiscal Years 2004–07**

Number	Project name	Country	Fiscal year	Project ID	Project type
1	"Promoting Growth with Equity—Country Economic Memorandum"	China	2004	24169-CHA	Economic report
2	"Inequality and Economic Development"	Brazil	2004	24487-BR	Sector report
3	"State-Level Public Expenditure Review: The Case of Veracruz-Llave"	Mexico	2004	25162-ME	Economic report
4	"The Pension System in Iran: Challenges and Opportunities"	Islamic Republic of Iran	2004	25174-IR	Sector report
5	"Household Risk Management and Social Protection"	Chile	2004	25286-CH	Sector report
6	"Poverty Assessment"	Bosnia and Herzegovina	2004	25343-BIH	Economic report
7	"Reforming Policies and Institutions for Efficiency and Equity of Public Expenditures"	Argentina	2004	25991-AR	Economic report
8	"Poverty Assessment"	Serbia and Montenegro	2004	26011-YU	Economic report
9	"The New Economic Agenda and Fiscal Sustainability"	Mauritius	2004	26152-MU	Economic report
10	"Poverty Assessment"	Romania	2004	26169	Sector report
11	"Poverty Assessment"	Albania	2004	26213-AL	Economic report
12	"Country Economic Memorandum: Towards Macroeconomic Stability and Sustained Growth," vol. 1 of 3	Turkey	2004	26301	Economic report
13	"Poverty Reduction Strategy Paper (PRSP) and Joint Staff Assessment," vol. 1 of 1	Mongolia	2004	26563	Poverty Reduction Strategy Paper
14	"El sistema previsional y la crisis de la Argentina," vol. 1 of 1 (Spanish)	Argentina	2004	26825	Working paper (numbered series)
15	"Development Policy Update"	Philippines	2004	26946-PH	Sector report
16	"Defining a Strategy for Social Protection Policy"	Paraguay	2004	27352-PA	Sector report
17	"Development Policy Report: Beyond Macroeconomic Stability"	Indonesia	2004	27374-IND	Sector report
18	"Development Policy Review—Growth, Inclusion and Governance: The Road Ahead"	Ecuador	2004	27443	Economic report
19	"Strategy for Public Debt Management"	Tunisia	2004	27599-TUN	Economic report
20	"Restoring the Multiple Pillars of Old-Age Income Security"	Peru	2004	27618-PE	Sector report

21	**"Public Expenditure Review: Fiscal Policies for Growth and Poverty Reduction"**	Kyrgyz Republic	2004	28123-KG	Economic report
22	**"Policies and Strategies for Accelerated Growth and Poverty Reduction: A Country Economic Memorandum," vol. 1 of 1**	Senegal	2004	28143	Economic report
23	**"Growth, Employment, and Living Standards in Preaccession Poland"**	Poland	2004	28233-POL	Poverty assessment
24	**"Poverty in Russia in Service Provision for the Poor: Public and Private Sector Cooperation," vol. 1 of 1**	Russian Federation	2004	28403	Publication
25	**"Development of Non-Bank Financial Institutions and Capital Markets in European Union Accession Countries," vol. 1 of 1**		2004	28404	Working paper (numbered series)
26	**"Subnational Administration in Afghanistan"**	Afghanistan	2004	28435-AF	Sector report
27	**"Developing Residential Mortgage Markets in the Russian Federation: Final Report"**	Russian Federation	2004	29014	Working paper
28	**"Preferences, Constraints, and Substitutes for Coverage Under Peru's Pension System"**	Peru	2004	29252	Working paper
29	**"Subnational Administration in Afghanistan: Assessment and Recommendations for Action"**	Afghanistan	2004	29415	Working paper
30	**"Modernizing an Advanced Pension System"**	Mauritius	2004	29588-MU	Sector report
31	**"Developing Institutional Investors in People's Republic of China"**	China	2004	30248	Working paper
32	**"Improving Mandatory Saving Programs"**		2004	30398	
33	**"Is There a Positive Incentive Effect from Privatizing Social Security? Evidence from Latin America"**		2004	30399	
34	**"The New Pensions in Kazakhstan: Challenges in Making the Transition"**	Kazakhstan	2004	30873-KZ	Sector report
35	**"Managing Labor Market Reforms: Case Study of Poland"**	Poland	2004	31365	Working paper
36	**"Report on the Observance of Standards and Codes (ROSC): Corporate Governance Country Assessment"**	Colombia	2004	35021	Sector report
37	**"Report on the Observance of Standards and Codes (ROSC): Corporate Governance Country Assessment"**	Panama	2004	35169	Sector report
38	**"Report on the Observance of Standards and Codes (ROSC): Corporate Governance Country Assessment"**	Peru	2004	35171	Sector report

(continued)

Table 4.B.3: **Economic and Sector Work, Fiscal Years 2004–07** (*continued*)

Number	Project name	Country	Fiscal year	Project ID	Project type
39	"Insurance Regulation in Jordan: New Rules, Old System"	Jordan	2004	WPS3298	Policy Research Working Paper
40	"Governance of Public Pension Funds: Lessons from Corporate Governance and International Evidence," vol. 1"		2004	WPS3110	Policy Research Working Paper
41	"Integrating Housing Wealth into the Social Safety Net: The Elderly in Moscow," vol. 1	Russian Federation	2004	WPS3115	Policy Research Working Paper
42	"The Use of 'Asset Swap' by Institutional Investors in South Africa"	South Africa	2004	WPS3175	Policy Research Working Paper
43	"A Conceptual Framework for Retirement Products: Risk Sharing Arrangements between Providers and Retirees"		2004	WPS3208	Policy Research Working Paper
44	"Labor Market Reforms, Growth, and Unemployment in Labor-Exporting Countries in the Middle East and North Africa"		2004	WPS3328	Policy Research Working Paper
45	"Public Expenditure Review"	Colombia	2005	25163-CO	Economic report
46	"The Quest for Jobs and Growth: A World Bank Country Economic Memorandum"	Latvia	2005	26768-LV	Economic report
47	"Public Expenditure Review"	Mexico	2005	27894-MX	Economic report
48	"Creating Fiscal Space for Poverty Reduction: A Fiscal Management and Public Expenditure Review"	Ecuador	2005	28911-EC	Economic report
49	"Financial Sector Assessment"	Chile	2005	29906	Economic report
50	"Fiscal Costs of Structural Reforms"	Russian Federation	2005	30741-RU	Economic report
51	"Republic of Uruguay Policy Notes"	Uruguay	2005	31338-UY	Economic report
52	"Republic of Paraguay Institutional and Governance Review: Breaking with Tradition—Overcoming Institutional Impediments to Improve Public Sector Performance"	Paraguay	2005	31763-PY	Sector report
53	"Colombia REDI: Recent Economic Developments in Infrastructure—Balancing Social and Productive Needs for Infrastructure"	Colombia	2005	32090	Working paper
54	"Ageing and Poverty in Africa and the Role of Social Pensions"		2005	32178	Working paper
55	"World Bank EU-8 Quarterly Economic Report"		2005	32598	Working paper
56	"Public Expenditure Reform Priorities for Fiscal Adjustment, Growth and Poverty Alleviation"	Lebanon	2005	32857-LB	Economic report

57	**"Pension Liabilities and Reform Options for Old-Age Insurance"**	China	2005	33116	Working paper
58	**"Pension Reform in Ukraine: Remedies to Recent Fiscal and Structural Challenges"**	Ukraine	2005	33225	Sector report
59	**"Notional Accounts"**		2005	33382	
60	**"Financial Sector Assessment Update"**	Uganda	2005	33422	Economic report
61	**"Financial Sector Review"**	Benin	2005	3440-BJ	Sector report
62	**"Report on the Observance of Standards and Codes (ROSC)"**	Dominican Republic	2005	35027	Working paper
63	**"Report on the Observance of Standards and Codes (ROSC) Tanzania: Accounting and Auditing"**	Tanzania	2005	35188	Economic report
64	**"Labor Market Issues in South Asia: Issues and Challenges"**		2005	36256	
65	**"Income Generation and Social Protection for the Poor"**	Mexico	2005	36853	Economic report
66	**"Corporate Governance Country Assessment"**	Pakistan	2005	38971	Working paper
67	**"Corporate Governance Country Assessment"**	Poland	2005	38972	Working paper
68	**"Social Protection in Transition: Labor Policy, Safety Nets, and Pensions"**	Iraq	2005	39030	Working paper
69	**"Disability in ECA"**		2005		Concept note
70	**"Mortgage Securities in Emerging Markets"**		2005	WPS3370	
71	**"Pension Funds and National Saving"**		2005	WPS3410	Policy Research Working Paper
72	**"The Transactions Costs of Primary Market Issuance: The Case of Brazil, Chile, and Mexico"**	Brazil, Chile, Mexico	2005	WPS3424	Policy Research Working Paper
73	**"Supervision of Financial Conglomerates: The Case of Chile"**	Chile	2005	WPS3553	Policy Research Working Paper
74	**"Joint Poverty Assessment Report"**	Turkey	2006	29619-TU	Economic report
75	**"Labor Market Update"**	Bosnia and Herzegovina	2006	32650-BA	Sector report
76	**"Income Generation and Social Protection for the Poor"**	Mexico	2006	32884-MX	Economic report
77	**"Managing Risks in Rural Senegal: A Multisectoral Review of Efforts to Reduce Vulnerability"**	Senegal	2006	33435-SN	Economic report

(continued)

Table 4.B.3: **Economic and Sector Work, Fiscal Years 2004–07** (*continued*)

Number	Project name	Country	Fiscal year	Project ID	Project type
78	"Development Policy Review"	Chile	2006	33501-CL	Sector report
79	"The Challenge of Increasing Fiscal Space to Meet Future Pressures"	Cape Verde	2006	34523-CV	Sector report
80	"Managing Public Finances for Development"	Afghanistan	2006	34582-AF	Economic report
81	"Labor Market Assessment"	Albania	2006	34597-AL	Sector report
82	"Public Expenditure Review: Making Public Finances Work for Growth and Poverty Reduction"	Djibouti	2006	34624-DJI	Economic report
83	"Ukraine Poverty Assessment: Poverty and Inequality in a Growing Economy"	Ukraine	2006	34631-UA	Sector report
84	"Report on Public Financial Management, Procurement, and Expenditure Systems in Iran"	Islamic Republic of Iran	2006	34777-IR	Economic report
85	"Social Protection in the Maldives: Options for Reforming Pensions and Safety Nets"	Maldives	2006	34818-MV	Sector report
86	"Pension Schemes for the Formal Sector: Emerging Challenges and Opportunities for Reform"		2006	34940	Other social protection study
87	"'Who Cares Wins': One Year On"		2006	34973	
88	"Rebuilding Iraq: Economic Reform and Transition"	Iraq	2006	35141-IQ	Sector report
89	"Modernizing Ukraine through Better Public Governance"	Ukraine	2006	35358	World Bank Institute working paper
90	"Moldova Poverty Update"	Moldova	2006	35618-MD	Sector report
91	"Serbia Social Assistance and Child Protection Note"	Serbia	2006	35954-YU	Other social protection study
92	"Pension System Note"	Bosnia and Herzegovina	2006	36459-BA	Policy note
93	"Sri Lanka: Selected Public Expenditure Issues, 2003/2004"	Sri Lanka	2006	36630-LK	Sector report
94	"Financing Infrastructure: Addressing Constraints and Challenges"	India	2006	36876	Working paper
95	"Rural Growth and Development Revisited: Postreform Situation of the Rural Financial Markets, Policy Gaps and Recommendations"	Philippines	2006	36995	Sector report
96	"Housing Finance Policy Note"	Poland	2006	37143	Working paper
97	"Infrastructure Strategy: Cross-Sectoral Issues"	Vietnam	2006	37184	Working paper

98	**"Development Policy Review"**	Chile	2006	37429	Sector report
99	**"The Republic of Serbia: A Policy Agenda for a Smaller and More Efficient Public Sector"**	Serbia	2006	38476	Working paper
100	**"Pilot Assessment of Governance of the Insurance Sector"**	Czech Republic	2006	38501	Working paper
101	**"Payments and Securities Clearance and Settlement Systems in Georgia"**	Georgia	2006	38859	Working paper
102	**"Pensions in Iraq: Issues, General Guidelines for Reform, and Potential Fiscal Implications"**	Iraq	2006	39024	Working paper
103	**"Sustainability and Sources of Economic Growth in the Northern Part of Cyprus"**	Northern Cyprus	2006	Draft	Country Economic Memorandum
104	**"Pension Reform Programme: Institutional Planning for Implementation of Multi-Pillar Reform"**	Arab Republic of Egypt	2006	Draft	Other social protection study
105	**"Affordable Health Insurance for High Risks in Low-Income Countries: A Conceptual Framework"**		2006	P092907	
106	**"Competition and Performance in the Hungarian Second Pillar"**	Hungary	2006	WPS3876	Policy Research Working Paper
107	**"An Analysis of Money's Worth Ratios in Chile"**	Chile	2006	WPS3926	Policy Research Working Paper
108	**"An Empirical Analysis of the Annuity Rate in Chile"**	Chile	2006	WPS3929	Policy Research Working Paper
109	**"Financial Development in Latin America: Big Emerging Issues, Limited Policy Answers"**		2006	WPS3963	Policy Research Working Paper
110	**"Brazil: Towards a Sustainable and Fair Pension System"**	Brazil	2007		
111	**"Jobs for Brazil's Poor: What Helps? Social Protection Programs and Labor Supply Impacts on the Poor in Brazil"**	Brazil	2007		Other social protection study
112	**"Socialist People's Libyan Arab Jamahiriya Country Economic Report"**	Libya	2007	30295-LY	Economic report
113	**"Kosovo Public Expenditure and Institutional Review"**	Kosovo	2007	32624-XK	Economic report
114	**"Country Economic Memorandum: Unlocking Djibouti's Growth Potential: The Road Ahead"**	Djibouti	2007	33115-DJ	Economic report
115	**"Addressing Fiscal Challenges and Enhancing Growth Prospects: A Public Expenditure and Institutional Review"**	Bosnia and Herzegovina	2007	36156-BA	Economic report

(continued)

Table 4.B.3: **Economic and Sector Work, Fiscal Years 2004–07** *(continued)*

Number	Project name	Country	Fiscal year	Project ID	Project type
116	**"Labor Market Assessment"**	Serbia	2007	36576-YU	Other social protection study
117	**"Towards Equality of Opportunity, 2006–2010: Policy Notes"**	Chile	2007	36583-CL	Sector report
118	**"Creating Fiscal Space for Growth: A Public Finance Review"**	Ukraine	2007	36671-UA	Economic report
119	**"Turkey Public Expenditure Review"**	Turkey	2007	36764-TR	Economic report
120	**"Social Insurance Review"**	Albania	2007	37594-AL	Other social protection study
121	**"Improving Public Expenditure Efficiency for Growth and Poverty Reduction"**	Moldova	2007	37933-MD	Sector report
122	**"Living Standards Assessment"**	Croatia	2007	37992-HR	Sector report
123	**"Vietnam Aiming High: Vietnam Development Report 2007"**	Vietnam	2007	38064-VN	Economic report
124	**"Financial Sector Review"**	Togo	2007	38146 -TG	Economic report
125	**"Evaluation of the Liaoning Social Security Reform Pilot"**	China	2007	38183	Working paper
126	**"Creating Better Jobs for Poverty Reduction in Burkina Faso"**	Burkina Faso	2007	38335-BF	Sector report
127	**"Municipal Finance Policy Note"**	Romania	2007	38357-RO	Policy note
128	**"Pension Reform and the Development of Pension Systems: An Evaluation of World Bank Assistance"**	Russia	2007	39137	Working paper
129	**"Pension Reform and the Development of Pension Systems: An Evaluation of World Bank Assistance"**	Peru	2007	39138	Working paper
130	**"Pension Reform and the Development of Pension Systems: An Evaluation of World Bank Assistance"**	Mexico	2007	39140	Working paper
131	**"Pension Reform and the Development of Pension Systems: An Evaluation of World Bank Assistance"**	Former Yugoslav Republic of Macedonia	2007	39141	Working paper
132	**"Pension Reform and the Development of Pension Systems: An Evaluation of World Bank Assistance"**		2007	39143	
133	**"Pension Reform and the Development of Pension Systems: An Evaluation of World Bank Assistance"**	Kazakhstan	2007	39144	Working paper

134	**"Pension Reform and the Development of Pension Systems: An Evaluation of World Bank Assistance**	Hungary	2007	39145	Working paper
135	**"Pension Reform and the Development of Pension Systems: An Evaluation of World Bank Assistance/Background Paper Regional Summary: Europe and Central Asia"**		2007	39146	
136	**"Pension Reform and the Development of Pension Systems: An Evaluation of World Bank Assistance**	China	2007	39147	Working paper
137	**"Pension Reform and the Development of Pension Systems: An Evaluation of World Bank Assistance"**	Bulgaria	2007	39148	Working paper
138	**"Pension Reform and the Development of Pension Systems: An Evaluation of World Bank Assistance/Background Paper Regional Summary: Asia"**		2007	39149	
139	**"Pension Reform and the Development of Pension Systems: An Evaluation of World Bank Assistance/Background Paper: Argentina Country Study"**	Argentina	2007	39150	Working paper
140	**"Pension Reform and the Development of Pension Systems: An Evaluation of World Bank Assistance/Background Paper: Bolivia Country Study"**	Bolivia	2007	39159	Working paper
141	**"Pension Reform and the Development of Pension Systems: An Evaluation of World Bank Assistance/Background Paper: South Korea Country Study"**	Republic of Korea	2007	39160	Working paper
142	**"Pension Reform and the Development of Pension Systems: An Evaluation of World Bank Assistance/Background Paper: Kyrgyz Country Study"**	Kyrgyz Republic	2007	39161	Working paper
143	**"Pension Reform and the Development of Pension Systems: An Evaluation of World Bank Assistance/Background Paper: Uruguay Country Study"**	Uruguay	2007	39162	Working paper
144	**"Kazakhstan Pension Report: From Policy Considerations to Practical Proposals"**	Kazakhstan	2007	Concept note	Policy note
145	**"Regulation, Enforcement, and Adjudication In Indian Labor Markets:"**	India	2007	Draft	Other social protection study
146	**"Pilot Diagnostic Review of Governance of the Supplementary Private Pension Fund Sector"**	Czech Republic	2007	Draft	Policy note
147	**"On the Financial Sustainability of Earnings-Related Pension Schemes with 'Pay-as-You-Go' Financing and the Role of Government Indexed Bonds"**		2007	WPS3966	Policy Research Working Paper

(continued)

Table 4.B.3: **Economic and Sector Work, Fiscal Years 2004–07** (*continued*)

Number	Project name	Country	Fiscal year	Project ID	Project type
148	**"Annuity Markets in Chile: Competition, Regulation, and Myopia?"**	Chile	2007	WPS3972	Policy Research Working Paper
149	**"Financial System Structure in Colombia: A Proposal for a Reform Agenda"**	Colombia	2007	WPS4006	Policy Research Working Paper
150	**"An Assessment of Reform Options for the Public Service Pension Fund in Uganda"**	Uganda	2007	WPS4091	Policy Research Working Paper
151	**"The Use of Derivatives to Hedge Embedded Options: The Case of Pension Institutions in Denmark"**	Denmark	2007	WPS4159	Policy Research Working Paper

Source: Authors' calculations, based on the Business Warehouse data and World Bank documents.

David Lindeman, Boguslaw D. Mikula, Marek Mora, Sergio Nisticó, Edward Palmer, David Robalino, Michal Rutkowski, Nicola Sartor, Ulrich Schuh, Ole Settergren, Sandra Stabiņa, Annika Sundén, Ingemar Svensson, Noriyuki Takayama, Salvador Valdés-Prieto, Tarmo Valkonen, Inta Vanovska, Carlos Vidal-Meliá, R. Kent Weaver, and Christina B. Wilke

Type of publication: Book

Year of publication: 2006

Abstract: The previous decade has been one of pension reform throughout the world. In high-income countries, the driving force has been the threat of current systems' becoming unaffordable in coming decades, with demographic developments presenting a major risk. In another setting, countries in the process of transition from a command economy to a market economy are confronted with the challenge of introducing a public pension system that will provide social security in old age but that also supports the fundamentals of a market economy. In the latter sense, it is important to examine carefully the experiences of developed market economies. Even in these countries, the driving force behind reform is demographic change and affordability. In a third setting, middle- and lower-middle-income countries are faced with the question of what system will best serve the interests of their specific country goals for the future.

In all these settings nonfinancial defined-contribution pension schemes have been on the agenda in discussions of possible options. Sweden is one of four countries to have implemented such a scheme in the 1990s, when the nonfinancial defined contribution came into its own as a concept (Italy, Latvia, and Poland are the other three). The nonfinancial defined-contribution pension scheme has become a reform option considered by many countries—understandably since most of Europe has a pay-as-you-go tradition, and the scheme constitutes a new way to "organize" a mandatory, universal pay-as-you-go pension system. With some experience in implementing such schemes, Sweden was particularly relevant to host a conference devoted to discussing both the conceptual and the institutional aspects of the nonfinancial defined contribution. The goal was even more ambitious, however: to contribute to creating a synthesis of current knowledge on this new topic. This book is the realization of that goal. It comprises discussion papers on the status of the nonfinancial defined contribution, its concept, and the the reform strategies that follow. Papers also discuss the conceptual issues of design and implementation and lessons from countries with nonfinancial defined-contribution schemes, and finalizes on the potential of these schemes in other countries' reforms.

Title: *Pensions Panorama: Retirement-Income Systems in 53 Countries*

Author: Edward Whitehouse

Type of publication: Book

Year of publication: 2007

Abstract: *Pensions Panorama* provides a compendium of facts and analysis that should inform policy making and public debate about retirement income systems around the world. The section following the introduction sets out a typology: a way of defining and classifying different kinds of pension schemes. It shows which countries have which types of pension schemes, covering all elements of the retirement income system, including resource-tested benefits and basic pensions, as well as public, earnings-related, and compulsory private pension plans. Next, the study sets out the institutional detail: the parameters and rules of different parts of the retirement income system. The next section presents the core, empirical results: future pension entitlements of today's workers with different levels of earnings from all sources. This section includes the familiar replacement rate indicator: individual pension entitlements as a proportion of individual earnings when working. The following section explores the important role that personal income taxes and social security contributions play in determining the relative incomes of older people. In particular, it shows net replacement rates (that is, pension net of taxes and any contributions, relative to earnings, net of taxes and contributions). The third section on empirical results looks at the link between pension entitlements in retirement and earnings in work. This analysis highlights the key differences in philosophy between different countries' retirement income systems. Moreover, changes to the pension-earnings link have been central to many recent reforms to retirement income regimes. The concluding section sets out a number of dimensions in which the pension systems of 53 countries differ.

Title: *Pensions in the Middle East and North Africa: Time for Change*

Editor: David A. Robalino

Authors: Alberto R. Musalem, David A. Robalino, Elizabeth Sherwood, Oleksiy Sluchynsky, and Edward Whitehouse

Type of publication: Book, *Orientation in Development* series

Year of publication: 2005

Abstract: This is the first comprehensive assessment of pension systems in the Middle East and North Africa. While other regions—Central Asia, Eastern Europe, and Latin America, in particular—have been actively introducing reforms to their pension systems, Middle Eastern and North African countries have lagged. This lag is explained, in part, by the common belief that, because demographics remain favorable (the countries are young and the labor force is expanding rapidly), financial problems are far in the future. As a result, pension reform does not need to be a priority in the broader policy agenda. However, the authors show that aging is not the only factor behind a financial crisis; the problem is the generosity of the current schemes. Moreover, badly designed benefit formulas and eligibility conditions introduce unnecessary economic distortions and make the systems vulnerable to adverse distributional transfers. The book does not present a general model that could solve the problems of all pension systems in Middle Eastern and North African countries. Instead, the authors focus on outlining a framework for guiding discussions on pension reform and making objective policy choices.

Title: *Keeping the Promise of Social Security in Latin America*

Authors: Indermit S. Gill, Truman Packard, Juan Yermo, and Todd Pugatch

Type of publication: Book

Year of publication: 2005

Abstract: Nations around the world (both large and small, rich and poor) are engaged in debate over how to reform their social security systems and care for the aged. For many countries, this debate requires speculation on hypothetical scenarios, but in Latin America, a rich body of experience on social security reform has been accumulating for more than a decade (for Chile, more than two decades). This report takes stock of those reforms, evaluates their successes and failures, and considers the lessons that can be drawn for the future of pension policy in the region. The authors draw on a series of background papers and surveys commissioned specifically for this inquiry, as well as on existing research conducted by themselves and other pension experts. In the debate on pension reform, there is no orthodoxy, as reflected in major differences of opinion among leading experts. Despite more than a decade of experience with pension reform in Latin America, reforms—although undoubtedly a major step forward—are still works in progress. This report further enriches the policy dialogue that is of crucial importance to the future of the region.

Title: *Old Age Income Support in the 21st Century: An International Perspective on Pension Systems and Reform*

Authors: Robert Holzmann and Richard Hinz

Type of publication: Book

Year of publication: 2005

Abstract: This book provides a comprehensive overview of the current policy framework that underlies the World Bank's work on pension systems and reforms and a discussion of the work to date in the area and the key issues going forward. It consists of an introduction and two main parts. Part I presents the conceptual underpinnings for the Bank's thinking on pension systems and reforms, including the structure of Bank lending in this area. Part II highlights key design and implementation issues where it signals areas of confidence and areas for further research and experience, and it includes a section on regional reform experiences, including those of Latin America and Eastern Europe and Central Asia.

Title: *Public Pension Fund Management: Governance, Accountability, and Investment Policies: Proceedings of the Second Public Pension Fund Management Conference, May 2003*

Editors: Robert J. Palacios and Alberto R. Musalem

Type of publication: Conference proceedings

Year of publication: 2004

Abstract: This volume highlights the key themes and findings of the Second Public Pension Fund Management Conference, which was organized by the World Bank and took place in May 2003. This book addresses issues of governance, accountability, and investment policies and aims to foster ongoing dialogue and exchange of experiences across regions and among emerging and developed economies.

Title: Pension Reform in Europe: Process and Progress

Editors: Robert Holzmann, Mitchell A. Orenstein, and Michal Rutkowski

Authors: Tito Boeri, Agnieszka Chłoń-Domińczak, Robert Holzmann, Florence Legros, Landis Mackellar, Marek Mora, Katharina Muller, Steven Ney, Mitchell A. Orenstein, and Michal Rutkowski

Type of publication: Book, *Directions in Development* series

Year of publication: 2003

Abstract: Pension reform is an important topic, high on the agendas of most European countries, which are profoundly affected by an aging population, lower fertility, increased life expectancy, changes in family structure, and globalization. This book presents seven papers on the political economy of European pension reform, where, clearly, major reforms are needed to ensure the sustainability of retirement income systems. However, reform programs will need to combine measures to delay retirement, introduce changes in the benefit structure, and diversify the sources of retirement income to better balance individuals' risks. Subjects address the need to accelerate the European pension reform agenda and compare pension privatization in Latin America with that in Eastern Europe. Furthermore, subjects look at democracy and structural pension reform in continental Europe, focusing on the aging population, the electoral behavior, and early retirement effects, on the basis of commitment to and consensus on—or the lack thereof—pension reform. Most interestingly, one of the subjects questions—and further analyzes—the wide differences of social policy models among transition economies, finalizing with a look at the diffusion of pension innovation. These subjects provide insight into the process and progress of European pension reform, to the benefit of the reform agenda in other regions as well.

Title: The Development and Regulation of Non-bank Financial Institutions

Authors: Jeffrey Carmichael and Michael Pomerleano

Type of publication: Book

Year of publication: 2002

Abstract: Nonbank financial institutions (NBFIs) are becoming an increasingly important segment of the financial system in some developing countries. This book aims to create awareness of the promise of NBFIs for developing countries and to assist policy makers in creating a coherent policy structure and a sound regulatory and supervisory environment for their development. The first chapter offers a coherent policy framework for addressing the regulation of NBFIs, and the second chapter addresses the principles for regulation. Subsequent chapters provide an overview of the insurance industry, mutual funds and pension schemes, leasing and real estate companies, and securities markets and discuss the specific regulatory framework for these institutions. The final chapter explores development policy challenges confronting emerging markets.

Title: *New Ideas about Old Age Security: Toward Sustainable Pension Systems in the 21st Century*

Editors: Robert Holzmann and Joseph E. Stiglitz

Type of publication: Conference proceedings

Year of publication: 2001

Abstract: Given the effect of the multipillar approach to pension reform and the diversity of its implementation, the authors, who presented papers at the 1999 conference on New Ideas about Old Age Security, reexamine the evidence and thinking on pensions and retirement security. This volume examines global issues on pension reform that help put in perspective three major sets of questions. A first set of questions deals with generic issues that concern policy makers worldwide, almost independently of approaches to reform. Most prominent but also least understood are the economic policy questions regarding the economic circumstances that are most conducive to the initiation of a reform and to its eventual success. Equally important are questions relating to the coverage of the labor force under a reformed system. Other questions concern the distributive effects of reformed systems with respect to generation, income group, and gender. A second set of questions is linked with a move toward funded provisions under a multipillar approach. A third set of questions concerns the multipillar reform approach itself. A wide consensus has emerged inside and outside the World Bank about the multipillar framework, but that consensus does not extend to several key issues regarding how the framework should be implemented in practice. The introduction to this report sums up each chapter and concludes with a discussion of policy issues and areas requiring further research.

NOTES

[1] Approximately 80 percent of the Brazil Programmatic Fiscal Reform Loan (Social Security Reform Project P086525) is used for reforming the pension system for public sector workers and private sector workers.

[2] West Bank and Gaza's Public Financial Management Reform Structural Adjustment Operation Project, P088754.

[3] Although the World Bank's (1994) publication *Averting the Old Age Crisis* was an essential part of the Bank's thinking in the 1990s, it was never suggested as a sector strategy.

[4] A recent report found that separate pension schemes exist for civil servants or other public sector workers in about half the world's countries, and those schemes tend to be more generous and less financially viable than those covering the rest of the formal sector. Furthermore, most available projections show that the situation will worsen without reform. See Palacios and Whitehouse (2006).

[5] One exception is Kazakhstan, where the implicit returns on the existing pay-as-you-go scheme would have been higher.

[6] Under such schemes, individuals accrue account balances, but such accumulations are "notionally" funded. All or part of the current contributions are used to finance the benefits of existing retirees, as is the case in most pay-as-you-go defined-benefit schemes. Individual accounts earn interest at a rate broadly equivalent to the growth of the payroll tax base, and when employees retire, their notional capital is converted into regular pension annuities, paid out of the contributions of current workers and not their own retirement savings. See Holzmann and Palmer (2006).

[7] See "Introduction and Executive Summary" in Holzmann and Hinz with others (2005: 10).

REFERENCES

Holzmann, Robert, and Richard Hinz, with Hermann von Gersdorff, Indermit Gill, Gregorio Impavida, Alberto R. Musalem, Robert Palacios, David Robolino, Michal Rutkowski, Anita Schwartz, Yvonne Sine, and Kalanidhi Subbarao. 2005. *Old-Age Income Support in the 21st Century: An International Perspective on Pension Systems and Reform.* Washington, DC: World Bank.

Holzmann, Robert, and Edward Palmer. 2006. *Pension Reform: Issues and Prospects for Non-Financial Defined Contribution (NDC) Schemes.* Washington, DC: World Bank. http://web.worldbank.org/WBSITE/EXTERNAL/TOPICS/EXTSOCIALPROTECTION/EXTPENSIONS/0,,contentMDK:20811726~pagePK:148956~piPK:216618~theSitePK:396253,00.html.

IEG (Independent Evaluation Group). 2006. "Pension Reform and the Development of Pension Systems: An Evaluation of the World Bank Assistance." World Bank, Washington, DC.

Palacios, Robert, and Edward Whitehouse. 2006. "Civil Service Pension Schemes around the World." Social Protection Discussion Paper 602, World Bank, Washington, DC. http://siteresources.worldbank.org/SOCIALPROTECTION/Resources/SP-Discussion-papers/Pensions-DP/0602.pdf.

World Bank. 1994. *Averting the Old Age Crisis.* Washington, DC: World Bank.

———. 2001. *Social Protection Sector Strategy: From Safety Net to Springboard.* Washington, DC: World Bank. http://go.worldbank.org/97LBYDY3U0.

CHAPTER 5 five

SOCIAL SAFETY NETS IN WORLD BANK LENDING AND ANALYTICAL WORK, 2002–07

Margaret Grosh and Annamaria Milazzo

INTRODUCTION

In 2007, World Bank management called for a review of the implementation of the social protection (SP) sector strategy (World Bank 2001). To support this assessment, the Human Development Network, Social Protection (HDNSP), inventoried World Bank lending and analytical work for social safety nets (SSNs) during fiscal years 2002 to 2007. In addition, HDNSP reviewed outputs of SP activities reported in implementation completion reports (ICRs) for projects that had closed during that time period.

This chapter summarizes the World Bank's lending and knowledge activities in SSNs and includes analysis by region, type of intervention involved, sector, and financing instrument. It describes briefly how the strategy for SSNs has evolved over the years and presents some key results that were achieved. This information is presented so that those interested may have a broad overview of the Bank's work in safety nets.

This chapter does not attempt to explain fully Bank policy or know-how on SSNs. Such detailed explanation is found in the safety net primer materials and the safety net Web site, which are ongoing public sources of information (see http://www.worldbank.org/safetynets), and in Grosh and others (2008).

Definitions of Key Terms

Conceptually, *social safety nets* may be defined as noncontributory transfer programs targeted in some manner to the poor and those vulnerable to poverty and shocks.[1] The terms *welfare* (especially in the United States) and *social assistance* (especially in Europe) are often used for the same concept. In the Bank's internal coding system, individual task team leaders assign codes to their projects. Sometimes they depart from the conceptual definition presented here. Thus, in the inventory that follows, a somewhat broader set of categories is used than this definition implies. Microfinance, for example, does not meet the SSN definition, but a few of the operations that provide microfinance were motivated to help households confront shocks and are therefore coded as safety nets and included in the analysis. Some training programs were also included under the same reasoning.

Table 5.1 shows the common types of SSN interventions—cash, noncash, and other interventions—and their subcategories.

The first group, cash interventions, includes programs that provide transfers in cash, whether they are means tested (such as need-based income-support programs) or categorical (such as child allowances, noncontributory pensions for the elderly, and disability benefits). It also

Margaret Grosh is lead economist and head of the Social Safety Nets Team of the World Bank's Social Protection and Labor Department. Annamaria Milazzo was a consultant at the World Bank; she is now working on her PhD at Bocconi University.

Table 5.1: Types of SSN Interventions

Type	Example of interventions
Cash	Conditional cash transfer programs
	Social assistance and income-support programs
	Family and child allowances
	Noncontributory pensions
	Disability benefits
Noncash	Food transfers
	Basic transfers: including in-kind transitional safety net assistance to cover the basic needs of former combatants and provision of "starter packs" (including fertilizers, tools, and the like)
	Education related: school vouchers, scholarships, and fee waivers
	Training for beneficiaries: mainly vocational and skills training
	Health related: fee waivers and exemptions for health care services
	Energy subsidies
	Housing: support for housing improvement, rent subsidies, and housing assistance[a]
Others	Public works
	Microcredit and income-generation opportunities
	Technical assistance[b]
	Other activities[c]

Source: Authors' representation.

a. Through housing assistance, the World Bank finances housing reconstruction or rehabilitation of destroyed or damaged houses in areas hit by a natural disaster (such as in areas recently affected by the earthquake in Pakistan or the tsunami in South Asia).

b. The technical assistance components include such things as providing (a) institutional development and support to strengthen the institutional capacity of key government agencies to improve the administration, coverage, and targeting of the SSN for the poor, as well as training programs aimed at upgrading the skills of officials and government staff members involved in SSN interventions, and (b) support to social sector reforms involving SSN-related activities of a system and performance evaluations and public monitoring of the main social sector programs.

c. This category includes employment services, job creation, and employment programs for youth at risk; social services; compensation funds for farmers; and HIV awareness an counseling activities.

includes conditional cash transfers (CCTs), which are an increasingly popular instrument of social assistance. CCTs provide cash transfers to poor families conditional on certain behavior, such as ensuring that the children regularly attend school and receive adequate preventive health care. CCTs aim at reducing poverty in the short term through cash transfers and promote investments in human capital that encourage the use of education and health facilities. Box 5.1 provides three examples of successful applications of CCTs.

The noncash category includes food-based programs (for example, school feeding, maternal-child supplements, and food rations); training opportunities for beneficiaries (vocational and skill training); interventions to lower the cost of accessing health and education facilities (fee waivers); and price subsidies for energy or housing.

The third set of interventions, labeled "other," consists of public works, microcredit, and other income-generating activities. Public works (or *workfare*) constitute the most important SSN intervention within this category. Public works typically provide low-skill employment opportunities (that is, construction or rehabilitation of much-needed public infrastructures) to poor people who are willing to work for a low wage paid in cash or in kind. Microcredit programs and other activities, such as support to initiate small-scale activities that facilitate access to income-earning opportunities, are also in this category.

In addition to lending to support the costs of the transfers themselves, the Bank supports SSNs through technical assistance (TA). TA is aimed at strengthening the capacity of government agencies involved in implementing SSNs. It may support the improvement of the targeting system, the

BOX 5.1

THREE STORIES OF SUCCESSFUL CCT PROGRAMS

BANGLADESH: FEMALE SECONDARY SCHOOL ASSISTANCE

Selina was enrolled in Mirpur Girls High School in 1995, which is about 5 kilometers from her home. She received a regular stipend while attending grades 6 to 10. She used a part of the stipend money to pay for her commute to school; she had to walk about 1.7 kilometers to the Kamaichauri Police Box, where she would catch a bus to the school. The commute was hard for Selina, but she knew that she had to maintain 75 percent attendance in school to continue getting the stipend, so she was seldom absent. Because of her regular attendance, she was able to improve her results every year; when she was first enrolled in grade 6 she was 72nd in her class, in grade 7 she was 6th, and in grade 8 she was 5th. In 2000, Selina passed the Secondary School Certificate exam in Humanities with a B average. According to Selina, although the amount of stipend is small, it played a crucial role in terms of enabling her to pursue education. "If I didn't get the stipend, then it would have been impossible for me to continue schooling," said Selina.

BRAZIL: BOLSA FAMÍLIA PROGRAM

Dinalva Moura, a mother of three, has been part of Brazil's Bolsa Família Program. She says, "The Bolsa Família helps me buy food—sometimes even fruit for the children. And they don't skip school, because they know the money depends on their going."

COLOMBIA: FAMILIAS EN ACCIÓN

Gloria Pedraza is a 36-year-old mother of six, who lives in Tolima, a municipality near Bogotá. She belongs to the poorest of the poor in Colombia. "Even though my husband is away, I have money for food," Pedraza stated, referring to the US$52 subsidy she receives from the government every month as a beneficiary of Familias en Acción. Thanks to these cash transfers, which are equivalent to US$6 a month for each child enrolled in elementary school and US$12 for secondary school (grades 7–9), close to a million children will be able not only to have an education, but also to eat properly.

SOCIAL RISK MITIGATION PROJECT: A SUCCESSFUL SSN PROJECT IN TURKEY

"I have five children; for three I receive education money. My daughter is in high school, the oldest boy is in the technical school and the younger boy is in the sixth grade. I have a baby of 18 months and another 6 years of age; I am not sure that I receive health support for them. I started getting the money in September 2004; received four payments so far: once YTL 44 and three times YTL 106. When I receive the money, I buy fruit juice for the children and give them pocket money. When I buy them clothing for the school, they change ... they become happy. Sometimes we spend YTL 2 to YTL 3 on the children, other times only YTL 0.25. They walk about 20 minutes to the school. Each child has a different problem." (A mother from Southeastern Anatolia)

Sources: Bangladesh, Ahmed 2004; Brazil, Zoellick 2007; Colombia, World Bank 2002. Kudat 2006.

development of operational manuals, and the establishment or enhancement of monitoring information systems as well as monitoring and evaluation systems.

How Bank Thinking on Social Safety Nets Has Evolved

Safety nets help redistribute income to the poorest and most vulnerable and have an immediate effect on poverty and inequality. They also contribute to social risk management,[2] thus playing a productive role in economies. In particular, SSNs play a productive role in the following:

- *Enabling households to make better investments in their futures.* In this role, safety nets basically act to remedy credit market failures by allowing households to take up investment opportunities that they would otherwise miss—both in the human capital of the children and in the livelihoods of the earners.
- *Helping households manage risk.* At minimum, safety net programs help households facing hard times avoid irreversible losses, allowing them (a) to maintain the household and business assets their livelihoods are based on and (b) to adequately nourish and school their children. At best, SSNs can provide an insurance element that allows households to make choices about livelihoods that yield higher earnings. SSNs thus both protect and promote independence.
- *Allowing societies to make choices that support efficiency and growth.* Safety nets support good policy in varying degrees

of directness. Most direct is that a good social assistance program can replace inefficient redistributive elements in other programs. Less direct but still widely recognized is that safety nets play a role in helping governments adopt or sustain sound macro, trade, and other policies. Also, safety nets can mitigate the negative effects that high inequality has on the development of sound institutions.

Safety nets fit into the wider array of policies involved in poverty reduction, risk management, and social protection (figure 5.1). Safety nets are part, but not the whole, of each, and poverty reduction and risk management strategies overlap substantially but not entirely. Safety nets are not the only, or even the principal, tool for achieving any of the ends they serve. Yet they can make a very important contribution. When situations are most dire, they can help save lives. When situations are less dire and programs especially good, they can save or help build livelihoods.

The productive, as opposed to the redistributive, role of safety nets is becoming more recognized. This shift in understanding has helped pave the way for increased work on long-term safety nets as well as for expansion of programs (especially CCT programs) in middle-income countries and increased interest in safety nets in low-income countries.

Because the Bank's engagement is increasingly geared to long-term social policy and not just immediate and temporary programs, the issues encompass not only the choice of programs but also the implementation and perfection of their targeting and administrative systems. Almost all safety net projects overseen by the Social Protection Sector Board contain elements to strengthen those elements. The best targeting systems in Bank client countries that worked with the Bank on SSNs, such as Brazil and Romania, have achieved levels of accuracy similar to those in the United Kingdom and the United States. This success demonstrates the potential for improvement in other client countries, where a fifth of programs with targeting instruments that can yield good results were still producing regressive outcomes as recently as 2004. The Bank's Europe and Central Asia (ECA) Region, for example, has made loans specifically for improving social protection administration capacity in a number of countries, including Armenia, Croatia, Georgia, Serbia, and Ukraine. The Latin America and Caribbean (LAC) Region carried out a special review of control and accountability mechanisms in Bank-financed CCT programs to identify areas for institutional strengthening.

Many countries—especially middle-income countries—are improving permanent safety nets, often using CCT programs

FIGURE 5.1: HOW SAFETY NETS FIT INTO THE BANK'S BROAD DEVELOPMENT STRATEGY

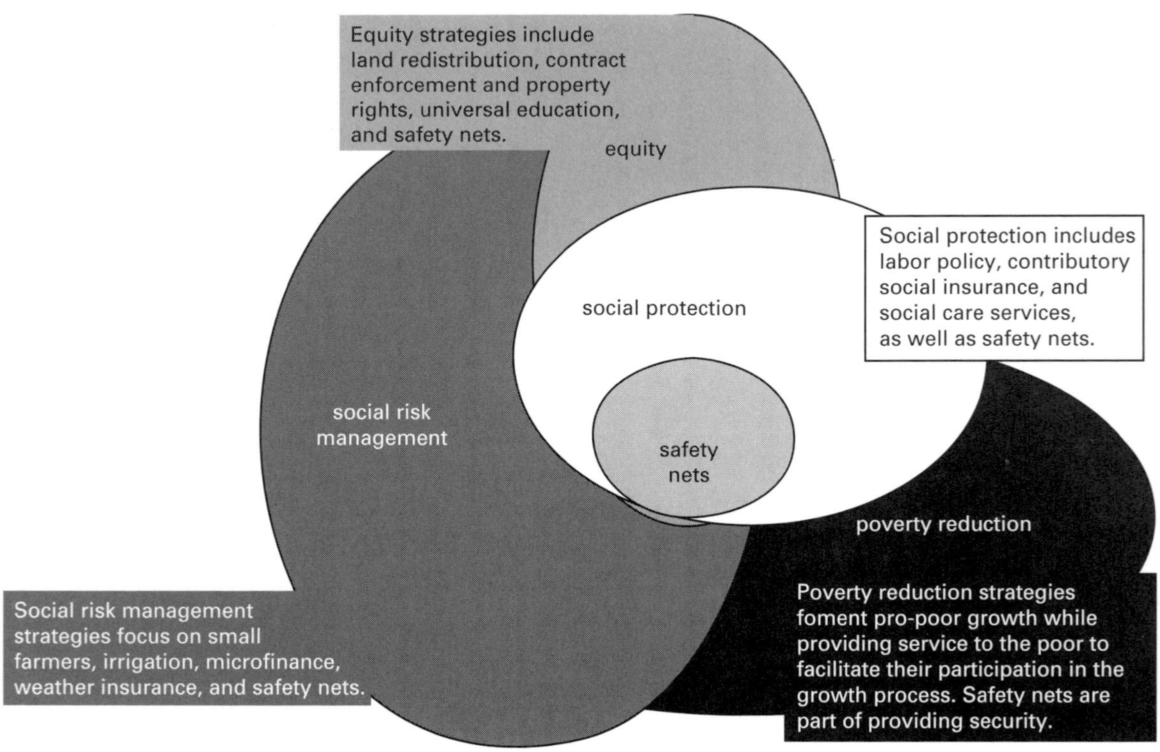

Source: Grosh and others 2008.

as the instrument of choice. These programs transfer cash to poor families on the condition that the families ensure that the children regularly attend school and receive prescribed standards of preventive health care. From only three countries with such programs a decade ago, two dozen now have full-scale programs or pilots, and as many more are considering them. The early programs had "gold-standard" experimental design evaluations, showing effective targeting, effects on poverty and inequality commensurate with the (varied) transfer size; largely positive effects on school enrollment and use of health services; and more muted but often positive effects on educational and health status (see the section titled "Results").

The Bank has been actively involved in this agenda. It is lending to 16 countries so far, with several other countries in the pipeline,[3] and is doing country-specific analytical and advisory activities (AAA), study tours, or evaluations for at least a dozen others. The Bank has convened three biennial international conferences for program officials and their counterparts. The June 2006 conference in Istanbul drew together about 375 delegates from 40 countries and a dozen donor agencies. Still more individuals were able to participate through the Webcast.

For low-income countries, especially in Sub-Saharan Africa and South Asia, dialogue on safety nets has increased substantially. More than a dozen African countries are either piloting or considering cash transfer programs. Social funds have recently been experimenting with innovative community-based approaches in delivering safety net services in low-income countries. For example, community institutions for implementing cash transfers are being piloted in Nigeria, Sierra Leone, Tanzania, and Uganda, and community targeting and participatory methods in public works programs are being piloted in Malawi, Tanzania, and Uganda.

METHODOLOGY

In inventorying the portfolio, the results will differ somewhat according to definitions and data sources. Here we explain those used in this chapter.

How the Bank Accounts for SSN Lending: Coding

Since December 2001, project task team leaders have assigned thematic codes to projects. The team leader may use up to five codes for each project. Thematic code 54, *Social Safety Nets,* is meant to capture safety net activities. The guidance note for coding defines thematic code 54 as

→ *Activities intended to provide social assistance (i.e., in-kind or cash assistance to poor and vulnerable individuals or families, including those to help cope with consequences of economic or other shocks). It includes: benefits in-cash to vulnerable groups; benefits in-kind to vulnerable groups; subsidies for goods to vulnerable groups; subsidies for services to vulnerable groups; workfare programs; other risk coping activities. (World Bank 2006a)*

Business Warehouse, an in-house World Bank database, provided the list that forms the universe of projects.[4] Additional documents for 180 projects were examined to supplement the information available from Business Warehouse. The review of project documents was based primarily on project appraisal or information documents. When those documents were not available, completion reports or other relevant available documents were used. All 145 projects identified as containing safety nets were included in the analysis[5] (see annex 5.E for further details on the methodology).

How the Bank Accounts for SSN Analytical Work

The goal of this analysis was to capture the full scope of World Bank analytical work on SSNs.[6] Official economic and sector work (ESW) tasks[7] were counted, encompassing both diagnostic reports (such as poverty assessments, risk and vulnerability assessments, public expenditure reviews, and development policy reviews) and advisory reports (such as general economy studies, other SP studies, other poverty studies, and other health studies).[8] Such reports do not deal exclusively with SSN programs but may provide an extensive diagnosis of different aspects (for example, poverty status, government spending, or reforms agenda) of a country or region. Also included in the search were working or discussion papers (World Bank numbered series), as well as other studies carried out within the Bank, such as books, *World Development Reports*, and Poverty Reduction Strategy Papers dealing with safety nets.

Several search strategies were used to identify SSN-related analytical work:

- Business Warehouse provided a list of all Bank-generated official ESWs with thematic code 54.[9]
- Bank-produced documents from thematic bibliographies on various safety net programs that were pulled together by the Safety Nets Team for other purposes were included. Most of these documents were working papers, discussion papers, World Bank journal articles, and the like.

- Information was included from an inventory of documents that outline safety net expenditures as part of a public expenditure review study.[10]
- A keyword search for *safety nets* on ImageBank under the "Publication and Research" and "Analytical and Advisory Work" search fields was conducted to incorporate items not already captured by the preceding sources.[11]

At the end of this exercise,[12] an inventory was produced that included 315 documents that addressed at least one type of SSN program or SSN-related issue. Still, some errors are probable, involving exclusion of items that were not cataloged in the official system or published in a publicly available series. The authors have personally peer reviewed a few such items and presume that many more exist.

REVIEW OF SSN PORTFOLIO, 2002–07

Overall Portfolio

During fiscal years 2002 to 2007, safety nets appear in 145 projects (see table 5.2). The total value of these projects is US$13.4 billion, of which 25 percent is dedicated to safety net activities. The safety net portfolio is US$3.4 billion (see table 5.3). Nine percent of all World Bank projects include safety nets, although they are usually a small share of the overall loan. The safety net portfolio accounts for 2.6 percent of total World Bank lending.[13]

The analysis can be extended back to 1998 by drawing on an inventory done before the current coding scheme was put in place (Amde 2003). The prior inventory was constructed from a project document search through key

Table 5.2: **Number of Projects with Safety Net Components by Region, Fiscal Years 2002–07**

Region	Fiscal year 2002	2003	2004	2005	2006	2007	Total
Africa	2	11	3	9	1	7	33
East Asia and the Pacific	0	1	0	4	1	1	7
Europe and Central Asia	8	5	5	4	5	3	30
Latin America and the Caribbean	3	10	8	7	9	6	43
Middle East and North Africa	2	2	3	1	0	5	13
South Asia	1	1	0	4	6	7	19
Total	16	30	19	29	22	29	145

Source: Authors' calculations, based on the Business Warehouse data and World Bank documents.

Table 5.3: **Lending Commitments for Safety Nets by Region, Fiscal Years 2002–07**

Region	Fiscal year (US$ millions) 2002	2003	2004	2005	2006	2007	Total (US$ millions)
Africa	58.9	123.3	39.7	112.4	5.5	93.3	433.2
East Asia and the Pacific	0.0	55.0	0.0	61.6	64.0	8.0	188.6
Europe and Central Asia	136.4	91.9	24.8	88.6	102.3	10.1	454.0
Latin America and the Caribbean	63.0	857.5	311.1	176.6	207.9	120.9	1,736.9
Middle East and North Africa	4.4	6.8	17.0	24.0	0.0	18.8	70.9
South Asia	30.2	39.2	0.0	96.5	158.5	192.7	517.0
Total	293.0	1,173.7	392.5	559.6	538.2	443.7	3,400.7

Source: Authors' calculations, based on the Business Warehouse data and World Bank documents.
Note: Because of rounding, totals may deviate slightly from the sum of the parts.

words related to safety nets. It resulted in a count of 95 projects from fiscal years 1998 to 2001. Then, as now, few projects were devoted solely to safety nets. However, the previous inventory did not assign a dollar value to the components or the activities within projects. Thus, the historical analysis is based only on the number of projects. The current social risk management strategy that guides SP and that shows SSNs are not only redistributive vehicles but also an important and productive part of a risk management strategy was published in 1999, a year in which the East Asian financial crisis necessitated increased lending. Thus, 1998 may serve as a reasonable base year for historical comparison. Although wide variation occurs, the general trend is an increase in SSN projects. The LAC, Africa (AFR), and ECA Regions generally have the highest number of SSN projects. Moreover, the South Asia Region (SAR) is recently experiencing a substantial increase in the number of projects involving SSN activities (figure 5.2).

Figure 5.3 reflects the effect of high-dollar-value loans on the variability of SSN shares. In fiscal year 2003, for example, large loans to Argentina's Jefes de Hogar program[14] (US$600 million for the program itself and an additional US$120 million to improve monitoring and transparency of *jefes* as the social component of a separate

FIGURE 5.2: NUMBER OF PROJECTS INVOLVING SSNs BY REGION AND FISCAL YEAR, FISCAL YEARS 1998–2007

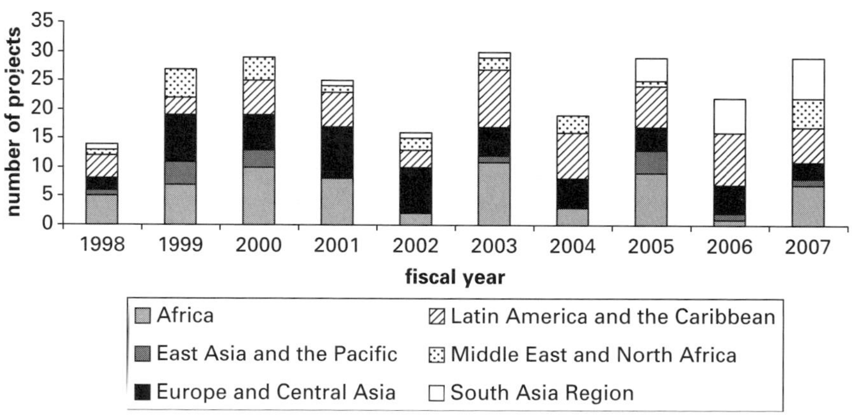

Source: Authors' calculations, based on the Business Warehouse data and World Bank documents.
Note: The total number of projects is 240.

FIGURE 5.3: SSN PORTFOLIO, FISCAL YEARS 2002–07

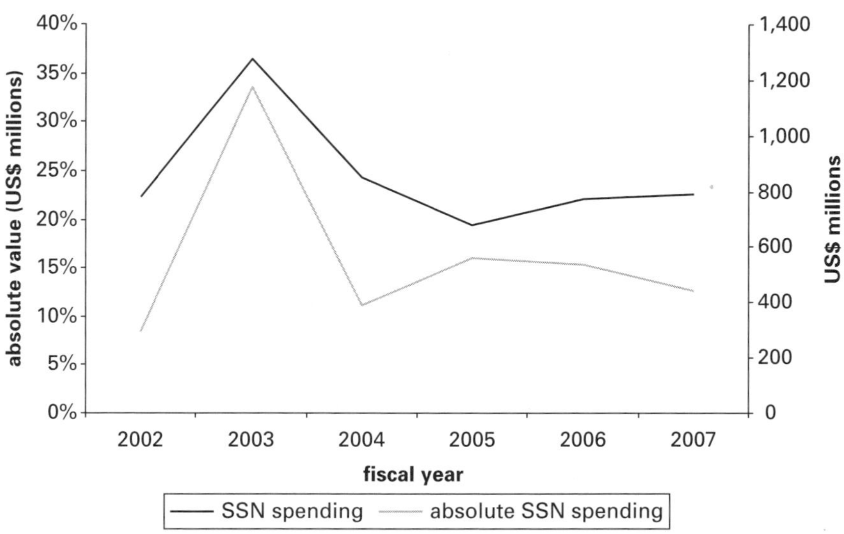

Source: Authors' calculations, based on the Business Warehouse data and World Bank documents.

Economic and Social Transition Structural Adjustment Loan Project) in response to the Argentine financial crisis resulted in a portfolio size nearly double the average for other years. Although the quantitative analysis presented here does not extend back so far, a similar spike occurred in fiscal year 1999 around the East Asian financial crisis, when large safety net loans were made to Indonesia, the Republic of Korea, and Thailand.[15]

Figure 5.4 shows the greater activity in the number of SSN-related analytical reports during fiscal years 2003 to 2007, compared with the activity during fiscal years 1999 to 2002. Two factors may account for this increase in activity: the timing of the financial crises and the release of the SP strategy paper in 2001. Analytical work was carried out to support countries in crisis, and additional effort was taken to do country-specific diagnostic work using the new SP strategic framework.

One area where the treatment of safety nets has unambiguously increased is in Country Assistance Strategies (CASs). Nsour (2007) analyzed the frequency and depth of SP themes in a sample of 18 strategic CASs published in fiscal years 2005 and 2006 and in the preceding CAS for each of the same countries. Increases had clearly occurred both in the number of countries covering safety nets and in the depth of their treatment. The results were especially marked in the diagnosis of country needs, with smaller but positive increases also found in the lending and analytical work proposed. In the more recent cycle of CASs, safety nets were considered in some way in 17 of 18 reviewed.

Distribution of Safety Net Lending and Analytical Work by Region

Sixty-eight countries[16] have at least one loan that involves safety nets, and half of those countries have more than one loan. At seven loans, Colombia and Pakistan have the highest number of loans involving safety nets.[17] The average number of loans per country is 2.1.

In 2002 to 2007, the LAC Region had the largest number of World Bank lending activities involving SSN interventions (43 projects, or 29 percent of the number of SSN projects in the inventory), followed by the AFR Region (33 projects), the ECA Region (30 projects), and the South Asia Region (19 projects). The Middle East and North Africa (MENA) Region and the East Asia and the Pacific (EAP) Region had only a few projects each (figure 5.5, panel a). By a wide margin, the LAC Region also claimed the highest share of lending of the SSN portfolio by dollar value (51 percent), followed by SAR (15 percent), the ECA and AFR Regions (13 percent each), the EAP Region (6 percent), and the MENA Region (2 percent) (figure 5.5, panel b).

Figure 5.6 shows that Latin America became dominant in the portfolio in the second part of the study period (fiscal years 2002–07). The LAC Region experienced a large increase (by 50 percent) in its share of total SSN

FIGURE 5.4: **ANALYTICAL PRODUCTS DEALING WITH SSN BY REGION AND FISCAL YEAR, FISCAL YEARS 1999–2007**

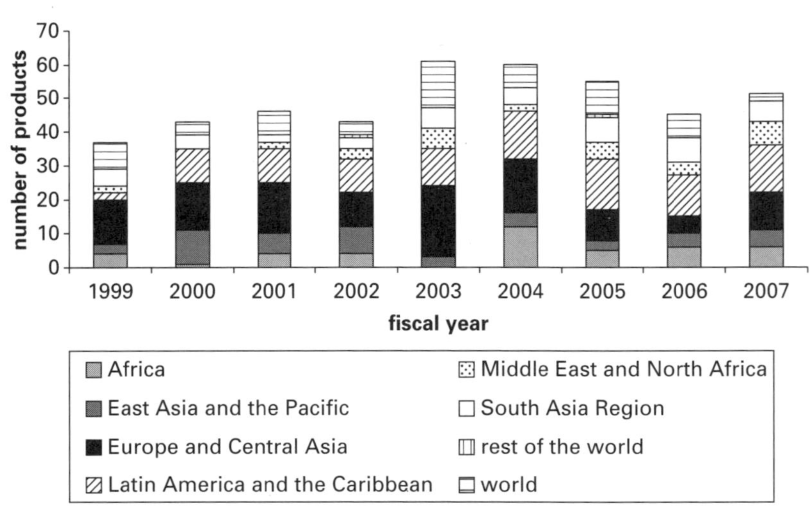

Source: Authors' calculations, based on the Business Warehouse data and World Bank documents.
Note: Total number of analytical products is 441.

FIGURE 5.5: **PROJECTS INVOLVING SSNs BY REGION, FISCAL YEARS 2002–07**

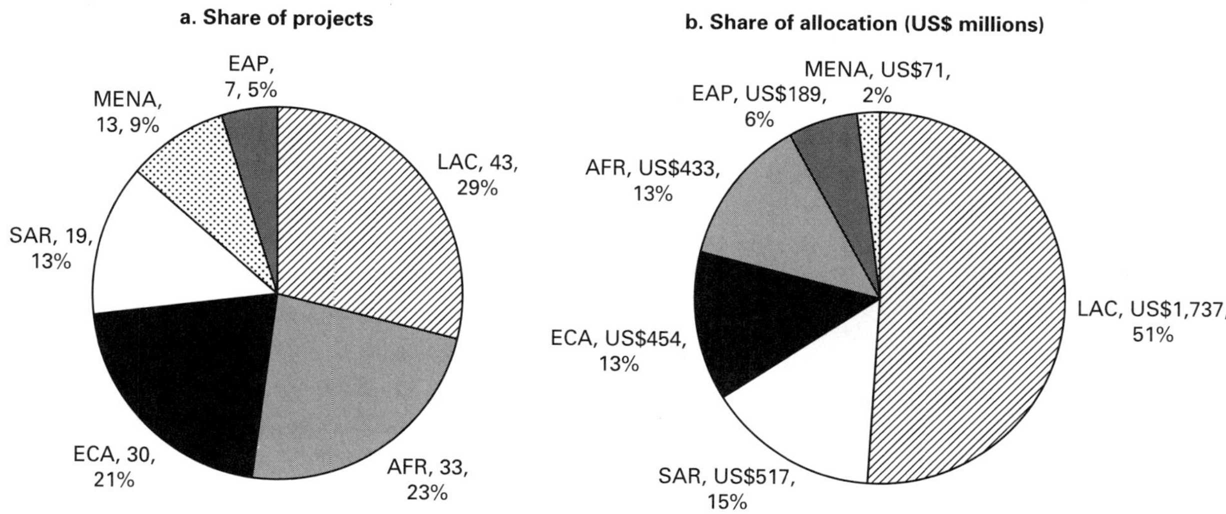

Source: Authors' calculations, based on the Business Warehouse data and World Bank documents.
Note: AFR = Africa; EAP = East Asia and the Pacific; ECA = Europe and Central Asia; LAC = Latin America and the Caribbean; MENA = Middle East and North Africa; SAR = South Asia Region. Panel a shows the number and share of total analytical products. The total number of products is 145. Panel b shows the U.S. dollar amount and share of allocation. The total amount of allocation was US$3.4 billion.

FIGURE 5.6: **AVERAGE NUMBER OF PROJECTS PER YEAR BY REGION, FISCAL YEARS 1998–2001 AND 2002–07**

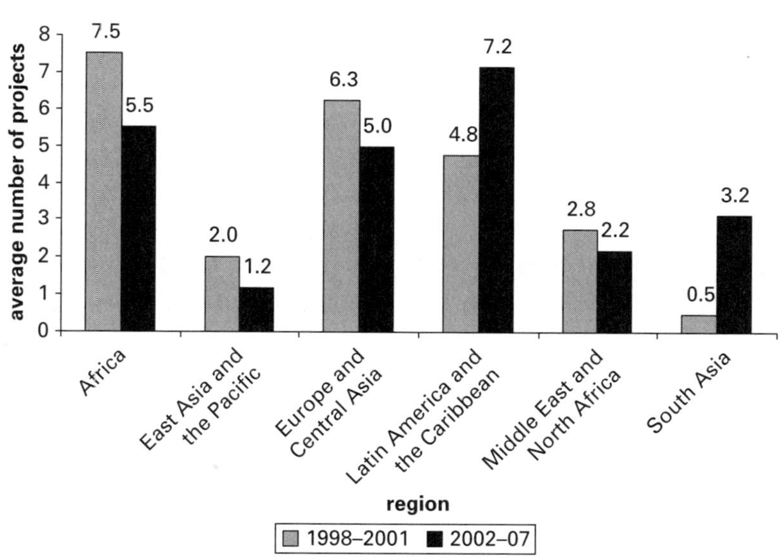

Source: Authors' calculations, based on the Business Warehouse data and World Bank documents.
Note: The total number of projects is 240.

projects when compared against the early and late inventories of average number of projects per year by region. Although South Asia has had a small share of the portfolio over the period, the average number of projects per year has increased considerably from 0.5 to 3.2 in the later years. These SAR programs, while providing support to government SP interventions, were mainly geared toward housing reconstruction and emergency assistance following recent natural disasters (the 2006 earthquake in Pakistan and 2005 tsunami in South Asia).

The regional pattern of analytical work is somewhat similar to that for lending—with Latin America and the Caribbean the most active region. The differentials are, however, somewhat smaller with the MENA and EAP Regions, which are

FIGURE 5.7: SHARE OF ANALYTICAL PRODUCTS DEALING WITH SSNs BY REGION, FISCAL YEARS 2002–07

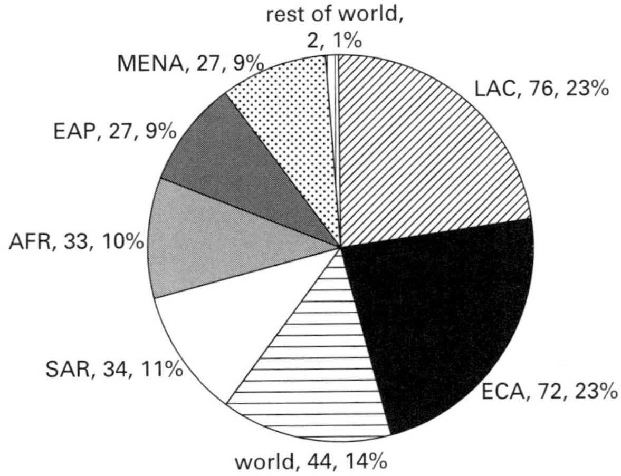

Source: Authors' calculations, based on the Business Warehouse data and World Bank documents.
Note: AFR = Africa; EAP = East Asia and the Pacific; ECA = Europe and Central Asia; LAC = Latin America and the Caribbean; MENA = Middle East and North Africa; SAR = South Asia Region. Figure shows the number and share of total analytical products.

comparatively more active in analytical work than in lending (figure 5.7). The ECA Region carries a heavier weight in analytical work than in lending. This emphasis on analytical work may reflect the fact that it has been more important to achieve greater efficiency and equity of ECA's already high level of spending on SP than to borrow additional funds for SP. Conversely, the relatively large and increasing lending commitments for the SAR are not reflected by a similar pattern in the analytical effort, which remains low in comparative terms.

Distribution of Lending and Analytical Work by Type of Lending: International Bank for Reconstruction and Development and International Development Association

A common perception is that only high- or middle-income countries can afford social protection. The Social Risk Management framework takes the opposite position, showing that risk management can be especially important for poor people and for poor countries. Therefore, this chapter examines the portfolio by level of country income, using the World Bank's International Development Association (IDA) and International Bank for Reconstruction and Development (IBRD) threshold for analysis.[18] Panel a of figure 5.8 shows that the number of projects containing SSNs is about evenly split between IDA (61 projects) and IBRD (51 projects) countries. Panel b of figure 5.8, however, shows that IBRD-eligible countries receive 62 percent of the lending by dollar amount for SSN activities. This share is about the same as the share of the overall Bank portfolio across all themes, where 58 percent of lending is to IBRD countries.

For analytical work, the largest share of products dealing with SSNs focused on IBRD countries (34 percent), while a relatively smaller share analyzed SSNs in IDA countries (27 percent) (figure 5.9). The category "not assigned" is large in the analytical category because many of the products analyze multiple countries that include both IDA and IBRD countries.

Distribution of SSN Lending and Analytical Work by Lending Instruments: Investment and Policy

Figure 5.10 illustrates the regional distribution of SSN projects and their dollar value for both investment and policy-based loans. Seventy percent of the projects approved over fiscal years 2002 to 2007 are investment loans, which represent 62 percent of the total spending on SSN activities; the remainder are policy-based or "adjustment" operations. The average adjustment loan is larger in lending amount than the average investment loan, with the exception of lending in the LAC and AFR Regions.

Figure 5.11 shows the many types of analytical work on safety nets. The largest category is working papers, which, together with the book category, total 43 percent of the whole and show an effort to disseminate information beyond the country most directly concerned so that others may learn from that country's experience—the "knowledge bank" side of the World Bank. Safety net issues seem well represented in cross-sector or due diligence work, with public expenditure reviews, poverty reduction strategy work, and poverty assessments accounting for 28 percent of safety nets analytics (also see annex 5.C for a breakdown of types of analytical work, by fiscal year and region).

In addition to supporting safety nets through lending and analytical work, the World Bank is active in capacity building through training. Most of this training is supplied by the World Bank Institute or the Social Protection Unit in the network anchor, most often working together on events. These groups sponsored about 20,000 training days over the fiscal years 2005 and 2006 in events that either dealt solely with safety nets or included significant treatment

FIGURE 5.8: **PROJECTS INVOLVING SSNs BY COUNTRY ELIGIBILITY, FISCAL YEARS 2002–07**

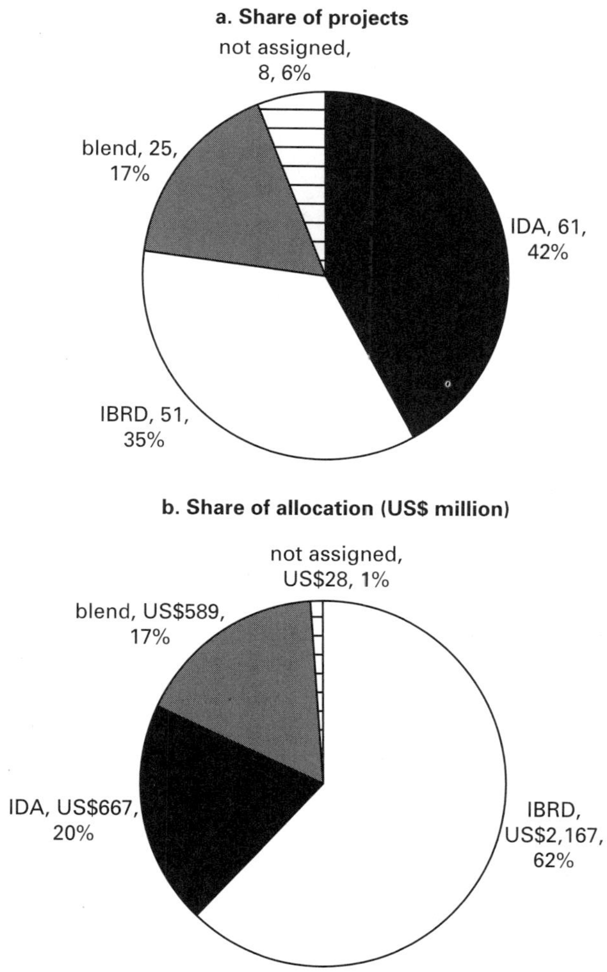

Source: Authors' calculations, based on the Business Warehouse data and World Bank documents.
Note: IBRD = International Bank for Reconstruction and Development; IDA = International Development Association. Panel a shows the number of projects and share of total projects. Panel b shows the U.S. dollar amount and share of total allocation.

of safety nets within a broader social protection setting. Most of the events were aimed at a joint audience of Bank staff members and external participants and often even at specific Bank-client teams, which could use the training to leverage policy action most effectively.

Distribution of SSN Lending and Analytical Work by Sector Board

Despite some recent developments, the World Bank organizational chart during fiscal years 2002 to 2007 had 17 sectors: 3 or 4 sectors grouped into each of six operational networks.[19] The group of managers from across the Bank

FIGURE 5.9: **SHARE OF ANALYTICAL PRODUCTS DEALING WITH SSNs BY COUNTRY ELIGIBILITY, FISCAL YEARS 2002–07**

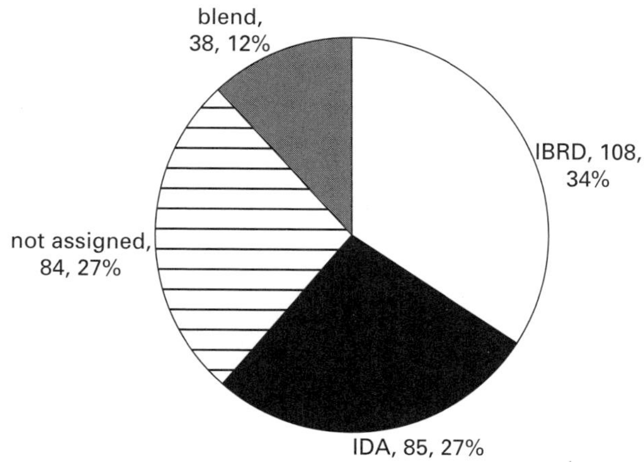

Source: Authors' calculations, based on the Business Warehouse data and World Bank documents.
Note: IBRD = International Bank for Reconstruction and Development; IDA = International Development Association. Figure shows the number of projects and share of total projects.

within a sector is referred to as a *sector board*. The sector board has certain responsibilities for oversight of the tasks mapped to that sector through sector and thematic codes, including quality assurance. Also, the central units responsible for much of the knowledge management and training done by the World Bank get input on their work program from the sector board.

Forty-two percent of the projects with safety net components were mapped to the Social Protection Sector Board, corresponding to 54 percent of the total spending on safety net activities (figure 5.12). The rest of the projects are scattered over a large number of other sectors, indicating that safety nets are used, as would be expected, in a wide range of policy reforms or tools to improve equity in sector-specific ways. For instance, the Urban Development Sector Board approved 10 percent of the projects (corresponding to 11 percent of the allocation) involving at least one safety net component (mostly disaster relief assistance). Box 5.2 illustrates some of the many projects containing safety nets handled outside the SP sector.

It is interesting to examine how the loans that are not mapped to the Social Protection Sector Board differ from those that are. First, the share of the total loan amount mapped to safety nets is smaller for projects mapped to other sector boards (19.6 percent compared with 33.5 percent). Second, the regional mix is quite different. Within loans mapped to the Social Protection Sector Board, the LAC Region dominates; it has nearly three-fourths of

FIGURE 5.10: **PROJECTS INVOLVING SSN ACTIVITIES BY LENDING INSTRUMENT AND REGION, FISCAL YEARS 2002–07**

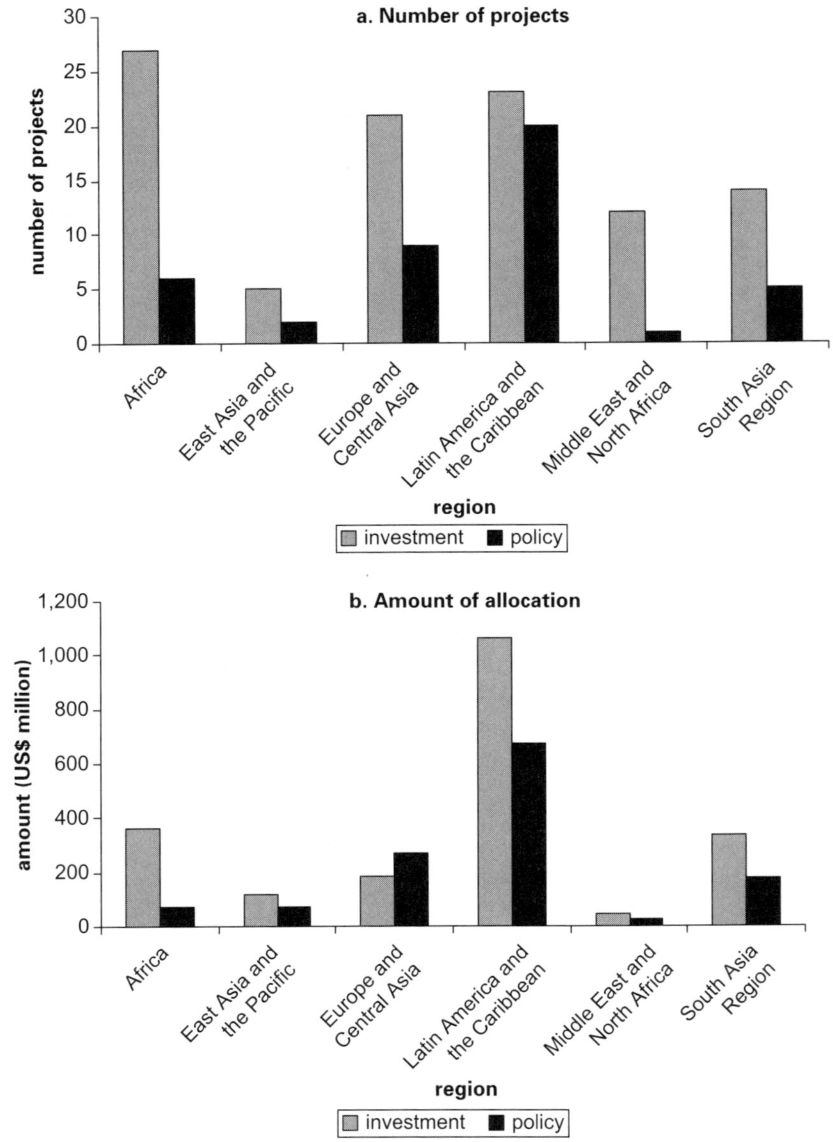

Source: Authors' calculations, based on the Business Warehouse data and World Bank documents.
Note: Policy instruments include development policy loans, poverty reduction credits, and programmatic structural adjustment loans.

SSN lending (figure 5.13, panel a). In contrast, for loans mapped to other sector boards, the LAC Region has less than a third of the total. Also interesting to note is that lending for SSNs in the South Asia and EAP Regions is almost exclusively supported through projects approved by sector boards other than the Social Protection Sector Board[20] (figure 5.13, panel b). Third, the types of safety net activities do vary somewhat by sector (figure 5.14). For example, within the category of cash transfers, the bulk of CCT activities are mapped through the Social Protection Sector Board, but the bulk of nonconditional income support is mapped through the Poverty Reduction and Economic Management (PREM) Sector Board. Within the noncash category, projects mapped to the Social Protection Sector Board include training, whereas those mapped to infrastructure contain housing. The Social Protection Sector Board approved most of the public works projects. TA is supported in loans mapped both to the Social Protection Sector Board and to the PREM Sector Board.

For analytical work, many networks—and, within them, sectors—are active in safety nets. The Human Development Network (HDN) is responsible for 45 percent of the analytical work produced on safety nets (figure 5.15), 94 percent of which is done by the SP sector (the education and health sector produces the remaining analytical products within the HDN). The PREM Sector Board[21] is responsible for

FIGURE 5.11: SHARES OF ANALYTICAL PRODUCT TYPES DEALING WITH SSNs, FISCAL YEARS 2002–07

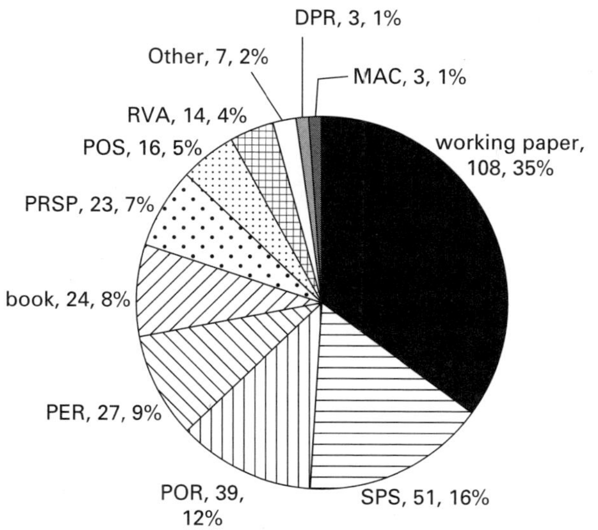

Source: Authors' calculations, based on the Business Warehouse data and World Bank documents.
Note: DPR = development policy review; MAC = general economy, macroeconomics, or growth study; PER = public expenditure review; POR = poverty assessment; POS = other poverty study; PRSP = Poverty Reduction Strategy Paper; RVA = risk and vulnerability assessment; SPS = other social protection studies. Figure shows number and share of SSN-related documents. The total number of documents is 315.

another 40 percent of the analytical work, presumably because it carries out most of the public expenditure reviews, poverty assessments, and poverty reduction strategy assessment exercises in which safety nets commonly figure as a theme. This distribution seems to indicate good mainstreaming of the topic.

The diversity of interventions and actors within the Bank poses challenges in knowledge management and quality assurance. Staff members across many sectors must have basic knowledge of safety net policy and practice as well as access to more detail on some parts of safety net policy when they need it. The safety net primer and associated Web site and the safety net thematic group are designed to help staff members acquire this basic knowledge of safety nets. Although they may not rise to the challenge in all dimensions, the primer and Web site either treat in depth or provide links to other Web sites that offer good treatment of most of the interventions involved in the portfolio.[22] The thematic group has a membership that reaches far beyond the SP sector; indeed, only 30 percent are from the SP sector, 36 percent are from the PREM Sector Board, and the remaining third from the range of other sectors. These tools provide a good means of disseminating what is learned in SP operations to others, although they do so more successfully probably to those in the PREM Sector Board and the education and health sectors than to those in housing or energy. The structural challenges in capturing learning in the more far-flung sectors and bringing it back to SP are greater, but not new, and they are partially addressed by the diversity in the thematic group and the comprehensive work in the safety nets primer.

Distribution of Safety Net Lending and Analytical Work by Types of Intervention

The total lending portfolio for SSNs covers many different types of intervention. Noncash assistance (for training, education, health, housing, and energy—see box 5.3) dominates the portfolio in terms of the number of activities (see figure 5.16), but it is slightly smaller in terms of dollar value than cash programs. Conversely, there are relatively few public works projects, but some are large (especially Argentina's Jefes program), which makes their total dollar value high. Figure 5.17, shows that, by dollar value, the portfolio is nearly evenly divided among a range of cash programs, various types of noncash programs, public works, and TA, in that order, with much smaller amounts going to microfinance, others, and food-related projects.[23] Box 5.4 provides two examples of successful public works activities.

Despite the ubiquitous appearance of CCTs in recent development writing, from serious evaluation literature to the popular press, the portfolio of CCTs is a rather small—just 6 percent by number of projects and 14 percent by dollar volume. Part of the reason for the lower measured shares is methodological.[24] If only loans approved by the Social Protection Sector Board are considered, taking those that have safety nets as a primary objective, and the full value of the loan is counted, then CCTs constitute about 30 percent of the portfolio. Even this percentage may seem low compared to the perceived domination of CCTs in the portfolio. This situation results in part because the Bank has engaged in AAA in a number of countries where it has not made loans (Mexico being a rather prominent example). Moreover, the first-generation CCT programs are well documented and evaluated; as a result, discussions of aspects of safety nets not uniquely pertinent to CCTs, such as targeting, evaluation, and accountability mechanisms, tend to be illustrated with examples from CCT programs. Thus, they get more "airtime" than is merited by their weight in the portfolio.

Detail by type of activity and region is presented in annex 5.A. Technical assistance is concentrated in the ECA and LAC Regions. Public works are found mostly in the LAC and AFR Regions, with the Africa Region having a slightly higher number of projects—but again the large loan to Argentina's Jefes program puts the bulk of the dollar portfolio

FIGURE 5.12: **PROJECTS INVOLVING SSN ACTIVITIES BY SECTOR BOARD, FISCAL YEARS 2002–07**

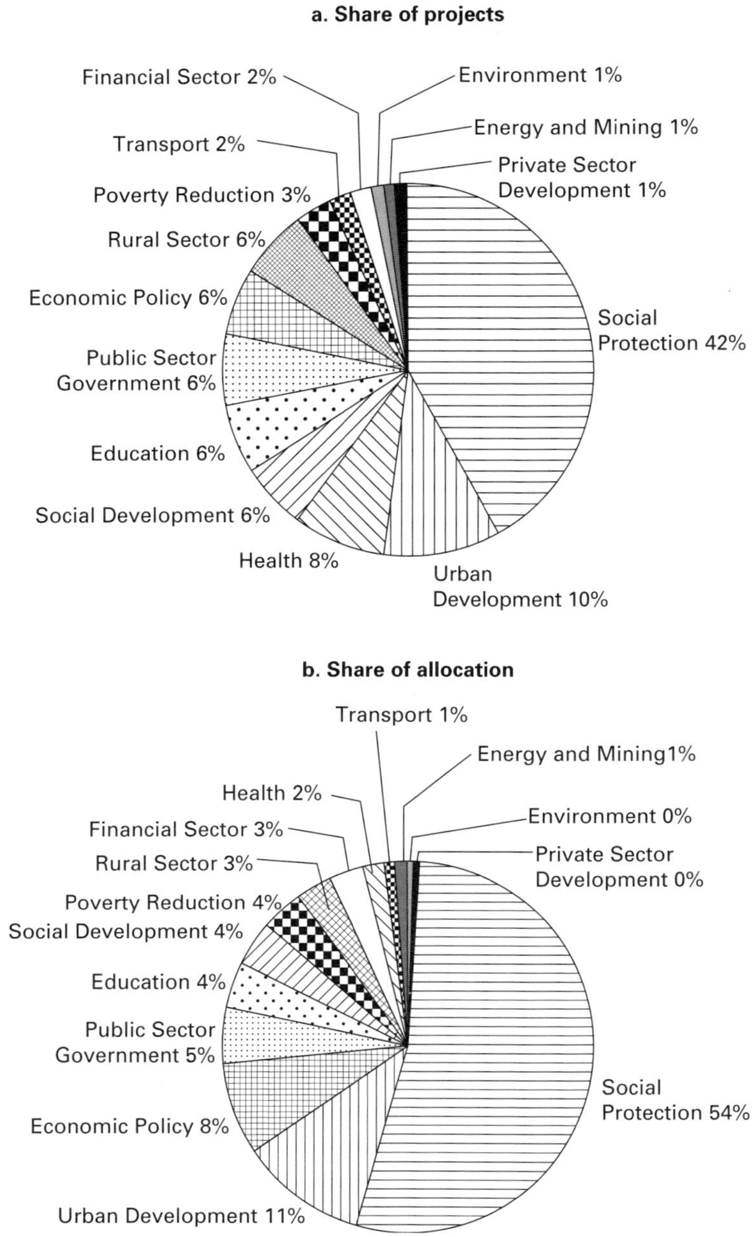

Source: Authors' calculations, based on the Business Warehouse data and World Bank documents.

of public works in the LAC Region. The bulk of CCT programs is implemented in the LAC Region (10 of a total 17 CCT components), with the SAR an increasingly active region. In terms of lending amount, the LAC Region accounts for 65 percent of the total amount committed to CCTs. Finally, the Bank's interest in helping the people affected by emergency situations in Africa with basic noncash assistance is illustrated by the number of such activities financed in that region.

Figure 5.18 shows that the most common theme in analytical work on safety nets is cash transfers (in all their various forms), with noncash programs running second and public works a distant third. In the regional breakdowns, the ECA Region leads in analysis of cash transfers, child allowances, disability allowances, and noncash energy programs. The LAC Region dominates work on CCT programs but has a diverse portfolio. The AFR and EAP Regions do little analysis on safety nets, although the AFR Region does some work on public works and food programs, whereas the EAP Region focuses mostly on cash transfers as well as fee waivers for health and education. Finally, the SAR leads the analysis of microcredit and income-generation activities and carries

BOX 5.2

PROJECTS CONTAINING SSNs FROM SECTORS OTHER THAN SOCIAL PROTECTION

HUMAN DEVELOPMENT NETWORK

Health

Burundi: Multisectoral HIV/AIDS and Orphans Adaptable Program Loan (US$36 million, 22 percent to SSNs)

This project provides orphans with scholarships for primary education and vocational training. It strengthens the economic and nutritional well-being of families that care for orphans through investments to supplement nutrition (such as gardening) and income-generating activities. The project also provides training for the informal job market to older adolescent orphans.

Education

Bangladesh: Female Secondary School Assistance II (US$120.9 million, 25 percent to SSNs)

This project increases access and retention of female students in secondary education by providing stipends conditional on school attendance and attainment of a certain level of test scores. It provides tuition assistance to all eligible girls in 119 rural *upazilas* (subdistricts) of Bangladesh.

INFRASTRUCTURE NETWORK

Urban Development

Republic of Yemen: Third Public Works Project (US$45 million, 29 percent to SSNs)

This project consists of about 800 subprojects (targeted mainly at the rural population) for the rehabilitation or extension of infrastructure works throughout the 20 governorates of the Republic of Yemen.

India: Emergency Tsunami Reconstruction Project (US$465 million, 17 percent to SSNs)

This project funds the repair and reconstruction of existing houses, the construction of new houses, and related services and community infrastructure, such as access roads, internal roads, water supply, latrines, storm drains, electrification, rainwater harvesting structures, and limited community infrastructure facilities, such as community halls, nursery schools, and primary schools. Families affected by the project are resettled. The project funds transit shelter, as needed, and the upgrading of services in temporary shelter sites.

Transport

Afghanistan: National Emergency Employment Program for Rural Access (US$39.2 million, no thematic allocation to SSNs)

This project creates productive, self-targeting, emergency employment opportunities in maintenance and rehabilitation of rural access infrastructures, using appropriate labor-intensive methods. It also finances TA services to build capacity of joint project management units to implement and manage the program.

Energy and Mining

Romania: Mine Closure, Environment and Socioeconomic Regeneration Project (US$120 million, 25 percent to SSNs)

This project is involved in job creation activities in mining regions (including employment and incentives schemes, microcredit, and employment services).

PREM NETWORK

Public Sector Governance

Guyana: Public Sector Technical Assistance Credit (US$4.76 million, 14 percent to SSNs)

This project improves the coverage, targeting, and efficiency of social safety nets and helps strengthen institutions.

Ukraine: Development Policy Loan (US$251.26 million, 13 percent to SSNs)

This project broadens social inclusion by improving access and quality of social services, by better targeting social assistance programs, by improving the fiscal sustainability of the pension system, by refining the system of local public finance and accountability, and by helping to ensure that land reform benefits rural landholders.

Economic Policy

Senegal: First Poverty Reduction Support Credit (US$30 million, 13 percent to SSNs)

This project supports the implementation of Senegal's Poverty Reduction Strategy, in particular health services. It focuses on improving financial and human resources management in the sector as well as accelerating access to basic health services, because these factors have been

(continued)

BOX 5.2 (Continued)

identified as the most important for determining the performance of this sector.

ESSD NETWORK

Rural Sector

Zambia: Emergency Drought Recovery Loan (US$50 million, 23 percent to SSNs)

This project provides in-cash assistance through a public works program to vulnerable groups, as well as an agricultural input package delivered to vulnerable, but viable, farmers.

Social Development

Indonesia: Kecamatan Development Project (US$249.8 million, 22 percent to SSNs)

This project provides block grants that communities allocate to proposals agreed to in the Intervillage Decision Forum. The project supports bottom-up planning in villages, including training for social and technical village facilitators, village cross-visits, and village operational costs for planning and management. It also provides support to microfinance institutions.

Environment

Africa: Emergency Locust Project (US$59.5 million, 17 percent to SSNs)

This project provides starter packs (seeds, fertilizers, and tools) and animal feed to rural populations. It also includes job creation for those who have lost crops or income to locust infestation. Such jobs are created through existing community-driven development or social projects, including small-scale local civil works.

Sources: Various World Bank project documents.

FIGURE 5.13: REGIONAL ALLOCATION OF THE PROJECTS MAPPED TO THE SOCIAL PROTECTION SECTOR BOARD COMPARED WITH OTHER SECTOR BOARDS, FISCAL YEARS 2002–07

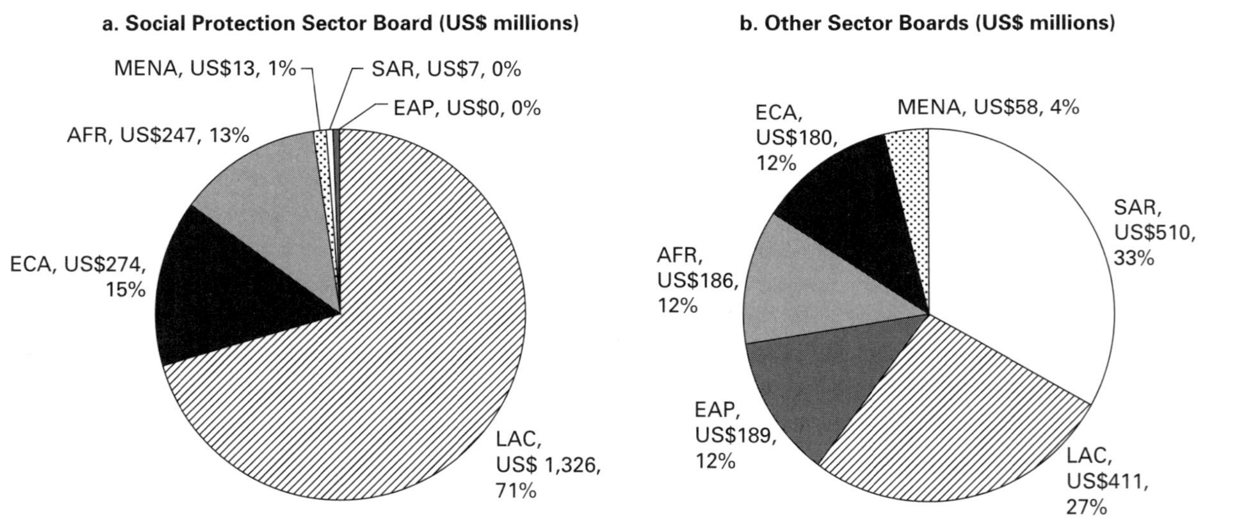

Source: Authors' calculations, based on the Business Warehouse data and World Bank documents.
Note: AFR = Africa; EAP = East Asia and the Pacific; ECA = Europe and Central Asia; LAC = Latin America and the Caribbean; MENA = Middle East and North Africa; SAR = South Asia Region. Panel a shows the allocation of the 63 projects mapped to the Social Protection Sector Board. The total value of these projects was US$1.866 billion. Panel b shows the allocation of the 82 projects mapped to other sector boards. The total value of these projects was US$1.534 billion.

out a substantial share of studies on public works, food-related programs, and CCTs (see annex 5.B).

Results

There are various ways to tell the story of the results of the portfolio. Unfortunately, as in other SP areas, global data on outcomes achieved are not available. Nevertheless, a substantial inventory of country- and project-specific quantitative and qualitative data exist on outcomes and outputs that might reasonably be expected to lead to good development outcomes. Where the attribution is most clear, the easiest way to evaluate is to look at the outputs and outcomes

FIGURE 5.14: TYPES OF SSN ACTIVITIES IN WORLD BANK PROJECTS APPROVED BY THE SOCIAL PROTECTION SECTOR BOARD COMPARED WITH OTHER SECTOR BOARDS, FISCAL YEARS 2002–07

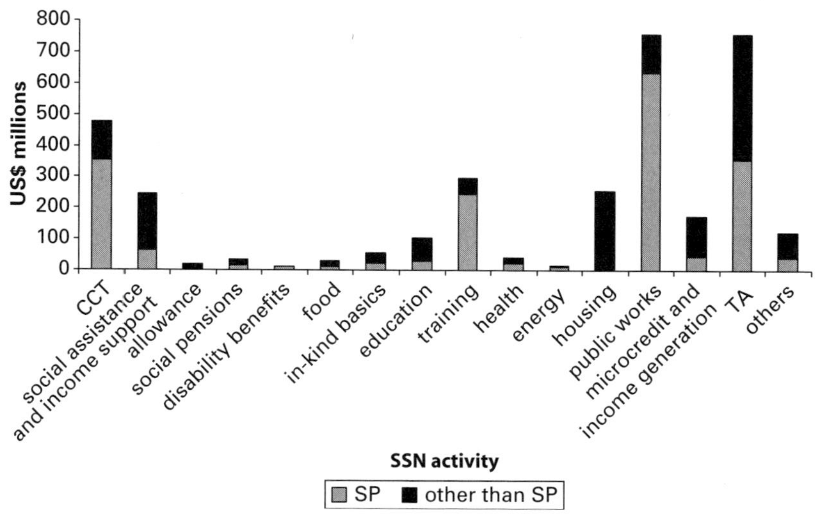

Source: Authors' calculations, based on the Business Warehouse data and World Bank documents.

FIGURE 5.15: NUMBER OF ANALYTICAL PRODUCTS DEALING WITH SSNs BY WORLD BANK NETWORK AND VICE PRESIDENCY, FISCAL YEARS 2002–07

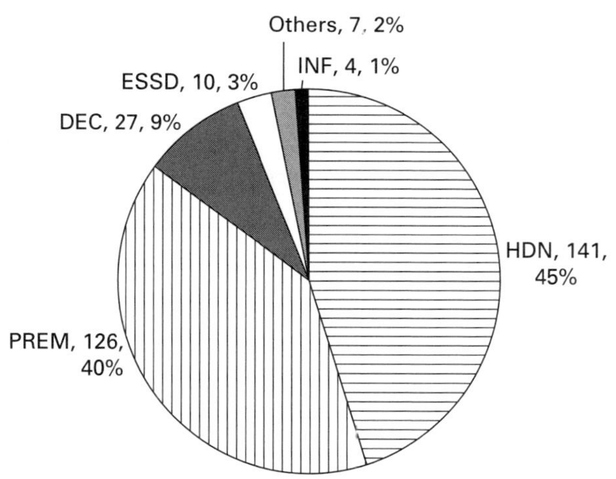

Source: Authors' calculations, based on the Business Warehouse data and World Bank documents.
Note: DEC = Development Economics Vice Presidency; ESSD = Environmentally and Socially Sustainable Development Network; HDN = Human Development Network; Poverty; INF = Infrastructure Network; PREM = Poverty Reduction and Economic Management Network. Figure shows the number of and share of analytical products.

presented in implementation completion reports.[25] Table 5.4 summarizes the results of ICRs for loans that closed during fiscal years 2002 to 2006.[26] This cohort of projects is a little older than the previous analysis of the portfolio because it includes only those projects that closed in that period, whereas the inventory contains many projects that are still active. The summary gives a flavor of what was accomplished. Here again, the portfolio's diversity by type of intervention can be seen in the beneficiaries column. The number of activities in the institutional strengthening and legal framework columns is not surprising, given the weight of technical assistance in the portfolio. The physical outputs are from the public works projects.

The indicators tabulated in ICRs are, however, often indicators of process or output, not the indicators of ultimate effect. For that, beneficiary assessments or impact evaluations tell a fuller story, although the attribution to the Bank's action is much less clear. Moreover, impact evaluations are not available for every project, especially where the intervention was a minor part of the loan. Nonetheless, the SSN portfolio has a good track record of credible impact evaluations for some of the main interventions—especially CCTs and public works programs. Of the CCT programs in 12 countries in this portfolio, credible evaluations are available or planned for 10 countries, and results to date are largely positive. (In Guatemala, a small secondary scholarship program is coded to safety nets in the context of a much larger education program and is not included in these evaluations. The emergency program in the West Bank and Gaza did not have a plan for a scientific impact evaluation, and indeed, circumstances have proved too difficult to even carry out the program as intended much less do a sound evaluation.)

Impact evaluations and beneficiary assessments of public works programs are available for only 5 of the 17 countries where the Bank supports this type of intervention, but these 5 countries account for more than 80 percent of the public works portfolio (of US$760 million), when the amount of

BOX 5.3

SELECTED EXAMPLES OF NONCASH BENEFITS INVOLVED IN SSN PROJECTS

TRAINING

Bosnia and Herzegovina: Employment Support 2 Project (US$12 million, 20 percent to SSNs)

This project supports active labor market programs or employment assistance programs, including on-the-job training, skills enhancement training, support for self-employment in agriculture, small business support, job fairs, and business advisory services.

Uganda: Uganda Social Action Fund (US$100 million, 20 percent to SSNs)

This project supports vulnerable groups through rehabilitation and expansion of training facilities to provide vocational skills. It provides sponsorships for youth to undergo vocational and life-skills training (for example, masonry, carpentry, tailoring, blacksmiths, and welding) and gives them toolkits upon their graduation to work on subprojects. The project finances new and ongoing income-generating activities and provides support services to female-headed households and other disadvantaged groups.

HOUSING ASSISTANCE

Brazil: Programmatic Loan for Sustainable and Equitable Growth: Supporting Housing Sector Policy (US$502.52 million, 17 percent to SSNs)

This project supports the government in its efforts to design and implement a unified federal housing subsidy system to address the affordability of housing solutions for the poor.

Sri Lanka: North East Housing Reconstruction Program (US$75 million, 14 percent to SSNs)

This project finances housing reconstruction through the transfer of a cash grant to eligible beneficiaries. The pace of installments is performance based, and the beneficiary is allowed four months to complete construction.

ENERGY AND UTILITIES ASSISTANCE

Armenia: Urban Heating Project (US$15 million, 16 percent to SSNs)

This project provides grants to the poorest households living in multiapartment buildings, thus enabling them to gain access to improved heating. It funds the investments necessary for connecting gas, heat, and hot water supply to apartments of the poor.

BASIC TRANSFERS

Eritrea: Emergency Demobilization and Reintegration Emergency Recovery Loan (US$60 million, no thematic allocation to SSNs)

This program supports reintegration of former soldiers and includes the provision of financial or in-kind assistance to cover basic needs of former soldiers' families (transitional safety nets) relative to the living standard of general population.

Zambia: Emergency Drought Recovery Loan (US$50 million, 23 percent to SSNs)

This project provides in-cash assistance through a public works program to vulnerable groups, as well as an agricultural input package to vulnerable, but viable, farmers.

EDUCATION

West Bank and Gaza: Emergency Services Support Project (US$20 million, no thematic allocation to SSNs)

This project provides textbooks to all students in basic education.

HEALTH (AND EDUCATION)

Madagascar: Emergency Economic Recovery Credit (US$50 million, 25 percent to SSNs)

This project finances part of the government's priority recovery program to support the most vulnerable and most affected by the crisis. It provides free access to social services, a fee waiver for primary school, medical care and essential drugs free of charge, and public works.

Sources: Various World Bank project documents.

---

allocation for public works is considered. Evaluations are done when the activity is central to the loan, as in the five cases with evaluation, and are less likely to be performed when the activity is only a minor component. Box 5.5 highlights some of the results from selected impact evaluations.

Another way to think about the results of the Bank's portfolio of lending and AAA is to look at it from the perspective of specific countries. In the following sections, the stories are told briefly of safety net development in two countries, one with low income, one with middle income, and both with a multiyear, multiproduct engagement with the Bank.

Figure 5.16: NUMBER OF TYPES OF SSN ACTIVITIES IN WORLD BANK PROJECTS, FISCAL YEARS 2002–07

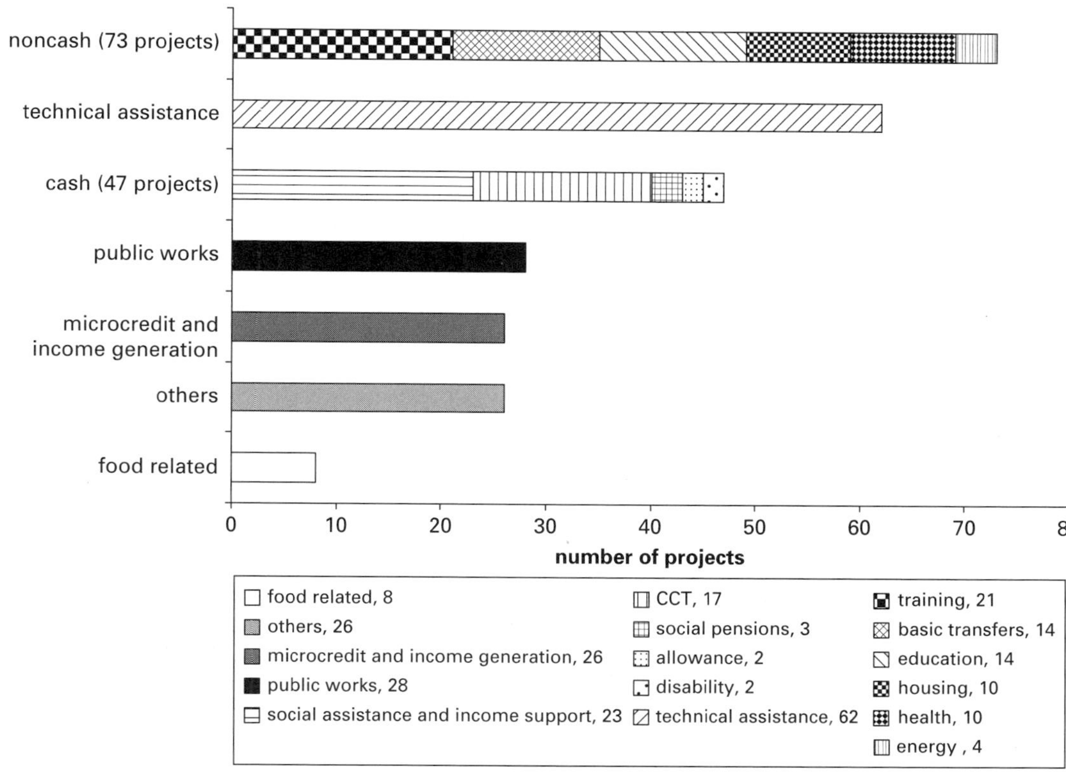

Source: Authors' calculations, based on the Business Warehouse data and World Bank documents.
Note: Figure represents 270 SSN activities in 145 loans.

Figure 5.17: U.S. DOLLAR VALUE OF TYPES OF SSN ACTIVITIES IN WORLD BANK PROJECTS, FISCAL YEARS 2002–07

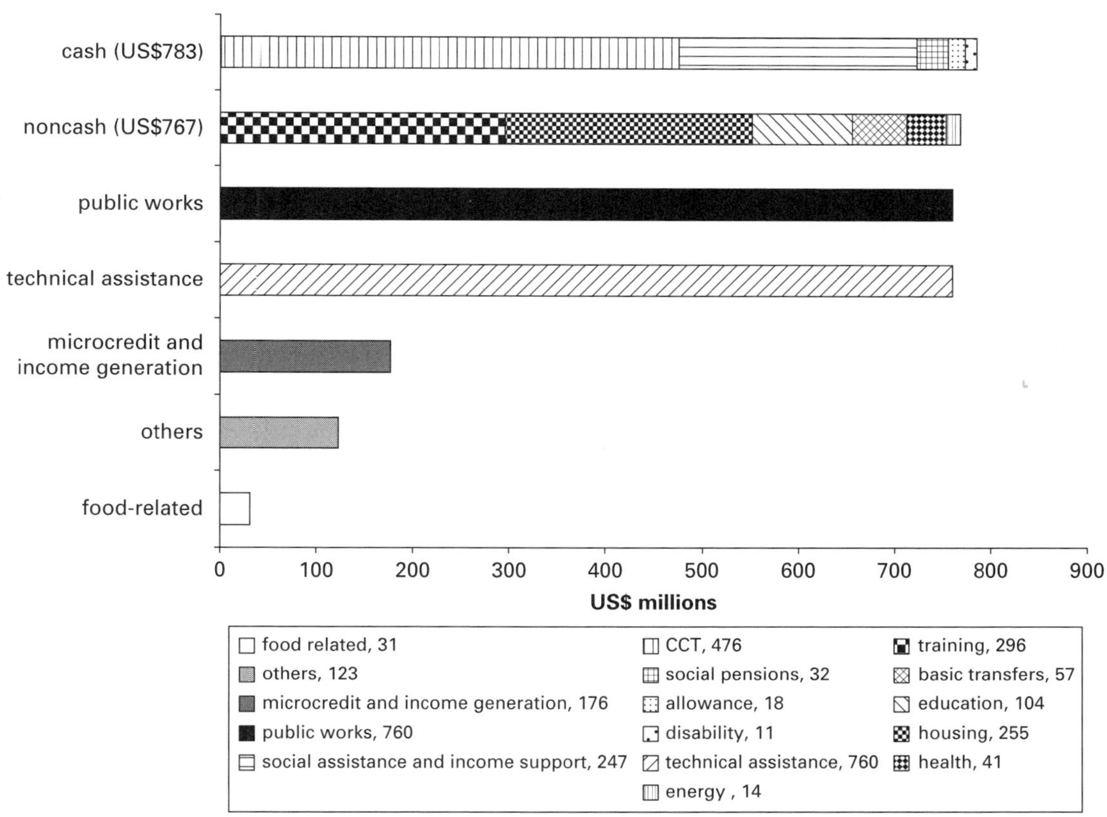

Source: Authors' calculations, based on the Business Warehouse data and World Bank documents.

BOX 5.4

TWO STORIES OF SUCCESSFUL PUBLIC WORKS PROGRAMS

MALAWI: MALAWI SOCIAL ACTION FUND (MASAF)

"Although the wage was little (reportedly MK 200 per month) and delayed, the money greatly helped us to buy food (for example, fish, which we could not afford before) and other things. We bought or shopped from the nearest trading centers at Thabwa, Chitakale, Chinakanaka, and Mulanje Mission. Prices of commodities did not go up because of the MASAF wages, but it was time they had to go up. Supply of goods and services did not change as a result of MASAF wages." (Beneficiaries of the Thabwa-Robeni Road)

"The construction of the road has eased communication problems which used to exist. For example, people had a lot of problems doing business. With the road it became easy for them to carry out their businesses." (Nonbeneficiaries of the Lunjika via Chasenga-M1 Road)

"MASAF wages helped some people to buy fertilizer, which enabled them to have increased food crop harvest." (Nonbeneficiaries of the Bwengu-Katope Road project).

ETHIOPIA: PRODUCTIVE SAFETY NET PROGRAM

"Before the safety net, I tried to get all the kids in school doing casual labor, but there were lots of gaps in their education. Now all three stay in school." (Widow and mother of four)

Source: Malawi, Mvula and others 2000; Ethiopia, Wiseman 2007.

Ethiopia. Ethiopia is a very poor country, with gross domestic product per capita of about US$100, at least 7 million to 8 million people chronically food insecure, and more than half the children malnourished.[27] Ethiopia has a long experience of safety nets and has garnered significant donor funding through a system of annual emergency appeals. By policy, 80 percent of the emergency aid was dedicated to public works programs, but problems existed with the programs, which were exacerbated by the aid arrangements. A World Bank (2004) public expenditure review summarized the problems as follows:

- *Food comes too late, the amount of food distributed is so diluted that each household receives too little to materially affect their welfare. In the case of works programs, the stop-start nature of programs prevents them having a sustained impact on the incomes of the poor; and the absence of counterpart funds and of integration with local capital plans means they often do not result in creation of lasting, productive assets.*

In 2005, the government launched the Productive Safety Nets Program (PSNP) to overcome several of these problems (table 5.5). It established a single government program for donors' aid to feed into and requested multiannual pledges. Together, these actions made possible development of permanent administrative capacity and adequate planning and integration of works into district development plans. Because aid is no longer delayed, works can take place in the dry season when construction is feasible. Moreover, 20 percent of funds are earmarked for nonlabor inputs so the technical quality of works can be higher.

In 2006, the PSNP made about six rounds of payments to about 7.3 million beneficiaries. In aggregate terms, the PSNP public works are operating on a large scale, generating more than 172 million person-days of labor per year in 2006. Most of these works are focused on soil and water conservation activities, with associated voluntary community agreements on grazing restrictions. The works have been found to bring demonstrable benefits to farmers from the conservation of moisture, which leads not only to visibly improved plant growth close to the bunds, but also to an increase in groundwater recharge such that dry springs have started to flow again and local stream flows have increased.

The 2005 beneficiary survey (Devereux and others 2006) found that the PSNP has had a positive, significant effect on the well-being of beneficiaries, as calculated through both subjective and objective indicators of well-being. The survey found that three in five beneficiaries avoided having to sell assets to buy food in 2005. Ninety percent of households explained that this outcome was a result of participation in the PSNP. Moreover, almost half the beneficiaries surveyed stated that they used health care facilities more in 2005/06 than in 2004/05, and 76 percent of these households credited the PSNP with this enhanced access. More than one-third of households enrolled more of their children in school, and 80 percent of this enrollment was attributed to participation in the PSNP.

From 2007, significant work has been started under the second phase of the program to further improve implementation capacity and to strengthen monitoring and evaluation as well as program governance, bringing systems to a level of functioning not previously possible with fragmented and temporary programs. Work is also

FIGURE 5.18: **TYPES OF SSN ACTIVITIES IN WORLD BANK ANALYSIS, FISCAL YEARS 2002–07**

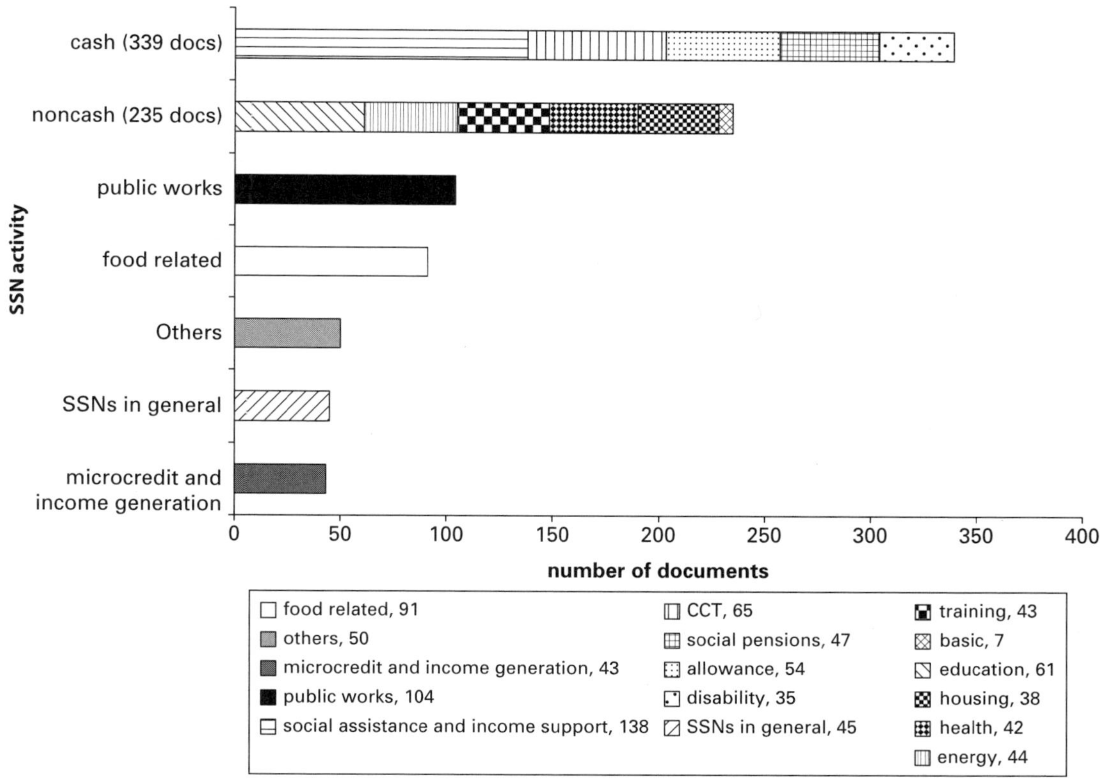

Source: Authors' calculations, based on the Business Warehouse data and World Bank documents.
Note: Figure represents 901 SSN activities in 315 analytical products.

beginning on a contingent grant mechanism to provide resources in the same districts so that they can accommodate transient food-insecure households in response to periodic droughts. The mechanism will use a rainfall-based index, relying on 30 years of rainfall data in Ethiopia to trigger and scale additional funding, and is a key element in the strategy to stop people from falling into destitution and chronic food insecurity.

The Bank has provided critical support to the government in its implementation of the reform of the safety net system. First, much of the analytical work underpinning the reform was undertaken by the Bank in the form of a public expenditure review and risk and vulnerability assessment. Second, the Bank has supported the program with significant IDA resources. It has developed a large, three-phase Adaptable Program Loan, now in the second phase of implementation, which has provided financing required both for transfers to beneficiaries and for capacity building. The financing provided by the IDA has been key in leveraging significant additional financing from other donors. Currently, seven other donor agencies support the program. Finally, the Bank has played a significant role in donor coordination, managing a large multidonor trust fund to harmonize donor technical assistance as well as additional trust funds for channeling donor program cofinancing to the government.

Brazil. The Bolsa Família Program (BFP) was launched in October 2003, through the merger of four preexisting cash transfer programs, in an effort to improve efficiency and coherence of the social safety net and to scale up assistance to provide universal coverage of Brazil's poor.[28] The program provides transfers ranging from R$15 to R$95 (US$7–US$45) per month to poor families.[29] Like other CCTs, the BFP seeks to help (a) reduce current poverty and inequality by providing a minimum level of income for extremely poor families and (b) break the intergenerational transmission of poverty by conditioning these transfers on beneficiary compliance with human capital requirements (school attendance, vaccines, and prenatal visits). The BFP also seeks to help empower BFP beneficiaries by linking them to complementary services.

Several factors make the BFP particularly complex:

- *Its size and speed of expansion.* With, as of June 2006, 11.1 million beneficiary families (about 46 million people), the BFP is larger than many nations and is the largest program if its kind. The program has expanded at an

Table 5.4: **Summary of ICR-Reported Outputs and Outcomes from 53 Operations with Thematic Code 54 (*Social Safety Nets*) Completed during Fiscal Years 2002–06**

Beneficiaries	Institutional strengthening	Legal framework and policy reform	Physical outputs
27 projects directly benefited 23 million beneficiaries mostly through ■ CCTs (2.3 million beneficiaries) ■ Other cash interventions (1.9 million beneficiaries) ■ Public works (4.8 million beneficiaries) ■ School feeding (1.6 million beneficiaries) ■ Health subsidy (9.0 million beneficiaries) Other interventions were the provision of ■ Training (3 million beneficiaries) ■ Social care services (922,129 beneficiaries) ■ Agricultural inputs (195,650 beneficiaries) ■ Documentations (52,883 beneficiaries) ■ Disability devices (2,453 beneficiaries)	33 projects supported institutional strengthening through (1 or multiple) a range of interventions, such as the following: ■ 27 projects contributed to improve the monitoring and evaluation systems ■ 15 projects supported the improvement of the targeting system ■ 11 projects supported training of staff from various ministries, officials, implementers, and contractors ■ 10 projects supported the establishment or improvement of the management information system ■ 8 projects supported the development of operational manuals ■ 4 projects provided staff members for implementation ■ 4 projects organized 139 seminars and workshops	13 projects supported changes in the legal framework through new legislation or decrees	10 operations contributed to build or rehabilitate (1 or multiple) physical infrastructure, such as the following: ■ 7 projects contributed to construct or improve 8,363.6 kilometers of roads and 46 rural roads ■ 5 projects contributed to construction of 422 classrooms and 57 education facilities and rehabilitation of 903 schools ■ 8 projects supported construction or rehabilitation of other infrastructure (1,028 facilities for people with disabilities, dams, water pipelines, and so forth)

Source: Authors' calculations, based on the Business Warehouse data and World Bank documents.

BOX 5.5

RESULTS FROM SELECTED IMPACT EVALUATIONS OF SSN PROGRAMS

JAMAICA: PROGRAMME OF ADVANCEMENT THROUGH HEALTH AND EDUCATION

The impact evaluation of Programme of Advancement through Health and Education (PATH) shows that the CCT program has been successful at targeting its benefits to the poorest households. In particular, 58 percent of benefits were found to go to the poorest quintile of the population (Levy and Ohls 2007). PATH was successful in increasing education attendance and use of preventive health care for children in PATH families. Levy and Ohls (2007) estimate that school attendance has increased by approximately 0.5 days per month and that health care visits for children ages 0 to 6 years have increased by approximately 38 percent as a result of PATH.

CAMBODIA: IMPACT EVALUATION FOR THE JAPAN FUND FOR POVERTY REDUCTION GIRLS' SCHOLARSHIP PROGRAM AND THE EDUCATION SECTOR SUPPORT PROJECT

In Cambodia, the Bank funded two CCT projects: the impact evaluation of the Japan Fund for Poverty Reduction (JFPR) program (Filmer and Schady 2008), which targets girls in seventh grade, the first year of lower secondary school, and the Education Sector Support Project.

The JFPR program provides cash to families, provided that their daughter is enrolled in school, maintains a passing grade, and is absent without "good reason" fewer than 10 days in a year. Filmer and Schady (2008) estimate that the JFPR program's effects on enrollment are large—between 22 and 33 percentage points. The effect appears to have been largest among girls who come from poorer households, have parents with less education, and live farther away from a secondary school.

A follow-on Bank program, the Education Sector Support Project scholarship program, was made available to boys as well as girls.

ARGENTINA: PROGRAMA JEFES DE HOGAR

In Argentina, in response to the deep social and economic crisis, the government launched the Programa Jefes de Hogar, or Heads of Household Program, for a lending amount of US$600 million, wholly devoted to SSNs. The government took this public works program to scale very quickly: to 574,000 beneficiaries in May 2002 and to nearly 2 million beneficiaries in May 2003 (World Bank 2007a). Lindert, Skoufias, and Shapiro (2006) show that the program had a good targeting performance, reaching 32 percent of the poorest 20 percent of the Argentine population. The impact evaluation (Galasso and Ravallion 2004) estimated that an additional 10 percent of the beneficiaries would have fallen below the food poverty line without the program and that the transfer also compensated participants partially from income loss. The impact evaluation also estimated that the program had a positive, but relatively small, effect of lowering the unemployment rate by 2.5 percentage points in late 2002.

The Bank also actively supported the government in strengthening the program's governance and accountability and in designing and implementing the transition process of the program (through the Heads of Household Transition Project, for a lending amount of US$115 million for the SSN fraction of the loan). The transition strategy (see Almeida and Galasso 2007 for the impact evaluation), which is currently under implementation, promotes self-employment for Jefes beneficiaries through a set of activities designed to strengthen their long-term capacity to generate income.

MALAWI: MALAWI SOCIAL ACTION FUND

In Malawi, the national public works program under Malawi Social Action Fund (MASAF) has been implemented since 1995. It has concentrated on construction of roads but has gradually shifted toward environment-related projects. The beneficiary assessment (Mvula and others 2000) provides evidence that the MASAF-funded public works projects in the 16 project sites considered have positive effects on the socioeconomic status of households, and the assets have enormous benefits to the community and rural economies. The public works activities created new wage employment for 39.9 percent of the beneficiaries covered in the study (who had not been employed 12 months before starting work in MASAF).

Among male beneficiaries and female beneficiaries, new wage employment was created for 29.1 percent and 55.5 percent, respectively. Participation in the MASAF-funded public works projects significantly improved beneficiaries' socioeconomic status, as reported by 70.9 percent of beneficiaries—77.4 percent among female beneficiaries and 65.1 percent among male beneficiaries. Beneficiaries best described the changes in the quality of

(continued)

BOX 5.5 (Continued)

life by reporting that they "can afford basic necessities" (54.1 percent) or they are "better off now" (50.6 percent). The number of meals taken by the household per day during this evaluation is higher compared with the findings in the baseline study. Finally, the study finds evidence that the nutritional status of the children covered during the study was better than that for children covered during the baseline study (Zgovu and Mvula 1998). The more critical measures of nutrition (wasting and underweight) showed fewer children were moderately and severely wasted and underweight. The gains in nutritional status, however, cannot be attributed to a single factor, such as income from the safety net.

ARMENIA: POVERTY FAMILY BENEFIT

Before 1998, Armenia had a system of 26 categorically targeted cash and in-kind social assistance programs for individuals who met various criteria, plus a large quasi-fiscal subsidy through electricity pricing. In 1998/99, a reform program transformed this system into a single program targeted to poor families through a proxy means test. Before and after the policy reform, the Bank supported the government by AAA and policy-based lending in 1997, 1998, 2001, and 2003 and by a TA loan in 2004. These activities yielded a number of improvements in capacity—development of operations manuals, staff training, improvements in the proxy means-testing systems and cross-checking with other databases, development of an appeals process, control of fraud and errors, and so on. The suite of reforms nearly doubled the coverage of the program (from 15 percent to 27 percent of the population), nearly tripled the share of the benefits going to the poorest quintile (from 16 percent to 43 percent), and increased the generosity of the benefit.

Source: Various World Bank project documents.

exponential rate since its inception in 2003 and is now sufficiently large that it has the potential to reach all of Brazil's poor.

- *Its implementation in a decentralized institutional context.* Although managed at the federal level, many aspects of BFP implementation are carried out by Brazil's 5,564 municipalities. The BFP has developed numerous innovative mechanisms to promote incentives for quality implementation, many of which merit documentation for potential adaptation by other countries with decentralized federal structures.
- *The complexity of the reform creating the BFP.* The BFP was created to integrate four preexisting CCTs into a single program, and it consolidated and inherited their systems from four separate ministries.
- *The promotion of the BFP as a "unifying" force for social policy.* The BFP is intended to unify social policy both vertically (unifying transfer programs across levels of government) and horizontally (linking the BFP with complementary actions and services at all levels of government).

Table 5.5: Sample of Public Works Supported in 2005 under the Ethiopia PSNP

Public works activity	Extent of support
Soil bund construction (kilometers)	10,320
Stone bund construction (kilometers)	244,673
Pond construction (number)	759
Pond maintenance (number)	18,958
Spring development (number)	310
Spring maintenance (number)	1,545
Hand-dug well construction (number)	407
Area closure (hectares)	39,450
Small-scale irrigation canal (kilometers)	3,467
Fruit seedling production (number)	7,900
Nursery site establishment (number)	48
Seedling planting (number)	17,228,942
Rural road construction (kilometer)	6,160
Rural road maintenance (kilometer)	4,887
School classroom construction (number)	756
Elementary school maintenance (number)	80
Health post construction (number)	342
Farmer training center construction (number)	121

Source: World Bank 2006b.

To date, the BFP has achieved some important efficiency gains and is showing exceptional targeting results, with 73 percent of transfers going to the poorest quintile and 94 percent going to the poorest two quintiles. Furthermore, studies have shown that the BFP played a significant role in the recent reduction in income inequality, which, in turn, has been instrumental in reducing extreme poverty, explaining 25 percent and 18 percent, respectively, of the reduction in extreme poverty and inequality in Brazil.[30] The quasi-experimental baseline suggests positive effects of the BFP on adult labor supply and a possible reduction in child labor, which is consistent with the findings of other evaluations.

To support Brazil in the reform, expansion, and consolidation of the Bolsa Família Program and in other aspects of safety net policy, the Bank used a number of instruments. A multiyear, multiproduct programmatic analytical and advisory program—the Brazil Social Assistance (BRASA) program—was one of the central elements underpinning the start of the process. The work of the BRASA program was then reinforced with a large loan that provided support to the budget and to specific further capacity building on administrative themes. Further programmatic AAA on allied themes of evaluation and on labor (and its nexus with social assistance) and preparation of a second loan continue the work. Figure 5.19 illustrates the scope and interrelations of the work.

CONCLUSIONS AND FUTURE ACTIVITIES AND STRATEGIES

In the Social Risk Management framework, safety nets play a role in improving efficiency and growth as well as in redistributing income. Awareness of this role has greatly increased in recent years. As a result of the wider acknowledgment of the need for safety nets, the range and sophistication of work have greatly increased. The World Bank has engaged with 118 countries on safety net issues over the six years under review, providing lending in 68 countries, analytical products in 86 countries, training in 87 countries, and a combined package of all three services in 42 countries. In the earlier years, Bank SSN activity was mainly in support of reform programs—and usually in times of crisis. This activity has evolved into a portfolio with significant analytical work and lending in support of safety nets as long-run parts of social policy.

One of the more intriguing aspects of this analysis is the diversity within the SSN portfolio, with respect to both the type of intervention supported and the range of sectors. Only 42 percent of projects with SSN components are mapped to the Social Protection Sector Board—54 percent by dollar value. The breadth of use of safety nets recognizes that safety nets are appropriate tools to improve equity in service delivery and to compensate losers in many kinds of reforms.

The broad array of activities in the SSN portfolio is driven by the thousands of decisions taken in the many countries concerned about safety net policy, by the services the countries would like from the Bank in support of those policies, and by the ways Bank management responds to those needs.

The assessment of the current trends, country needs, and other factors with respect to SSNs is that an active portfolio will exist in the future. The portfolio may be more balanced regionally because of the growing interest in safety nets in low-income countries in the world, which may help support more work in Africa. In South Asia, the Bank has been working very actively on AAA in recent years, which may continue and translate into lending. In the Middle East and North Africa, some signals have been given of interest in strengthening the role of cash transfers in the social protection system.

The substance of the portfolio would be expected to focus on several areas identified in this report:

- Work on implementing safety nets in the low-income countries of South Asia and Sub-Saharan Africa
- Lending for CCTs in additional countries
- Further work throughout the portfolio, especially in middle-income countries, on institutional issues, targeting, decentralization, improved service delivery, and the like
- Policy issues throughout the portfolio—particularly how safety nets fit in the poverty reduction and social policies of each country.

A high share of nonlending activities relative to lending would be anticipated, because governments often prefer to finance safety nets from own or donor funds rather than taking on debt to support them (outside times of crises). This shift to nonlending activities suggests that there may be considerable scope for work with partners in providing collaborative programs to support safety net policy. A great deal of the work on safety nets has already been done with partners. Joint work is expected to grow. Countries are more often interested in the development of high-quality permanent safety nets, not just those that are part of quick emergency programs, hence making donor collaboration both more feasible and more important. Moreover, a number of partner organizations are placing more emphasis on safety nets now than they did 5 or 10 years ago.

FIGURE 5.19: **THE BRASA PROGRAM: RESULTS AGREEMENT VISION, ELEMENTS, AND LINKS TO OTHER WORK**

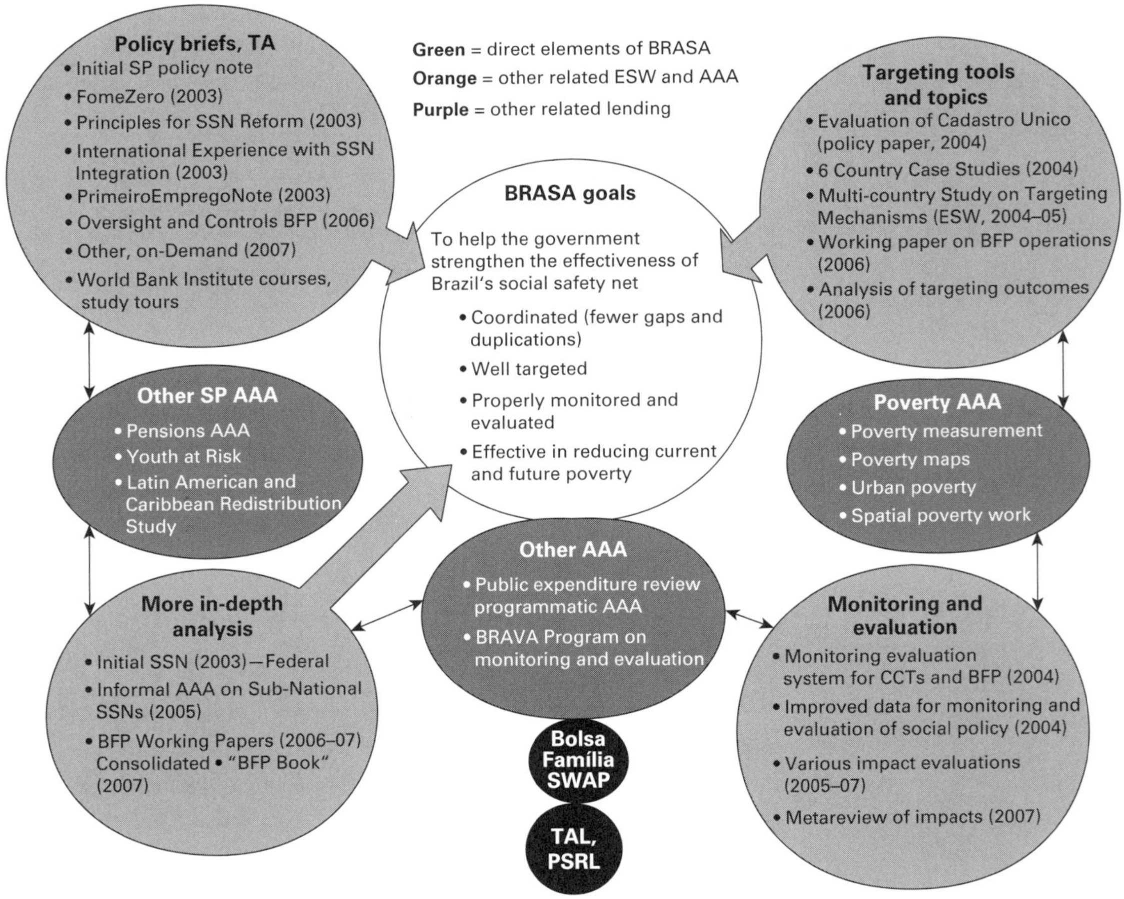

Source: Lindert 2006.

ANNEX 5.A: REGIONAL DISTRIBUTION OF SSN ACTIVITIES IN WORLD BANK LENDING

Annex table 5.A.1 shows the regional distribution of 270 safety net activities involved in 145 projects. Annex table 5.A.2 shows the U.S. dollar amount of allocation out of a total safety net portfolio of US$3.4 billion.

ANNEX 5.B: REGIONAL DISTRIBUTION OF SSN ACTIVITIES IN WORLD BANK ANALYTICAL PRODUCTS

Annex table 5.B.1 shows the regional distribution of 907 safety net activities described in 315 documents.

ANNEX 5.C: TYPES OF ANALYTICAL PRODUCTS, BY REGION AND FISCAL YEAR, FISCAL YEARS 2002–07

Annex table 5.C.1 shows the analytical work conducted by the Bank by region. Annex table 5.C.2 shows the analytical work by fiscal year.

ANNEX 5.D: SELECTED CCT PROGRAMS

Annex table 5.D.1 shows selected conditional cash transfer programs by thematic and sectoral allocation.

The chapter included all lending activities with thematic code 54 (*Social Safety Nets*), yielding 122 projects with nonzero budgets. Some of the activities coded 54 are at the boundaries of safety nets, labor, and finance. These activities were not recoded but were included so that the analysis of interventions covered a commensurately wide set of categories, including, for example, retraining, microcredit, or income-generating schemes.

Program documents were reviewed for a number of operations not coded by their task teams as SSNs to identify possible errors of exclusion; such loans were included in the inventory if they were judged to have a safety net component. In the search for "excluded" projects, a review was conducted of all projects that were approved by the Social Protection Sector Board during fiscal years 2002 to 2007 and that were not coded 54. Among the 56 projects meeting those criteria, 22 projects were identified with at least one safety net component. Among the 22 projects so identified, 13 involve technical assistance (exclusively or among the other components) for the strengthening of the SSN system. Other projects include a public works program for unemployed youth, demobilized soldiers, and other vulnerable groups in Sierra Leone and a school feeding and emergency workfare program in West Bank and Gaza. Thirty-one projects with thematic code 56, *Other Social Protection and Risk Management*, approved by sector boards other than the Social Protection Sector Board were also reviewed. Among them, only one project was identified that contained safety net components (namely, a workfare program for rural areas in Afghanistan complemented by TA services).

The result of this exercise was an inventory including a total of 145 (122 + 22 +1) projects that have at least one safety net component for the period between fiscal year 2002 and fiscal year 2007.

All 145 projects identified as containing safety nets were included in the analysis, but a sensitivity analysis was also done, repeating the analysis for only the 93 projects officially given thematic code 54 (over fiscal years 2002–06). The qualitative results on mix by region, type of intervention, and diversity in actors are quite robust. Moreover, the size of the portfolio changes little. The SSN components in the 23 projects not originally coded to safety nets comprise about 10 percent of the portfolio by dollar volume.

Categories of SSN Components

It is important to know both whether a loan supports an activity that acts as a safety net and what that activity is. In many projects, the components related to safety net activities actually involve more than one type of SSN intervention, thus totaling 270 SSN activities within the 145 projects. The classification in table 5.1 has been used.

Assignment of Monetary Amounts to Project Components

All but two of the projects with SSN components were assigned multiple codes. Thus, to estimate a dollar value of the portfolio, some assignment of the share of the loan to be attributed to safety nets was needed. Business Warehouse does this imputation on the basis of the number and combination of codes assigned by the task team.[31] That information was not fully sufficient for this chapter's purpose for two reasons. First, it was not assigned for the 23 projects considered as having safety net components but not so coded by their task teams. Second, in this analysis of which safety net activities are included in the portfolio, projects were disaggregated within the thematic code, assigning project shares within the multiple safety net activities involved in a single project.

The amount of the allocation to each activity was estimated using the following criteria:

- When the task team assigned code 54 and there was only one safety net activity, then the share of the activity is the share of the theme in the full dollar value of the loan.

Table 5.A.1: **Distribution of SSN Activities in World Bank Projects by Type of Activity and Region, Fiscal Years 2002–07**

	Cash activities					Noncash activities										
Region	Conditional cash transfers	Social assistance or income support	Allowances	Social pensions	Disability benefits	Food-related activities	In-kind basic	Education	Training	Health	Energy	Housing	Public works	Microcredit and income generation	General technical assistance	Others	Total
Africa	0	6	0	0	1	1	9	5	9	4	0	0	13	10	7	7	72
East Asia and the Pacific	1	2	0	0	0	1	0	1	0	2	0	0	0	3	3	0	13
Europe and Central Asia	1	4	1	0	1	1	1	3	4	2	2	0	1	4	20	10	55
Latin America and the Caribbean	10	5	1	3	0	3	1	2	7	2	2	3	8	3	25	6	81
Middle East and North Africa	1	1	0	0	0	1	0	1	1	0	0	1	4	3	3	2	18
South Asia	4	5	0	0	0	1	3	2	0	0	0	6	2	3	4	1	31
Total	17	23	2	3	2	8	14	14	21	10	4	10	28	26	62	26	270

Source: Authors' calculations, based on the Business Warehouse data and World Bank documents.

Table 5.A.2: **Distribution of the Allocation to SSNs in World Bank Projects by Type of Activity and Region, Fiscal Years 2002–07**

	Cash activities (US$ millions)					Noncash activities (US$ millions)											
Region	**Conditional cash transfers**	**Social assistance or income support**	**Allowances**	**Social pensions**	**Disability benefits**	**Food-related) activities (US$ millions)**	**In-kind basic**	**Education**	**Training**	**Health**	**Energy**	**Housing**	**Public works (US$ millions)**	**Microcredit and income generation (US$ millions)**	**General technical assistance (US$ millions)**	**Others (US$ millions)**	**Total (US$ millions)**
Africa	0.00	36.30	0.00	0.00	4.08	2.33	44.30	39.24	32.47	18.04	0.00	0.00	152.97	36.82	48.78	17.88	433.2
East Asia and the Pacific	4.80	50.70	0.00	0.00	0.00	7.70	0.00	7.70	0.00	9.90	0.00	0.00	0.00	49.30	58.60	0.00	188.6
Europe and Central Asia	60.00	41.60	0.30	0.00	7.40	5.00	0.50	9.60	16.50	9.10	6.20	0.00	5.00	20.30	205.10	67.40	454.0
Latin America and the Caribbean	309.90	49.10	17.30	32.10	0.00	8.70	0.50	18.60	246.80	3.90	8.10	86.90	532.10	22.70	371.70	28.50	1,736.9
Middle East and North Africa	2.90	1.40	0.00	0.00	0.00	0.90	0.00	0.80	0.20	0.00	0.00	24.00	20.30	7.50	4.60	8.40	70.9
South Asia	98.10	67.60	0.00	0.00	0.00	6.00	11.80	28.00	0.00	0.00	0.00	144.40	49.90	39.80	70.90	0.70	517.0
Total	475.60	246.60	17.60	32.10	11.50	30.60	57.00	104.00	296.00	41.00	14.30	255.30	760.20	176.40	759.70	122.80	3,400.7

Source: Authors' calculations, based on the Business Warehouse data and World Bank documents.
Note: Because of rounding, totals may deviate slightly from the sum of the parts.

Table 5.B.1: **Distribution of Analytical Work Dealing with SSNs by Type of Activity and Region, Fiscal Years 2002–07**

	Cash activities					Noncash activities											
Region	Conditional cash transfers	Social assistance or income support	Allowances	Social pensions	Disability benefits	Food-related activities	In-kind basic	Education	Training	Health	Energy	Housing	Public works	Microcredit and income generation	General technical assistance	Others	Total
Africa	0	9	0	3	1	16	3	6	4	8	0	0	16	5	2	6	79
East Asia and the Pacific	4	13	4	5	4	6	0	12	2	9	2	3	5	5	4	3	81
Europe and Central Asia	1	55	36	11	13	3	3	5	8	4	20	14	11	1	4	17	206
Latin America and the Caribbean	42	27	8	18	4	31	0	21	17	12	11	12	30	2	9	7	251
Middle East and North Africa	1	15	3	2	4	12	0	2	9	4	6	5	14	9	5	7	98
South Asia	10	13	0	5	6	19	1	10	0	2	2	3	21	18	2	3	115
Rest of the world	0	1	0	0	0	0	0	0	0	0	0	0	0	0	1	0	2
World	7	5	3	3	3	4	0	5	3	3	3	1	7	3	18	7	75
Total	65	138	54	47	35	91	7	61	43	42	44	38	104	43	45	50	907

Source: Authors' calculations, based on the Business Warehouse data and World Bank documents.

Table 5.C.1: **Analytical Work by Document Type and by Region, Fiscal Years 2002–07**

Document type	Europe and Central Asia	Latin America and the Caribbean	World	South Asia Region	Africa	East Asia and the Pacific	Middle East and North Africa	Rest of the world	Total
Working Papers	11	30	36	9	10	9	1	2	108
SPS	12	13	1	7	2	6	10	0	51
POR	15	10	0	5	1	4	4	0	39
Book	8	4	6	2	1	1	2	0	24
RVA	3	2	0	0	7	2	0	0	14
POS	4	4	0	2	0	2	4	0	16
PER	13	8	0	1	1	1	3	0	27
PRSP	3	3	0	5	10	1	1	0	23
DPR	2	0	0	1	0	0	0	0	3
MAC	0	2	0	0	0	0	1	0	3
HLT	0	0	0	0	0	1	1	0	2
OED	1	0	0	0	1	0	0	0	2
Esmap	0	0	0	1	0	0	0	0	1
RDA	0	0	0	1	0	0	0	0	1
WDR	0	0	1	0	0	0	0	0	1
Total	72	76	44	34	33	27	27	2	315

Source: Authors' calculations, based on the Business Warehouse data and World Bank documents.
Note: DPR = development policy review; HLT = other health study; MAC = general economy, macro economics; or growth study; OED = operation evaluation department study; PER = public expenditure review; POR = poverty assessment; POS = other poverty study; PRSP = poverty reduction strategy paper; RDA = rural development assessment; RVA = risk and vulnerability assessment; SPS = other social protection studies; WDR = world development report.

- When the task team assigned code 54 and there was more than one safety net activity, then information from the project appraisal or other documents was used to assign shares to each activity within the dollar value of code 54 activities in the loan.
- In the few cases when the task team assigned code 54 and the project had more than one safety net activity, but the project documents did not allow the allocation to safety nets to be clearly assigned (for example, there was no appraisal document or other detailed description of the component allocation, and a cost breakdown was not available), any ancillary information available was used to estimate an allocation.
- When the task team did not assign thematic code 54, then the share assigned to the other social protection codes (51, 55, 56, and 87)[32] was used to allocate dollar value, if needed, among multiple safety net activities.

The assignment of the dollar value to the component is important because, with three exceptions, the highest share that safety nets gets is 50 percent of the whole loan, the lowest is 2 percent, and the average is 24 percent.

Three basic cases are possible:

1. *Loan is wholly about one intervention and coded to safety nets.* For example, the US$600 million loan to support Argentina's Jefes de Hogar program was coded 100 percent to safety nets. Within it, 70 percent was allocated to public works and 30 percent to training. Interpretation is quite straightforward in this case.

Table 5.C.2: **Analytical Work by Document Type and by Fiscal Year, Fiscal Years 2002–06**

	Fiscal year						
Document Type	**2002**	**2003**	**2004**	**2005**	**2006**	**2007**	**Total**
Working Papers	12	24	22	24	15	11	108
SPS	8	8	5	4	8	18	51
POR	5	7	10	5	6	6	39
PER	4	7	4	8	2	2	27
Book	5	5	4	5	2	3	24
PRSP	4	2	7	1	4	5	23
POS	3	6	0	5	1	1	16
RVA	0	1	5	2	4	2	14
DPR	0	1	2	0	0	0	3
MAC	0	0	0	0	2	1	3
HLT	1	0	0	0	0	1	2
OED	0	0	1	1	0	0	2
Esmap	1	0	0	0	0	0	1
RDA	0	0	0	0	0	1	1
WDR	0	0	0	0	1	0	1
Total	43	61	60	55	45	51	315

Source: Authors' calculations, based on the Business Warehouse data and World Bank documents.
Note: DPR = development policy review; HLT = other health study; MAC = general economy, macro economics; or growth study; OED = operation evaluation department study; PER = public expenditure review; POR = poverty assessment; POS = other poverty study; PRSP = poverty reduction strategy paper; RDA = rural development assessment; RVA = risk and vulnerability assessment; SPS = other Ssocial protection studies; WDR = world development report.

2. *Loan covers multiple activities, and codes are assigned to each.* Most of the loans included in the inventory followed this pattern. For instance, Rwanda's Multisectoral HIV/AIDS Project, which is part of a multicountry HIV/AIDS program in Africa, aims at strengthening preventive measures to slow the spread of HIV/AIDS and at expanding support and care for those infected. The project entails a wide range of activities, from strengthening the diagnosis, care, and treatment of the disease, which includes the prevention of mother-to-child HIV transmission and the provision of HIV voluntary testing and counseling services, to providing financial support to orphans and vulnerable children, including training programs for community volunteers, counselors, and home-based caregivers.[33] Accordingly, the project was coded to several themes: *HIV/AIDS* and *Population and Reproductive Health* for 29 percent, and *Safety Nets, Participation and Civic Engagement,* and *Gender* for 14 percent.

3. *Loan is wholly about one intervention but coded to multiple themes.* Many of the loans to support CCT programs follow this model. For example, the loan to Brazil in support of the Bolsa Família Program provides about US$550 million for the CCTs themselves and about US$15 million for institutional strengthening for improvements in targeting, monitoring, evaluation, administration, and experimentation with new systems. Although the loan supports a single program, it is assigned four codes to reflect the multiple objectives of the program. *Safety Nets* is listed first and accorded 29 percent of the whole; *Vulnerability Assessment and Monitoring,* 29 percent; *Poverty Strategy, Analysis, and Monitoring,* 28 percent; and *Administrative and Civil Service Reform,* 14 percent.[34] That safety nets receive a minority share in coding of CCT programs is not uncommon; indeed, 29 percent to safety nets is the highest share accorded in any of the loans in support of

CCT programs, although the ancillary codes used differ considerably, often including those for child health, education, gender, social risk management, or administrative reform (see annex 5.D for details on coding of CCT programs). Thus, the dollar size of the CCT portfolio is, in a different perspective, about four times what it is listed as in this chapter's tables.

Methodology for Compiling the Inventory of Analytical Work for SSNs

This analysis needed to identify uniform criteria to classify the whole inventory of documents by fiscal year, sector board (or Bank network), and type of document. This information is provided for those documents listed in Business Warehouse, but for other documents, the information must come from the project document itself and may not be strictly comparable. The following procedure was used to handle this classification:

- *Fiscal year.* The fiscal year was approximated by looking at the publication date on the front cover of each document.[35] Thus, the inventory includes documents published between July 1, 2001, and the end of June 2007.
- *Sector board or network.* The sector board was not easily discernible for most documents (especially the nonofficial ones), and often only the broad Bank network to which the item is mapped could be identified. In general, when the unit was not reported on the document, the sector board or network was assigned according to *ESW Report: Sector and Thematic Codes* (World Bank n.d.; see also World Bank 2006a). This system indicated that, typically (even if there are a few exceptions), poverty assessments are mapped to the PREM Sector Board and risk and vulnerability assessments to HDN (the Social Protection Sector Board). For other types of documents—for example, working and discussion papers,[36] books, and other publications such as Poverty Reduction Strategy Paper joint assessments—the network was inferred, depending on the topic of the document, authors' unit, and so on.
- *Document type.* When the type of document was not easily traceable from the document, *ESW Report: Sector and Thematic Codes* (World Bank n.d.) was used, cross-checking the consistency of the type of document with the assigned sector board. Documents were also classified according to the topic, using categories of documents such as "other social protection studies," or "other poverty studies," depending on the focus of the report.

Classification of SSN Activities

In the inventory of SSN components, a similar classification has been used to that of Bank lending, with two exceptions. First, the technical assistance category used in lending is replaced by a generic "social safety nets" category,[37] which includes documents dealing with general crosscutting issues and not with a specific safety net activity. Second, the "others" category includes the following activities: early childhood development (6 such cases), emergency disaster response (1 case), private transfers and informal safety nets (5 cases), employment generation and job services (4 cases), social care services (12 cases), other privileges (3 cases), and other social programs for specific groups (1 case).

Table 5.D.1: **Selected CCT Programs by Thematic and Sectoral Allocation, Fiscal Years 2002–06**

Fiscal Year	Country and Project Title	Allocation to SSN (54)	Full Amount	All themes applied to project and % thematic allocation						
				Thm 1	Thm 1 %	Thm 2	Thm 2%	Thm 3	Thm 3%	Thm 4
2002	Jamaica, SSN Project	10.00	40.00	Safety Nets	25%	Child Health	25%	Education for all	25%	Social Risk Mitigation
2002	Turkey, SRMP	100.00	500.00	Education for all	20%	Social Analysis & Monitoring	20%	Labor Markets	20%	Safety Nets
2003	Ecuador, Human Dev. Reform PSL	14.50	50.00	Public Expenditure	29%	Safety Nets	29%	Child Health	14%	Participation & Civic Engagement
2004	Chile, SP Adjustment Loan	58.00	200.00	Safety Nets	29%	Poverty Strategy	29%	Participation & Civic Engagement	14%	Administrative Reform
2004	West Bank & Gaza, SSN Reform Project	2.90	10.00	Safety Nets	29%	Social Risk Mitigation	29%	Child Health	14%	Education for all
2004	Dominican Republic, Social Crisis SAL	13.00	100.00	Social Risk Mitigation	25%	Education for all	25%	Access to urban services & housing	24%	Safety Nets
2004	Brazil, Bolsa Familia	165.94	572.20	Safety Nets	29%	Vulnerability Assessment & Monitoring	29%	Poverty Strategy	28%	Administrative Reform
2005	Cambodia, Education Sector Support	4.76	28.00	Education for all	33%	Gender	17%	Indigenous people	17%	Safety Nets
2005	Colombia, Labor reform and Social SAL	44.00	200.00	Labor Markets	23%	Safety Nets	22%	Other Social Protection	22%	Education for all
2006	Colombia, SSN Project	25.06	86.40	Safety Nets	29%	Other Social Protection	29%	Child Health	14%	Education for all
2006	Ecuador, BDH	13.80	60.00	Safety Nets	23%	Vulnerability Assessment & Monitoring	22%	Child Health	22%	Education for all

Source: Business Warehouse data and World Bank documents.

			All sectors covered in project and percentage of sectoral allocation									
Thm4%	**Thm 5**	**Thm 5%**	**Sec 1**	**Sec 1 %**	**Sec 2**	**Sec 2 %**	**Sec 3**	**Sec 3 %**	**Sec 4**	**Sec 4 %**	**Sec 5**	
25%	#	#	Other social services	73%	Central Government Administration	27%	#	#	#	#	#	#
20%	SMEs support	20%	Other social services	74%	Education Sector	12%	Health	6%	Central Government Administration	4%	General Industry & Trade	4%
14%	Nutrition & Food security	14%	Other social services	40%	Education Sector	25%	Health	20%	Health insurance	8%	Compulsory Pension & Unemployment Insurance	7%
14%	Law Reform	14%	Other social services	75%	Central Government Administration	10%	Education Sector	5%	Health	5%	Sub-national government administration	5%
14%	Other public sector government	14%	Other social services	90%	Central Government Administration	10%	#	#	#	#	#	#
13%	Child Health	13%	Other social services	50%	Health	30%	Central Government Administration	15%	Education Sector	5%	#	#
14%	#	#	Other social services	97%	Central Government Administration	2%	Sub-national Government Administration	1%	#	#	#	#
17%	Decentralization	16%	Secondary Education	45%	Other social services	25%	Primary Education	14%	General Public administration	9%	Tertiary education	7%
22%	Education for knowledge economy	11%	Health	40%	Primary Education	30%	Other social services	20%	Secondary Education	10%	#	#
14%	Other public sector government	14%	Other social services	100%	#	#	#	#	#	#	#	#
22%	Managing for Development Results	11%	Other social services	93%	Central Government Administration	6%	Sub-national government administration	1%	#	#	#	#

NOTES

[1] See Grosh and others (2008) for an extensive treatment of several topics relating to SSNs, including their role in social policy, know-how on specific features of design and implementation, international experience, and challenges and options to help manage them.

[2] *Social risk management* refers to how society manages risks, a conceptual framework introduced by Holzmann and Jørgensen (2001).

[3] This count includes programs that were not included in the inventory of SSN projects either because they were mapped to a sector board other than the Social Protection Sector Board and did not have a 54 thematic code or because they had a very small CCT component. It also includes a CCT in Panama for fiscal year 2008.

[4] The list was pulled from Business Warehouse on August 6, 2007.

[5] A sensitivity analysis was also carried out, repeating the analysis for only the 93 projects carried out between fiscal years 2002 and 2006 and officially given thematic code 54. The qualitative results on mix by region, type of intervention, and diversity in actors are quite robust. Moreover, the size of the portfolio changes little. The SSN components in the 23 projects not originally coded to safety nets compose about 9 percent of the portfolio by dollar volume.

[6] The World Bank undertakes a range of knowledge activities intended for different purposes and external audiences. Collectively, these are known as AAA and include the following product lines: economic and sector work, nonlending TA, donor and aid coordination, research services (which includes the Policy Research Working Paper Series), *World Development Report*, and impact evaluation. In this chapter, analytical work means AAA excluding nonlending TA and donor and aid coordination.

[7] According to Operations Policy and Country Services, an activity qualifies as ESW if the following considerations are met: (a) the activity involves original analytical effort (defined as work that has new added value, such as new information, a new methodology, or conclusions and recommendations, as opposed to being a replication of existing work or ideas); (b) the activity is undertaken with the intent of influencing an external client's policies and programs; and (c) the activity is "owned" by a specific Bank unit (that is, the output must represent the views of the Bank rather than be attributed to individual authors, whether Bank staff members or consultants).

[8] ESW reports can be divided into two main categories: diagnostic reports and advisory reports. Diagnostic reports (both core and other diagnostic reports) underpin the Bank's dialogue with clients and provide upstream analysis for lending. Advisory reports provide advice to clients on specialized topics.

[9] The list was pulled from Business Warehouse on August 6, 2007. The criterion used was whether the document was coded 54. The listed documents should have been available from ImageBank, but most were not, so the units or authors that managed the documents were contacted to obtain copies. Of the 150 listed items, 25 did not result in a paper of the sort that could be included in the inventory. A document or explanatory contact was achieved for all 150 of the listed items. Some of the documents obtained (10 ESWs) are confidential and are not displayed in the inventory, even though they were included in the analysis.

[10] This inventory is posted at http://siteresources.worldbank.org/INTPERGUIDE/Resources/551579-11465 81904088/AllRegions_SocialSpendingGDP.xls.

[11] This search produced a list of more than 200 publications. Each relevant document was examined, adding a small fraction to the total number of documents (there was a large overlap with what was already included in the inventory).

[12] Once all data sources were taken into account, a wide range of analytical work not given thematic code 54 was screened (at least 200 more than those included in the final inventory).

[13] Overall World Bank lending figures are from the *World Bank Annual Report 2007* (World Bank 2007b).

[14] The Jefes de Hogar (Heads of Household) program is the workfare part of an SSN launched by Argentina in April 2002 to alleviate the effect of rising unemployment caused by the worsening economic crisis.

[15] The World Bank provided a series of Structural Adjustment Loans in response to the East Asian economic crisis. These programs largely addressed financial sector reforms, corporate restructuring, privatization programs, and liberalization. To ameliorate the direct impact of the

crisis on the poorest, the programs also included other components such as the following: (a) strengthening of SSNs in Korea (as part of one of the several Structural Adjustment Loans provided over fiscal years 1998 and 1999, with a recurrent value of US$2 billion); (b) support of existing SSN programs (such as public works, the health care scheme, and training programs) in Thailand (as part of a social investment project with a total value of US$300 million); and (c) Indonesia's SSN adjustment (total value US$600 million) for improving the targeting and monitoring of the existing SSN.

[16] This number includes one multicountry operation in West Africa: the Africa Emergency Locust Project.

[17] The corresponding total loan amounts (counting the SSN portion of the loan) are US$231 million and US$261 million for Colombia and Pakistan, respectively.

[18] According to the definition of lending category from the World Bank's Web site, IDA countries are those that had a per capita income in 2005 of less than US$1,025 and lacked the financial ability to borrow from the IBRD. IDA loans are deeply concessional: interest-free loans and grants are provided for programs aimed at boosting economic growth and improving living conditions. IBRD loans are nonconcessional. "Blend" countries are eligible for IDA loans because of their low per capita incomes but are also eligible for IBRD loans because they are financially creditworthy.

[19] The networks and the sectors they cover are as follows: Environmentally and Socially Sustainable Development Network, covering Environment, Rural Sector, and Social Development; Human Development Network, covering Education, Health, Nutrition and Population, and Social Protection; Poverty Reduction and Economic Management Network, covering Economic Policy, Gender and Development, Poverty Reduction, and Public Sector Governance; Infrastructure Network, covering Energy and Mining, Urban Development, Water Supply and Sanitation, Transport, and Global Information and Communications Technology; Financial Sector Network; and Private Sector Development Network. In 2006, the Sustainable Development Network was created, merging the environment and social development units with the infrastructure and energy units.

[20] In the SAR, two of the three largest projects were mapped to the Urban Development Sector Board (India: Emergency Tsunami Reconstruction Project and Pakistan: Earthquake Emergency Recovery Credit) and one to the Poverty Reduction Sector Board (Second Poverty Reduction Support Credit Project). In the EAP Region, the largest projects were in Indonesia: the Second Development Policy Loan, which was mapped to Economic Policy Sector Board, and the Kecamatan Development Projects, which were mapped to the Social Development Sector Board.

[21] The categorization can be done well only at the network level as opposed to the sector level.

[22] For more information on the safety nets primer and Web site, see http://www.worldbank.org/safetynets.

[23] This pattern does not necessarily mean that total Bank lending in these categories is low. Microcredit, for example, would often be given thematic code 41, *Small and Medium Enterprise Support*, or 75, *Rural Markets*, which include support for microfinance institutions. Likewise, income-generating activities are likely given thematic code 76, *Rural Nonfarm Income Generation*.

[24] This inventory was constructed from all loans Bank-wide, not just from loans approved by the Social Protection Sector Board, and the method prorates the share of the total project according to its multiple objectives and excludes CCT projects that are not coded to safety nets at all.

[25] The Bank prepares an ICR for every project. The ICR is reviewed by the Independent Evaluation Group, which reports to the Bank Executive Board. This report includes an evaluation of project performance by the implementing agency and contains the results of stakeholder and beneficiary consultations.

[26] The review of ICRs is based on a list of ICRs for 53 projects mapped to the Social Protection and other Sector Boards with thematic code 54 (either primary or secondary) and completed during fiscal years 2002 to 2006. The projects were reviewed by the SSNs thematic group (16 projects) and by Operations Policy and Country Services (37 projects).

[27] This section is condensed from the project appraisal document for the second World Bank loan in support of the Productive Safety Nets Program (World Bank 2006b).

[28] This section is condensed from Lindert and others (2007) and Lindert, Skoufias, and Shapiro (2006).

[29] The benefit level is adjusted from time to time to handle inflation. This level prevailed in October 2007.

[30] The Gini coefficient, which measures inequality, fell from a three-decade average of 60.0 to 56.6 by 2006, its lowest level in the three decades. Poverty has fallen from 34.1 percent in 2003 to 29.5 percent in 2005, and extreme poverty has fallen from 14.5 percent to 11 percent over that same period. Transfers from the well-targeted BFP explain 25 percent and 18 percent, respectively, of the reduction in extreme poverty and inequality in Brazil (Paes de Barros 2007).

[31] The algorithm ensures that all primary codes get the same weight as one another, all secondary codes get the same weight as one another, and all primary codes get double the weight of any secondary code. For example, if a project has one primary code and two secondary codes, the codes would be assigned 50, 25, and 25 percent of the value of the project, respectively. Similarly, the value of a project with two primary codes and two secondary codes would be allocated as 33, 33, 17, and 17 percent, respectively, across the codes.

[32] The SP thematic codes are *Improving Labor Markets* (51); *Social Safety Nets* (54); *Vulnerability Assessment and Monitoring* (55); *Other Social Protection and Risk Management* (56); and *Social Risk Mitigation* (87).

[33] Specific safety net activities are demand-side subsidies targeted to orphans and vulnerable children covering school fees and related expenses, access to health services, income-generating activities for the older youth, and psychosocial support.

[34] The share of the loan coded to the various objectives speaks to the balance of objectives within the loan. It is not directly related to the administrative costs of accomplishing them in the program supported.

[35] This procedure is not completely accurate, however, because analytical works are often finally printed either before or after their targeted year.

[36] The Development Economics Vice Presidency, though not a sector board, produces a range of research studies, among which the Policy Research Working Paper Series is encompassed by this inventory.

[37] This category includes design, development, and strengthening of safety net programs in general (they can deal with a country or region or just be general, but not with one SSN intervention in particular); SSN implemented in a particular country context (for example, measures to mitigate negative effects of a reform and measures in transition, postconflict, or very-low-income countries); specific design features (for example, more gender sensitive); SSN to deal with targeting; and delivery mechanisms.

REFERENCES

Ahmed, Akhter U. 2004. "Assessing the Performance of Conditional Cash Transfer Programs for Girls and Boys in Primary and Secondary Schools in Bangladesh." Project report prepared for the World Bank, International Food Policy Research Institute, Washington, DC.

Almeida, Rita, and Emanuela Galasso. 2007. "Jump-Starting Self-Employment? Evidence among Welfare Participants in Argentina." Policy Research Working Paper 4270, World Bank, Washington, DC.

Amde, Yisgedullish. 2003. "Safety Nets in World Bank Lending and Analytic and Sector Work." Social Protection Unit, Human Development Network, World Bank, Washington, DC.

Devereux, Stephen, Rachel Sabates-Wheeler, Mulugeta Terefa, and Hailemichael Taye. 2006. "Trends in PSNP Transfers within Targeted Households." Institute of Development Studies, Sussex, U.K., and Indak International, Addis Ababa.

Filmer, Deon, and Norbert Schady. 2008. "Getting Girls into School: Evidence from a Scholarship Program in Cambodia." *Economic Development and Cultural Change* 56 (April): 581–617.

Galasso, Emanuela, and Martin Ravallion. 2004. "Social Protection in a Crisis: Argentina's Plan Jefes y Jefas." *World Bank Economic Review* 18 (3): 367–99.

Grosh, Margaret, Carlo del Ninno, Emil Tesliuc, and Azedine Ouerghi, with Annamaria Milazzo and Christine Weigand. 2008. *For Protection and Promotion: The Design and Implementation of Effective Safety Nets.* Washington, DC: World Bank.

Holzmann, Robert, and Steen Jørgensen. 2001. "Social Risk Management: A New Conceptual Framework for Social Protection, and Beyond." *International Tax and Public Finance* 8 (4): 529–56.

Kudat, Ayse. 2006. *Evaluating the Conditional Cash Transfer Program in Turkey: A Qualitative Assessment.* Washington, DC: International Food Policy Research Institute.

Levy, Dan, and Jim Ohls. 2007. "Evaluation of Jamaica's PATH Program: Final Report." Mathematica Policy Research Inc., Washington, DC. http://www.mathematica-mpr.com/publications/redirect_pubsdb.asp?strSite=pdfs/JamaicaPATH.pdf.

Lindert, Kathy. 2006. "Brazil: Analytic and Advisory Program for Social Assistance (the "BRASA" Program) Annual Report, BRASA Phase 3." World Bank, Washington, DC.

Lindert Kathy, Anja Linder, Jason Hobbs, and Bénédicte de la Brière. 2007. "The Nuts and Bolts of Brazil's Bolsa Família Program: Implementing Conditional Cash Transfers in a Decentralized Context." Social Protection Discussion Paper 0709, Social Protection Unit, Human Development Network, World Bank, Washington, DC.

Lindert, Kathy, Emmanuel Skoufias, and Joseph Shapiro. 2006. *Redistributing Income to the Poor and the Rich: Public Transfers in Latin America and the Caribbean.* Washington, DC: World Bank. http://web.worldbank.org/WBSITE/EXTERNAL/COUNTRIES/LACEXT/0,,contentMDK:20871694~pagePK:146736~piPK:146830~theSitePK:258554,00.html.

Mvula, Peter M., Evious K. Zgovu, Ephraim W. Chirwa, and Esme Kadzamira. 2000. "Malawi Social Action Fund (MASAF) Second Beneficiary Assessment of the Public Works Programme (PWP) Final Report, November 2000." Wadonda Consult, Zomba, Malawi. http://www.masaf.org/reports/PWP%20BA2%20MASAFII%20Final%20Report-Nov%202000.pdf.

Nsour, Surat. 2007. "Study of Country Assistance Strategy (CAS) Alignment with Social Protection Sector Strategy." Social Protection Unit, Human Development Network, World Bank, Washington, DC.

Paes de Barros, Ricardo. 2007. "The Recent Decline in Income and Inequality in Brazil and Its Consequences on Poverty." Seminar presentation to the Latin America Poverty Reduction Sector Unit, World Bank, Washington, DC, September.

Wiseman, William. 2007. "Case Study on Ethiopia's Productive Safety Net Programme." Presentation at the Workshop on Fraud and Error Control in Social Protection Programs, World Bank, Washington, DC, May 17.

World Bank. 2001. *Social Protection Sector Strategy: From Safety Net to Springboard.* Washington, DC: World Bank. http://go.worldbank.org/97LBYDY3U0.

———. 2002. "Protecting People with Social Safety Nets." *Spectrum* (Winter), World Bank, Washington, DC.

———. 2004. *Ethiopia Public Expenditure Review: The Emerging Challenge (in Two Volumes)—Volume I: Public Spending in the Social Sectors 2000–2020.* Report 29338-ET. Washington, DC: World Bank. http://www-wds.worldbank.org/external/default/WDSContentServer/WDSP/IB/2004/07/14/000012009_20040714101156/Rendered/PDF/293380ET.pdf.

———. 2006a. "Guidelines for Using World Bank Theme Codes." World Bank, Washington, DC.

———. 2006b. *Project Appraisal Document on a Proposed Grant in the Amount of SDR 118.5 Million (US$175 Million Equivalent) to the Federal Democratic Republic of Ethiopia for a Productive Safety Net APL II Project in Support of the Second Phase of the Productive Safety Net Program, December 1, 2006.* Report 37224. Washington, DC: World Bank. http://www-wds.worldbank.org/external/default/WDSContentServer/WDSP/IB/2007/01/17/000020953_20070117142245/Rendered/PDF/37224.pdf.

———. 2007a. "Argentina Jefes de Hogar (Heads of Household) Program." Implementation Completion and Results Report, World Bank, Washington, DC.

———. 2007b. *World Bank Annual Report 2007.* Washington, DC: World Bank.

———. n.d. *ESW Report: Sector and Thematic Codes.* Washington, DC: World Bank.

Zgovu, Evious K., and Peter Mvula. 1998. "MASAF Safety Net Baseline Study." Malawi Social Action Fund, Lilongwe.

Zoellick, Robert B. 2007. "An Inclusive and Sustainable Globalization." Speech by World Bank Group president to National Press Club, Washington, DC, October 10.

CHAPTER 6 six

SOCIAL FUNDS AS AN INSTRUMENT OF SOCIAL PROTECTION: AN ANALYSIS OF LENDING TRENDS, 2000–07

Samantha de Silva and June-wei Sum

INTRODUCTION

Objectives

This review of World Bank lending for social funds covers fiscal years 2000 to 2007 and comes 20 years after the establishment of the first World Bank–funded social fund in Bolivia (1987). Its objective is to assess the evolution of the social funds portfolio, with a specific focus on the fiscal years 2000 to 2007, and the portfolio's role in implementing the social protection sector strategy. Lending trends, the evolution of the social funds model, and future implications of the review's major findings are also discussed. The paper was initially prepared as part of the Social Protection unit's September 2006 Sector Strategy Implementation Update.

Definition of Key Terms

The definition of the term *social fund* has changed over time and is often used to describe similar but distinct development activities. Social funds are agencies or programs that channel grants to communities for small-scale development projects. Social fund subprojects involve the active participation of local actors, such as community groups, local governments, and nongovernmental organizations (NGOs). Social funds typically finance some mixture of socioeconomic infrastructure (such as building or rehabilitation of schools, health centers, water supply systems, and feeder roads); productive investments (such as microfinance and income-generating projects); social services (such as nutrition campaigns, literacy programs, youth training, and programs for support to the

Samantha de Silva is Senior Social Protection Specialist in the World Bank's Social Protection and Labor Department. June-wei Sum was a consultant at the department. This paper was written as part of the Social Protection Sector Strategy Implementation Update. It was reviewed by Adolfo Brizzi (Sector Manager, South Asia Agriculture and Rural Development Department); Laura Frigenti (Country Director, Latin America and the Caribbean Region); Steen Lau Jørgensen (Director, Social Development Department); and Laura Rawlings (Lead Specialist, Latin America and the Caribbean Human Development Department). The paper benefited from inputs and advice from Julie Van Domelen. The authors would also like to acknowledge the contribution of Randa El-Rashidi for analysis of implementation completion report data; Ravi Cherukupalli and Feruza Abduazimova, who helped with data retrieval and compilation; the task team leaders who provided information about individual projects; the Social Funds Team in Human Development Network, Social Protection Unit; and the Community-Driven Development Group in the Sustainable Development Network.

elderly and people with disabilities); and capacity-building programs (such as training for community-based organizations, NGOs, and local governments).

The relationship between the social funds portfolio and community-driven development (CDD) is an important one that merits clarification. *Social fund* was originally a generic term, dating back to the late 1980s, that denoted multisector, demand-driven mechanisms financed by the World Bank and others. As the number of social funds grew, mainly in the Human Development Network (HDN), the term began to be used to describe a brand of operations managed by the HDN under its Social Protection Unit. At the same time, a number of "close cousins"—that is, similar demand-driven, multisector projects, such as rural investment funds and empowerment funds—were established primarily within the Environmentally and Socially Sustainable Development (ESSD) Network (now part of the Sustainable Development Network).

In the early 2000s, an effort was made to better understand the potential of these community-driven programs within poverty reduction strategies, as part of *A Sourcebook for Poverty Reduction Strategies* (Klugman 2002). CDD was the internal term coined to denote this broad class of interventions that transferred control over resources and decision making from central agencies to communities (Dongier and others 2002). CDD is thus an approach to development. Social funds, in contrast, are instruments that in many cases use a CDD approach (that is, many social fund activities are driven by community demand). The greater the role of community-level groups in social fund operations is, the stronger the presence of the CDD approach.[1]

Evolution of the Social Fund Model

This section covers the evolution of social fund objectives over time, as well as the adaptation of the institutional model to meet the changing needs of social fund agencies.

Evolution of Social Fund Objectives. The first World Bank–supported social fund, the Fondo Social de Emergencia (Emergency Social Fund) in Bolivia, was established in 1987. This fund was the first in a series of short-term emergency funds used to mitigate the effects of the World Bank's support to highly visible structural adjustment programs in the late 1980s and early 1990s. Although social funds continue to respond to emergencies (such as Hurricane Mitch in Central America, the aftermath of conflict in Timor-Leste and the Democratic Republic of Congo, and the economic crisis in Thailand), their main role is as freestanding social protection instruments that target underserved populations.

Although the objectives of social funds have shifted over time, many core characteristics persist: social funds are demand-driven, multisectoral operations that are typically managed by a semiautonomous body (often established by decree or law). The broad evolution of social fund activities and objectives is illustrated in figure 6.1. These activities and objectives are not mutually exclusive, and most funds support several objectives and activities.

During the fiscal years 2000 to 2007, a diversification of social fund goals occurred. The most common trend has been to increase the role of social funds in governments' decentralization processes by shifting more responsibility for managing local-level investments and by providing more direct training and capacity building so that local govern-

FIGURE 6.1: EVOLUTION OF SOCIAL FUND OBJECTIVES AND ACTIVITIES, 1987 TO PRESENT

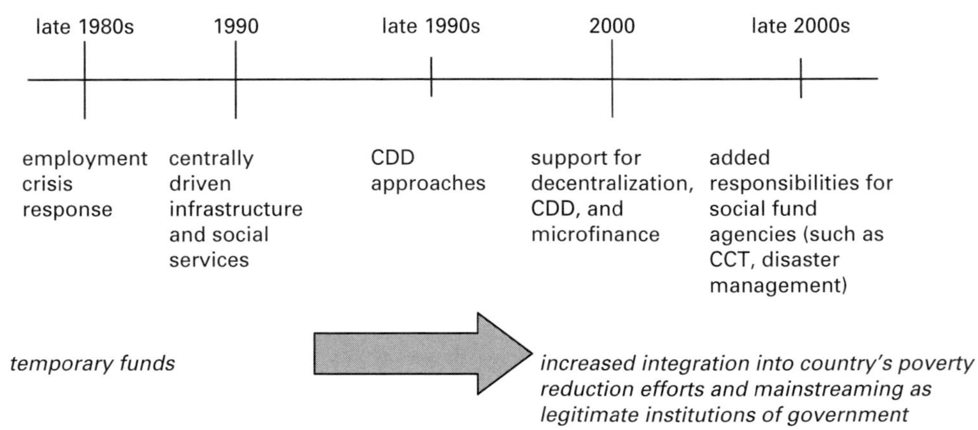

Source: Authors.
Note: CCT = conditional cash transfer.

ments can better oversee these investments. In some instances, the community management of resources deepened, with community contracting leading to grassroots-level participatory planning and a search for social capital outcomes (as occurred in Argentina, Romania, and Senegal). In some cases, divergent and even conflicting goals developed. For example, in some countries (such as Honduras, Jamaica, Madagascar, and Nicaragua), social funds that were becoming more integrated with local decentralization efforts were recentralized to respond to short-term emergency rehabilitation needs. This change was led primarily by country circumstances. Social funds became the instrument of choice in postconflict countries where weak capacity and the need for quick results combined to make the direct financing of small-scale investments imperative.

The fit of social funds in middle-income countries came about increasingly because of their social protection–related role of reaching certain vulnerable groups and marginalized segments of society. For example, conditional cash transfer programs were piloted out of selected social funds in Latin America and the Caribbean, and ethnic minority issues were addressed by social funds in the former Yugoslav Republic of Macedonia and Romania.

The timeline in figure 6.1 captures the evolution of social fund objectives over time and reflects changes across the entire portfolio of projects.

A systematic review of social fund documents for projects mapped to the Social Protection Sector Board that were approved between fiscal years 2000 and 2007 found that the most frequently cited project development objectives were as follows:[2]

1. *Increase access to services by building or rehabilitating of socioeconomic infrastructure for underserved populations.* This objective is often considered a defining feature of social funds and was found in virtually all the social funds reviewed.
2. *Strengthen and support* community institutions and local governments. This objective evolved as a response to increased use of CDD approaches and the decentralization process.
3. *Assist groups affected by specific external shocks, such as natural disasters, or economic shocks.* This objective was a defining goal of most of the first wave of social funds and is still relevant in some social funds today.
4. *Provide microfinance services.* This objective is a fairly new feature of social funds, but it is already included in social fund projects in several countries, including Albania, Kosovo, Morocco, Tajikistan, and the Republic of Yemen.
5. *Target vulnerable groups, including women, children, youth, indigenous peoples, ethnic groups, and people affected by conflict.* Again, this objective is considered a core feature of social funds. Poverty and vulnerability targeting is an area to which social funds specifically contribute.

Evolution of the Institutional Model. Depending on their legal status, social fund agencies enjoy varying degrees of operational and financial autonomy (see figure 6.2). Social funds can often hire staff members under market-driven terms of employment and make use of private sector–like management approaches (such as market salaries, performance contracts, competitive recruitment, effective monitoring and evaluation systems, and effective communications strategies) that translate into higher institutional performance than found in many other institutions of government. The 2002 Operations Evaluation Department (OED) evaluation of social funds states:

→ *Social fund implementing agencies have gained capacity as effective and innovative organizations using transparent procedures to channel resources to communities. Much of*

FIGURE 6.2: INSTITUTIONAL DISTRIBUTION OF SOCIAL FUND AGENCIES, FISCAL YEARS 1999–2007

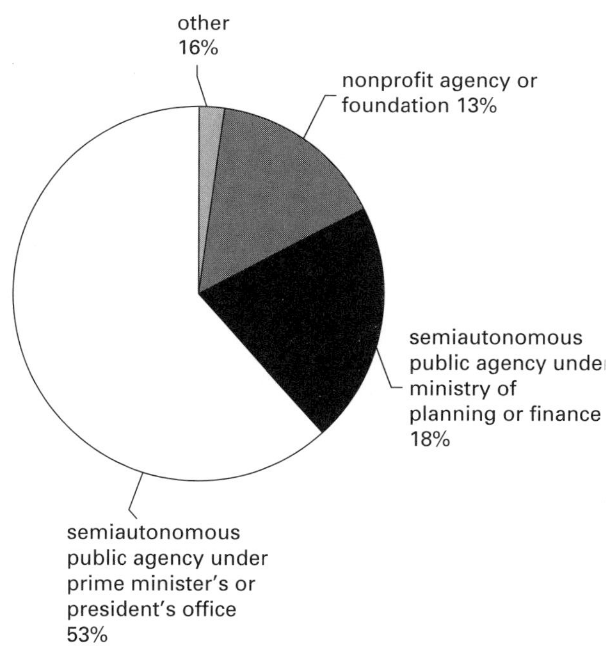

Source: World Bank project appraisal documents.
Note: The data reflect the institutional setup that was designed for the project but do not take into account whether the social fund agency maintained its intended operational structure or reporting lines in the course of project implementation. A review of Bank implementation completion reports of closed social fund projects in this period found that such a shift in operational structure or reporting lines is not uncommon.

this effectiveness is attributed to their autonomous status, which gives them independence in recruiting and operating procedures. They have developed innovative procedures for project management—including management information systems, use of poverty maps, and procurement and disbursement procedures which have been adopted in other Bank projects. (World Bank 2002: xxix)

Although the model was sometimes tagged as "parallel" and undermining the core institutions of government, it has, in practice, sustained itself, and governments have retained the model because of the results it produces. Many governments argue that they need a diversity of institutional models within government, especially in low-capacity countries. In such contexts, social funds are often seen as islands of high performance that can inspire the rest of the system, as opposed to undermining it.

Figure 6.2 shows the distribution of the institutional model for fiscal years 1999 to 2007 for social fund agencies.[3] These data were obtained primarily through information from each project's project appraisal document.[4] The majority of social funds are governed by a board of directors or steering committee comprising representatives of line agencies, the private sector, and NGOs, thus allowing broad cross-sector collaboration and dialogue with civil society.

Social Funds as Part of the Social Risk Management Framework

Since 2001, the policy context for the Bank's work on social funds has been *Social Protection Sector Strategy: From Safety Net to Springboard* (World Bank 2001a). The strategic directions for social protection by product type are summarized from this paper in table 6.1.

The strategy articulated in the 2001 publication committed the Bank to support clients in their attempts to scale up CDD as part of social fund lending. In addition, the strategy paper stated that the World Bank would support social funds for these purposes:

- To expand the menu of eligible subprojects
- To target vulnerability in addition to poverty
- To strengthen the means to enhance the flow of services from existing infrastructure

Table 6.1: Strategic Directions for Social Protection Products According to the 2001 Social Protection Sector Strategy Paper

Product	Shifts in strategy required by social risk management approach
Country strategy work	Promote risk management as a theme in the overall discussion of poverty reduction. Use tools such as the social protection chapter of *A Sourcebook for Poverty Reduction Strategies* (Coudouel and others 2002; Klugman 2002) to encourage the incorporation of social protection instruments into country strategies.
Analytical and advisory services	Move to more comprehensive and action-oriented sector analyses. Improve dynamic vulnerability aspects of poverty assessments, especially from a gender perspective.
Portfolio management and quality enhancement	Maintain the sector's portfolio in a quality leadership position. Evaluate the explosive growth in lending, and rework existing operations against the new risk management benchmark.
Knowledge management	Expand and maintain reform "primers," which compile current analytical thinking, operational lessons, and case studies into an accessible handbook format.
Lending	Explore new dissemination technologies. Undertake more pilot programs. Employ adjustment operations in countries still in need of first-generation sector reform, and initiate second-generation reforms. Scale up community-driven development through social funds.
Information	Support dissemination of the new risk management and social protection communication approach, including through *World Development Report 2000/2001* (World Bank 2001b) and the World Bank Institute.
Evaluation	Refine evaluation criteria and benchmarks. Adjust household surveys to better reflect vulnerability indicators, including intrahousehold data. Assess the appropriateness of different risk management instruments.

Source: World Bank 2001a.

- To further explore methods to ensure that the voices of women and other marginalized groups are better heard in setting the development priorities.

Role of Social Funds within the Social Protection Sector Strategy. Social protection approaches within the Bank have focused on three typologies: (a) public sector approaches, (b) market-based interventions, and (c) informal community-based solutions. Traditional social protection interventions have tended to focus on the national and household levels (for example, delivery of social assistance benefits, development of pension systems, and development of labor market policies). Communities and community-based organizations, which are often the first line of defense for individuals and households in crisis, have received little attention as a unit of analysis. However, access to community-level services and infrastructure, as well as to social networks, can be critical to a household's ability to smooth consumption and protect assets in the face of shocks, particularly in low-income countries. For example, proximity to health centers is a critical component of mitigating the risks of malaria and its resulting economic consequences on the household. Access to microfinance institutions has been found to reduce the consumption loss from health shocks. In postconflict settings, stabilizing community institutions is a means of mitigating risk of future violence.

Social funds, as discussed by Jørgensen and Van Domelen (2001), are uniquely positioned to enable community-based institutions to manage risk, given their close involvement with a range of community, public, and market agents and the rapidity and flexibility of their response. In addition, conceptual work on community-based, informal risk management arrangements was put forth by Holzmann and Jørgensen in World Bank (2001a) and was built on in *World Development Report 2000/2001: Attacking Poverty* (World Bank 2001b).

As discussed in the 2001 strategy paper (World Bank 2001a), social funds can deliver a range of social risk management functions for poor and vulnerable populations. They can strengthen local institutions (risk mitigation), increase access to basic services (risk reduction), and assist groups affected by external shocks through public works programs and support to conditional cash transfers (risk coping). Over time, social funds have evolved in the functions they serve for social risk management. The early generation of social funds mainly focused on risk-coping mechanisms by providing support for employment-creating public works programs. However, by using CDD approaches, social funds have increasingly focused on promoting a whole range of community-level risk management interventions, including risk reduction (improved access to preventive health care, water supply and sanitation, and basic education) and risk mitigation (microfinance and support for productive assets). Examples of social risk management interventions implemented by social funds are captured in table 6.2. In the table, these examples are juxtaposed onto the Social Risk Management Matrix; the matrix itself lays out a set of strategies and arrangements conceptualized in the Bank's 2001 social protection sector strategy. Table 6.2 demonstrates that social funds use all three social risk management strategies (prevention, mitigation, and coping) and also support all three types of risk management arrangements (informal, public, and market based).

In *World Development Report 2000/2001* (World Bank 2001b), social funds are categorized as a publicly provided, formal risk management mechanism. It is important to note that although social funds are publicly provided, they can support informal mechanisms for managing risk. Hence, they are distinct from other social protection instruments traditionally financed by the Bank, such as pension systems, labor market interventions, and insurance, which primarily serve the formal market and operate at the individual or household level. By supporting informal risk management strategies at the community level, social funds occupy a unique niche within the social protection sector and provide a balance in the risk management arrangements used in a country, as called for in the 2001 strategy. Social funds have also been able to deliver interventions in the area of risk reduction, which historically has received less attention (World Bank 2001a: 16).

How to Put the Sector Strategy to Work? With regard to the social funds portfolio, the sector strategy agreed to "support social funds in becoming integral to community-driven development and … improve project design and implementation to better address vulnerability" (World Bank 2001a: 54). The analysis of lending trends demonstrates that social funds have delivered on the goal of focusing on CDD and local governance, with nearly all of the social fund projects now including a major focus on building social capital and local organizational capacity. Lending trends also show that many social funds have become more focused on the very poor and vulnerable, have developed poverty and vulnerability targeting methods (box 6.1), and have adapted the menu of eligible investments to better meet the needs of the critically vulnerable (support for people with HIV/AIDS or disabilities, widows, the elderly, orphans, and so forth). As demonstrated earlier, targeting vulnerable groups, including women, children, youth, indigenous peoples, ethnic groups,

Table 6.2: **Integration of Social Fund Activities within the Social Risk Management Matrix**

Arrangements and strategies	Social fund interventions: Informal	Market based	Public
Risk reduction	■ Strengthening informal community-based institutions ■ Building links between community and public or private actors ■ Enhancing social capital by establishing processes that promote trust and cooperation at the community level		■ Providing support for socially inclusive policies and legislation ■ Increasing access to basic services (such as preventive health care, water supply, and primary education) ■ Promoting participatory local planning processes ■ Promoting public awareness campaigns for positive behavior change (such as health awareness raising, HIV/AIDS prevention, and better nutrition) ■ Providing support to community-based disaster risk reduction strategies
Risk mitigation			
Portfolio	■ Supporting informal community savings groups ■ Enhancing social capital by establishing processes that promote trust and cooperation at the community level	■ Increasing access to microfinance services ■ Investing in income-generating activities	■ Providing land-titling training and related support ■ Increasing access to legal assistance and legal literacy programs for women and marginalized groups ■ Providing training for community members (such as vocational training for unemployed youth and adult literacy classes)
Insurance	■ Supporting community risk management arrangements (such as providing matching grants to burial societies in Africa)		
Risk coping	■ Enhancing social capital by establishing processes that promote trust and cooperation at the community level		■ Supporting public works programs ■ Supporting conditional cash transfers ■ Generating temporary employment to help cope with economic crisis ■ Providing interventions to support relief and reconstruction after natural disasters (such as the Pakistan earthquake, Malawi drought, and Honduras floods)

Source: World Bank 2001a.

and people affected by conflict, is cited frequently as a core project development objective in a majority of social funds.

METHODOLOGY

The cohort of projects for this review consists of 49 social funds that were managed by regional social protection units and approved between fiscal years 2000 and 2007 (annex 6.A). A complete stock of social funds approved during 1987 to 2007 is listed in annex 6.B. This list includes projects approved before fiscal year 2000 that remained active during part or all of fiscal years 2000 to 2007. Of the social funds approved between fiscal years 2000 and 2007, 28 are active as of the date

BOX 6.1

POVERTY AND VULNERABILITY TARGETING METHODS IN SOCIAL FUNDS

As a class of investment instruments, social funds have been at the forefront of using poverty maps to direct resources and to identify vulnerable populations through inclusive and participatory processes at the local level. A six-country study (Rawlings, Sherburne-Benz, and Van Domelen 2004) found that geographic targeting performance of social funds tended to be better than that of other public programs, with the poorest districts or provinces receiving at least their population's share according to poverty ranking. A more recent evaluation of social fund and community-driven development operations in East Asia used evidence from programs in three countries—Indonesia, the Philippines, and Vietnam—to conclude that targeting performance is better in social fund and community-driven development programs.

Many social funds successfully use a combination of poverty and vulnerability targeting strategies, including (a) geographic targeting using poverty maps, (b) menu and eligibility criteria, and (c) an inclusive and participatory microproject identification and implementation process. Use of several targeting methods is necessary to optimize targeting results and to better control for the limitations of any one method.

Source: Van Domelen 2007.

of this review and 21 are closed. The funds are regionally diverse and include 21 from the Africa Region, 15 from the Eastern and Central Europe (ECA) Region, 5 from the Middle East and North Africa (MENA) Region, 2 from the East Asia and the Pacific (EAP) Region, and 6 from the Latin America and the Caribbean (LAC) Region. No social funds were managed by social protection units in the South Asia Region.[5] Annex 6.A contains a complete list of projects reviewed.[6]

Lending data were obtained from the Bank's Business Warehouse data system and were generated under several social protection themes. The thematic code used most frequently was 51 (which stood for *Social Risk Reduction* prior to late 2004), followed by 56 (*Other Social Protection and Risk Management*). For the purposes of this review, only projects mapped to the Social Protection Sector Board were included. Projects mapped to other sector boards (namely, the Social Development, Rural Development, and Financial and Private Sector Development Sector Boards) are referenced but not included in the analysis if they have a similar approach—that is, they are multisectoral, community-driven development projects.

The data were disaggregated and analyzed by volume, year, region, lending instrument, loan type, and number of loans per country for social fund operations during fiscal years 2000 to 2007. The majority of this chapter's analyses take into account only those social funds described previously. Where relevant, the broader CDD portfolio figures are also provided (projects with an approach similar to that of social funds and mapped to sectors other than the social protection sector).

The documents reviewed included World Bank project appraisal documents, implementation completion reports, and formal evaluations of social funds.[7] Interviews with task team leaders were also conducted, and the findings were incorporated into the analysis.

REVIEW OF SOCIAL FUND PORTFOLIO, FISCAL YEARS 2000–07

This section covers overall lending for social funds as well as its distribution by region and by lending instrument. It also reviews social fund lending within the broader CDD portfolio.

Overall Levels of Social Fund Lending

From 1987, when the first social fund was financed, through fiscal year 1999, the World Bank committed approximately US$3.5 billion to social funds. This lending covered 98 projects in 57 countries (more than one-third of Bank client countries), representing an extremely rapid expansion of a new institutional model across many different country circumstances. This expansion occurred without a central directive or a formal Bank strategy. Instead, the rapid growth can be attributed to demand by governments of developing countries for social fund programs. Most of these early social funds had one or more cofinanciers, which included regional development banks and bilateral agencies. During this period, social funds were usually established as temporary agencies with short- to medium-term time horizons, often in response to external shocks. However, as the need for efficient resource transfer mechanisms persisted and the relative efficiency of social funds was recognized, many social funds were institutionalized and became mainstream agencies of government, albeit often set up as semiautonomous institutions so that they could adopt efficient management systems.

During fiscal years 2000 to 2007, the Bank financed 49 social fund projects, committing US$1.9 billion in five of the Bank's six regions. Social fund activity is summarized in table 6.3. Average annual lending during this period was US$238 million, although there were wide variations from year to year, as well as a gradual reduction in overall lending by fiscal year 2007.

Lending and borrowing for social fund operations appears to be cyclical in nature. The peaks and valleys in Bank lending for social funds seem to reflect the average three- to four-year project cycle for social funds. The data indicate a spike in social fund lending around fiscal years 2000 and 2001, then a lull in new lending as the projects were implemented, followed by an increase in fiscal year 2005, as a round of new or repeater projects was approved. All of the lending in fiscal year 2007 was for either repeater projects or supplemental credit. More than US$800.5 million in planned lending for social funds is in the pipeline of projects for fiscal years 2008 and 2009.[8] This lending volume represents a substantial increase in the lending levels for social funds in recent years. The Africa Region makes up more than half the portfolio of potential new lending with US$405.5 million.

Twenty-one of the 49 social funds implemented during fiscal years 2000 to 2007 were repeater projects or follow-on projects with an expanded mandate. *Repeater projects* are projects whose basic design and effectiveness have been proven and that a borrower proposes to augment or scale up. Social fund repeater projects are scaled up by extending activities into different geographic regions or by increasing the types of services they provide, or both. *Follow-on projects with an expanded mandate* can be described as new projects that have objectives distinct from the original social fund but are implemented by the same social fund agency. They benefit from the institutional and managerial capacity developed within social fund agencies during the implementation of the original project. Box 6.2 contains examples of both repeater and follow-on projects.

The large proportion (43 percent) of repeater projects and follow-on projects with an expanded mandate is evidence of the success of and demand for social funds. Although social funds were originally established as short-term crisis

Table 6.3: **Social Fund Lending by Region, Fiscal Years 2000–07**

Fiscal year	AFR	EAP	ECA	LAC	MENA	Total World Bank Financing of Social Funds
FY00	114	21	20	103	75	333
FY01	260	0	25	120	20	425
FY02	100	19	194	0	5	318
FY03	88	0	65	0	0	153
FY04	75	0	24	15	60	174
FY05	310	0	0	21	0	331
FY06	0	0	58	0	0	59
FY07	48	0	44	0	15	107
Total	996	40	431	259	175	1901

Source: Authors.

Note: IBRD = International Bank for Reconstruction and Development; IDA = International Development Association. Because of rounding, totals may deviate slightly from the sum of the parts.

a. The fiscal year 2002 portfolio for Europe and Central Asia included a US$500 million Specific Investment Loan to the Turkey Social Risk Mitigation Project (P074408). For this table, only the social fund component of the project was counted—that is, Component III: Local Initiatives (Investment Portion)—which was equivalent to US$105 million in lending. This stock of lending (both active and closed projects) includes only social fund projects mapped to the Social Protection Sector Board and not those mapped to other sector boards, most commonly the Environmentally and Socially Sustainable Development, Infrastructure, and Finance and Private Sector Development Sector Boards. The integration of the Environmentally and Socially Sustainable Development and Infrastructure Networks into a single network—the Sustainable Development Network—was announced at the beginning of fiscal year 2007. The Finance Network and the Private Sector Development Network were consolidated at the same time.

BOX 6.2

EVOLUTION OF SOCIAL FUND PROJECT SCOPE: THREE CASES

Zambia

The Zambia Social Investment Fund (ZAMSIF) grew out of the social fund component of the First and Second Social Recovery Projects in Zambia, which were implemented between 1991 and 2000. ZAMSIF, the third incarnation of the operation, scaled up by increasing the geographic reach of activities. ZAMSIF closed in fiscal year 2006, but a follow-on project is now in preparation. The Zambia Local Development Fund Project will expand its mandate not only to fund local investments but also to support the national decentralization policy, and it will be implemented by the ZAMSIF agency.

Honduras

The Nuestras Raices Project in Honduras (fiscal year 2004) is a follow-on project to the Honduras Social Investment Project, which itself generated four repeater projects after the success of the original project. The Nuestras Raices Project has a clear mandate to target vulnerable groups, by strengthening the participation and influence of indigenous and Afro-Honduran groups in local development processes, including providing training and technical assistance to these groups in subproject management. The Nuestras Raices team is located within the Fondo Hondureño de Inversión Social, the original social investment project implementing agency.

Malawi

The Malawi Social Action Fund (MASAF) is in its third phase and has also inspired similar projects in neighboring Tanzania and Uganda. MASAF I was approved in 1996 and MASAF II in 1999. MASAF III began in November 2003 as a 12-year program with US$60 million in the pipeline for the first three years. In addition, requests from local communities and civil society groups for a social fund–type mechanism to fund productive investments resulted in a new follow-on project to acquire and administer land. This project was approved in fiscal year 2004, and the Malawi Community-Based Rural Land Development Project, a rural development sector operation, is being delivered through the existing MASAF system.

Source: Authors.

management tools, in many countries they have evolved into more permanent public institutions that deliver a range of social services and deal systematically with problems of social exclusion and social assistance, while partnering with local institutions to implement activities that benefit vulnerable communities.

Social Fund Lending within the Social Protection Portfolio

In fiscal years 2000 to 2007, the social funds portfolio accounted for 18.5 percent of social protection lending (see table 6.4). It is important to note that social funds constitute the largest share of International Development Association (IDA) lending (that is, lending in low-income countries) within the social protection portfolio. Indeed, they comprise 61 percent of total IDA financing for social protection operations in fiscal years 2000 to 2007. In contrast, social funds accounted for 5.4 percent of loans for social protection operations in countries borrowing on International Bank for Reconstruction and Development (IBRD) terms (figures 6.3 and 6.4).

Distribution of Social Fund Lending by Region

Regional emphasis of social fund lending has varied widely during the period under review. Throughout fiscal years 2000 to 2007, the Africa Region was the largest borrower for social fund operations among the six Bank regions (table 6.3 and figure 6.5). Loans in the Africa Region have also been spread among a larger number of projects than those in other regions (figure 6.6). The ECA Region was the second-largest borrower for social funds during this period, although loan amounts are only about 40 percent of those of the Africa Region. Social fund financing in the LAC Region for the period totaled US$259 million. In the MENA Region, it totaled US$175 million, and in the EAP Region, it totaled US$40 million. The trend of the past two fiscal years shows that demand for social funds in Africa remains strong. The region had US$358 million of lending during fiscal years 2005 to 2007 and another US$252 million in the pipeline for fiscal years 2008 to 2009.[9]

Several key observations can be made from the regional portfolio data:

- East Asia and the Pacific has the fewest social fund projects: one each in Timor-Leste (closed) and Lao People's Democratic Republic (active as of the date of this review). The CDD approach, however, is well established in projects such as the Kecamatan Development Project in

Table 6.4: Social Fund Lending as a Share of Social Protection Lending, Fiscal Years 2000–07

Fiscal year	Social funds (US$ millions)	Social protection as a whole (US$ millions)	Percentage in each fiscal year
2000	333.4	880.0	38.0
2001	425.0	1,340.0	32.0
2002	318.3	822.0	39.0
2003	126.1	1,323.0	10.0
2004	169.0	1,635.0	10.0
2005	297.7	2,108.0	14.0
2006	58.5	991.0	6.0
2007	107.3	802.0	13.0
Total	1,835.3	9,901.0	18.5

Source: Authors.

FIGURE 6.3: **SOCIAL FUNDS AS A PROPORTION OF TOTAL IDA FINANCING FOR SOCIAL PROTECTION OPERATIONS, FISCAL YEARS 2000–07**

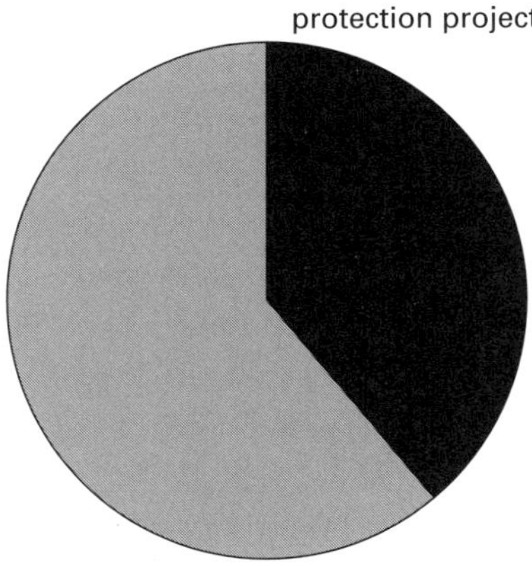

Source: Authors.

FIGURE 6.4: **SOCIAL FUNDS AS A PROPORTION OF TOTAL IBRD FINANCING FOR SOCIAL PROTECTION OPERATIONS, FISCAL YEARS 2000–07**

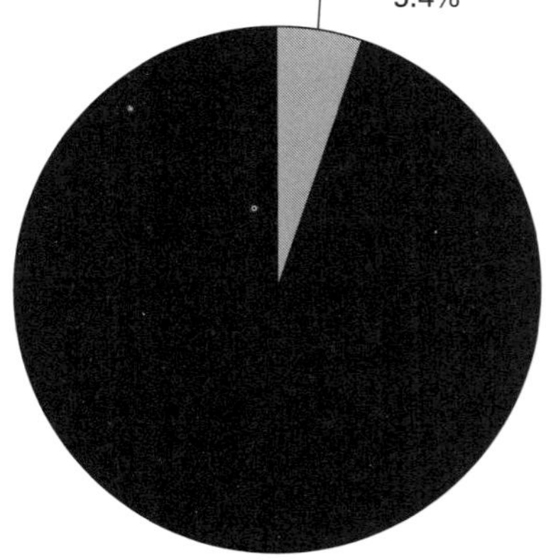

Source: Authors

Indonesia and in the large CDD operations in the Philippines and Vietnam that are managed by the Sustainable Development Network.

- Africa has the most social fund projects, which account for 50 percent of its current social protection portfolio (as of February 2006). With a 96 percent satisfactory rating by the OED (World Bank 2005),[10] the social funds portfolio is one of the best-performing portfolios in Africa.
- The ECA Region relies on social funds as an important part of the social protection portfolio, with 40 percent of all social protection projects being social investment funds (as of February 2006). The social funds model itself appears to be well accepted. In at least two countries, Serbia and Slovakia, social funds have been established with funds from sources other than the World Bank.
- The Middle East and North Africa social protection portfolio during fiscal years 2000 to 2007 has consisted

FIGURE 6.5: **REGIONAL DISTRIBUTION OF SOCIAL FUND LENDING, FISCAL YEARS 2000–07**

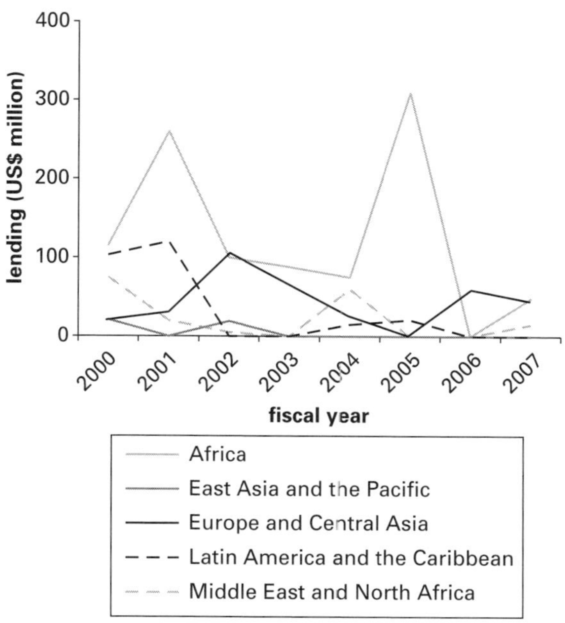

Source: Authors.

FIGURE 6.6: **REGIONAL DISTRIBUTION OF SOCIAL FUND PROJECTS, FISCAL YEARS 2000–07**

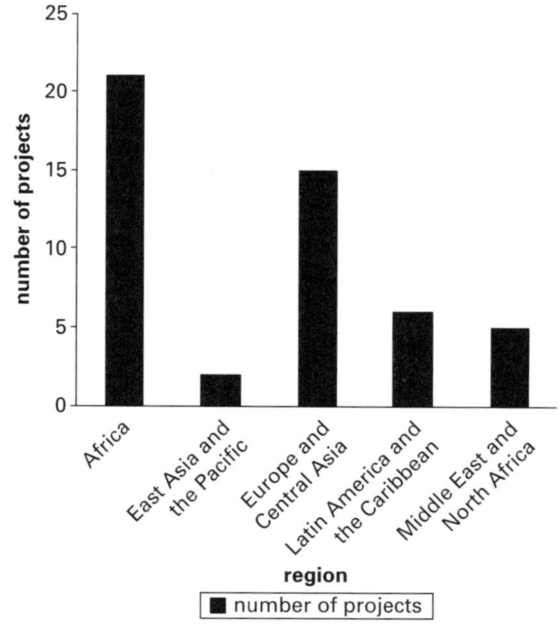

Source: Authors.

almost entirely of social fund operations. Of social protection lending (IBRD and IDA) in the region during this period, 100 percent was for social fund operations. The other five (out of a total of nine) projects mapped to the Social Protection Sector Board were in the West Bank and Gaza and were financed by emergency grants for a range of social protection activities. Within the countries that borrowed for social funds, the social fund operation was often an important part of the country's overall social protection efforts. For example, the Republic of Yemen Social Fund for Development accounted for more than 40 percent of public expenditure on social protection in 2005. The Arab Republic of Egypt Social Fund for Development accounted for about 13 percent of public expenditure on social protection for 2004, whereas the Morocco Social Development Agency accounted for 4 percent of that country's public spending on social protection in 2003.

- The Latin America and Caribbean region led the development of social funds in the 1990s and initially had the largest portfolio of social fund lending across all regions. As of the date of this analysis, social fund lending in the LAC Region is much lower than in earlier years, but none of the regional funds has closed. This continuity in activity has largely been a result of new financing from the Inter-American Development Bank (IDB) and other donors, whereas the World Bank has reduced its support. Moreover, as a result of participatory processes becoming mainstreamed in local governments in the region, many social funds have been used to support decentralization processes. For example, the Bolivian Social Investment Fund was initially financed through stand-alone investment operations, then through components of sector investment operations, and subsequently through decentralization programmatic lending. In some countries in the region, social funds have also been instrumental in providing an institutional platform for developing innovative social assistance and other social protection interventions, such as conditional cash transfer programs in El Salvador and Nicaragua and emergency community feeding programs in Argentina.

Distribution of Social Fund Lending by Lending Instrument

A wide variety of lending instruments has been used to support social funds. In terms of IDA credit versus IBRD lending for social funds, the number of projects is concentrated most heavily in IDA countries: 37 of the 49 social fund projects reviewed were financed by IDA credits, 11 projects used IBRD financing, and 1 (in St. Lucia) used a blend of

IDA and IBRD financing. Two social fund projects in IDA countries—the Democratic Republic of Congo and Timor-Leste—were financed by trust funds.

Five types of lending instruments were used to finance the social funds reviewed: Specific Investment Loans, Sector Adjustment Loans, Learning and Innovation Loans, Adaptable Program Loans, and Emergency Recovery Grants and Loans.[11] The majority of social funds in fiscal years 2000 to 2007 were financed by Specific Investment Loans (38 projects). Sector Adjustment Loans were used in Angola and Turkey following economic crises in both countries, whereas Learning and Innovation Loans were used in Lesotho and St. Lucia as a means to test the approach.[12] Multiphase Adaptable Program Loans were used in Malawi, Romania, Senegal, and Zambia. For example, in Malawi, the social fund program takes a medium-term rather than short-term view of the Malawi Social Action Fund (MASAF) as a social policy instrument, moving from a series of sector investment loans to an Adaptable Program Loan format. MASAF III began in November 2003 as a 12-year program and is scheduled to end in 2015. Timor-Leste and the Democratic Republic of Congo used Emergency Recovery Grants, whereas Liberia undertook an Emergency Recovery Loan.

Social Fund Lending within the Broader CDD Portfolio

The social fund model has had a significant effect on Bank projects far beyond social protection. In preparation for this analysis, an estimate was made of World Bank financing for CDD projects that are similar to social funds and that are managed by sectors other than the social protection sector. These operations are based on the social fund model and support central or state-level agencies for the provision of grants to communities and local governments for multisectoral subprojects. These figures do not include single-sector operations that use a CDD approach. The total estimate of lending for such projects for fiscal years 2000 to 2007 is US$14.4 billion (see regional breakdown in table 6.5) and is more than seven times the amount of social fund lending managed by the Social Protection Sector Board between fiscal years 2000 and 2007.[13]

Although table 6.3 shows that social fund lending mapped to the Social Protection Sector Board has been decreasing in most regions—particularly in the ECA, MENA and EAP Regions—table 6.5 shows that multisector CDD operations continue to be implemented in these three regions but are mapped to other sectors. Most significantly, in the EAP Region, between fiscal years 2000 and 2007, more than US$2.5 billion has been loaned for multisector CDD operations mapped to other sector boards. The majority of these projects were mapped to the Sustainable Development Network. Lending to these projects was much greater than the US$40 million EAP Region social fund loan portfolio in fiscal years 2000 to 2007 that was mapped to the Social Protection Sector Board. In the LAC Region, the amount of lending for multisector CDD operations was about eight times that of financing mapped to the Social Protection Sector Board (US$2 billion versus US$259 million). The majority of that region's multisector CDD operations mapped to other sector boards were

Table 6.5: Estimated World Bank Lending for Multisector CDD Projects Mapped to Other Sectors, Fiscal Years 2000–07

	Estimated CDD lending (US$ millions)		
Region	**Total**	**Fiscal years 2000–03**	**Fiscal years 2004–07**
Africa	3,851.5	1,727.4	2,124.1
Europe and Central Asia	1,013.9	721.4	292.5
Middle East and North Africa	716.5	388.9	327.6
East Asia and the Pacific	2,545.5	1,105.7	1,439.8
Latin America and the Caribbean	2,040.2	1,347.1	693.1
South Asia	4,189.9	1,368.3	2,821.6
All regions	14,357.5	6,658.8	7,698.7

Source: Authors.

mapped to the Sustainable Development Network. Lending for similar projects was actually greatest in South Asia for this period, with US$2.8 billion made in loans that were primarily mapped to the Sustainable Development Network. No lending was mapped to the Social Protection Sector Board for such operations in South Asia.

Long-Term Stability of the Model

In assessing the stability of the social fund model, one must look beyond Bank lending figures. The model's stability can by analyzed by looking at the status of social funds that are no longer financed by the Bank.

The general conclusion can be drawn that, with or without Bank financing, governments have managed to sustain social funds. Of the 48 social funds that received support from the Bank between fiscal years 1987 to 2000, the vast majority (35) still operate in some form (see annex 6.B). For example, in the LAC Region, of the 14 countries that had social funds financed by the Bank during that period, only 2 still receive funding through Bank operations managed by the Social Protection Sector Board. Although 13 funds still exist, the majority of them are financed by IDB.

In the Africa Region, few external financiers are filling the gap for withdrawal of Bank financing, but the substitution of operations managed by other sector boards for operations previously managed by the Social Protection Sector Board is an increasing phenomenon (as occurred, for example, in Senegal). A number of factors appear to drive this trend. First, the overall impressive results of social funds have earned them a permanent position in many governments' institutional responses to poverty reduction. Most governments recognize that social funds have been one of the few institutions to successfully deliver results in poor communities and, therefore, do not close them on completion of shorter-term objectives as was originally intended. Second, although the HDN has had an increasingly smaller "market share," the total portfolio of similar CDD operations is expanding. Additionally, with the rise of other networks claiming resources for CDD initiatives, part of the HDN portfolio has migrated to other networks. However, the basic task of perfecting the demand-driven community-level investment mechanisms has continued.

Social Fund Knowledge Products and Analytical Work

A significant number of knowledge management products related to social funds were published by the Social Protection and Labor Network Anchor (Social Protection Unit) in fiscal years 2000 to 2007. All of the publications are classified as knowledge management rather than economic and sector work. Products are produced for the use of social fund task teams and client governments and primarily constitute operational guidance and technical advice. Products and topics are identified on the basis of an annual survey of social fund thematic group members (about 200 members).

As can be tracked by the requests received by the Social Protection Advisory Service, the knowledge management products produced by the Social Funds Anchor Team have been used widely by task teams working on social fund and CDD operations across the Bank. They are also used by the technical staff of client governments (such as the social fund and CDD implementing agency staff) and by policy makers. All of the operational guidance provided has contributed to the high quality of the social funds portfolio. For example, a portfolio review conducted by the Bank's Quality Assurance Group (QAG) in March 2005, which was based on a sampling of 90 operations from quality at entry (QEAEA 4–7) and quality of supervision (QSA 5–6) social fund CDD operations, highlighted that such operations are a strong cohort (better satisfactory outcomes and quality of supervision) than HDN and Bank-wide averages, despite being designed and implemented under challenging country circumstances. (A more detailed discussion of the QAG review of social funds is presented later.) In Africa, the Independent Evaluation Group rated 96 percent of the social funds as satisfactory, hence making them one of the best-performing portfolios of the region.

A recent example of a knowledge management product is "Evaluating Social Fund Impact: A Toolkit for Task Teams and Social Fund Managers" (Adam 2006). Produced in May 2006, the toolkit aims to increase the number, expand the topical coverage, and improve the quality of social fund impact evaluations. "Reaching the Poor and Vulnerable: Targeting Strategies for Social Funds and Other Community-Driven Programs" (Van Domelen 2007) aims to enhance program design to better serve the poor. The toolkit approach is designed to provide technical staff members in the Bank and in client governments with concepts, empirical evidence, noteworthy case studies of different approaches, and operational elements necessary to better design and manage social funds operations. "Communities Taking the Lead: A Handbook on Direct Financing of Community Subprojects" (de Silva 2002), with more than 2,000 requests, was one of the most popular publications of the Social Protection Anchor. It was reprinted twice—in 2002 and 2005. In addition, the Social Funds Thematic Group publishes informally a series of four- to six-page notes. The

Social Funds Innovation Notes capture experiences and innovations of specific social fund projects.

The anchor unit also carries out social fund analytical work, most notably the 2004 cross-country impact evaluation of social funds (Rawlings, Sherburne-Benz, and Van Domelen 2004). This study was the first systematic cross-country impact evaluation of social funds using survey data and accepted evaluation methodologies. The research was carried out in Armenia, Bolivia, Honduras, Nicaragua, Peru, and Zambia. The regions have also produced smaller-scale reviews or evaluations of individual social fund projects, whereas the network anchor has provided support to larger regional studies of social funds. For example, an in-depth review of the role and relevance of social funds in the ECA Region was completed in fiscal year 2007 (Serrano-Berthet 2007), and a similar review of social funds in Africa is currently under way and should be completed within fiscal year 2008.

Given the demand-driven nature of social funds, systematic feedback from beneficiaries is an essential evaluation tool. Beneficiary assessments have been used extensively in social funds. "Getting an Earful: A Review of Beneficiary Assessments of Social Funds" (Owen and Van Domelen 1998) reviewed 15 beneficiary assessments conducted in eight countries. The study was divided into two sections: an evaluation of the use of beneficiary assessments as an evaluation tool and observations on social funds based on information from the end users. In addition, between 2000 and 2007, impact evaluations were carried out by many individual social funds including funds in Honduras, Jamaica, the Lao People's Democratic Republic, Moldova, Nicaragua, Pakistan, Peru, St. Lucia, and the Republic of Yemen, with technical assistance provided by the Bank. An interesting study to assess the effect of the Thailand Social Investment Fund on social capital and the ways CDD approaches can enhance it was carried out in 1996.

Results and Lessons Learned from Implementation of the Fiscal Years 2000–07 Portfolio

Assessing Portfolio Quality. The OED (now the Independent Evaluation Group, or IEG) conducted a portfolio review of social funds that assessed effects, including institutional development issues, such as integration with broader poverty reduction strategies. *Social Funds: Assessing Effectiveness* (World Bank 2002) reviewed the development effectiveness of social fund projects and implications for future Bank support. Overall, the report found that the operational focus of social fund projects was broadly consistent with Bank and government poverty reduction objectives (World Bank 2002: xv). Social fund agencies, the report observed, have developed capacities as "effective and innovative organizations" (World Bank 2002: xi). However, the report highlighted several areas where social fund performance warranted more attention and outlined the following recommendations: (a) strengthen integration of social funds into country and sector strategies and Poverty Reduction Strategy Papers, (b) pay more attention to long-term effects, (c) ensure efficiency of resource allocation, and (d) develop policy requirements for support to social funds (World Bank 2002: xix–xxi). Of the 23 closed projects at the end of fiscal year 2000, 96 percent were rated satisfactory on outcome in the review. This outcome rating compared favorably with those of all World Bank projects—71 percent satisfactory on average (World Bank 2002: 6).

In 2005, the OED (now IEG) reviewed the broader CDD portfolio (World Bank 2005). Many of the themes from the social fund evaluation were echoed in this later report. The outcome ratings of Bank-supported community-based development (CBD) and CDD projects were found to, on average, have been better than those for non-CBD and CDD projects between 1994 and 2003 (World Bank 2005: xi). In addition, between 1999 and 2003, the outcome rating for CBD and CDD projects in postconflict countries was better than the rating for such projects in nonconflict countries.

The overall recommendations for future Bank support for CBD and CDD were to (a) strengthen operational guidance and management oversight at the corporate level, (b) design the CBD and CDD program as an integral part of the overall Country Assistance Strategy, and (c) give priority to helping countries build up existing indigenously mature initiatives (World Bank 2005: xiv).

More recently, in March 2006, the Bank's Quality Assurance Group carried out a portfolio review that was based on a sampling of 90 operations from quality at entry (QAE 4–7) and Quality of Supervision (QSA 5–6) social fund and CDD operations. The results highlighted that social fund and CDD operations are a strong cohort (better satisfactory outcomes and quality of supervision) than HDN and Bank-wide averages, despite being designed and implemented under challenging country circumstances (Garg 2006):

- Development effectiveness ratings were better than HDN and Bank-wide ratings.
- A lower percentage of unsatisfactory outcomes compared with HD and Bank-wide ratings.

- Likely sustainability was higher than HDN and Bank-wide averages.
- Institutional development was substantially stronger than HDN and Bank-wide averages.
- In terms of portfolio management, social fund and CDD operations generally do better than the Bank-wide projects in recognizing risks, as reflected in high realism and proactivity ratings.
- In terms of quality at entry, social fund and CDD projects are on par with the Bank for strategic relevance and approach, technical financial and economic aspects, poverty and social aspects, fiduciary aspects, policy and institutional aspects, and risk assessment.
- Overall ratings with respect to quality of supervision are ahead of the HDN's performance and the Bank's overall performance.

Measuring Performance. Given the rapid scale-up of social funds through the late 1990s, measuring the performance of this portfolio became a priority. In 2004, the Social Protection Anchor (that is, Human Development Network, Social Protection) supported a six-country impact evaluation, which was based on household and other survey data and used accepted evaluation methodologies (Rawlings, Sherburne-Benz, and Van Domelen 2004).

The general findings of the study showed several positive effects of social funds:

- Social fund resources are pro-poor, and targeting has improved over time. Despite some leakage to better-off households and regions, social fund performance compares favorably with that of other public programs.
- Investments largely reflected community needs and priorities, and beneficiaries were satisfied with the results.
- Results were consistent in showing increased access to, quality of, and use of basic social infrastructure.
- Social fund benefits are generally translated into improvements in the health and education status of households, but specific effects varied by country, sector, and region.
- The vast majority of facilities supported by social fund agencies were operating several years after completion, but long-term sustainability in some sectors—particularly water supply and sanitation—was sometimes problematic given insufficient cost recovery.

Data on the results of the social funds portfolio have been analyzed using various evaluative approaches. The most basic approach is to count outputs: the physical outputs financed and built by social fund projects, beneficiaries reached, trainings conducted, and so forth. Much of these data are captured in the implementation completion report written when the project closes. Table 6.6 summarizes the outputs of 20 social fund projects that closed between fiscal years 2002 and 2006 on the basis of a review of the project implementation completion reports.[14]

The data show an impressive number of beneficiaries affected by the 20 projects—76 million—and more than 90,000 subprojects were implemented to improve access to a range of social services. However, the indicators tabulated in the implementation completion reports are primarily indicators of process or outcome and do not capture the full effect of the project. Social funds have attempted to investigate their effect using various approaches since their introduction in Latin America at the end of the 1980s (see, for example, Goodman and others 1997; Khadiagala 1995; Marc and others 1993, all as cited in Chase 2002).

"Getting an Earful: A Review of Beneficiary Assessments of Social Funds" (Owen and Van Domelen 1998: 30), an eight-country review of beneficiary assessments, found that

→ *the impacts of social fund interventions were largely positive. Moreover, the assessments were able to identify factors that contributed to these results. Impacts were concentrated mainly in providing access to and improving the quality of basic services, with some evidence of ancillary capacity effects (both at the community and individual level). Potential indirect income effects were less clear, or not explicitly explored in the [beneficiary assessments].*

As the trend for assessing outcomes increased within the Bank in the 1990s, social funds began experimenting with using quantitative techniques as part of their evaluations. Bolivia was the first social fund to conduct an evaluation using quantitative methods (Newman and others 2002; Pradhan, Rawlings, and Ridder 1998). To provide deeper, more diverse evidence on the effect of social funds, the World Bank initiated a multicountry analysis in 1997 (Rawlings, Sherburne-Benz, and Van Domelen 2004). Since then, a growing number of impact evaluations have been conducted for social funds, including funds in Armenia (Chase 2002), Honduras (Walker and others 1999), Jamaica (Rao and Ibáñez 2001), Malawi (JIMAT Development Consultants 2008), Nicaragua (World Bank 2000), Peru (Paxson and Schady 1999), the Republic of Yemen (Walker and others 2003), and Zambia (Chase and Sherburne-Benz 2000). See box 6.3 for selected examples.

Table 6.6: **Implementation Completion Report Outputs and Outcomes for Social Funds, Fiscal Years 2002–06**

Area	Outcome
Beneficiaries	Twenty projects financed 90,098 multisector, demand-driven subprojects that increased access to local infrastructure and services for about 76 million direct and indirect beneficiaries.
Institutional strengthening	Twelve projects provided direct and on-the-job training to about 400,000 poor and vulnerable people who were formed into community management committees. These committees were responsible for the identification, management of resources, and monitoring and evaluation of small-scale development investments. Twelve projects built capacity within local and national governments to implement comprehensive management information systems and monitoring and evaluation systems. Five projects were able to conduct impact evaluations using data collected during the project implementation process.
Legal framework and policy reform	Five operations mainstreamed CDD approaches into the decentralization policy framework, thereby introducing more transparency and accountability. Four operations piloted innovations in decentralized service delivery, and one piloted innovations in social inclusion of marginalized ethnic groups. Two operations supported dialogue around social protection policies. One operation piloted a CDD approach in land reform that increased government political support for land reform.
Physical outputs	Of the 90,098 subprojects delivered, 43 percent were for roads, 35 percent were microfinance initiatives, 21 percent were for water and sanitation, 23 percent involved social assistance, 21 percent were for schools, 10 percent were other subprojects, and 6 percent were for health. (The total exceeds 100 percent because each community-managed subproject can finance several different interventions.)

Source: World Bank Implementation Completion Reports.

KEY LESSONS AND IMPLICATIONS FOR THE FUTURE

The key lessons learned from this review include the following:

- The evaluative evidence (IEG, QAG, and anchor evaluations) of social funds points to a significant development outcome from delivering basic social and economic services in poor communities and strengthening local-level capacities for improved local governance.
- In many countries, social fund agencies have demonstrated the merits of their institutional model as efficient, semiautonomous bodies focused on promoting concrete results at the local level. Because of their effectiveness, social funds have continued to exist beyond their originally intended short-term horizon, often funded from government budgets or by other donors after World Bank financing ended. They have become an important element of the national system of service delivery.
- Social funds are flexible institutional instruments. Social funds' objectives have evolved over time in line with the changing country context and government needs. Although, they were often created for specific purposes (such as safety nets for vulnerable groups during a crisis), they gradually took on a larger number of development objectives (such as delivery of basic services and capacity-building of local institutions).
- Although the social funds portfolio of the social protection sector has decreased in size in recent years, it remains significant—particularly in IDA countries, where social funds represent 61 percent of social protection lending.
- The social fund model has had a significant effect on Bank projects far beyond social protection. Characteristics of the social fund model have been absorbed by operations supported by several other sectors, including infrastructure, rural development, social development, and finance, and by the private sector, as well as by other donors.
- Although the HDN has had a decreasing "market share," the total portfolio of multisector, demand-driven CDD operations is expanding, especially in the Sustainable Development Network.
- Although social funds are publicly provided, they can support informal mechanisms for managing risk. This feature is distinct from other social protection instruments traditionally financed by the Bank, which primarily serve the formal market and operate at the individual or household level. By supporting informal risk management strategies at the community level, social funds occupy a unique niche within the social protection sector

BOX 6.3

RESULTS FROM SELECTED IMPACT EVALUATIONS OF SOCIAL FUND PROJECTS

Bolivia

The investments in health centers made by Bolivia's Fondo de Inversión Social (Social Investment Fund, or FIS) brought about significant improvements in the centers' physical characteristics and use. Both the share of women's prenatal care and the share of births attended—two important factors affecting mortality in children under age five—increased significantly. Nineteen percent of the women in the treatment group (those living in communities with FIS-financed health projects) received prenatal care versus 7 percent of women in the comparison group. Close to 7 percent of births were attended by trained personnel in the treatment group, compared with only 2 percent in the comparison group. Investments in small community-managed water systems were found to have no major effect on water quality until they were combined with community-level training. However, such investments increased the access to and the quantity of water. The increase in quantity appears to have been sufficient to generate declines in under-five mortality similar in size to those associated with the health interventions. Data from before and after the FIS water supply investments in Chaco and the Resto Rural show that the main changes were a reduction in the distance to the water source (for example, in Chaco the distance was reduced from about 598 meters to 211 meters) and, in the Resto Rural, a substantial improvement in sanitation facilities (the fraction of households with sanitation facilities increased from 27 percent to 71 percent between 1993 and 1997).

Armenia

The results show that the Armenia Social Investment Fund (ASIF) reached poor households, particularly in rural areas. Education projects increased school attendance. In treatment communities, 87 percent of primary school–age children attended school. This finding was higher than the 79 percent attending school in communities where an ASIF project had been approved but not yet completed (termed ***pipeline communities***). Potable water projects increased household access to water and had mild positive effects on health. For example, in ASIF treatment communities, 93 percent of households had access to cold running water, compared with 85 percent in matched communities and 72 percent in pipeline communities. Furthermore, 92 percent of households in ASIF communities had central water systems, significantly more than in both matched communities (83 percent) and pipeline communities (68 percent).

Communities that completed a social fund project were less likely than the comparison group to complete other local infrastructure projects, suggesting that social capital was expended in these early projects. By contrast, communities that joined the social fund later and had not yet completed their projects took more initiatives not supported by the social fund.

Jamaica

This impact evaluation developed and used an evaluation method that combined qualitative evidence with quantitative survey data analyzed with propensity score methods, on matched samples, to study the effect of a participatory community-driven social fund in Jamaica on preference targeting, collective action, and community decision making. The qualitative data revealed that the social fund process is elite driven, and decision making tends to be dominated by a small group of motivated individuals. However, by the end of the project, there was broad-based satisfaction with the outcome. The quantitative data from 500 households mirrored the findings by showing that ex ante the social fund did not address the expressed needs of the majority of individuals in the majority of communities. By the end of the construction process, however, 80 percent of the community expressed satisfaction with the outcome.

Sources: For Bolivia, Newman and others 2002; for Armenia, Chase 2002; for Jamaica, Rao and Ibáñez. 2001.

and provide a balance in the risk management arrangements used in a country.

- Despite the positive effect of social funds, outstanding questions remain regarding their comparative advantage as part of national development strategies:
  —How can social funds be better positioned as part of national systems of social protection?
  —Given the de facto importance of social funds as government institutions, what is their logical place in the institutional fabric of developing countries?

—How can the social protection sector continue to learn from the operational experiences of the many social funds that continue to exist after World Bank support has ended and from similar institutional instruments supported by other sector units?

—How should social funds be strengthened to play constructive roles in fragile states and postconflict contexts?

On the basis of the above findings, four directions for the future are proposed:

1. A key direction is to better embed social funds as part of the social protection policies and programs that form a cornerstone of national development strategies. Experience shows that social funds have the potential to efficiently deliver a range of social risk management functions for vulnerable groups: risk-coping safety nets, such as conditional cash transfer and public works programs; risk-mitigating programs supporting community-driven delivery of basic social and economic services; and risk-reducing programs developing capabilities of community institutions and local governments as part of demand-based efforts to strengthen local governance. Social funds are particularly well suited to support informal, community-based risk management mechanisms that often fit well within contexts where formal social protection programs (such as pensions or labor market policies) are not sufficient.
2. Given the dispersion of the portfolio of social funds and similar instruments across sectors and given that the Bank has now exited from a number of social fund programs, learning efforts should focus on the broad range of multisector programs working in support of local institutions managed by the different World Bank networks (in particular the HDN and the Sustainable Development Networks), as well as on social fund programs no longer supported by the Bank.
3. An important comparative advantage of the social fund programs is that they are semiautonomous institutional models, able to achieve levels of efficiency often higher than traditional central institutions of government. Learning efforts should therefore include attention to the place of social fund instruments as part of the central-level institutional fabric of the state and their ability to complement longer-term efforts aiming to reform the ministries and to decentralize authority and institutional capacity at subnational and local levels of government.
4. It will also be important to focus learning efforts on lessons learned from the experience of social funds and similar instruments in fragile and postconflict environments—often characterized by weak institutions and by the need for rapid and visible results. The relevance of social funds to such contexts comes from the ability of the model both to rapidly establish strong professional capacity at the central level and to build capacity at the community and local government levels.

ANNEX 6.A: PROJECTS REVIEWED, FISCAL YEARS 2000–07

Table 6.A.1: **Projects Reviewed, Fiscal Years 2000–07**

Fiscal year	Country	Project ID	Project title
Africa			
2000	**Angola**	P056393	Second Social Action Fund Project
2000	**Burundi**	P064510	Second Social Action Project
2000	**Lesotho**	P058050	Community Development Support Project
2000	**Zambia**	P063584	Zambia Social Investment Fund
2001	**Madagascar**	P055166	Community Development Project
2001	**Nigeria**	P069086	Community-Based Poverty Reduction Project
2001	**Senegal**	P041566	Social Development Fund Project
2001	**Tanzania**	P065372	Social Action Fund Project
2002	**Uganda**	P002952	Northern Uganda Social Action Fund Project
2003	**Ethiopia**	P077457	Ethiopia: Social Rehabilitation and Development Fund Project—Supplemental
2003	**Malawi**	P075911	Third Malawi Social Action Fund Project
2004	**Angola**	P081558	Third Social Action Fund Project
2004	**Comoros**	P084315	Services Support Project
2004	**Rwanda**	P074102	Decentralization and Community Development Project
2005	**Benin**	P081484	National Community Driven Development Project
2005	**Democratic Republic of Congo**	P086874	Emergency Social Action Project
2005	**Madagascar**	P088978	Community Development Project Supplemental Credit
2005	**Tanzania**	P085786	Tanzania Second Social Action Fund
2007	**Madagascar**	P096296	Community Development Fund 4 (Additional Financing)
2007	**Liberia**	P105683	Community Empowerment Project II
2007	**Nigeria**	P102966	Community-Based Poverty Reduction (Additional Financing)
East Asia and the Pacific			
2000	**Timor-Leste**	P069762	East Timor Community Empowerment and Local Governance Project
2002	**Lao People's Democratic Republic**	P077326	Lao Poverty Reduction Fund Project
Europe and Central Asia			
2000	**Armenia**	P057952	Second Social Investment Fund Project
2001	**Albania**	P055383	Social Services Delivery Project
2001	**Bosnia and Herzegovina**	P070995	Bosnia and Herzegovina Community Development Project
2001	**Kosovo**	P072814	Community Development Fund Project

(continued)

Table 6.A.1: **Projects Reviewed, Fiscal Years 2000–07** *(continued)*

Fiscal year	Country	Project ID	Project title
2002	Former Yugoslav Republic of Macedonia	P076712	Community Development Project
2002	Romania	P068808	Second Social Development Fund Project
2002	Tajikistan	P008860	Poverty Alleviation Project II
2002	Turkey	P074408	Social Risk Mitigation Project
2002	Ukraine	P069858	Social Investment Fund Project
2003	Bulgaria	P069532	Social Investment and Employment Promotion Project
2003	Georgia	P074361	Second Georgia Social Investment Fund
2004	Kosovo	P079259	Second Community Development Fund Project
2004	Moldova	P079314	Social Investment Fund II Project
2007	Armenia	P094225	Social Investment Fund III
2007	Bulgaria	P104272	Social Investment and Employment Promotion Project (Supplement)
Latin America and the Caribbean			
2000	Colombia	P068762	Community Works and Employment Project
2000	St. Lucia	P054939	Poverty Reduction Fund Project
2001	Honduras	P064895	Fifth Social Investment Fund Project
2001	Nicaragua	P064906	Poverty Reduction and Local Development Project
2004	Honduras	P083244	Nuestras Raices Program
2005	El Salvador	P088642	El Salvador Social Protection Project
Middle East and North Africa			
2000	Republic of Yemen	P068830	Second Social Fund for Development
2001	Lebanon	P071113	Community Development Fund
2002	Morocco	P073531	Morocco Social Development Agency Project
2004	Republic of Yemen	P082498	Third Social Fund for Development
2007	Republic of Yemen	P102181	Third Social Fund for Development (Supplement)

Source: Authors.
Note: No social fund projects were approved in fiscal year 2006.

ANNEX 6.B: IMPLEMENTATION STATUS OF SOCIAL FUND PROJECTS, FISCAL YEARS 1987–2006

Table 6.B.1: **Implementation Status of Social Fund Projects, Fiscal Years 1987–2006**

Fiscal year	Country	Project ID	Project title	Implementation status
Africa				
1989	**São Tomé and Príncipe**	P002540	Multisector Credit Project: Social and Infrastructure Fund	Project closed in fiscal year 1997; repeater project approved in fiscal year 1991
1991	**São Tomé and Príncipe**	P002548	Second Multisector Project	Project closed in fiscal year 1998; Third Multisector Project canceled during preparation because of government's reluctance to allow an independent agency to implement public works
1991	**Zambia**	P003242	First Social Recovery Project	Project closed in fiscal year 1999; repeater project implemented
1993	**Burundi**	P000227	First Social Action Project	Project closed in fiscal year 2000; followed by second project in fiscal year 2000
1993	**Comoros**	P044824	Social Fund Project	Project closed in fiscal year 2004; implementing agency now implementing Services Support Project starting in fiscal year 2004
1993	**Madagascar**	P001553	Food Security and Nutrition Project	Project closed in fiscal year 1999; project established the Fonds d'Intervention pour le Developpement, which was basis for follow-on social fund projects
1995	**Zambia**	P003210	Second Social Recovery Project	Project closed in fiscal year 2001; follow-on project approved in fiscal year 2000
1996	**Angola**	P000061	First Social Action Fund Project	Project closed in fiscal year 2001; follow-on project approved in fiscal year 2000
1996	**Eritrea**	P039264	Community Development Fund Project	Project closed in fiscal year 2002; social fund agency dissolved approximately 2 years after end of Bank financing
1996	**Ethiopia**	P000771	Ethiopia: Social Rehabilitation and Development Fund Project	Project continued with supplemental credit in fiscal year 2003
1996	**Madagascar**	P035669	Second Social Fund Project	Project closed in fiscal year 2001; follow-on community development project approved in fiscal year 2001
1996	**Malawi**	P001668	Social Action Fund Project (MASAF I)	Project closed in fiscal year 2002; repeater projects implemented
1998	**Benin**	P035645	Social Fund Project	Project closed in fiscal year 2004; follow-on project, National Community-Driven Development Project, approved in fiscal year 2005, of which the social fund is one component
1998	**Mali**	P035617	Grassroots Initiative to Fight Hunger and Poverty Project	Project closed in fiscal year 2004; follow-on CDD operation, Rural Community Development Project, approved in fiscal year 2006, mapped to the Africa Region ESSD, with social fund as one component

(continued)

Table 6.B.1: **Implementation Status of Social Fund Projects, Fiscal Years 1987–2006** *(continued)*

Fiscal year	Country	Project ID	Project title	Implementation status
1998	**Zimbabwe**	P045031	Community Action Project	Project closed in fiscal year 2004; government then funded scaled-down project for a couple of years but was unable in short term to clear its arrears and reengage with the Bank; project unit staff not rehired on expiry of annual contracts and closure of project
1999	**Ghana**	P040659	Community-Based Poverty Reduction Project	Project closed in fiscal year 2006 and merged into Poverty Reduction Support Credit
1999	**Madagascar**	P064305	Third Social Fund Project	Project closed in fiscal year 2003
1999	**Malawi**	P049599	Second Social Action Fund Project (MASAF II)	Project closed in fiscal year 2004; repeater project implemented
1999	**Togo**	PO52263	Pilot Social Fund Project	Project closed in fiscal year 2002; originally funded in north Togo by United Nations Development Programme and European Union; new operation to complete community investments initiated by original fund in the south, being prepared as low-income country under stress project
2000	**Angola**	P056393	Second Social Action Fund Project	Project closed in fiscal year 2004
2000	**Burundi**	P064510	Second Social Action Project	Project active
2000	**Lesotho**	P058050	Community Development Support Project	Project closed
2000	**Zambia**	P063584	Zambia Social Investment Fund	Project closed in fiscal year 2006; follow-on project, Local Development Fund Project, in preparation for approval in fiscal year 2007
2001	**Madagascar**	P055166	Community Development Project	Project active
2001	**Nigeria**	P069086	Community-Based Poverty Reduction Project	Project active
2001	**Senegal**	P041566	Social Development Fund Project	Project active
2001	**Tanzania**	P065372	Social Action Fund Project	Project closed; repeater project approved in fiscal year 2005
2002	**Uganda**	P002952	Northern Uganda Social Action Fund Project	Project active
2003	**Ethiopia**	P077457	Ethiopia: Social Rehabilitation and Development Fund Project—Supplemental	Project closed; social fund agency dissolved
2003	**Malawi**	P075911	Third Social Action Fund Project (MASAF III)	Project active
2004	**Angola**	P081558	Third Social Action Fund Project	Project active

(continued)

Table 6.B.1: **Implementation Status of Social Fund Projects, Fiscal Years 1987–2006** *(continued)*

Fiscal year	Country	Project ID	Project title	Implementation status
2004	**Comoros**	P084315	Services Support Project	Project active
2004	**Rwanda**	P074102	Decentralization and Community Development Project	Project active
2005	**Benin**	P081484	National Community-Driven Development Project	Project active
2005	**Democratic Republic of Congo**	P086874	Emergency Social Action Project	Project active
2005	**Madagascar**	P088978	Community Development Project Supplemental Credit	Project active; supplemental to fiscal year 2001 project
2005	**Tanzania**	P085786	Tanzania Second Social Action Fund	Project active
2007	**Liberia**	P105683	Community Empowerment 2	Project active
2007	**Madagascar**	P096296	Community Development Fund 4: Additional Financing	Project active
2007	**Nigeria**	P102966	Nigeria Community-Based Poverty Reduction: Additional Financing	Project active
East Asia and the Pacific and South Asia				
1991	**Sri Lanka**	P010368	Poverty Alleviation Project	Project closed in fiscal year 1998; social fund agency dissolved
1995	**Cambodia**	P037088	Social Fund Project	Project closed in fiscal year 2000; repeater project implemented
1998	**Philippines**	P051386	Special Zone of Peace and Development Social Fund Project	Project closed in fiscal year 2003; lessons learned incorporated into the fiscal year 2003 Autonomous Region in Muslim Mindanao Social Fund Project, mapped to EAP Rural Development
1999	**Cambodia**	P050601	Second Social Fund Project	Project closed in fiscal year 2005; social fund agency dissolved
1999	**Thailand**	P056269	Social Investment Project	Project closed in fiscal year 2004; social investment fund component closed in late 2002 in part because of a change in government and the government's decision not to seek additional Bank financing for social protection programs; local development funded since 2001 by a government village fund (microlending) program, considered a populist hallmark program of the Thaksin administration
2000	**Timor-Leste**	P069762	East Timor Community Empowerment and Local Governance Project	Project closed; no follow-on activities
2002	**Lao People's Democratic Republic**	P077326	Lao Poverty Reduction Fund Project	Project active

(continued)

Table 6.B.1: Implementation Status of Social Fund Projects, Fiscal Years 1987–2006 *(continued)*

Fiscal year	Country	Project ID	Project title	Implementation status
Europe and Central Asia				
1993	**Albania**	P008264	Rural Poverty Alleviation Project	Project closed in fiscal year 1996; financing continued by KfW, European Union, and others
1995	**Armenia**	P035768	First Social Investment Fund Project	Project closed in fiscal year 2001; repeater projects implemented
1997	**Bosnia and Herzegovina**	P045310	Emergency Public Works and Employment Project	Project closed in fiscal year 2000; lessons learned incorporated into design of the fiscal year 2001 Community Development Project
1997	**Georgia**	P039929	First Social Investment Fund	Project active
1997	**Tajikistan**	P044202	Pilot Poverty Alleviation Project	Project closed in fiscal year 2002; repeater project implemented
1998	**Bulgaria**	P055156	Regional Initiatives Fund Project	Project closed; originally a pilot project scaled up in a fiscal year 2003 social fund project
1999	**Moldova**	P044840	First Social Investment Fund Project	Project closed in fiscal year 2005; repeater project implemented
1999	**Romania**	P049200	First Social Development Fund Project	Project closed in fiscal year 2002; repeater project implemented
2000	**Armenia**	P057952	Second Social Investment Fund Project	Project closed in fiscal year 2006; third project in the pipeline
2001	**Albania**	P055383	Social Services Delivery Project	Project active
2001	**Bosnia and Herzegovina**	P070995	Community Development Project	Project active
2001	**Kosovo**	P072814	Community Development Fund Project	Project closed; repeater project implemented
2002	**Former Yugoslav Republic of Macedonia**	P076712	Community Development Project	Project active
2002	**Romania**	P068808	Second Social Development Fund Project	Project active
2002	**Tajikistan**	P008860	Poverty Alleviation Project II	Project active
2002	**Turkey**	P074408	Social Risk Mitigation Project	Project active
2002	**Ukraine**	P069858	Social Investment Fund Project	Project active
2003	**Bulgaria**	P069532	Social Investment and Employment Promotion Project	Project active
2003	**Georgia**	P074361	Second Georgia Social Investment Fund	Project active
2004	**Kosovo**	P079259	Second Community Development Fund Project	Project active
2004	**Moldova**	P079314	Social Investment Fund II Project	Project active

(continued)

Table 6.B.1: **Implementation Status of Social Fund Projects, Fiscal Years 1987–2006** *(continued)*

Fiscal year	Country	Project ID	Project title	Implementation status
2007	**Armenia**	P094225	Social Investment Fund 3	Project active
2007	**Bulgaria**	P104272	Social Investment and Employment Promotion Project Supplement	Project active
Latin America and the Caribbean				
1987	**Bolivia**	P006176	Emergency Social Fund Project	Project closed; second project approved in fiscal year 1998
1991	**Haiti**	P007321	Economic and Social Fund Project	Financing continued by IDB
1991	**Honduras**	P007389	First Social Investment Fund Project	Project closed in fiscal year 1994; repeater projects implemented
1992	**Guatemala**	P007220	Social Investment Fund Project	Financing continued by IDB from fiscal year 1999
1992	**Guyana**	P007254	Social Impact Amelioration Program and Agency	Financing continued by IDB from fiscal year 1998
1992	**Honduras**	P007394	Second Social Investment Fund Project	Project closed in fiscal year 1996; repeater projects implemented
1992	**Nicaragua**	P007786	First Social Investment Fund Project	Project closed in fiscal year 1997; repeater projects implemented
1994	**Ecuador**	P007106	Third Social Development Project: Emergency Social Investment Fund	Financing continued by IDB from fiscal year 1997
1994	**Peru**	P008062	Social Development and Compensation Fund Project	Financing continued by IDB from fiscal year 1997
1995	**Argentina**	P035495	First Social Protection Project	Project closed in fiscal year 1999; repeater projects implemented
1995	**Honduras**	P037709	Third Social Investment Fund Project	Project closed in fiscal year 2000; repeater projects implemented
1996	**Nicaragua**	P038916	Second Social Investment Fund Project	Project closed in fiscal year 1998; repeater project implemented
1997	**Argentina**	P049268	Second Social Protection Project	Project closed in fiscal year 1999; repeater projects implemented
1997	**Belize**	P039292	Social Investment Fund	Project closed in fiscal year 2003; financing continued by Caribbean Development Bank and others
1997	**Jamaica**	P039029	Jamaica Social Investment Fund Project	Project closed in fiscal year 2002, but fund still exists and is the implementing agency for the Bank-financed National Community Development Project established in 2002, which is still active and mapped to the LAC finance and private sector development sector
1997	**Panama**	P007837	Social Investment Fund Project	Project closed in fiscal year 2004

(continued)

Table 6.B.1: **Implementation Status of Social Fund Projects, Fiscal Years 1987–2006** *(continued)*

Fiscal year	Country	Project ID	Project title	Implementation status
1998	**Bolivia**	P006175	Second Emergency Social Fund Project	Project closed in fiscal year 1992; demand-driven approach of fund provided model and catalyzed other Bank-financed projects (not mapped to the social protection sector), such as Bolivia Rural Communities Development Project (fiscal year 1995) and Bolivia Participatory Rural Investment Project (fiscal year 1998); social fund agency still a government program, Bolivia Fondo Nacional de Desarrollo Regional
1998	**Honduras**	P048651	Fourth Social Investment Fund Project	Project closed in fiscal year 2003; repeater project implemented
1999	**Argentina**	P006058	Fourth Social Protection Project	Project closed in fiscal year 2006; fund objectives amended to include community kitchens during economic crisis; fund still financed jointly by European Union and government
1999	**Nicaragua**	P040197	Third Social Investment Fund Project	Project closed in fiscal year 2003; spin-off project, Poverty Reduction and Local Development Project, implemented in fiscal year 2001
2000	**Colombia**	P068762	Community Works and Employment Project	Project continued by Ministry of Social Development (Manos a la Obra)
2000	**St. Lucia**	P054939	Poverty Reduction Fund Project	Financing continued by United Nations Development Programme and European Union
2001	**Honduras**	P064895	Fifth Social Investment Fund Project	Project closed; spin-off project, Nuestras Raices Program, being implemented by the social fund agency
2001	**Nicaragua**	P064906	Poverty Reduction and Local Development Project	Spin-off project now closed; financing continued by IDB, KfW Bankengrappe and others
2004	**Honduras**	P083244	Nuestras Raices Program	Spin-off project still active
2005	**El Salvador**	P088642	El Salvador Social Protection Project	Project still active
Middle East and North Africa				
1991	**Arab Republic of Egypt**	P005158	Social Fund for Development Project I	Project closed in fiscal year 1997; second and third repeater projects implemented in fiscal years 1996 and 1999
1996	**Algeria**	P004978	Social Safety Net Support Project	Project closed in fiscal year 2001
1996	**Arab Republic of Egypt**	P043102	Social Fund for Development Project II	Project closed in fiscal year 2002; followed by third project in fiscal year 1999
1997	**West Bank and Gaza**	P047110	First Community Development Project	Project closed in fiscal year 2000; repeater project implemented

(continued)

Table 6.B.1: **Implementation Status of Social Fund Projects, Fiscal Years 1987–2006** *(continued)*

Fiscal year	Country	Project ID	Project title	Implementation status
1997	**Republic of Yemen**	P041199	Social Fund for Development Project	Project closed; second and third repeater projects implemented in fiscal years 2000 and 2004
1999	**Djibouti**	P044584	Social Development and Public Works Project	Project active
1999	**Arab Republic of Egypt**	P052705	Third Social Fund for Development Project	Project closed; repeater fourth project is in pipeline for fiscal year 2007
1999	**West Bank and Gaza**	P058684	Second Community Development Project	Project closed in fiscal year 2003
2000	**Republic of Yemen**	P068830	Second Social Fund for Development	Project closed; repeater third project undertaken in fiscal year 2004
2001	**Lebanon**	P071113	Community Development Fund	Project active
2002	**Morocco**	P073531	Morocco Social Development Agency Project	Project active
2004	**Republic of Yemen**	P082498	Third Social Fund for Development	Project active
2007	**Republic of Yemen**	P102181	Social Fund for Development 2 (Supplement)	Project active

Source: Authors.

NOTES

1 More than half of the funds in the social fund portfolio used community contracting, whereby community groups directly managed microproject resources. This model was a truer expression of the CDD approach than social funds for which a central agency retained many of the responsibilities.

2 Project development objectives are paraphrased from project appraisal documents. Such documents are mandatory for World Bank project preparation.

3 An additional fiscal year, 1999, was included in this analysis and covers a total of 56 social fund agencies.

4 Fifty-six social fund projects and project appraisal documents were reviewed (for the fiscal years 1999–2007); additional information was provided by individual task team leaders.

5 Before fiscal year 2000, at least two social funds in South Asia were mapped to the Social Protection Sector Board—in Pakistan and in Sri Lanka. South Asia CDD operations are now largely mapped to the Sustainable Development Network.

6 Many social fund operations are also mapped to other sector boards, including the Social Development, Finance and Private Sector Development, Rural Development, and Urban Development Sector Boards. Examples of such projects in fiscal years 2000 to 2007 include the Bangladesh Social Investment Fund (Rural Development), Pakistan Poverty Alleviation Fund (Finance and Private Sector Development), Jamaica Social Investment Fund (Infrastructure), and Kecamatan Development Project (Social Development).

7 Three particularly important multicountry reviews were carried out in the 2000 to 2007 period, including the Social Protection Unit's six-country impact evaluation of social investment funds, a Quality Assurance Group portfolio review of social funds (2006), and an Independent Evaluation Group portfolio review of CDD operations (2005).

[8] Pipeline figures are preliminary.

[9] Pipeline figures are subject to change.

[10] The OED was renamed the Independent Evaluation Group in 2005.

[11] Sector Adjustment Loans were replaced by Sector Investment and Maintenance Loans as of fiscal year 2005. Of the current loan types, Technical Assistance Loans and Financial Intermediary Loans have not been used to finance social funds. Technical Assistance Loans are used specifically to support institutional capacity building, whereas social funds also require infrastructure investment, and Financial Intermediary Loans are not used because social funds are not financial institutions.

[12] Learning and Innovation Loans are loans of US$5 million or less that finance small, experimental, risky, or time-sensitive projects. They are used to pilot promising initiatives and to build consensus around those initiatives or to experiment with an approach and develop locally based models before a larger-scale intervention.

[13] These figures are indicative.

[14] The review of implementation completion reports is based on a list of reports for 20 projects that were mapped to the Social Protection Sector Board under thematic code 56, *Other Social Protection*, and were closed between fiscal years 2002 and 2006.

REFERENCES

Adam, Sarah. 2006. "Evaluating Social Fund Impact: A Toolkit for Task Teams and Social Fund Managers." Social Protection Discussion Paper 0611, Social Protection Unit, Human Development Network, World Bank, Washington, DC.

Aiyar, Swaminathan, and Binswanger, Hans P. 2003. "Scaling Up Community-Driven Development: Theoretical Underpinnings and Program Design Implications." Policy Research Working Paper 3039, World Bank, Washington, DC.

Bhatia, Mukhmeet. 2005. "Social Funds: A Review of Public Sector Management and Institutional Issues." Social Protection Discussion Paper 0508, Social Protection Unit, Human Development Network, World Bank, Washington, DC.

Chase, Robert. 2002. "Supporting Communities in Transition: The Impact of the Armenia Social Investment Fund." *World Bank Economic Review* 16 (2): 219–40.

Chase, Robert, and Lynne Sherburne-Benz. 2000. "Zambia Social Recovery Project: Evaluating the Household Impact." Social Funds 2000 Study, World Bank, Washington, DC.

Coudouel, Aline, Kene Ezemenari, Margaret Grosh, and Lynn Sherburne-Benz. 2002. "Social Protection." In *A Sourcebook for Poverty Reduction Strategies*, ed. Jeni Klugman, 163–200. Washington, DC: World Bank.

de la Brière, Bénédicte, and Laura B. Rawlings. 2006. "Examining Conditional Cash Transfer Programs: A Role for Increased Social Inclusion?" Social Protection Discussion Paper 0603, Social Protection Unit, Human Development Network, World Bank, Washington, DC.

de Silva, Samantha. 2002. "Communities Taking the Lead: A Handbook on Direct Financing of Community Subprojects." World Bank, Washington, DC.

———. 2005. "Leveraging Social Funds for a Broader Risk Management Agenda." Paper presented at the World Bank Social Protection Retreat, Washington, DC, December.

———. 2007. "Social Funds as Social Protection Instruments." Presentation at Africa Social Protection Retreat, World Bank, Social Protection Unit, Washington, DC, March 2007.

Dongier, Philippe, Julie Van Domelen, Elinor Ostrom, Andrea Rizvi, Wendy Wakeman, Anthony Bebbington, Sabina Alkire, Talib Esmail, and Margaret Polski. 2002. "Community-Driven Development." In *A Sourcebook for Poverty Reduction Strategies*, ed. Jeni Klugman, 301–31. Washington, DC: World Bank.

Frigenti, Laura, and Alberto Harth, with Rumana Huque. 1998. *Local Solutions to Regional Problems: The Growth of Social Funds and Public Works and Employment Projects in Sub-Saharan Africa*. Washington, DC: World Bank.

Garg, Prem. 2006. "Operational Quality of Social Fund/CDD Operations: Some Trends and Issues." Presentation to World Bank staff, March 15, Washington, DC.

Goodman, Margaret, Samuel Morley, Gabriel Siri, and Elaine Zuckerman. 1997. *Social Investment Funds in Latin*

America: Past Performance and Future Role. Washington, DC: Inter-American Development Bank.

Holzmann, Robert, and Steen Jørgensen. 2000. "Social Risk Management: A New Conceptual Framework for Social Protection and Beyond." Social Protection Discussion Paper 0006, Social Protection Unit, Human Development Network, World Bank, Washington, DC.

JIMAT Development Consultants. 2008. "MASAF 3 APL I Impact Evaluation." JIMAT Development Consultants, Harare.

Jørgensen, Steen, and Julie Van Domelen. 2001. "Helping the Poor Manage Risk Better: The Role of Social Funds." In *Shielding the Poor: Social Protection in the Developing World,* ed. Nora Lustig, 91–108. Washington, DC: Brookings Institution Press.

Khadiagala, Lynn. 1995. "Social Funds: Strengths, Weaknesses, and Conditions for Success." Environment and Social Protection Department, World Bank, Washington, DC.

Klugman, Jeni, ed. 2002. *A Sourcebook for Poverty Reduction Strategies.* Washington, DC: World Bank.

Lenneiye, N. Mungai. 2005. "Who Has the Yam, and Who Has the Knife? Social Action Funds and Decentralization in Malawi, Tanzania, and Uganda." Social Protection Discussion Paper 0518, Social Protection Unit, Human Development Network, World Bank, Washington, DC.

Marc, Alexandre, Carol Graham, Mark Schachter, and Mary Beth Schmidt. 1993. "Social Action Programs and Social Funds: A Review of Design and Implementation in Sub-Saharan Africa." Discussion Paper 274, World Bank, Washington, DC.

Newman, John, Menno Pradhan, Laura B. Rawlings, Geert Ridder, Ramiro Coa, and José Luis Evia. 2002. "An Impact Evaluation of Education, Health, and Water Supply Investments by the Bolivian Social Investment Fund." *World Bank Economic Review* 16 (2): 241–74.

Owen, Daniel, and Julie Van Domelen. 1998. "Getting an Earful: A Review of Beneficiary Assessments of Social Funds." Social Protection Discussion Paper 9186, Social Protection Unit, Human Development Network, World Bank, Washington, DC.

Paxson, Christina, and Norbert Schady. 1999. "Do School Facilities Matter? The Case of the Peruvian Social Fund (FONCODES)." Policy Research Working Paper 2229, Poverty Division, Poverty Reduction and Economic Management Network, World Bank, Washington, DC.

Pradhan, Menno, Laura Rawlings, and Geert Ridder. 1998. "The Bolivian Social Investment Fund: An Analysis of Baseline Data for Impact Evaluation." *World Bank Economic Review* 12 (3): 457–82.

Rao, Vijayendra, and Ana-María Ibáñez. 2001. "The Social Impact of Social Funds in Jamaica: A Mixed-Methods Analysis of Participation, Targeting, and Collective Action in Community-Driven Development." Working paper, Development Research Group, World Bank, Washington, DC.

Rawlings, Laura B., Lynne Sherburne-Benz, and Julie Van Domelen. 2004. *Evaluating Social Funds: A Cross-Country Analysis of Community Investments.* Washington, DC: World Bank.

Schmidt, Mary Beth, and Alexandre Marc. 1998. "Social Investment Funds in Transition Economies: Opportunities and Risks." World Bank, Washington, DC.

Serrano-Berthet, Rodrigo. 2007. "From Social Funds to Local Governance and Social Inclusion Programs: A Prospective Review from the ECA Region." Human Development Sector Unit, Europe and Central Asia Region, World Bank, Washington, DC.

Van Domelen, Julie. 2007. "Reaching the Poor and Vulnerable: Targeting Strategies for Social Funds and Other Community-Driven Programs." Social Protection Discussion Paper 0711, Social Protection Unit, Human Development Network, World Bank, Washington, DC.

Van Domelen, Julie, and Randa El-Rashidi. 2002. "A Review of Social Funds in Africa: Implementation Experience and Issues for the Future." Social Protection Unit, Human Development Network, World Bank, Washington, DC.

Walker, Ian, Rafael del Cid, Fidel Ordóñez, and Florencia Rodríguez. 1999. "Ex-Post Evaluation of the Honduras

Social Investment Fund (FHIS 2)." Report prepared for the World Bank by ESA Consultores International, Honduras.

Walker, Ian, Vincent David, Fidel Ordóñez, and Freddy Velásquez. 2003. "Yemen Social Fund for Development: 2003 Impact Evaluation Study." Report prepared for the World Bank by ESA Consultores International, Tegucigalpa, Honduras.

World Bank. 2000. *Nicaragua Ex-Post Impact Evaluation of the Emergency Social Investment Fund (FISE).* Human Development Sector Management Unit, Latin America and the Caribbean Region, World Bank, Washington, DC.

———. 2001a. *Social Protection Sector Strategy: From Safety Net to Springboard.* Washington, DC: World Bank. http://go.worldbank.org/97LBYDY3U0.

———. 2001b. *World Development Report 2000/2001: Attacking Poverty.* Washington, DC: World Bank.

———. 2002. *Social Funds: Assessing Effectiveness.* Washington, DC: Operations Evaluation Department, World Bank.

———. 2005. "The Effectiveness of World Bank Support for Community-Based and -Driven Development: An OED Evaluation." Operations Evaluation Department, World Bank, Washington, DC.

———. 2006a. "Opportunity, Security, and Equity in the Middle East and North Africa." *Spectrum* (Summer), Social Protection Unit, Human Development Network, World Bank, Washington, DC.

———. 2006b. "Show and Tell Seminar on Social Protection: Social Protection at the World Bank." Presentation by the Social Protection Unit at International Labour Organization Headquarters, Geneva, February.

———. 2007. "Enabling East Asian Communities to Drive Local Development: East Asia Region CDD Flagship Report." World Bank, Washington, DC. December 1.

CHAPTER 7 seven

DISABILITY AND DEVELOPMENT IN THE WORLD BANK, 2002–07

Jeanine Braithwaite, Richard Carroll, Daniel Mont, and Karen Peffley

INTRODUCTION

People with disabilities compose a significant portion of the population. Estimates show that there are at least 600 million people with disabilities in the world, of which at least 400 million live in developing countries and are disproportionately represented among the poor. In most countries, people with disabilities have historically been stigmatized and denied the opportunities that have benefited other poor people. Governments have ignored this population and have failed to enforce their own laws where such laws exist. People with disabilities living in poverty, therefore, benefit least from the expanding opportunities that economic development brings, are least likely to achieve empowerment even when other poor groups do, and are most likely to remain vulnerable to economic shocks and other sources of insecurity.

Since about 1996, awareness in the World Bank about the two-way causality between poverty and disability has increased. The World Bank has made efforts to direct part of its lending to projects targeted specifically at people with disabilities (*disability-specific projects*). In addition, the Bank is working on increasing the degree to which concerns about disability issues are reflected in all of its development activities, including strategies, policies, programs, and projects in light of the economic and social benefits of ensuring the participation of people with disabilities in the development process and providing opportunities for those people.

Disability issues extend across many sectors of the Bank's work. The Disability & Development (D&D) team was created in 2002 by the Social Protection and Labor Unit of the Human Development Network (HDN) to help ensure that disability issues are appropriately addressed in the World Bank's mainstream poverty alleviation efforts. A key function of the team is to coordinate and seek synergies (a) among the various areas of social protection (social insurance, social funds, social safety nets, and labor markets); (b) within HDN more broadly (education, health, nutrition, and population); and (c) across the Bank (poverty reduction, gender, social development, postconflict recovery, transportation and communications, and so forth).

Objectives

This chapter's objectives are (a) to present the record of the World Bank's involvement in disability as part of its overall development strategy; (b) to share with development partners some of the good practices the Bank has discovered and fostered; and (c) to stimulate new ways to address the issues facing people with disabilities through partnerships, better

Jeanine Braithwaite is senior economist at the World Bank and is head of the Disability & Development team of the Social Protection and Labor Department. Daniel Mont, Senior Economist, and Karen Peffley, Program Assistant, are on this team. Richard Carroll is a consultant at the World Bank.

practices, and the further mainstreaming of disability into the work of the Bank.

How the Theme Fits in the Social Risk Management Framework and How Bank Thinking on Disability Has Evolved

As both a cause and a consequence of poverty, disability is an issue central to the mission of the Bank as well as to the Millennium Development Goals (MDGs). For example, as many as one-third of all primary schoolchildren not attending school have a disability, and lack of maternal health care is a major cause of disability in developing countries (World Bank 2003b). A paper commissioned by the Bank estimates that gross domestic product lost as the result of labor costs alone is in the range of 5 to 7 percent worldwide (Metts 2004). This loss results both from the inadequate access to the labor market and from the lack of services for people with disabilities, which compels other household members to withdraw from the labor market.

Disability is not a rare event but is rather a normal part of the life cycle and something that all people are likely to experience. The World Bank estimates that roughly 10 to 12 percent of the world's population has a disability, and as many as one-fourth of all households have a member with a disability (Mont 2007). People with disabilities face major barriers that prevent them from working, attending school, building families, or even participating in civic activities.

Disability was a neglected topic in the World Bank before 2001. Without a formal sector or structure, regional vice presidential units had taken up disability on an ad hoc basis, as a component in a few projects or as a reference in a poverty report or other research. In 2001, in *Social Protection Sector Strategy: From Safety Net to Spring Board* (World Bank 2001), the Bank introduced a new social risk management approach that helped focus the World Bank's work on fighting poverty of the more vulnerable groups in society, including people with disabilities. In pursuing this new focus, the Bank has become aware that people with disabilities are disproportionately represented among the world's poor and that the poverty of people with disabilities is both deeper and more difficult to overcome.

In response to this challenge, a small Disability & Development team was created at the Human Development Network, Social Protection (HDNSP), and an adviser on Disability and Development was appointed in 2002. Regional vice presidential units began to designate regional disability coordinators for regional working groups on disability, and all regions now have disability coordinators. Initially, the team focused its efforts on raising awareness and organizing training events to sensitize the World Bank staff to the issue. Success was mixed. Training events were attended by few task team leaders, and unrealistic expectations were raised among nongovernmental organizations (NGOs) and disabled persons' organizations (DPOs) by two high-profile international conferences (in 2002 and 2004). Nevertheless, the World Bank was able to advocate for disability as an issue, which raised awareness internally and also among other development agencies. In addition, the Bank helped NGOs better make their case to address disability from an economic development framework.

The World Bank began to move into specialized areas that were necessary to develop the evidence base for the case to include disability in World Bank operations: data and disability prevalence, inclusive education, accessibility, legal issues and safeguards, health, conflict management, and natural and human-made disasters. A list of papers, notes, toolkits, and training events undertaken is available on the HDNSP D&D Web site (http://www.worldbank.org/disability) and excerpts are provided in annex 7.A. As a result, the World Bank has been able to raise awareness that disability is a key issue for development, given the vicious circular nature of poverty and disability. Poverty causes many disabilities that are prevented in more developed countries, and households with members who have disabilities are often poorer than average.

In 2004, HDN management realized that D&D work at the World Bank needed to be reoriented toward mainstreaming by incorporating disability concerns and inclusive policies in World Bank lending and economic and sector work, thus making D&D work more operationally relevant. The first measure was to produce operational toolkits. In 2005, activities shifted more toward improving the evidence base and results framework for interventions in disability-inclusive policies. These efforts are focused in several key areas: monitoring disability in World Bank operations, data, and prevalence and developing disability indicators; evaluating the relationship between disability and poverty; promoting inclusive education; using health and rehabilitation to reduce disability; ameliorating disability in countries affected by conflict; increasing accessibility; supporting social protection (disability pensions, disability grants, and labor market protection); developing operational tools and guidelines; and fostering partnerships.

In 2005, the first loan dedicated to disability, the Iraq Emergency Disabilities Project, was established to promote the delivery of rehabilitation services and orthotic and prosthetic services that improve physical functioning.

Types of Interventions and Activities

The World Bank's comparative advantage in supporting disability interventions lies in its capacity to address complex, multisectoral issues in a consistent, coordinated, fiscally responsible, and operational manner. The World Bank's strengths lie in the following areas: (a) helping countries understand the economic reasons and advantages for pursuing inclusive development; (b) providing the analytical work to develop policies, programs, and targeted safety nets; and (c) ensuring that Bank programs and projects help with incremental implementation of the United Nations (UN) Convention on the Rights of Persons with Disabilities, which entered into force on May 3, 2008.

The World Bank has undertaken a three-pronged approach to pursue the D&D objectives. This approach includes continuing its efforts of the past several years to mainstream disability into existing programs and research; improving the evidence base through data measurement, collection, and program and policy analysis; and continuing outreach and awareness building of disability as a development issue that is crucial for achieving sustainable reduction of poverty as well as reaching some key MDGs. The specific areas of D&D that the Bank will address are described later in this chapter.

METHODOLOGY

Because disability is not a World Bank sector or thematic code, D&D activities cannot be quantified and analyzed in the same way as other social protection and labor (SP&L) activities. A baseline of World Bank activity in disability was undertaken in 2006 and 2007. In the case of D&D, a simple criterion was adopted to estimate the D&D portfolio: if the lending documentation or report mentioned disability in any way, the activity was counted.

D&D PORTFOLIO ACTIVITIES AT THE WORLD BANK, 2002–07

During fiscal years 2002 to 2007, 6.7 percent of World Bank projects by number and 6.65 percent of new lending commitments mentioned disability, although a precise amount dedicated to specific disability aspects could not be determined. The total volume of these new lending commitments was US$4.8 billion. Disability was mentioned in 6 percent of economic and sector work during fiscal years 2002 to 2006. Another indicator of progress is that many World Bank country offices and public information centers now provide both physical and communications access. Figure 7.1 and table 7.1 show the increasing importance of D&D activities in Bank lending operations.

Types of D&D Activities

The history of D&D activities at the World Bank is not as long, nor is the volume of associated lending as high, as that of other areas of SP&L. Furthermore, lending volume is not a good measure of the importance of D&D activities in the Bank's work, partly because providing access to persons with disabilities can be low cost, particularly for new construction. For example, for an additional cost of 1 to 2 percent of school construction, a building can be accessible to all (World Bank 2003a). The Bank's D&D activities are growing. Major disability activities include the following:

- Developing disability indicators, statistics, and measurement capacity
- Supporting inclusive education

FIGURE 7.1: **PROJECTS THAT REFER TO DISABILITY, FISCAL YEARS 2002–07**

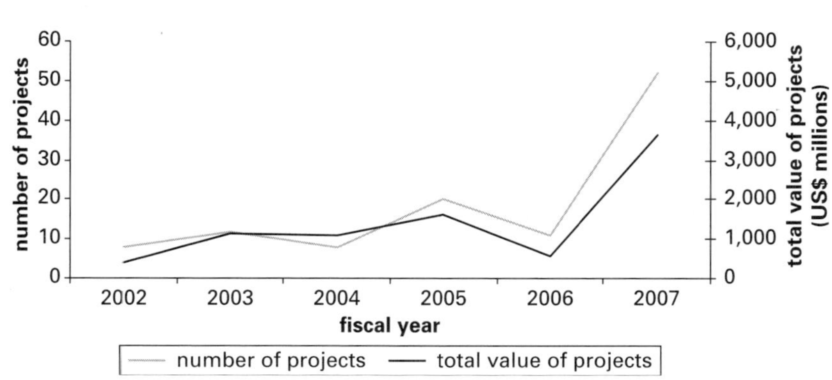

Source: Authors' calculations, based on the Business Warehouse data and World Bank documents.

Table 7.1: **Projects that Refer to Disability by Region, Number, and Lending Amount, Fiscal Years 2002–07**

	Number of projects mentioning disability							Lending commitments for projects mentioning disability (US$ millions)						
Region	**2002**	**2003**	**2004**	**2005**	**2006**	**2007**	**Total**	**2002**	**2003**	**2004**	**2005**	**2006**	**2007**	**Total**
Africa	0	4	0	2	0	20	26	0.0	240.5	0.0	85.0	0.0	1,058.6	1,384.1
East Asia and the Pacific	1	1	0	3	2	4	11	0.0	138.8	0.0	79.0	104.0	579.4	901.2
Europe and Central Asia	4	1	1	4	2	11	23	44.2	300.0	100.0	197.0	147.3	532.8	1,321.3
Latin America and the Caribbean	3	2	3	4	5	7	24	347.0	72.0	218.7	702.5	194.8	730.0	2,265.0
Middle East and North Africa	0	4	0	4	1	3	12	0.0	388.5	0.0	178.1	10.0	120.0	696.6
South Asia	0	0	4	3	1	7	15	0.0	0.0	765.7	357.0	120.0	605.0	1,847.7
Total	8	12	8	20	11	52	111	391.2	1,139.8	1,084.4	1,598.6	576.1	3,625.8	8,415.9

Source: Authors' calculations, based on the Business Warehouse data and World Bank documents.
Note: Because of rounding, totals may deviate slightly from the sum of the parts.

- Promoting health and rehabilitation
- Ameliorating disability caused by conflict and natural disasters
- Increasing accessibility for persons with disabilities to community life and to economic empowerment
- Pursuing disability activities within the three core areas of SP&L
- Developing operational tools and guidelines
- Creating regional initiatives
- Forging partnerships.

Developing Disability Diagnostics, Statistics, and Measurement Capacity. A working group on improved disability measurement and statistics was begun by the UN Statistical Commission and supported by the World Bank through a US$235,000 development grant facility (DGF) and also through donated staff time. Known as the Washington City Group, it is working actively to improve the measurement of disability and statistical systems. More than 50 countries have participated in these activities.

The World Bank aims to assist countries in providing reliable data for making more inclusive policies and in implementing, monitoring, and evaluating those policies. Definitions, measurements, and prevalence of disabilities vary substantially across countries. Many developing countries significantly underestimate the prevalence of disability. Often families hide children or other family members with disabilities because of associated social stigma. Where people with disabilities are not visible in society, prevalence is even more difficult to assess. Recent studies in selected developing countries indicate a disability prevalence of 10 to 12 percent of the population, with about 2 to 3 percent of the entire population having severe impairments (Mont 2007). The World Bank promotes a modern, functional approach to disability, which is a better platform for designing inclusive policies than the previously predominant medical approach. Additional details of the World Bank's work in this area are provided in annex 7.B.

The Disability & Development team has produced a survey paper about disability and poverty, which is based on a review of all 154 poverty assessments undertaken by the World Bank (Braithwaite and Mont 2008). This survey found that a surprisingly high percentage of poverty assessments (80.5 percent) had some mention of disability, but fewer than 10 percent (11 by count) had information detailed enough to assess the relative poverty rate among households with and without members with disabilities, and all of those assessments were in only one World Bank region—the Europe and Central Asia Region. The team is also working on an empirical analysis of poverty and disability—work that can now be done because new data are now available.

Supporting Inclusive Education. Universal primary education by 2015 is one of the MDGs. Universal primary education cannot be obtained unless all children are in school, including those with disabilities. Inclusive education is the education framework for including all hard-to-reach children, including those with disabilities; it was originally based on a principle stating that all should have the opportunity to learn together. The team produced a series of Education Notes on inclusive education and the cost of making schools accessible both in terms of physical layout and for information and communications technology. Furthermore, a project to include disability indicators in the Education Management Information Systems of four East Asian countries was recently completed and will be expanded to three more countries in the region. In addition, the World Bank has actively been engaged in the policy dialogue on inclusive education in Cambodia, Indonesia, and Vietnam.

Promoting Health and Rehabilitation. The World Bank has a strong commitment to achieve good health, nutrition, and population outcomes. The MDGs and the adoption of the Poverty Reduction Strategy Framework underscore the importance of inclusive health policies. Supporting more inclusive public health policies involves collecting evidence, developing such policies, and ensuring access to health services, especially for rehabilitation. The Disability & Development team has provided technical support to operations and studies on disability and health in some of these areas. Knowledge gained is available on the World Bank's intranet and Internet sites. Since 2006, the World Bank has been partnering with the World Health Organization (WHO) on the first *World Report on Disability and Rehabilitation*, coauthoring several chapters as well as working on the report's editorial and advisory committees. This joint report is expected to be launched in 2009.

Ameliorating Disability Caused by Conflict and Natural Disasters. Conflict and disaster are two important causes of disabilities. The emphasis on disability in these settings is often on the emergency phase, with a focus on reintegration of former combatants and medical rehabilitation of physical injuries. Much data on disability in these situations has been limited to the specific case of land mines and amputations. The problem, however, is much more complex and greatly influences the affected countries' opportunity for sustainable and equitable growth. The World Bank has unique comparative advantages to address this issue at all phases—from emergency to reconstruction, and from fragile states to sustainable development. The Disability & Development team has also worked on mental health and conflict.

Several operational tools and publications are available in this area, and the team has revised a draft toolkit on disability in conflict-affected countries. With support from the Trust Fund for Environmentally and Socially Sustainable Development and from other trust funds, the Disability & Development team and operational teams in the regions are presently working in this area, especially in Sub-Saharan Africa. In the South Asia Region, the World Bank was very active in addressing disability aspects of natural disasters (such as the Pakistan earthquake and the Southeast Asia tsunami).

Increasing Accessibility for Persons with Disabilities to Community Life and to Economic Empowerment. Accessibility is a very important part of the inclusion of people with disabilities. An accessible environment is essential to the enjoyment of the rights of people with disabilities to participate in community life. Community participation includes access to transportation, water supply and sanitation, technology, civil and political participation, appropriate sources of communication and media to obtain information, and accessible infrastructure. Increasingly, World Bank country offices and public information centers are accessible to people with disabilities.

The International Finance Corporation and European Bank for Reconstruction and Development are adopting policies and guidelines on the accessibility of new construction. The cost of new construction is only 1 to 3 percent (World Bank 2003a). In the World Bank, a joint guidance note on disability-inclusive social analysis between D&D and the Social Development Department was completed, and dissemination is taking place. The International Finance Corporation and European Bank for Reconstruction and Development are adopting policies and guidelines on the accessibility of new construction. The Disability & Development team is collaborating with other units—namely, the Legal Network, Operations Policy and Country Services, and the Sustainable Development Network—to develop an action plan for increasing accessibility by phasing universal design into all World Bank–financed construction. *Universal design* is "the design of products and environments to be usable by all people, to the greatest extent possible, without the need for adaptation or specialized design" (Center for Universal Design 1997). Additionally, HDNSP partnered with the Social Development Department to produce *Social Analysis and Disability: A Guidance Note* (Social Development Department and Human Development Network 2007).

The World Bank has done extensive work on bus, rapid transit, and other forms of accessible transportation, including guidelines for accessible transportation done by the Social Development Department with support from the Disability & Development team.

Pursuing Disability Activities within the Three Core Areas of SP&L. The Disability & Development team has also undertaken some initial work in the three core areas of social protection:

- *Expanding opportunities.* Helping create good jobs through better labor market regulations, active and passive labor market policies, and wage-setting processes
- *Providing security.* Assisting people with disabilities in better managing their risks to reduce their vulnerability, helping them secure an asset base, and enabling them to engage in higher-risk but higher-return activities
- *Enhancing equity.* Providing minimum levels of subsistence and helping correct market-based distributive outcomes.

In the area of "providing security," the team supported work on disability systems in Latin America and India, in addition to earlier work on Poland on disability insurance in general and on social safety nets. It also looked at employment practices in the countries of the Organisation for Economic Co-operation and Development (OECD) in the context of "expanding opportunities."

Developing Operational Tools and Guidelines. The Disability & Development team focused on providing operational tools, such as a toolkit for including disability in operations. The toolkit includes a database of international and national legislation. At present, the toolkit is available only internally to World Bank staff members, but the team is working to make it available publicly. Many short notes on operationally relevant topics are already publicly available on the external Web site (http://www.worldbank.org/disability). Additionally, the team collaborated on the aforementioned *Social Analysis and Disability: A Guidance Note.*

Regional Initiatives and D&D-Specific Projects

Regional and country initiatives in disability have been gaining momentum. The World Bank's regions are particularly active and developed regional strategies or working groups: the Europe and Central Asia (ECA) Region, the East Asia and Pacific (EAP) Region, the Africa (AFR) Region, the Middle East and North Africa (MENA) Region, the Latin American and Caribbean (LCR) Region, and the South Asia Region (SAR). Each region has a disability focal-point person, who works across sectors and helps link sector colleagues with the Disability & Development team's expertise. Primary areas of work in lending and nonlending activities include the following:

- Supporting national disability strategies or policies and their related action plans for implementation
- Providing technical assistance for collecting baseline data, developing management information systems, and mapping disability prevalence
- Carrying out analytical and advisory activities assessing technical aspects of programs, conducting economic analysis and projections, and examining disability in relation to conflict situations
- Sponsoring high-level, high-visibility conferences on disability
- Committing a country-based development marketplace to disability and creating small-grants programs to support DPOs
- Mainstreaming disability into education, community-based rehabilitation, transportation, microfinancing, community-driven development, and other projects and social funds
- Developing a few stand-alone disability projects in disaster and postconflict situations
- Generating knowledge and guidelines on HIV/AIDS and disability.

Partnerships

The World Bank has provided and continues to provide significant support to the Global Partnership for Disability and Development (GPDD), "a dynamic new initiative to accelerate inclusion of people with disabilities and their families into development policies and practices" according to the GPDD Web site (http://www.worldbank.org/disability/GPDD) hosted by HDNSP:

→ *The GPDD was formed to increase collaboration among development agencies and organizations to reduce the extreme poverty and exclusion of a substantial number of children, women, and men with disabilities living in poor countries. This population includes those born with disabilities and people who become disabled through wars and other violence, traffic or work injuries, diseases, disasters, and other causes.*

The World Bank has supported the GPDD through a DGF. Initially obtained for one year to finance activities on better disability data, the DGF was recently extended for two additional years (U$$700,000) to assist the GPDD in its interim operations until a permanent secretariat can be formally established.

Other important partnerships include continuation of and new financial commitments from donors such as Denmark, Finland, Italy, Japan, Norway, the Bank-Netherlands Partnership Program (BNPP), and the Bank's Environmentally and Socially Sustainable Development (ESSD) Network through the Social Development Department (ESSD disability window, ESSD general call, and secondees). These funds support the work of the regions on disability projects such as country studies and analytical work.

Summary of Results of D&D Activities

The Bank has had some notable achievements. Through the Disability & Development team, the Bank has contributed significantly to the improvement of disability data collection through surveys, censuses, and administrative data and has provided knowledge management and operational tools designed to help task team leaders make their projects more inclusive (see annex 7.C). Currently, the Disability & Development team is collaborating with WHO on the first *World Report on Disability and Rehabilitation.*

In the regions, a growing number of activities are emerging, such as the following:

- The Multi-country Demobilization and Reintegration Program in Africa targets an estimated 450,000 former combatants in seven countries. Services include the provision of physical rehabilitation assistance (prostheses and orthotics), counseling, vocational training, and support for microenterprise activities.
- The Primary Education for Disadvantaged Children Project in Vietnam has combined project funds of US$243 million for technical support to improve administration, enhance delivery of acceptable quality education, and develop a policy on inclusive education and accessible schools.
- The Disability and Child Protection Project in Bangladesh will establish a US$30 million social fund to finance NGOs and private provision of services, training, and empowerment for people with disabilities.
- Data collection in the Latin America and Caribbean (LAC) Region—including a pilot of disability questionnaires in the household surveys of Bolivia and Ecuador—and awareness and outreach through a video demonstrate the importance and complexity of data on disability.

- The Arab Republic of Egypt's Social Protection Initiative Project contains a disability component to develop and test integrated programs for children with disabilities and at-risk youth through a range of providers and to use the experience of the programs to develop a new strategy for improving services.
- An ECA Region disability study, which comprises work in four countries (including a disability survey piloted in Uzbekistan), is analyzing the economic costs of disability. Results will be published in book form.

Other projects include development of microfinance initiatives, social funds, national disability policies, classroom tools promoting inclusive education, and support for development marketplaces that are entirely focused on DPOs. Interest expressed by the Bank's client countries is growing daily, spurred in part by the UN Convention on the Rights of Persons with Disabilities but also by a strong and growing movement within civil society. Boxes 7.1 to 7.6 provide additional examples of D&D activities by region.

BOX 7.1

AFRICA REGION D&D ACTIVITIES

- Three country surveys are under way—in Uganda, South Africa, and Zambia—on disability and HIV/AIDS.
- Three country studies have been conducted on the economic and social status of people with disabilities in Angola, Burundi, and Sierra Leone.
- A policy note has been written on people with disabilities in Sierra Leone.
- A pilot was done with the OECD on disability prevalence, with referrals for children with disabilities in and out of school in Ethiopia.
- The Multicountry Demobilization and Reintegration Program supports the demobilization and reintegration of former combatants in the greater Great Lakes region of Central Africa. The largest program of its kind in the world, the work currently targets an estimated 450,000 former combatants in seven countries. Support will also be extended to two additional countries if and when appropriate. Services typically include the provision of physical rehabilitation assistance (prostheses and orthotics), counseling, vocational training, and support for microenterprise activities.

Source: Information provided by the World Bank Africa regional disability coordinator.

BOX 7.2

EAST ASIA AND PACIFIC REGION D&D ACTIVITIES

Regionwide

- All public information centers in the region are ensuring information is accessible. They supported the translation of the UN Educational, Scientific, and Cultural Organization toolkit on embracing diversity into at least three languages in the region. Accessible public information centers resulted in increased use of the centers by people with disabilities in the Philippines.
- A transportation project addresses disability from the perspective of prevention and road safety.

Cambodia

- Socially inclusive materials in Cambodia, including books and television and radio slots, have been developed.
- A workshop on inclusive education was held in Cambodia in May 2007.

Cambodia, Indonesia, Mongolia, and Vietnam

- Administrative capacity has been built, and an inclusive educational management information system has been developed.

Indonesia

- BNPP trust funds were provided for baseline data collection on children with disabilities in the education sector. Some policy directives supporting inclusive education are envisioned as a result of this study.

Philippines

- The Social Expenditure Management Project included a component of social assistance for disadvantaged groups (US$25 million).
- Development marketplace support was provided for access to justice for the deaf. Several other development market competitions distributed grants to various stakeholders working on independent living.
- A DGF was awarded for children with disabilities in the Philippines.

Thailand

- The Japan Social Development Fund funded post-tsunami reconstruction work.

Vietnam

- The Primary Education for Disadvantaged Children Project combined project funds of US$243 million for technical support to improve administrative planning and management, to enhance delivery of acceptable quality education, to provide links to communities, and to produce a national-level child development report and policy on inclusive education and accessible schools.
- Disability questions have been introduced on the national census.
- An HIV/AIDS project run by young people with disabilities received support from the Bank. This project is a fully mainstreamed project through which young people with disabilities raise awareness.

Source: Information provided by the World Bank EAP regional disability coordinator.

BOX 7.3

EUROPE AND CENTRAL ASIA REGION D&D ACTIVITIES

Armenia

- The Armenian Democratic Forum prepared a National Disability and Poverty Action Plan.

Lithuania

- A Lithuania education improvement project is making 62 schools accessible to children with disabilities and is fully renovating the Vilnius School for the Deaf, as well as providing teacher training (US$25.29 million).

Romania

- A component of the Social Sector Development Project supports the rehabilitation of people with disabilities by strengthening the capacity of the National Institute for Medical Expertise and Work Capacity Recovery. It also bolsters the local medical expertise offices of the National House of Pensions and Other Social Insurance Rights (US$50 million, US$6.32 million of which targets people with disabilities).
- Under a social inclusion project, assistance is given to existing or emerging programs that address the needs of the vulnerable, including people with disabilities, through four components:
  - Priority interventions program
  - Inclusive early childhood education of Roma
  - Social assistance programs
  - Capacity building for Roma social inclusion

Turkey

- A program has provided training to 6,678 special education teachers, who themselves reach 150,000 students, 35,000 of whom are students with disabilities.
- Visually and hearing impaired primary schoolchildren are receiving specialized equipment through phase 2 of a basic education project. The project is building 70 special education primary schools and installing 770 computers. Special educational materials and teacher training will cover 1,340 preschool classrooms.

Uzbekistan

- A regional disability study is in print. It includes four country studies, including a disability survey piloted in Uzbekistan.

Source: Information provided by the World Bank ECA regional disability coordinator.

BOX 7.4

LATIN AMERICA AND THE CARIBBEAN REGION D&D ACTIVITIES

Principle

- Mainstreaming disability measurement to promote effective policy making for social inclusion

Main Outputs

- Pilot of disability questionnaires in the household surveys of Bolivia and Ecuador
- Support for the inclusion of statistical data on disability in the national strategies for the development of statistics in Central America
- Awareness and outreach through video to demonstrate the importance and complexity of data on disability

Source: Information provided by the World Bank LAC regional disability coordinator.

BOX 7.5

MIDDLE EAST AND NORTH AFRICA REGION D&D ACTIVITIES

Arab Republic of Egypt Social Protection Initiative Project Disability Component

Project objective: Develop and test integrated programs for children with disabilities and at-risk youth through a range of providers, and use the experience of these programs to develop a new strategy for improving services.

Main results:

- Exposure to new inclusive approaches
- Awareness of issues for policy formulation

Main outputs:

- A total of 36 subprojects were developed with an average cost of approximately US$100,000 per subproject.
- 1,028 facilities were rehabilitated to adapt the infrastructure to the needs of children with disabilities.
- Numerous resource materials were developed to support future interventions.

Institutional development:

- Effect on Ministry of Insurance and Social Affairs
- Effect on the service providers and the communities
- Effect on future international collaborations

Source: Information provided by the World Bank MENA regional disability coordinator.

BOX 7.6

SOUTH ASIA REGION D&D ACTIVITIES

Principles

- Use mainstreaming in inclusive development.
- Have a two-country focus (India and Pakistan), with others on demand.
- Build on existing momentum.

Strategy

- Mainstreaming through prevention and inclusion
- Improving data and information
- Emphasizing awareness and outreach

India

- The Andhra Pradesh Rural Poverty Reduction Program targeted 560 disadvantaged ***mandals*** in 16 districts on the basis of levels of human, economic, and infrastructural development indicators. People with disabilities were then specifically selected, and the targeting was facilitated by NGOs and DPOs, as well as by self-help groups of people with disabilities.
- Interventions included providing surgical corrections and assistive devices, family support programs, and training to paraprofessionals in community-based rehabilitation; reviving defunct rehabilitation centers and establishing bridge residential schools for children with disabilities; and providing microcredit loans, small enterprise development, and vocational training.
- A draft document, "People with Disabilities in India: From Commitments to Outcomes," was produced in June 2006.

Pakistan

- For the Earthquake Disability Project, a US$5 million grant from International Bank for Reconstruction and Development surplus supported community-based rehabilitation through contracting NGOs.
- Two Japan Social Development Fund grants provided US$1.6 million for Handicap International and Milestone (a national DPO) to establish resource and information centers for community-based rehabilitation and independent living.

Source: Information provided by the World Bank South Asia regional disability coordinator.

FUTURE ACTIVITIES AND STRATEGIES

Developing a Results Framework

The overall strategic objective of the Bank's D&D work is to support the creation of more inclusive societies in client countries. Such societies will improve opportunities, security, and equity for people with disabilities and their families. This strategic, higher-level objective needs to be measured in a way that is attributable to the Bank's activities. Because barriers to labor-market participation keep persons with disabilities from participation, an indicator for *opportunity* would be a decrease in the difference between the employment, access to basic health and education services, and poverty rates of people with disabilities and others. An indicator for *security* could be the establishment of disability pensions and caregiver allowances in middle-income countries. An intermediate outcome indicator for *equity* could be the percentage of public buildings with physical and communications access as an important step toward a higher-level and longer-term objective: full inclusion and no difference in poverty incidence among people with or without disabilities. These indicators are important to gauge progress toward inclusion at global and national levels. Collecting comparable data for these indicators would require serious efforts because currently they are still not routinely monitored in borrowing countries.

Key outcome and process indicators include the following:

- Strategy and plan approved by the Bank's Board and resources allocated
- Increased number of people trained and an increased number of Poverty Reduction Strategy Papers, national development plans, and Country Assistance Strategies (CASs) that include disability as an issue.
- Global networks, universities, and training institutions that include disability in their work
- Knowledge easily accessible at all levels, Web page use, and use of other formats
- Adoption of a policy on infrastructure by the Bank with support to the field
- Strengthened international collaboration and increased appreciation from other donors, banks, and civil society regarding the Bank's role in such collaboration as a result of the GPDD progress and process
- All infrastructure and new construction supported by Bank funding to be accessible by people with disabilities
- Increased percentage of people with disabilities employed by the Bank and other development partners, as well as an increased percentage of people with disabilities in national governments, universities, and community-based organizations.

Emerging Opportunities for D&D

A number of business opportunities could be exploited on the basis of past efforts and if adequate resources are made available:

- Implementing the UN Convention on the Rights of Persons with Disabilities
- Building the interest of governments, international organizations, and the private sector in creating business and partnership opportunities
- Strengthening cooperation with civil society
- Strengthening multisectoral collaboration within and outside the Bank—for example, strengthening the collaboration between the Health, Education, and SP&L Sector Boards; strengthening collaboration between HDN, ESSD, the Development Economics Vice Presidency, the Poverty Reduction and Economic Management Vice Presidency, and others within the Bank; and increasing collaboration with UN agencies such as the United Nations Children's Fund, the UN Development Programme, the International Labour Organization (ILO), and WHO
- Addressing the large needs for dealing with mental, physical, sensory, and psychosocial disabilities in countries in conflict and postdisaster situations
- Strengthening international cooperation at global, regional, and national levels in addressing disability in development—thus enhancing equity in development
- Involving people with disabilities in development
- Ensuring that all new construction and rehabilitation of existing construction is inclusive and accessible
- Strengthening knowledge management, including accessibility for people with disabilities
- Strengthening human rights, equity, and poverty alleviation in international aid
- Increasing the understanding and use of inclusive development within international development.

As part of these activities, the Disability & Development team aims to raise the presence of disability considerations and activities in the World Bank portfolio and to provide task team leaders with the evidence base and operational tools they need to make compelling arguments to borrowing governments for incorporating disability into World Bank operations and to assist governments to measure whether these results are achieved. There are many more opportunities for D&D than the team could address. Following is only a selected subset.

Global Partnership for Disability and Development. As noted in the retrospective, the Bank played a key role in establishing the GPDD and is a very active member in this coalition of NGOs, DPOs, multi- and bilateral development agencies, governments, the private sector, and civil society. The Disability & Development team will continue to support the GPDD by providing fiduciary oversight for the multidonor trust fund that supports the GPDD; implementing the DGF, which HDN recently obtained for the GPDD; helping the task force of the GPDD to navigate Bank procedures; and participating regularly in GPDD meetings and telephone conferences.

United Nations. The Bank will continue to partner with the UN agencies, particularly the UN Department of Economic and Social Affairs (UNDESA), ILO, WHO, and the UN Washington City Group.

Implementation of the UN Convention on the Rights of Persons with Disabilities. As noted in the Implications of the UN Convention Note (Guernsey, Nicoli, and Ninio 2007) countries that sign and ratify the convention will look to the Bank and other international organizations for guidance and assistance in its implementation. The Bank's primary contribution could be to assist countries in understanding how to implement the ambitious goals of the convention incrementally, given the resource constraints they face. A demand-driven response to country needs is an obvious basis for future Bank strategy. This response could be supported by cross-support and other services by the Disability & Development team. In addition, the Bank could provide a global monitoring service, similar to its *Global Monitoring Report* for the implementation of the MDGs. Monitoring and evaluation is a very important part of the convention, which creates governance for monitoring but leaves open the technical and institutional questions of how to do it. UNDESA, one of the agencies supporting the implementation of the convention, has already indicated its interest in cooperating with the Bank in constructing a results framework. The Disability & Development team at HDNSP is capable of providing low-cost assistance to the construction of this framework. It would, however, need to work more extensively with other Bank sectors and networks to develop a set of monitorable indicators for countries that ratify the convention and to strengthen national statistics to collect better data on disability, should the Bank decide to engage in this activity.

ANNEX 7.A: DISABILITY PUBLICATIONS AND TRAINING EVENTS, 2003–07

Disability Publications

The publications listed in this annex are available at http://go.worldbank.org/L7EYWC6G40 or as otherwise noted.

2008

Braithwaite, Jeanine, and Daniel Mont. 2008. "Disability and Poverty: A Survey of World Bank Poverty Assessments and Implications." Social Protection Discussion Paper 0805, Social Protection Unit, Human Development Network, World Bank, Washington, DC.

Filmer, Deon. 2008. "Disability, Poverty, and Schooling in Developing Countries: Results from 11 Household Surveys." *Economic Review* 22(1): 141–63.

Mont, Daniel, and Mitchell Loeb. 2008. "Beyond DALYs: Indicators to Assess the Impact of Public Health Interventions on the Lives of People with Disabilities," Social Protection Discussion Paper 0815, Social Protection Unit, Human Development Network, World Bank, Washington, DC.

2007

Mont, Daniel. 2007. "Measuring Disability Prevalence." Social Protection Discussion Paper 0706, Social Protection Unit, Human Development Network, World Bank, Washington, DC.

———. 2007. "Measuring Health and Disability." *Lancet* 369 (9573): 1658–63.

Rickert, Thomas. 2007. *Bus Rapid Transit Accessibility Guidelines*. Washington, DC: World Bank. (Available in English and Spanish.)

Social Development Department and Human Development Network, Social Protection, Disability & Development Team. 2007. *Social Analysis and Disability: A Guidance Note—Incorporating Disability-Inclusive Development into Bank-Supported Projects*. Washington, DC: World Bank.

2006

Disability & Development Team, Human Development Network, Social Protection. 2006. "Disability and Development Team Brochure." World Bank, Washington, DC. http://siteresources.worldbank.org/DISABILITY/Resources/280658-1172606907476/BrochureDDteam.doc.

Global Partnership for Development and Disability. 2006. "Global Partnership for Disability and Development Brochure." World Bank, Washington, DC. (Available in hard copy only.)

Guernsey, Katherine, Marco Nicoli, and Alberto Ninio. 2006. *Making Inclusion Operational: Legal and Institutional Resources for World Bank Staff on the Inclusion of Disability Issues in Investment Projects*. Washington, DC: World Bank.

2005

Civil Society Team, World Bank. 2005. *Issues and Options for Improving Engagement between the World Bank and Civil Society Organizations*. Washington, DC: World Bank.

———. 2005. *World Bank–Civil Society Engagement: Review of Fiscal Years 2002–2004.* Washington, DC: World Bank.

Human Development Department, Middle East and North Africa Region, World Bank. 2005. "A Note on Disability Issues in the Middle East and North Africa." World Bank, Washington, DC.

Menckhoff, Gerhard. 2005. "Inclusive Design of Bus Rapid Transit: Experience from Latin America." PowerPoint presentation, Latin America and Caribbean Region, World Bank, Washington, DC.

Mitra, Sophie. 2005. "Disability and Social Safety Nets in Developing Countries." Social Protection Discussion Paper 0509, Social Protection Unit, Human Development Network, World Bank, Washington, DC.

Roggero, Paola, and Rosanna Tarricone. 2005. "Employment and Youth with Disabilities: Sharing Knowledge and Practices." Report of the E-discussion on Youth and Disabilities, World Bank, Washington, DC.

World Bank. 2005. *Development Outreach* 7(3) (2005). Special issue on Disability and Inclusive Development, World Bank, Washington, DC.

———. 2005. "Examining Inclusion: Disability and Community Driven Development." Social Development Note 100, World Bank, Washington, DC.

2004

Bonnel, René. 2004. *Poverty Reduction Strategies: Their Importance for Disability.* Washington, DC: World Bank.

Groce, Nora. 2004. "HIV/AIDS and Disability: Capturing Hidden Voices." World Bank/Yale University Global Survey on HIV/AIDS and Disability, World Bank, Washington, DC.

Jadin, Olivier. 2004. *La Situation des Personnes Handicapées au Bénin: Diagnostic préliminaire et propositions d'action.* Washington, DC: World Bank.

MacNeil, Joan M., and Nora Groce. 2004. "HIV/AIDS and Disability: The Hidden Risk." Global HIV/AIDS Program, World Bank, Washington, DC.

Metts, Robert. 2004. "Background Paper Prepared for the Disability and Development Research Agenda Meeting in the World Bank, November 16, 2004, World Bank Headquarters, Washington, D.C." World Bank, Washington, DC.

Mont, Daniel. 2004. "Disability Employment Policy." Social Protection Discussion Paper 0413, Social Protection Unit, Human Development Network, World Bank, Washington, DC.

Roberts, Peter, and Julie Babinard. 2004. "Transport Strategy to Improve Accessibility in Developing Countries." World Bank, Washington, DC.

Simeonsson, Rune J. 2004. *Early Childhood Development and Children with Disabilities in Developing Countries.* Chapel Hill, NC: School of Education and FPG Child Development Institute, University of North Carolina.

Voss, Maj-Lis. 2004. *Disability and Development: Inventory of Organizations Working on Disability.* Washington, DC: World Bank.

World Bank. 2004. "Disability and HIV/AIDS at a Glance Factsheet." World Bank Public Health at a Glance Web site. http://go.worldbank.org/922L4WKL70.

2003

Baingana, Florence. 2003. "Mental Health and Conflict." Social Development Note 13, World Bank, Washington, DC.

Bhambani, Meenu, and Maj-Lis Voss. 2003. "The World Bank and Disability in South Asia: A Portfolio Review." South Asia Human Development, World Bank, Washington, DC.

Groce, Nora. 2003. "Adolescents and Youth with Disability: Issues and Challenges." Global Health Division, Yale School of Public Health, New Haven, CT.

Grushka, Carlos O., and Gustavo Demarco. 2003. "Disability Pensions and Social Security Reform: Analysis of the Latin American Experience." Social Protection Discussion Paper 0325, Social Protection Unit, Human Development Network, World Bank, Washington, DC.

Rousso, Harilyn. 2003. "Education for All: A Gender and Disability Perspective." Background report prepared for the *Education for All Global Monitoring Report, 2003/04.* Washington, DC: World Bank.

Takamine, Yutaka. 2003. "Disability Issues in East Asia: Review and Ways Forward." East Asia and Pacific Region, World Bank, Washington, DC.

World Bank. 2003. "HIV/AIDS and Youth at a Glance Factsheet." World Bank Public Health at a Glance Web site. http://go.worldbank.org/PLSIWLONX0.

———. 2003. "Mental Health at a Glance Factsheet." World Bank Public Health at a Glance Web site.

Training Events

2007

November 8–9, 2007: "Disability and Disaster," Milan, Italy
Speaker: Pia Rockhold, World Bank

November 2007: "Measuring Disability and Health," American Public Health Association, Washington, DC
Speaker: Daniel Mont, World Bank

October 29–November 2, 2007: Inclusive Research (Global Health Research and Disability) Global Forum for Health Research, China
Speaker: Pia Rockhold, World Bank

October 2007: "Measuring Disability Prevalence," Bangladesh National Statistical Offices
Speaker: Daniel Mont, World Bank

October 2007: "What Is Disability and What Should We Capture in the EMIS?" Conference on Inclusive Education, Phnom Penh, Cambodia
Speaker: Daniel Mont, World Bank

October 2007: "Measuring Disability," presentation to various stakeholders in New Delhi
Speaker: Daniel Mont, World Bank

April 11, 2007: "Preparation of the First Joint World Health Organization–World Bank World Report on Disability, Rehabilitation, and Inclusion"
Speaker: Jennifer Madans, United Nations Washington Group on Disability Statistics

January 23, 2007: "A Function-Based Framework for Emergency Management and Planning"
Speaker: Jennifer Madans, United Nations Washington Group on Disability Statistics

2006

December 2006: "The International Classification of Functioning, Disability, and Health," UN Special Programme for the Economies of Central Asia Conference on Disability Measurement, Bishkek, Kyrgyzstan
Speaker: Daniel Mont, World Bank

December 2006: "Measuring Disability," presentation to Pakistani Census Bureau
Speaker: Daniel Mont, World Bank

November 9, 2006: "Measuring Disability on Censuses and Surveys"
Speakers: Jennifer Madans, United Nations Washington Group on Disability Statistics; Daniel Mont, World Bank

October 2006: "Disability and Employment Policy," course on the Labour Market Integration of Disabled Persons for Professionals from Latin America and the Caribbean, Turin, Italy
Speaker: Daniel Mont

October 11, 2006: "Mental Health" at Harvard University, Cambridge, MA
Speaker: Pia Rockhold, World Bank

July 11, 2006: "Inclusive Development: Tools for Operationalization (East Asia)"
Speakers: Christopher J. Thomas, sector manager, East Asia and Pacific Region Human Development Sector; Charlotte McClain-Nhlapo, East Asia and the Pacific disability adviser; Alberto Ninio, lead counsel, World Bank Legal Department; Jean-Roger Mercier, Environmental Assessment, Quality Assurance, and Compliance Unit; Marco Nicoli, Human Development Network, Social Protection; Katherine Guernsey, consultant

July 5–6, 2006: "Disability and Development," the Danish Association of Disability Organizations and Ministry of Foreign Affairs
Speaker: Pia Rockhold, World Bank

June 19–23, 2006: "Disability, Chronic Disease, and Lymphatic Filariasis," National Research Institute, Ghana
Speaker: Pia Rockhold, World Bank

June 14, 2006: "Inclusive Development and the Law: Challenges and Opportunities for the World Bank" (staff only event)
Speakers: Gerard Quinn, professor of Law, National University of Ireland, Galway; Michael Stein, visiting

professor, Harvard Law School; John Wodatch, chief, Disability Rights Section, Civil Rights Division, U.S. Department of Justice; Alberto Ninio, lead counsel, Environmental and International Law Unit, World Bank; Charlotte McClain-Nhlapo, coordinator for SAR and EAP, Disability Working Group, World Bank; Jeanine Braithwaite, senior social protection economist, World Bank; Katherine Guernsey, international lawyer and consultant

June 14, 2006: "Inclusive Development: Tools for Operationalization (Africa)"
Speakers: Jeeva Perumalpillai-Essex, Disability Focal Point, AFR; Emmanuel Akpa, sector manager, Poverty Reduction and Economic Management Sector, AFR; Charles Di Leva, chief counsel, World Bank Legal Department; Johannes Hoogeveen, Human Development Network, Social Protection, Dar es Salaam; Jean-Roger Mercier, Environmental Assessment, Quality Assurance, and Compliance Unit; Marco Nicoli, knowledge officer, Human Development Network, Social Protection; Katherine Guernsey, consultant

June 12–16, 2006: "Disability and Development, Kenya, NGOs"
Speaker: Pia Rockhold, World Bank

May 4, 2006: "Rio de Janeiro: Experiences on CBR and Deinstitutionalization"
Speaker: Leda de Azevedo, president, FUNLAR

April 24–May 5, 2006: "Disability, Development, Health, and Rehabilitation," Kenya Associations of Disability Organizations and Ministry of Health
Speaker: Pia Rockhold, World Bank

April 4, 2006: "Microfinance and Disability"
Speakers: Roy Mersland, consultant, Leonard Cheshire International; Enzo Martinelli, resource development manager, Leonard Cheshire International; Mike Goldberg, senior microfinance specialist, World Bank; Christopher Magarian, director, Finance Group, Japonica Intersect

March 2006: "Measuring Disability Prevalence," Meeting of Central American National Statistical Offices, Panama City
Speaker: Daniel Mont, World Bank

March 23, 2006: "Educational Inclusion/Exclusion: Seen through the Eyes of a Child"
Speaker: Ian Kaplan, research associate, University of Manchester

February 28, 2006: "The Disability Adviser in Kosovo: Key Lessons and Limitations"
Speaker: Mary F. Hayden, president, LBH Institute

February 22, 2006: "Overview of Perkins International Programs: Educating Children Who Are Deafblind and Blind with Multiple Disabilities—Building Capacity of Organizations for the Blind"
Speakers: Michael Collins, director, Hilton/Perkins Program; Aubrey Webson, regional consultant for Africa and the Caribbean; Steven M. Rothstein, president, Perkins School for the Blind

February 2, 2006: "Introducing the Employers' Forum on Disability"
Speaker: Susan Scott-Parker, founder and chief executive, Employers' Forum on Disability

2005

December 20, 2005: "Technology International: The CITTI Project"
Speaker: Bridgett Perry, project director, Colorado Institute for Technology Transfer and Implementation

December 15, 2005: "Pakistan: Impact of the Earthquake on the Lives of Disabled People"
Speakers: Susan Hirshberg, senior education specialist, World Bank; Charlotte McClain-Nhlapo, coordinator for South Asia and East Asia and the Pacific, Regional Disability Working Group, World Bank

December 3, 2005: "Fact-Finding Event on Postdisaster Situations: Opportunities for an Accessible Built Environment"
Roundtable discussion for the International Day of Disabled Persons

November 30, 2005: "Orphans, Education, Disability, and Deaf Empowerment: Implications for Development in Tanzania and Nigeria"
Speakers: K. P. Perkins, Bunmi Aina, and Respicius Batamula, Gallaudet University

November 3, 2005: "Developing Opportunities for Education and Economic Empowerment with People with Disabilities in Latin America: Methodologies and Approaches Promoted by LCI"
Speakers: Enzo Martinelli, resource development manager, Leonard Cheshire International; Désirée Roman Stadthagen, Latin American and Caribbean regional program manager, Leonard Cheshire International

October 25, 2005: "Disability in Emergency Response: An Analysis of Early Tsunami Relief Efforts"
Speakers: Maria Veronica Reina, president, Center for International Rehabilitation; Katherine J. Dorsey, director of publications, Center for International Rehabilitation; Anne Hayes, international coordinator, Center for International Rehabilitation

October 22–27, 2005: "Disability and Medical Rehabilitation," WHO, Geneva.
Speaker: Pia Rockhold, World Bank

September, 2005: "Purpose of Testing Census Questions on Disability," Regional Meeting of Washington Group on Disability Statistics, Rio de Janeiro.
Speaker: Daniel Mont, World Bank

September 2005: "Disability and Health Measurement," discussion paper presented to the Global Health Research Forum, Mumbai
Speaker: Daniel Mont, World Bank

August 19, 2005: "Disability and Development," International Committee of the Red Cross, Geneva
Speaker: Pia Rockhold, World Bank

August 16–18, 2005: "Inclusive Research (Global Health Research and Disability)," Global Forum for Health Research, Council on Health Research Development, and Special Programme for Research and Training in Tropical Diseases, Geneva
Speaker: Pia Rockhold, World Bank

July 2005: "Measuring Disability," Interministerial Meeting on Disability, Hanoi
Speaker: Daniel Mont, World Bank

July 27, 2005: "International Accessibility Standards for Persons with Disabilities"
Speaker: Betty Dion, chair, International Commission on Technology and Accessibility, Rehabilitation International

June 29, 2005: "Disability and Sports"
Speaker: Elise C. Roy, cofounder and director, Ready-Set-Go

June 20–22, 2005: "An Analysis Plan for Testing the UN Washington Group Census Questions on Disability," Regional Meeting of Washington Group on Disability Statistics, Nairobi
Speaker: Daniel Mont, World Bank

June 14, 2005: "Sharing of Experiences: USAID's Efforts to Accelerate the Inclusion of People with Disabilities"
Speakers: Lloyd Feinberg and Rob Horvath, U.S. Agency for International Development

May 26, 2005: "Psychosocial and Mental Health after Disaster: The Aid Program for Tsunami Affected Countries by JSPN"
Speaker: Tsuyoshi Akiyama, International Communication Office, Japanese Society of Psychiatry and Neurology

April 21, 2005: "ADA Fifteen Years Later: Lessons for Legal Frameworks in Developing Countries"
Speaker: John Wodatch, chief, Disability Rights Section, Civil Rights Division, U.S. Department of Justice

April 20, 2005: "Equity in Education: Students with Disabilities, Learning Difficulties and Disadvantages"
Speaker: Dr. Peter Evans, senior specialist, Organisation for Economic Co-operation and Development Centre for Educational Research and Innovation

March 30, 2005: "A National Commitment to Inclusive Education"
Speaker: Manuel Campos, director, National Secretariat for the Social Inclusion of Persons with a Disability

March 14, 2005: "Disability and Social Safety Nets"
Speaker: Sophie Mitra, assistant professor, Fordham University

February 24, 2005: "Post-Polio Syndrome"
Speaker: Lauro Halstead, director, Post-Polio Program, National Rehabilitation Hospital

February 15, 2005: "Inclusion of People with Disabilities and Sustainable Development: Mobility International USA"
Speaker: Karen Heinicke-Motsch, program manager, Mobility International USA

2004

November 10, 2004: "Independent Living Movement in Asia" and "Activities of Self-Help Groups in Asia"
Speakers: Yukiko Nakanishi, president, Asia Disability Institute; Shoji Nakanishi, chair, Disabled People International Asia-Pacific Regional Council

November 4, 2004: "Improving Postsecondary Education for Deaf Men and Women around the World"
Speakers: T. Alan Hurwitz, vice president, dean, and chief executive officer, National Technical Institute for the Deaf, Rochester Institute of Technology; James J. DeCaro, professor and director, Postsecondary Education Network–International, E. William Clymer, coordinator, Postsecondary Education Network–International

October 26, 2004: "What Constitutes Disabilities: Comparisons between the Global North and the Global South"
Speaker: Karen Saba, vulnerable population specialist

October 13, 2004: "Is Community-Based Rehabilitation a Sound Strategy for Disabled Persons in Developing Countries? Lessons Learned from CBR Experiences in Ghana and Benin"
Speaker: Olivier Jadin, rehabilitation specialist

June 10, 2004: "Vietnam through a Disability Lens: Finding a Prescription for Greater Clarity and Action"
Speakers: Yen Vo and Glen W. White, University of Kansas

May 25, 2004: "Disability in India: Implication for Reproductive Health Programming"
Speaker: Maitreyi B. Das, World Bank

May 6, 2004: "HIV/AIDS and Disability: Experience from Handicap International"
Speaker: Florence Thune, Handicap International

April 22, 2004: "Preparing Teachers to Educate Children with Disabilities in Inclusive Settings in LAC and ECA: A Presentation of 'Teacher Centered' Training Modules Developed by the Joseph P. Kennedy, Jr. Foundation"
Speakers: Maggie J. McLaughlin, University of Maryland; Alfredo Artiles, Vanderbilt University

April 14, 2004: "Training and Employment of People with Disabilities: Perspectives from Asia and the Pacific Region"
Speaker: Debra A. Perry, International Labour Organization

March 10, 2004: "Action for Ability, Development, and Inclusion: Experience from India"
Speaker: Syamala Gidugu, Action for Ability, Development, and Inclusion

March 4, 2004: "Making the Business Case for Disability Management and Integrated Health Benefits in Middle-Income Countries"
Speaker: Shelly Wolff, Watson Wyatt

February 10, 2004: "Orphans and Vulnerable Children with Disabilities"
Speakers: Kevin Bales, United Nations; Judy Heumann, World Bank

January 22, 2004: Integrating Disability Messages into the Mainstream Media
Speaker: Barbara Duncan, Rehabilitation International

September 1, 2004: "Disability and Development: Gathering Empirical Evidence"
Estadísticas sobre Personas con Discapacidad Program for the Improvement of Surveys and the Measurement of Living Conditions in Latin America and the Caribbean, Instituto Nacional de Estadística y Censos Meeting, Managua
Speaker: Daniel Mont, World Bank

ANNEX 7.B: KEY EXAMPLES OF ROLES FOR THE BANK AT DIFFERENT LEVELS

Bank-wide Roles: Operations Policy and Country Services, Networks, Independent Evaluation Group, and Development Economics

- Develop "good practice" case studies on successful interventions in disability across sectors from developing countries that explain how countries made progress in the area. This work could include strategy development, training programs, financing mechanisms, and other required technical support.
- Provide support for designing and implementing pilots.
- Continue support for data collection and for monitoring and evaluation.
- Help generate resources to support the regions in disability research (including financing Disability & Development team members' participation in regional efforts).

Regions: Regional Management Teams

- Encourage identification of country and sector point persons to engage with the disability teams in their regions and at the center.
- Specific policy decisions to ensure mainstreaming disability in the Bank's work:
  —Financing only infrastructure that is accessible (transport, roads, public buildings, technology)

—Ensuring reform programs include the needs of people with disabilities

—Ensuring in the review process of analytical and advisory activities (AAA) and projects that disability issues have been considered and evaluated (much like gender, environment, or social issues).

Countries

- Ensure a strategy for disability is included in the CAS with a few key actionable and measurable targets.
- Provide support to national disability policy development and action plans and law reform.
- Ensure disability issues have been addressed in AAA and projects during the review process.
- Allow for flexible budgeting to ensure cross-sectoral input and support for disability.

Sectors and Cross-Sectoral Programs

- Develop a checklist in each sector for projects, programs, and AAA that covers aspects of disability that should be mainstreamed.
- Approach disability in cross-sectoral ways—for example, transportation projects that include education and health components on road safety and emergency road services or education programs that include accessible infrastructure and school health components.
- Ensure accessibility to all infrastructure, services, and technology as well as economic and social participation.
- Conduct more economic analysis on disability and poverty, as well as on the cost of providing disability-friendly services and infrastructure.

ANNEX 7.C: DISABILITY DATA AND MEASUREMENT

The Disability & Development team has been very active in improving the quality and quantity of data on people with disabilities living in developing countries. These efforts have taken place in every region and involve quantitative, qualitative, and administrative data. Accomplishments include the following:

- The team secured a DGF for the UN Washington Group on Disability Statistics to support its efforts to develop and test internationally comparable census questions on disability. The team has been an active member of that group, including chairing its analytical working group and being involved in regional training sessions in Africa and Latin America to develop countries' capacity.
- The team has assisted in the development of quantitative data on disability collected by the World Bank in Ecuador, India, Pakistan, Panama, Uzbekistan, and Vietnam.
- The team oversaw the development of a qualitative data instrument that was then used in Georgia, Kenya, and the Republic of Yemen. The results of the Kenya data will inform the development of the country's national disability survey. In the other two countries, the results are feeding into government workshops aimed at developing a national disability policy. Earlier, the team also had a combined qualitative-quantitative study in Indonesia that assessed service delivery for people with disabilities in that country.
- Using BNPP funds, the team developed a methodological paper that used poverty-mapping techniques to develop a technique to estimate poverty rates for small populations using matched census and survey data. This technique was used in Mozambique, Tanzania, and Uganda. The team also helped the Development Economics Vice Presidency secure some funds to test the applicability of the Living Standards Measurement Study for data collection on disability.
- Using BNPP funds, the team is currently helping to integrate disability into the educational management information systems (EMIS) in Cambodia, Indonesia, Mongolia, and Vietnam. In conjunction with this project, the team has also advised on the Child Development Record component of Vietnam's Primary Education for Disadvantaged Children project. Education Program Development Fund support has been secured to extend the EMIS project to the Lao People's Democratic Republic, Timor-Leste, and Tonga.
- The team has supported efforts by the HDN Education Department and the OECD to adapt a technique for measuring disability in children to developing countries. The technique has been successfully pilot tested in Cambodia and Ethiopia. In Cambodia, the early identification and assessment of children with disabilities has been mainstreamed under the Education for All Fast-Track Initiative and funded by the Catalytic Funds. Plans are under way to implement data collection in many countries.
- The team is involved in many capacity-building activities, such as training in Central Asia (Armenia, Kazakhstan, Kyrgyz Republic, Tajikistan, and Uzbekistan) and South Asia (Bangladesh, India, and Pakistan); individual meetings with census bureaus in Pakistan and Vietnam; production of a video on disability data collection with the LAC Region; and individual consultations with numerous

countries, including (in addition to those mentioned above) The Bahamas, Guyana, Paraguay, and Peru.

- The team has published Social Protection Discussion Papers on measuring disability prevalence and on designing disability indicators for evaluating public health interventions, as well as a piece in *The Lancet* on issues involved with using disability-adjusted life years to assess the impact of public health interventions on disability. A paper on disability prevalence in Zambia has been published by *ALTER: The European Journal on Disability (2007)*. The team also spoke on developing disability data for policy purposes at the 2007 American Public Health Association meetings and the 2008 American Statistical Association meeting. Another paper coauthored with members of the Washington City Group on cognitive testing protocols was presented at the 2008 International Conference on Survey Methods in Multicultural, Multinational, and Multiregional Contexts in Berlin.

REFERENCES

Braithwaite, Jeanine, and Daniel Mont. 2008. "Disability and Poverty: A Survey of World Bank Poverty Assessments and Implications." Social Protection Discussion Paper 0805, Social Protection Unit, Human Development Network, World Bank, Washington, DC.

Center for Universal Design. 1997. "Principles of Universal Design." North Carolina State University, Raleigh.

Guernsey, Katherine, Marco Nicoli, and Alberto Ninio. 2007. "Convention on the Rights of Persons with Disabilities: Its Implementation and Relevance for the World Bank." Social Protection Discussion Paper 0712, Social Protection Unit, Human Development Network, World Bank, Washington, DC.

Metts, Robert. 2004. "Background Paper Prepared for the Disability and Development Research Agenda Meeting in the World Bank, November 16, 2004, World Bank Headquarters, Washington, DC." World Bank, Washington, DC.

Mont, Daniel. 2007. "Measuring Disability Prevalence." Social Protection Discussion Paper 0706, Social Protection Unit, Human Development Network, World Bank, Washington, DC.

Social Development Department and Human Development Network, Social Protection and Labor, Disability & Development Team. 2007. *Social Analysis and Disability: A Guidance Note—Incorporating Disability-Inclusive Development into Bank-Supported Projects.* Washington, DC: World Bank.

World Bank. 2001. *Social Protection Sector Strategy: From Safety Net to Springboard.* Washington, DC: World Bank. http://go.worldbank.org/97LBYDY3U0.

———. 2003a. "Education Notes: Education for All—Building the Schools." World Bank, Washington, DC.

———. 2003b. "Education Notes: Education for All—Including Children with Disabilities." World Bank, Washington, DC.

INDEX

Boxes, figures, notes, and tables are denoted by b, f, n, and t.